CANCELLED AND SOLD BY
FRIENDS OF THE
EUCLID PUBLIC LIBRARY
FOR
THE BENEFIT OF THE LIBRARY

EUCLID PUBLIC LIBRARY

PONSELLE

A SINGER'S LIFE

PONSELLE
A SINGER'S LIFE

BY ROSA PONSELLE
& JAMES A. DRAKE

FOREWORD BY LUCIANO PAVAROTTI

DOUBLEDAY & COMPANY, INC.
GARDEN CITY, NEW YORK
1982

Design by Beverley Vawter Gallegos

Library of Congress Cataloging in Publication Data
Ponselle, Rosa, 1897–1981.
Ponselle: A singer's life.
"Discography by Bill Park": p. 248
Includes index.
1. Ponselle, Rosa, 1897–1981.   2. Singers—United States—Biography.
I. Drake, James A.   II. Title.
ML420.P825A3   782.1'092'4   [B]
AACR2
ISBN: 0-385-15641-3
Library of Congress Catalog Card Number 79–6628

Copyright © 1982 by Elayne Duke and Michael Abromaitis,
Executors of the Estate of Rosa Ponselle and James A. Drake
All rights reserved
Printed in the United States of America

EUCLID PUBLIC LIBRARY

MA 83   191   MAR 1 0 1983

TO THE MEMORIES OF

MY MOTHER

AND MY SISTER

There be none of Beauty's daughters
With a magic like thee!

—Lord Byron, Stanzas for Music

CONTENTS

FOREWORD BY LUCIANO PAVAROTTI

As a boy in Italy, growing up in my hometown, Modena, I can hardly remember a time when the name Rosa Ponselle was unfamiliar to me. Even though this Queen of Queens had sung only one opera in Italy in her entire career—an incomparable *La Vestale,* two performances of which Florence audiences heard in 1933 at the first *Maggio Musicale*—the Italian people revered her as if she had sung all her great roles there. In Italy and in every corner of the world, her phonograph recordings assured her immortality, and it was as a young student that I first heard them. Nearly every aspiring young soprano in my hometown owned copies of her recordings. Though only a boy alto, how well I remember being urged to listen to them, note by note, one after the other.

One can imagine how I felt, having grown up admiring an artist whom I had known only from a series of prized phonograph records, meeting her in person—and not only meeting her, but actually *singing* with her! No doubt every contemporary opera singer, man and woman alike, occasionally wonders what his or her voice would have sounded like opposite one of the immortals of the Golden Age. One can imagine a great soprano of our day wondering how her voice would have sounded in a duet with Enrico Caruso, or a contemporary Wagnerian singer wondering how his voice and the legendary Kirsten Flagstad's might have blended. Where others have had to content themselves with wondering, I was accorded the privilege of raising my voice in song with the incomparable Rosa Ponselle.

It was at Villa Pace, her magnificent home in the Greenspring Valley near Baltimore, that I met her and sang with her. My visit to her villa was the culmination of a telephone-and-letter friendship that had begun a few years earlier. Even today my pulse quickens as I recall making my way up the long driveway to Villa Pace, all the while wondering what she would be like. I had always been told by those who knew her well that she was very lively, very magnetic as a person, yet silently I had to remind myself that I would be meeting a lady who would soon celebrate her eightieth birthday. Believe me, I was totally unprepared for the experience that awaited me behind the immense carved doors of her villa. On that treasurable day I met not an elderly lady but a young woman, a woman still very much in the springtime of her life. We were colleagues that day, she and I; there wasn't a hint of any age difference between us.

After much animated conversation and a splendid meal, we made our way into her expansive music room, where, before she sat down at the piano, she said to me apologetically, "Luciano, I'm not in form today. Every day when I get up in the morning I try out my *pianissimo*. If it's there, I'm in top form, and I can do anything. Today, it isn't there, but we'll sing together anyway, in full voice." And sing we did! From fragments of arias and snippets of duets to the beloved Tosti songs so dear to us both, we let our voices mate in one long shimmering line of harmony. My only wish was that we could have been transported magically into a modern recording studio, so that the whole world could have shared this once-in-a-lifetime experience.

Hearing Rosa Ponselle in person verified my judgments about her uniqueness in the annals of singing. Two qualities, one relating to her voice and the other to her musicianship, account for her artistic uniqueness. Of her voice it has often been said that she was Caruso's counterpart, among female voices "A Caruso in petticoats," as one critic put it. There is a great deal of truth in this because her voice, as with his, was a genuine *voce d'oro*—a voice of pure gold. In describing singing voices, we often resort to color metaphors to explain what we hear, and I think this is an appropriate way to try to characterize the Ponselle voice. I think of her voice as having been brown in color, amber-like in its purity. This is the color of voice every singer would like to have (myself included, yet my voice seems to tend more toward a sparkly silver than the rich brown color I so admire), although very, very few are naturally endowed with it. But Rosa Ponselle's natural endowments hardly ended there. She was among the most profoundly musical of all the singers who have ever lived, and her approaches to virtually everything she sang were instinctively perfect and musically flawless. Even the simplest songs took on new dimensions when she sang them.

There is a real sense in which Ponselle, though she sang her first performance sixty years ago, is still among the most modern of opera singers. Play one of her recordings made in the mid-1920s for the novice operagoer and, not knowing the age of the recording, the listener will invariably say, "This is a contemporary singer, a soprano of our day." Like Caruso's her musical style is timeless, and even a hundred years from now critics will marvel at how modern their singing will seem. Ponselle, almost more than any other singer, had the unique combination of voice and musical profundity to advance operatic interpretation by decades, simply by the sheer genius of her artistry.

She is also among the most copied of any singer in history. I doubt that there is a single living soprano, mezzo-soprano, or contralto who hasn't strived to sing like her at some early point in her career. She is an ideal, an almost mythical figure in opera singing. And even if one is not endowed with the vocal gold with which she entered this world—and who is?—one can still strive to use his or her instrument in the stylistically supreme way that she used hers. It is with this ideal in mind that whenever young singers approach me and ask whom they should pattern their singing after, I always respond, "Make a sincere study of the recordings of Rosa Ponselle." To every young singer in any age—ours, or some distant one—this will always be excellent advice.

Luciano Pavarotti

PREFACE

THOUGH THIS IS ESSENTIALLY an autobiography, the research underlying this book was extensive, and its format is somewhat unusual. The body of the book contains Rosa Ponselle's own narrative, illuminated where appropriate by footnotes on my part. Otherwise, I have introduced and, at the end, capsulized her story in my own first-person singular, as her collaborator. Both the research and the format were made necessary by the complexity of Miss Ponselle's life and career. As any biographer knows (or quickly learns), a living subject is sometimes the least reliable source for the sequence, detail, and perspective necessary to retelling specific events. This is especially true of celebrities, about whom legends sprout like wildflowers and who, in some cases, begin to confuse fact with their managers' press releases.

Rosa Ponselle's basic sense of realism allowed her to escape the latter problem, although legends did, in fact, surround her career—especially its Horatio Alger beginning and its premature ending. In the main, her own recollections were accurate, except where something highly emotional might have caused her to blot out a particular incident or event. In such instances it fell to me, as her collaborator, to search memoirs, archives, or, in the case of living relatives or colleagues, the recollections of those who were a part of these incidents and events. By doing so and then comparing various accounts with Miss Ponselle's recollections, she and I were almost always able to agree on the recording of the event in these pages. Where we might have disagreed, she allowed me the opportunity to express alternate viewpoints or accounts in footnotes or in the Postscript.

In several places, therefore, the contents of these chapters may be at variance with other accounts she might have given in past or recent interviews. This does not reflect badly on her memory or her accuracy for details, and can often be explained by two important considerations. First, almost none of the statements attributed to her in newspaper or magazine accounts published during her career were, in fact, said or written by her. Her managers (William Thorner and later Libbie Miller) or her secretary, Edith Prilik Sania, gave or wrote such statements with an eye to creating specific images for Rosa Ponselle. Hence, little in these published interviews is to be taken literally, and many are contradictory.

Preface 🎵

Second, many of the interviews Ponselle gave in retirement (which, after all, were numerous because she retired more than forty years ago) were printed or placed in archives without her final approval, and without the illumination of the recollections of others who were part of her life and career. In some cases the absence of the latter was understandable; oral history projects, university archives, and the like, were interested only in Ponselle's own recollections as they were recorded on tape or in transcripts. But those which were printed or placed in archives without her being allowed to check them for accuracy and perspective have caused, and will continue to cause, considerable difficulties to serious researchers. Ponselle herself was quick to realize that her memory was fallible, and that she rarely had time to reflect on her answers in interview situations. For this reason, she invariably requested a second look at what she had said—and especially a second look at how various writers used what she had told them in their news stories or features. Relatively few writers and interviewers honored her requests.

What appears in these chapters is, then, the factual story of Rosa Ponselle, told in her words after she had time to reflect on them, and with the illumination of necessary documents, personal recollections of family members, personal friends, business associates, artists, and colleagues. A list of them, along with our sincere thanks, appears in the following pages.

Tampa, Florida   JAMES A. DRAKE

ACKNOWLEDGMENTS

O<small>N</small> R<small>OSA</small> P<small>ONSELLE</small>'s behalf, as well as my own, I want to thank her many friends, colleagues, and family members whose honesty and cooperation made this book possible. Special thanks are owed posthumously to Carmela Ponselle and Antonio Ponzillo, her sister and brother, and to the late Libbie Miller, her manager. Our thanks also extend to Lena Tamburini (Mrs. Henry) Angle and to Edith Prilik (Mrs. Albert) Sania.

We also wish to thank (in alphabetical order) Kira Baklanova; Irving Caesar; George Cehanovsky; Igor Chichagov; Emily Coleman; the late Milton Cross; George Cukor; Joseph A. Gimma and his wife, Licia Albanese Gimma; the late Gustave Haenschen; Bette Hankin; Norma Heyde; the late May Higgins; the late Alexander Kipnis; Charles Kullman; the late Giacomo Lauri-Volpi; Luigi Lucioni; Carol Lynn; Luciano Pavarotti; Jack Pearl; Wilfred Pelletier and his wife, Rose Bampton Pelletier; Stella Roman; Ruth (Mrs. Romano) Romani (Sr.); Dr. Romano Romani, Jr.; Bidú Sayão; Beverly Sills; Valentina (Mrs. George) Schlee; the late Bruno Zirato and his wife, Nina Morgana Zirato; and others whose insights and recollections of Rosa Ponselle's artistry helped illuminate these pages. We appreciate their permission to be quoted.

In a similar vein we are grateful to Michael J. Abromaitis; Walter E. Afield, M.D.; Ida and Louise Cook; Myron Ehrlich; Dr. Bernard Gropper; Carle A. Jackson; Charles Jahant; Dragi Jovanovski, M.D.; George McManus; Michael Mott; Bill Park; the late Sonia (Mrs. Ral) Parr; William Seward; Aidan E. Walsh, M.D.; William Yannuzzi; and others who provided insights, anecdotes, or assistance relating to Rosa Ponselle's life from the early 1930s onward.

In my research I also wish to thank the staff of the Schenectady (New York) Public Library; the Yale University Library; the Meriden (Connecticut) Public Library; the New York Public Library, and especially author-critic David Hall and his staff; the U. S. National Archives; the Pratt Library of Baltimore, in particular Ms. Marion Johnson; the Metropolitan Opera, especially the late Francis Robinson and the late Dario Soria; *High Fidelity* magazine and its editor-in-chief, Leonard Marcus; Dr. Thomas G. Stockham, of Soundstream, Inc.; the editorial staff of the Baltimore *Sun,* especially Harold A. Williams; critics Harold C. Schonberg, Paul Hume, Max de Schauensee, and Martin Bookspan; and Warren F. Gardner, retired editor of the Meriden

(Connecticut) *Morning Record* and *Daily Journal.* Special thanks also go to *Time* magazine's Nancy Newman, and *Reader's Digest*'s Hannah Campbell, as well as Theresa Salisbury of WBJC in Baltimore.

Finally, I am indebted to Senator Charles Mathias (R-*Md.*) for having entered a portion of my work on Rosa Ponselle into the *Congressional Record.* I am also grateful to two ethnic historians, Dr. Bruno A. Arcudi, editor of *Italian Americana,* and Dr. Paul W. McBride, for their helpful suggestions at various points of my research; I am also grateful to Dr. Regina Soria, of the College of Notre Dame of Baltimore, for her insights into Rosa Ponselle as an Italian-American. A score of friends, colleagues, and family also merit my mention, including Don Martin Jager; Carl Gutekunst; Millie Armstrong Drake; Lydia M. Acosta; Dr. Maria Scajola Swenson and Dr. Edward E. Swenson; Eugene H. Cropsey; my literary agent, Howard Buck; and Doubleday & Company's Louise Gault, all of whom were helpful to me. Lastly, I offer inestimable thanks to my parents for their devotion; my debt to them goes far beyond these pages.

Miss Ponselle wished especially to thank four people without whom this book would not have been possible. First among them are Licia Albanese and Joseph A. Gimma, who numbered among her closest friends. Her profound admiration for Licia Albanese, both as an artist and as a person, is reflected in these pages. Both Mme. Albanese and Mr. Gimma, her husband, played a key role in the negotiations surrounding the publication of this book.

Inestimable thanks also go to Elayne Duke, whose role in the very conception of this book deserves direct acknowledgment. It was she who encouraged Miss Ponselle (whom she served as personal representative) to reconsider her longtime opposition to collaborating on a book about her life and career. Too, it was she who eventually urged Miss Ponselle to expand what was to have been a monograph into a full biography. And, finally, it was she whose assistance, planning, and development, as regards our interviewing and research sessions at Villa Pace, made our work both pleasant and efficient.

In the five years of research and writing that this book required, Rosa Ponselle was the essence of cooperation, making any number of suggestions as to persons I might wish to contact. She stipulated only that I consult and work directly with her longtime friend, Hugh M. Johns, because, in her words, "Hugh knows my artistry and understands my thoughts, my roles and the events in my career better than anyone." With this singular endorsement, an endorsement augmented by his having studied voice with Romano Romani, her coach, Mr. Johns proved to be an irreplaceable asset to the writing of this book. Equally at home in discussions of opera repertoire, opera singers, and the history of operatic recordings, his awesome memory and penetrating editing led Miss Ponselle to entrust to him the structure and recording of many details of her life and career, which, in turn, he conveyed to me at her request. Because he conferred regularly with her on matters of operatic history for more than three decades, and because for many years he had served with her on the auditions committee of the Baltimore Opera Company, he was a paramount resourceperson to me and I am profoundly grateful to him.

Those of us associated with the preparation of this book, and Rosa Ponselle in particular, would have hoped to be able to acknowledge here the cooperation of the late Robert Joy Collinge, general manager of the Baltimore Opera Company. As early as 1973, when I first met her, Miss Ponselle suggested that I meet Mr. Collinge and interview him. As is explained in the Introduction, I was then at work on an oral history project and was fortunate to be able to interview Miss Ponselle at Villa Pace. Originally, Mr. Collinge indicated that he would be present at the interview session, but he did not meet with me on that occasion; instead, I interviewed him by telephone, but was unable to secure his further cooperation. For reasons covered amply in Chapter Twelve and the Postscript, he remained inaccessible as an interviewee. Hence, I was forced to rely on correspondence and newspaper columns in my attempts to supplement Miss Ponselle's recollections of the events that triggered her resignation from the company as its Artistic Director.

Only two weeks before her sudden death on Memorial Day, 1981, I met with Miss Ponselle to review the final chapters of our manuscript. At the end of our session, I had the privilege of thanking her for having entrusted to me the story of her life. Posthumously, I thank her again.

Tampa, Florida   JAMES A. DRAKE

INTRODUCTION

BALTIMORE, MARYLAND, and the Greenspring Valley that borders it are a study in contrasts. The city, a port cradling the Patapsco estuary near Chesapeake Bay, is a teeming metropolis housing a third of the state's total population. The valley, by contrast, is a sparsely settled stretch of hills in which scenes reminiscent of Hudson Valley School canvases abound. Atop one of these hills, in a villa rather than a house, lives one of the state's most distinguished residents. The early morning hours to which others in these hills awaken will pass her by unnoticed. Her personal clock, the biological one within her, was never regulated to accommodate them. Night is her prime time, and this night—icy, bitter cold, and otherwise forbidding—will be one of the happiest she has known in recent years. The date is January 22, 1977, the evening of her eightieth birthday.

Outside her villa, Villa Pace, the white masonry walls are bathed by floodlights as doormen relieve waiting limousines of their well-dressed passengers. Once the guests make their way past the villa's elaborate entranceway, they will be met by a uniformed guard who will check their invitations against the master list on his clipboard. Inside the villa, in the restaurant-size kitchen that occupies one arm of the cross-shaped home, a team of volunteer chefs headed by Edward Byer, vice president of a local bank and a close friend of the singer's, are busy putting the finishing touches on the menu items that will be served the hundred twenty guests during the course of the evening. In the dining room, behind closed doors, assistants carry in immense silver trays, placing them in rows on the hand-carved twelve-foot table that dominates the room. "Chicken Ponselle"—an Edward Byer creation, a pasta dish made with linguine cooked *al dente* and prepared with a cream sauce of sautéed mushrooms, green olives, grated Cheddar, finely cut chicken, and liberal quantities of dry sherry—will be the main course. At each end of the dining table the assistants place serving trays holding twelve-pound salmon, each freshly poached and encased in a molded aspic glaze. Nearly ten pounds of hand-ground steak tartare and sugar-cured hams baked in ornate pastry shells complete an array of hors d'oeuvres that includes hot crab balls, select imported cheeses, and an assortment of European breads. Fine wines complement the exquisite menu.

In the library of the villa, reclining at one end of the ivory and red davenport that faces the room's immense fireplace, rests the lady for whom the party is being given. She is dressed in a black-velvet gown embroidered in gold. A handful of admirers and friends are seated with her, among them George (now Baron) McManus, and Elayne Duke, who has planned and coordinated what she hopes will be a surprise party. So far her ploys have worked: Rosa Ponselle is oblivious to the goings-on in the rest of her villa and is expecting only a dozen or so close friends. Yet she begins to wonder when Hugh Johns enters the library in formal evening wear. Thinking quickly, he assures her that he has donned a tuxedo merely out of respect for her and for the formality of the occasion. She seems satisfied with his explanation. Soon she asks to be handed a stack of letters and telegrams that have arrived during the past few days. Scanning their contents, she asks to have some of them read aloud to her.

One letter is from the White House and carries the familiar signature of the President. "Mrs. Ford and I were delighted to learn that you will be celebrating the grand occasion of your eightieth birthday," the letter says, "and we want to be sure to be included among those expressing congratulations to you at this time." Vice-President Rockefeller's letter, sent three days after the President's, has a philosophical tone to it. "On marvelous occasions like this," he writes, "we judge others not only by how long they have lived but how well they have lived. By both of these measures, you have had a full and inspiring life."

Eugene Ormandy's is among the first messages she has received from the musical world. "I am pleased to have the opportunity to send you my personal congratulations and those of the members of the Philadelphia Orchestra on your great contribution to American music as one of the renowned stars of the Metropolitan Opera Company," the eminent conductor writes. In another letter the Cleveland Orchestra's Lorin Maazel extends his "warm wishes and cordial greetings to a great lady, extraordinary artist and a significant force in the development of vocal artistry in the twentieth century." Leonard Bernstein, in his greeting, credits her with changing the direction of his young life. "Yours was the first operatic voice I ever heard, at age eight, on an old Columbia 78, singing 'Suicidio,'" he tells her. "Even through all the scratchiness and surface noise, that voice rang through in such glory that it made me a music-lover forever. I thank you every day of my life." In another letter, Vladimir and Wanda Horowitz add their "admiration and appreciation of your great artistry and your unceasing efforts in behalf of music and the arts."

There are messages of a lighter kind, too. "A Rosa is a Rosa is a Rosa," wires Victor Borge, borrowing liberally from Gertrude Stein and expressing his gratitude "for the opportunity to join in this tribute to she who is *R*-adiant *O*-ff *S*-tage *A*-lso." George Burns's letter gives her a hearty laugh. "They tell me you'll be eighty in January," he writes to the woman he first saw as a headliner in vaudeville sixty years earlier. "Well, I'm one up on you, I'll be eighty-one on the twentieth of January. What a team we would make! I don't think I could manage 'Madame Butterfly,' but we'd have them rolling in the aisles with the 'Red Rose Rag.' If you ever need a straight man, let me know. I've got a trunk full of hair for any occasion." Lapsing into seriousness for a rare moment, he asks that he be allowed to "join your many, many admirers in this tribute to a great artist and a lovely person." "Right after we sing 'Red Rose Rag,' we go into this little sand dance. It's very simple and they'd love it."

Beverly Sills (who, like Marilyn Horne and Aida Favia-Artsay, has sent an elegant floral display), Joan Crawford, Gloria Swanson, and Lillian Gish have all sent messages, each asking to "join the multitude in thanking you," as Miss Gish writes, "for the great beauty your artistry has brought to the world in our century." Amid the many warm and loving letters is one from a woman whose words evoke a happy period in the singer's retirement years. "Dear Rosa Ponselle," the writer begins, shaping her words in florid longhand: "I would like to join the other admirers of yours in wishing you a very happy birthday. We are nearly the same age, but I would be a couple of months ahead of you. We have seen many wonderful things come to pass in the last eighty years. I shall always remember your generous singing for Ike and me in 1952 and your letting the world know you were for my beloved. Again, best of everything on your natal day, from Mamie Doud Eisenhower."

It is now six-thirty and the guests are assembled in the villa's foyer. To its right, in the music room, television crews from the local CBS affiliate are arranging their lights and testing their sound equipment. It is now time to unveil the surprise, and the lady about to be fêted is told that a few more guests have arrived, unannounced. She asks to have them shown in, and the large walnut doors of the library are swung open. Francis Robinson, the Metropolitan Opera's tour director, is the first person she sees.

"Why, Francis, you mean you've come all the way from New York to—" She is unable to finish the sentence as the crowd of guests makes its way into the room.

Licia Albanese's smile catches her eye, and Stella Roman is standing next to her. The elegant Max de Schauensee greets her, and Sara Tucker, widow of the great tenor, soon embraces her. In a moment Nanette Guilford, who was first at her side in *L'Africaine* in 1923, is again at her side. She now sees Rose Bampton, her colleague in the last years of her Metropolitan career; beside Miss Bampton stands her husband, conductor Wilfred Pelletier.

"Is—is that you, Pellie?" she asks in wonderment, trying to adjust the mental picture she retains of a young, brown-haired man who had once helped to coach her in *La Juive*.

"Sì, Rosa, son'io," he answers in Italian, his snow-white hair falling across his forehead as he nods his assent. Decades have passed since he has seen her and the advanced years show on both their faces.

The rest of the guests—some, like Clementine Peterson, key figures in Baltimore society, others like Gerald Wise and Russell Wonderlic, executives and patrons of the Baltimore Opera Company, and still others who, like Ric Aloi and Joe Puglisi, are just plain friends—are shown into the library and pay their respects, one by one. Dinner is served, and afterward the guests and their honored hostess are directed into the music room, where a television interview is filmed. Rosa is cooperative, as usual, and balks only when the interviewer, Merle Comer, asks her to go to the piano and sing. Not even the presence of Igor Chichagov, a distinguished pianist-conductor, can induce her to sing. "Believe me, I'd do it if I weren't so overcome with emotion," she tells the attractive Miss Comer. Later in the weekend she will astound her guests with full-bodied portions of "I Love You Truly" and "Drink to Me Only with Thine Eyes," each one revealing the same ruby-rich tones that had led critic Harold C. Schonberg to once venture that hers may have been the greatest voice in modern opera history.

Her own opinion, expressed to her interviewer, is far more modest. "Now that I have had time to read what has been written about opera and opera singers," she says, "I think I can honestly say that I am considered *one* of the artists who the critics seem to think are the great ones. But, don't forget, I'm only one among many." Washington *Post* critic Paul Hume, standing near Francis Robinson, is heard to say in a stage whisper, "If there are more around like her, I'd like to know where to find them!"

The interview now completed, drinks are replenished and attention is called to a tape recording; through longtime friend Myron Ehrlich, some of those who have been unable to attend the party have arranged to convey their greetings by tape. As the machine is started, the voice of Luciano Pavarotti is heard. "My dear Rosa, I am here in my dressing room at the Metropolitan," he tells the lady he cannot see. "I am singing *Trovatore* and have just finished 'Di quella pira,' and I am happy to tell you that everything is going fine. But for now, dear Rosa, my thoughts are with you as you are seated at the table with your friends on your eightieth birthday." The genial tenor now makes her a promise. "I will not tell anybody that you are eighty because you don't look like it, and because I am an Italian and a gentleman . . . and to me you will always look like you did when I met you at your lovely house."

"Dear Madame Ponselle," speaks the next singer in clear, English-accented tones, "I want to compliment you on your wonderful birthday, and wish that you have many, many more. All the best wishes from your avid antipodeal fan, Joan Sutherland." Richard Bonynge's voice is heard next. "The operatic world owes you so much, Madame Ponselle, because you've been an inspiration to all of us. Many, many happy returns, and much love to you."

"This is Alexander Kipnis speaking from Westport, Connecticut," comes the next message as the recorder's speakers strain to accommodate the Russian basso's gargantuan voice. "Although I never had the privilege of singing with the great Rosa Ponselle, how well I remember sitting in a rehearsal at Covent Garden in 1929 and hearing her unique, wonderful voice. The range, the color, and the power of her voice were completely unique, as was her phrasing. I am only sorry that I cannot be there to shake the hand of the greatest soprano I ever heard in my life."

Peggy Wood, the genteel actress whose *I Remember Mama* made television history, is heard next. "I notice that people have spoken mostly here about the voice of Rosa Ponselle. I would like to say that as an actress, she was an inspiration, too. And as a person to look at she was an inspiration. She was stately and beautiful, and the way her voice came out of that beauty, it seemed to me just the right thing." Telling her audience that her very first listening experience at the Metropolitan as a young girl—a *Faust* with Melba and the two De Reszkes—had compelled her to go again and again, "there were many times that I stood behind the rail at the Old Met to hear and admire that genius of an artist, Rosa Ponselle."

A familiar voice now fills the room. "Vas you dere, Sharlie?" asks Jack Pearl, the Baron von Munchausen of radio's heyday in the 1930s. "Yes, I *was* there," he says, answering his famous question. "I was there at the Palace Theater when you sang Victor Herbert's 'Kiss Me Again,' and earned the great applause that you so richly deserved. On your birthday, this is my wish for you: May you live as long as you want, and may you never want as long as you live."

Renata Scotto now offers *"Cent' anni"*—"May you live a hundred years"—and there are "love and kisses from your friend, Jerome Hines." James Morris, one of her prized pupils, identifies himself as "your Jimmie"; speaking from his dressing room at the Metropolitan, he assures her that "if it weren't for you, I wouldn't be here—I wouldn't be on any stage, anywhere." Listeners strain now to hear the low whisper of a lady who identifies herself as "Rosa Ponselle's Number One Fan." "You have heard from my lips, in person, what you have meant to me and what an inspiration you have been in the forming of my vocal technique." The woman who speaks these words now identifies herself as she concludes her birthday greeting. "I send to you all my love, my deepest admiration, and my very best wishes for a happy birthday. This is Marilyn Horne."

Recorded messages from Nicolai Gedda, Bidú Sayão, Eleanor Steber, and Eva Turner are heard as the evening goes on. Soon, the birthday cake is displayed and captures everyone's attention. Shaped in the form of a page of music, it is decorated with a rose-colored clef bearing the opening notes of "Pace, pace mio Dio," the aria that had sealed her fame six decades before in *La Forza del destino*. The sides of the cake are decorated with the names of the operas in which she starred during her nineteen Metropolitan seasons. On top, letters made of lavender icing spell out the message "Happy Birthday, Rosa." At first no one is willing to put a cake knife to such a work of art, but eventually visual delights give way to gustatory ones.

The party comes to an end at two in the morning, as the last group of guests is driven to the Cross Keys Inn, where a full two floors have been designated the "Ponselle Wing." As the lady being honored contemplates making her way up the long, tiled staircase to her bedroom, she knows that she will be unable to sleep. Regular sleep has always eluded her, and this night will be no exception. This night she is in a mood to talk, not to sleep.

Would we mind listening? she asks.

We are her audience for as long as she wishes, we reassure her. One by one our small group—Elayne Duke, Hugh Johns, Dr. Dragi Jovanovski, Romano Romani, Jr., and his wife, Yara—ease back into our chairs because we are eager to listen to her. By now, she is long accustomed to talking to me, usually in the presence of a tape recorder. She knows that I am studying her, that I want to write a book about her life and career.

I came into her life just after her seventy-fifth birthday. I had no reason to think that my association with her would extend beyond my first visit to her home. That first visit had been taxing enough. I was doubling as a professor and administrator at Ithaca College, in upstate New York, where the late Gustave Haenschen, a pioneer recording executive and popular musical director on radio, had commissioned a colleague and me to begin an oral history project for entertainment industry personalities.

Although we recorded detailed interviews with a number of opera singers under the aegis of the Haenschen Collection, I pursued an interview with Rosa Ponselle singlehandedly. I did so because Gus Haenschen, though he had collaborated on a song that Ponselle had once recorded ("Rosita," written under one of his pseudonyms, Paul Dupont), had worked only with Carmela Ponselle and thus had no direct link to Rosa. But one of his longtime friends—Milton Cross, whose radio career Haenschen had helped foster—had such a link, and we called upon him for advice.

"She'll see you," Mr. Cross told me, "but just be prepared for a wait. She does nothing on impulse, as far as interviews go, and so she may want to see just how serious you are. But I know she'll eventually see you."

I wrote her a letter and explained that at twenty-nine I was too young to have had the privilege of hearing her onstage at the Old Met; but, I said to her, I had memorized every note, word, and inflection on her recordings. I said I knew she was very busy, but hoped that she might make room for my interview. I assured her that I would be well organized and would not waste her time.

Four weeks passed till I had received a letter with the familiar return address and Stevenson, Maryland, postmark on it; the letter was typewritten on delicate robin's-egg-blue stationery, and was signed by her secretary. "Miss Ponselle will be happy to speak with you in the near future," it said, "when her crowded schedule might permit her the kind of time you indicate you would like." I was elated, naturally, and prepared myself for a brief wait.

A year and a half later, I was still waiting.

Soon I learned from Francis Robinson that she was in guarded condition in the Greater Baltimore Medical Center. I phoned there and was told only that she was recovering from complications caused by a virus. Month after month crawled by, until I had nearly given up all hope of meeting her. I was being given the polite brush-off. Then, at one o'clock in the morning in the middle of March 1973, the telephone jarred me from my sleep. The conversation went like this:

"Is this Professor Drake I'm talking with?" inquired the low-pitched voice at the other end of the line.

"Yes," I responded groggily.

"Good. This is Rosa Ponselle."

Rosa Ponselle? My eyes shot open and a siege of nervousness instantly overtook me. My voice quickly showed my nerves; normally about as deep as John Denver's or Dennis Day's, my voice rose a third upward in pitch. With all the aplomb of a star-struck teenager in a similar situation, all I managed to squeak out was, "This isn't some kind of joke is it? I mean, you're *really* Rosa Ponselle, aren't you?"

At that I heard her hand cover the receiver. She said to Elayne Duke, who was in the room with her, "This is no professor, this is some thirteen-year-old boy!" Sensing that I was losing ground, I tried to lower my voice in a vain attempt to sound like a man of authority.

"Now, what is it that you want to talk to me about?" she asked, seeming to want to cut the conversation short.

"I—I'd like to interview you," I muttered in my inept *basso profundo* imitation.

"I sort of guessed that," she said wryly, "because that's what you said in your letter. What I need to know is what you want to interview me *about.*" Now there was a deadly pause in the conversation.

What the hell do I say now? I thought, cursing the fact that it was one in the morning and that I couldn't think fast enough.

"Oh, I'd like to ask you about your famous debut at the Metropolitan, and then I'd—"

"I've only told that story five hundred times over the years, and I really don't want to make it five hundred and one."

Now I was really off-track and vainly looked for the route back on.

"Well, of course, that isn't *all* I want to ask you," I said, hoping to stall for time.

"Okay, what else do you want to know about me?"

That was just what I was afraid she would say. Grasping for straws, I brought up her sister's and her vaudeville career.

"You see, I just gave all that information to the New York *Times,*" she said with an apologetic laugh. "I'll tell you what, I'll have Miss Duke send you a copy of the newspaper article and that way you can read about it firsthand."

There I was, going down for the third time. In desperation I told her that I had to interview her myself, in person, because there would be things I might want to know that the *Times* might not have printed.

"Well, like what?" she wanted to know.

I was sure I was finished now—I couldn't think of a single thing to say. Figuring that I was about to lose a golden opportunity, I decided to go for broke. Whatever came to mind, I would say it and hope to keep her on the phone long enough for my head to clear.

A name from the past popped into my head.

"Stracciari—I want to ask you about Riccardo Stracciari," I said, assuring myself that she would tell me to go to the library and look up his name in the card files. To my surprise, just the opposite happened.

"What a baritone!" she exclaimed. "You know, I sang several joint concerts with him, even a concertized *Aida*. That must have been around, oh, 1920 or 1921. And, you know, we made a recording together of the big duet from *Trovatore*. It's too bad it wasn't made under modern circumstances so that you could hear what we *really* sounded like. But what an artist he was! His voice was just like a shower of diamonds. Brilliant, just brilliant. It penetrated you when you heard it—it went right to the heart."

"Madame Ponselle," I tried to interrupt, to no avail.

"Of course, there was a lot of terrific baritones around then. Amato, for instance. And Danise, and de Luca—and we wouldn't want to leave Mario Basiola out of the list, either. And right on top was Titta Ruffo. They were all different, and each had his strengths. You couldn't imagine a greater Rigoletto than Giuseppe de Luca's, nor a greater Figaro than Stracciari's. Amato was stunning in *Pagliacci*. So was Antonio Scotti, particularly in *Tosca* or in *L'Oracolo*. But there was *nobody* like Titta Ruffo. He could sing it all, high notes and low notes, *piano* as well as *forte*."

"Madame Ponselle," I finally managed to interject, *"that's* the kind of thing I want to interview you about." With that I ran through as many famous names as I could spew out in one long breath.

"In that case," she said brightly, "I guess we have some business to take care of."

"Does that mean that I can come and interview you?" I said gingerly, wanting to be sure that I had interpreted her correctly. Yes, she said, that's what she meant. She suggested that we schedule it then and there. Naturally, I asked what part of the month might be best for her.

"Tomorrow, around four o'clock," she said. "We'll work till about six-thirty, and we'll take a dinner break. Then maybe we'll talk some more. Okay?"

"But Madame Ponselle," I said, afraid that she'd forgotten where I was, "I'm in upstate New York and you're way down there in Baltimore."

"Don't worry about it," she said offhandedly. "I'll have a driver call for you at the airport, and if your plane is late we'll wait for you."

With that she said a hasty goodbye; afterward, at quarter past one in the morning, I began making plane reservations to go to Baltimore the next day. Her chauffeur met me at the airport at three o'clock the next afternoon. An hour later, having been shown through Villa Pace and its lovely grounds, I found myself standing in the midst of its foyer as she descended its long staircase.

She was dressed in a floor-length velvet gown; the jewelry she wore, sparse but elegant, caught the light of the foyer's chandelier. Her walk was firm and proud, and as I studied her face from a distance I recognized its features very easily. As I moved toward her I could see that the years had been especially kind to her. Her energy and vitality quickly made one dismiss her chronological age.

The color and shape of her eyes made an immediate impression upon me. They were like coffee-colored gems set in fine china, and they seemed capable of infinite expression. The bow of her lips and the two rows of perfect pearl-like teeth they soon unveiled struck me similarly. They would have been marvelous instruments of expression for any actress.

For all the exquisiteness of her features, it was her voice that set her apart, even in her mid-seventies. I heard it for the first time when a tape recording I played of Caruso and Louise Homer singing "Ai nostri monti" from *Trovatore* prompted her to sing, while sitting down, Homer's measures as Azucena. Though she confined herself to a lower range, her voice was as powerful, shimmering, and prismatically colored as her old recordings suggested in its prime. Even the vibrato in her tones gave no clue of her age; it was as even and steady as a young girl's.

Listening to her sing, I thought back to a tribute that Alexander Kipnis, the distinguished Russian bass, had once paid her.

"Pick at random one hundred people," Kipnis said, "and out of the group perhaps a half-dozen, at most, will be able to produce *one tone* that an opera critic would consider a 'vital' tone. Go and find a hundred people who can produce good, ringing, vital tones in any part of their singing voices, and out of that one hundred maybe a handful will have the quality of voice and kind of intellect and personality that professional study requires.

"Out of that handful, with the proper training perhaps one, maybe two, can become great vocalists. But voice alone is not enough. Find one hundred great voices, ones which *sound* like a youthful Gigli or Galli-Curci or Ruffo, and perhaps only a dozen of them will have the innate musicianship, acting ability, and drive to become internationally respected performers.

"Out of that dozen, a real *genius* of an artist—a Caruso, a Battistini, a Journet—may be found, but once in a generation, perhaps once in a lifetime. Rosa Ponselle was one such artistic genius."

In the end, my interview with her lasted, at her invitation, two full days. After parts of the interview began to be published, I saw more and more of her, and each time I saw a dimension to her that I hadn't seen before. I learned that she was intense in everything she said and did. She seemed to relax only when she was tired from some sort of exercise (swimming, walking, and riding an exercise bicycle were her favorite pastimes), or, even more, when she listened to recordings. Few engineers in a recording studio could have listened with more precision than she exhibited when she riveted her attention to a recorded opera. Still blessed with near-total recall of all the opera scores she sang (the *whole* vocal score, not merely her part), she never needed to reach for a bound copy. Instead, she listened from memory, keeping an A-440 tuning fork nearby to check whether the performers were staying in original keys as they sang.

The voice of Caruso, especially, could transport her to heights that eluded the rest of us, perhaps because she knew his singing so intimately and respected the way he used his marvelous gifts. Caruso's name has been mentioned often on this, her eightieth birthday. Earlier in the evening, amid the glare of television lights, interviewer Merle Comer had wanted to know about Caruso. A bit later, Max de Schauensee recalled for the guests a performance of Halévy's *La Juive* with Caruso and Ponselle. "Your two voices," he told Rosa, "seemed like two marble pillars rising from the floor of the stage to the roof of the auditorium."

It is now past two in the morning, and we are a small group. The crackle of new logs in the blazing fireplace commands everyone's attention while I set the volume levels on my tape recorder. Rosa Ponselle knows that I have subjected to the microphone the people who have mattered to her. Each has told me something about her life and career. Tonight, buoyed by the warmth of old friends and cradled in the soft embrace of the past, she wants to tell her own story—the peaks and the valleys, the good times and the bad ones.

As I ready the tape reels, I wonder where she will begin.

Her childhood is on her mind tonight, she says. She wants to talk about Connecticut. About Meriden, where she passed her childhood seventy-odd years ago. We begin there, in her words.

Tampa, Florida   JAMES A. DRAKE

PONSELLE

A SINGER'S LIFE

A REAL LIVE BABY DOLL

MERIDEN, CONNECTICUT, was a city of twenty-three thousand when my father and mother came there in the summer of 1895. An industrial community lying some eighteen miles down the railway line from New Haven, Meriden lived and breathed industry. The city listed more than two hundred and thirty factories in its 1890 report to the Census Bureau; the town fathers estimated that each year those factories turned out more than $12,000,000 of exportable goods.

Boomtown that it was, Meriden was a "house divided" at the turn of the century. Elderly people who had married and raised their families when the town was an unassuming farm community resented the new turn that their once peaceful hamlet had taken since the Civil War. They didn't resent the trainloads of tinware, hardware, cutlery, brass work, iron castings, glassware, and ornate silverware that its factories turned out; Meriden billed itself as "The Silver City" and its citizens were proud of its products. No, what the elderly resented were the illiterate, rowdy immigrants who, like my father, had made their way up the coast from Castle Garden and, later, Ellis Island in search of steady work.

The parlors of Meriden's pure-blooded Old Guard buzzed with the same refrain in the 1890s. "Of what use," they would ask each other, "would our library system and our Bostonian schools be to these dregs of German, Slavic, Irish, and Italian society?" My father's generation had no answer for them; his people couldn't read or write English, and had been relegated to the town's seamier neighborhoods by the middle 1890s. Italians, like other immigrants, were castoffs; Meriden, like other towns, made them feel it.

My father, Benardino Ponzillo—"Ben" to his family and friends—was an Italian "from the Boot," a southerner whose face, dialect, and bearing all marked him a *Napuletan'*. His roots lay in Naples, though it wasn't his birthplace; he was born in Caserta, the capital of the district of Terra di Lavoro, part of the province of Naples. It was a farm region, mainly, and the only thing that made it different from others in the province was the extraordinary palace that the eighteenth-century architect Vanvitelli had built there for Charles III. It was a maze of marble staircases, travertine walls, and lush cascading gardens, and my father had seen it several times as a boy.

Knowing my father's pedestrian tastes, I doubt that Vanvitelli's masterpiece made any real impression on him. My mother, by contrast, would have memorized every detail of that palace.

1

Mother was twelve years younger than my father; she was still in her teens when she married him in 1886. Her name was Maddalena Conti, and she too was a Neapolitan from Caserta. Her family's social standing was higher than my father's, and it was only a matter of chance that the two of them happened to fall in love. From the time of Mamma's confirmation, her parents, Fortunata and Patrizio Conti, had arranged for her to marry a cooper's son, a boy five years older than she. Until my father first took notice of her, Mamma had no objections to the arrangement, even though she had had nothing to say about it.

Father became aware of her as a young *bersagliere,* a corpsman, and no doubt his ornate uniform and military ways attracted her to him. Young, romantic, and naïve, she saw in him a rugged manliness that she imagined was tempered by a tenderness similar to her own. The years proved her wrong; from his rawboned physique to the depths of his personality, he was iron-hard in every respect.

His attraction to Mamma was physical—and understandably so, considering what she looked like. Few men could have resisted her. She was fair-haired, light-skinned, and no doubt supremely alluring in her pubescence. The earliest photographs I have of her highlight her delicately formed lips and her flawless pearl-like teeth. She was just over five feet tall, and her youthful body—slim legs and hips, wasp-like waist and ample, rounded breasts—would have turned any man's head, and certainly my father's. For although he was unaffectionate and steely by the time I best remember him, I learned later that he had been a "hayloft Casanova" in his younger days. My mother was the last, and I'm sure the finest, of the young women he found attractive.

America claimed them in the summer of 1885. Though they weren't married when they crossed the Atlantic (her parents sailed with them, suggesting that they marry in the States to avoid an ugly situation with the family of the cooper's son she had jilted), they married a few months after they arrived. Schenectady was their first home, because Mamma's older sister had married and settled there several years before.

Once a sleepy little Dutch town, Schenectady had been transformed by the railroads into a sprawling mercantile center by the time Mamma and Papa got their start there. It was on the threshold of becoming the electrical capital of the country, though its Locomotive Works was then its largest manufacturer. The General Electric Company would arrive in 1892, a few years after its inventor-founder, Thomas Alva Edison, established the Edison Machine Works there. From then on, Schenectady and Electricity were synonymous.

Mamma and Papa and her parents shared a rented flat with her older sister and brother-in-law. Like most immigrant Italians in Schenectady, they lived in the city's first ward, in a dingy area called Myers Alley. My sister Carmela, their firstborn, came into the world there on June 7, 1887, at ten o'clock in the morning; Mamma was sixteen years old at the time.

Beautiful and healthy as Carmela was as a baby, Mamma and Papa had wanted a boy rather than a girl.* It was three years before they got their wish. My brother, born in mid-June, 1890, and christened Antonio Patrizio, entered the world in more prosperous circumstances than my sister had. By 1890 Papa owned his own boardinghouse and saloon on Myers Alley, and was doing well enough to make him want to try his luck elsewhere. Mamma had no qualms about leaving Schenectady by the time my brother was born. Two years before, in 1888, the city had been paralyzed by a four-day blizzard. With no fuel to keep them warm, and very little food to eat, they had nearly frozen to death. The worst was yet to come: early in 1890, when Mamma was pregnant with Tony, a typhoid epidemic broke out, lasting nearly a year. Mamma wanted to move.

Papa's older brother rescued them in 1891. A saloonkeeper in Waterbury, Connecticut, my uncle—Alfonso Ponzillo by name—had edged his way into the Italian community there. He and my father made a good pair—Papa the brains, and Uncle Alfonso the muscle of the partnership.

My uncle was a fearsome-looking man. Squat and bull-necked like many Neapolitans, he had a penchant for street fighting that earned him a peculiar kind of respect among northern and southern Italians alike. A bloody reputation had followed him to Waterbury. He had been run out of nearby Southington, where he had worked in a factory, after he had beaten a co-worker nearly senseless in a fistfight. Uncle Alfonso was a dangerous man and everyone who dealt with him knew it. Oddly, neither my sister nor I ever saw that side of him; with us, and especially when Mamma was near, he was gentle, talkative, and respectful. But around men, especially men who patronized the saloon he ran, his temper made him as unpredictable as a caged tiger.

Papa went to work in Uncle's saloon and soon became his partner. The two of them never had a harsh word, probably because they were motivated by the same purpose in life. Money was their goal, and how they got it was unimportant to them. Their brains-and-brawn combination enabled them to better most of their competitors. I remember Papa telling me in later years that their competitors used to undercut each other's prices by watering the liquor and beer they sold. But Papa and his brother never had to dilute their stock; they sold only the best, and at prices lower than most of their competition.

The catch was that Uncle Alfonso got most of their stock illegally, buying it

---

* In November 1940, after her brief Metropolitan Opera career had faded, Carmela Ponselle decided to write her memoirs. Six double-spaced pages into the manuscript and, for reasons known only to her, she abandoned the project and relegated it to a moldy trunk in the basement of her New York apartment house. "Dear Mother told me she didn't look at me for two weeks," Carmela wrote of her mother's reaction to her. "Soon she crushed me to her breast and sobbed from guilt for lack of love for her first unwanted baby girl." Although the grandiose promises of the manuscript's title page were never delivered ("Romancing with the Gods, or How the Dreams of a Little Girl of Five Came True . . . Revealing the Life and Loves of the First American Mezzo-Star"), Carmela's abortive autobiography's account of Maddalena's reactions are believable and mirror the immigrant Italians' concern for strong sons to help the family as workers. J.A.D.

at a third of the usual cost through a stolen-goods chain. I don't know whether their clientele ever caught on. If they did, they never bothered to say so. For one, a good drink was a good drink, no matter where it had come from. For another, Uncle Alfonso might have bashed in their heads if they had raised too many questions.

Mamma raised some questions of her own. An intensely moral woman, she was never content with the increased comforts that Papa's "shady money," as she used to call it, provided; especially for my sister's and brother's sake, as young children growing up, she wanted them to have the security of an un-tarnished family name.

Because Waterbury's Italian community was relatively small, and because Uncle had such a fearsome reputation as a so-called businessman, Mamma couldn't help hearing about the way he and Papa got their goods. As a child Carmela would hear Mother question Papa about what was going on, and would then hide under the covers of her bed when Mamma and Papa would fight over it.

"Idiota!" he would scream at her. "How dare you question *anything* I do, especially when you and the children live better thanks to me!"

"But do you have to go against the law with Alfonso and—"

"To hell with the law!" he would shout at her, his face beet-red and his hands flailing at anything within reach. "The law is an enemy, not a friend!"

Mamma would let her eyes drop and sit quietly on the edge of their bed, having heard Papa's litany a hundred times.

"Eight years ago you stood before God and vowed to obey me for the rest of your life. *Do you remember that?"*

Mamma would nod her head.

"Now you have forgotten your vow, and you dishonor me by questioning the way I provide for my children!"

She would say nothing, hoping his rage would pass.

"Have I earned your dishonor, woman?" he would ask her acidly. "Have I failed to provide for you? Well, *have* I?"

Again Mamma would say nothing.

"Your silence tells me your secret thoughts," he would say to her, knowing that he had reduced her to the point of tears. "By your silence, as with your questions, you are saying that you don't love me, that you are not fit to be the mother of my children!"

Papa was half right. She didn't love him. She loved her children, but long ago had stopped loving the man who had fathered them. She wanted out, but couldn't find a way.

Desperate, she went to her parish priest. All through Lent, she confessed to him, she had prayed to the Virgin for guidance. Always her innermost feelings stayed the same.

As she poured out her frustrations, the priest warned that except in extreme cases the Church routinely discouraged marital separations. Divorce, he reminded her, was completely out of the question; Church law expressly forbade it. Mamma held her ground, pressing for a separation. The priest wouldn't consent but suggested a compromise: if she and Papa would allow him and two fellow priests to interview them at length, a separation would be granted if their marriage seemed irreconcilable.

Mamma agreed, if reluctantly, and then faced the prospect of having to take the compromise to Papa.

The hearing eventually took place, but not without Papa's violent protests. Taking family problems outside the home was a violation of tradition among southern Italians. Taking one's problems to the clergy, a group mockingly regarded as "half-men" by my father's generation, made Mamma's actions almost unforgivable.

Papa put aside his contempt for the priests long enough to plan a way to sabotage the hearing. Carmela was his weapon. She was seven years old, the age at which the Church deemed that children were rational; Papa knew that the priests would want to question her. Antonio, four at the time, was too young to be asked anything substantive. But Carmela was another matter, and Papa would need her on his side. Gradually, he began playing upon her feelings until he was sure that she would say what he wanted her to say.

The day for the hearing came and, just as Papa suspected, the small committee of priests asked to talk with her.

"Are you a happy child?" one of them asked her.

It was an odd question to a seven-year-old's ears, but she nodded yes. Then came a question from a second priest, a silver-haired southern Italian who had been in the States only a few months.

"The Mamma *good* Mamma you, yes? No?" he sputtered in broken English. Carmela looked at him quizzically as one of the other priests reminded the old fellow that she understood and spoke Italian. The older man switched languages and explained that he wanted to know whether Mamma had been a good mother to Carmela.

Confused and uneasy in the priests' presence, she said nothing. The old priest asked again.

"Papa is good to me," she said haltingly, squirming in her seat, "but Mamma isn't."

The others asked her for details, but she quickly broke into tears and instinctively ran to Mamma, as she had always done. Mamma, though devastated by what Carmela had said, clutched her and stroked her silken hair until she calmed down. The hearing ended soon afterward, with the priests refusing to grant Mamma a separation. The incident only deepened her estrangement from Papa.

After the hearing, their leaving Waterbury was a foregone conclusion. Their marital troubles were too public now, and everyone around them made it a point to give them advice, solicited or not. Papa got more than advice; the saloon "regulars," as well as a handful of Neapolitans whom Alfonso indiscreetly involved in Papa's troubles, ridiculed him for not putting his maverick wife in her place.

"What kind of man tolerates this!" they would rant at him, assuring each other over glasses of whiskey that if Mamma were *their* wife . . . well, a razor strop would soon settle her down. Papa felt emasculated by this hounding and soon began looking for another town to work in. At dinner one evening he announced that they would move to nearby Meriden.

When Mamma asked why Meriden had to be their new home, Papa said it was because saloons were beginning to proliferate there. Mamma offered little resistance, and as a salve he assured her that he would try very hard to minimize the tension between them. Even if there was no mention of love in his promise to try harder, Mamma contented herself that he seemed willing to forgive her for involving priests in their problems. Too, she reminded herself, Papa was at least devoted to Carmela and little Tonio.

They arrived in Meriden in mid-August, 1895, moving their meager furnishings onto the third floor of a three-family house near the intersection of Lewis Avenue and Bartlett Street in Meriden's West Side. Through Uncle Alfonso, Papa had managed to get a letter of introduction from a Waterbury *padrone* to the Donderos, a well-to-do Italian family in Meriden. The letter enabled Papa to rent from the Donderos, with the option to buy it, a thriving saloon on Pratt Street.

Within four years Papa would own not only the saloon but a small farm on Gracey Avenue, a thriving neighborhood bakery, and even a small grocery store. Mamma and the children helped, and Papa ran these businesses with the rigor of a *bersagliere*.

Mamma became pregnant for the third time in the spring of 1896. Life in Meriden had already yielded its rewards, and so she looked upon the prospect of a third child with an inner satisfaction. Papa, no longer influenced by his easily corrupted brother, had grown attentive to her and had begun to accumulate money. The children were rewarding in every respect. At nine years old Carmela was already striking-looking, and her teachers had nothing but praise for her sunny disposition and her unflagging obedience. Little Tony, though not yet in school, was no more mischievous than other boys and, like Carmela, he was even-tempered and was a neighborhood favorite.

With Carmela and Tony growing up so happily, Mamma thought, surely God wouldn't have given her a third child unless He had wanted it to grow up in a happy family. Mamma carried me with pride, believing me to be a good sign from the Almighty.

A few weeks before Christmas my grandmother, Fortunata Conti, sailed from Caserta hoping to be with Mamma when I was born. Grandmother arrived in time for the traditional Feast of the Three Kings and took delight in Carmela's fantasy that before very long either the Kings or Santa Claus—she wasn't sure which—would be bringing her "a real live baby doll." I, the "baby doll," arrived more or less on schedule on January 22, 1897;* my grandmother served Mamma as a midwife. The next day, drinks were reduced to half price at the Pratt Street saloon, and all afternoon toasts were drunk to Papa's enduring masculinity.

I was eighteen months old when Papa moved us to 159 Springdale Avenue in Meriden, the first and last home he and Mamma were to own. Springdale Avenue lay in a cross-grid of peaceful-sounding streets—Pine, Garden, North, Windsor, Botsford, Hickory—that had been populated, until the 1890s, by a group of rough-and-tumble Irish families. They had settled there after escaping their country's mid-century potato famine. A small group of German immigrants made their way into the area just before the Civil War, and though the Irish outnumbered them they managed to coexist with their aggressive, hard-drinking neighbors. By the middle 1890s they found themselves intermixed with Jews, Slavs, and especially Italians.

Papa bought the Springdale Avenue property for several reasons, but mainly for our family's need for more space. It was a need that neither the Lewis Avenue attic apartment nor his and Mamma's next home, a rented second floor in a frame house on Foster Street, had been able to fill. The Springdale property would provide the added space, and could be added to in time. Meantime, Papa thought of clearing the acreage he owned on Gracey Avenue and planting there a series of vegetable gardens from which he would sell the produce. The trees he would have to cut down he could sell as firewood, he thought.

Selling fresh produce and cords of firewood would require a certain amount of office and storage space, and this the cottage-like house at 159 Springdale could be made to accommodate. He also thought of getting into the lucrative baking business, and if so there would be plenty of space in back of the house where he could build the necessary ovens. Wine-making, or at least growing the grapes from which others could make it, also fascinated him. Here too the Springdale property had its advantages; the house sat on a deep, spacious lot, one big enough to accommodate the network of arbors he would need.

Mamma liked Springdale Avenue for different reasons. The house at 159 was close to Lewis Avenue, the area's larger thoroughfare from which streetcars to Main Street and the downtown area ran. Just as important, the parish church was close by. Our Lady of Mount Carmel Church, a frame building facing Lewis from Goodwill Avenue, was only a block way. The two-story brick schoolhouse on Lewis Avenue was even closer.

By the turn of the century Papa had realized many of his business plans. He

* *Ponselle's actual birthdate has been the subject of conjecture in opera circles, with various writers, colleagues, and others suggesting that she was born in 1894 rather than in 1897. It was Carmela, not Rosa, who subtracted from her age, usually giving 1892 (rather than 1887) as her birth year. County as well as Church records in Meriden list Rosa Ponzillo as having been born on January 22, 1897, and baptized the following March.* J.A.D.

had built on second and third floors to the Springdale house, and had converted the first floor to a grocery store. The second floor encompassed an eat-in kitchen, a good-sized living room, and two bedrooms; Carmela and I shared one of them, and Mamma and Papa slept in the other. The third floor housed a sewing room and two more bedrooms; Tony was given one of them, and when Grandmother came to stay with us she was given the other.

In back of the house, in a small frame extension, stood a wood-fired oven capable of baking one hundred and ten loaves at a time. Francesco Cocchiaio, a Neapolitan whom Papa had befriended in Schenectady, was hired to man the oven six days a week. Cocchiaio, whom we always called "Cheech," often acted as a buffer between Mamma and Papa, and more than once incurred Papa's wrath for telling Mamma where some extra cash was hidden. She had given it to a hard-luck family on Lewis Avenue.

In 1903, just before I turned six, Papa gave Cheech another responsibility. Tony, now thirteen and old enough to work, would become Cheech's apprentice, Papa said. Tony obeyed accordingly, and for a while liked the idea of learning a trade.* But at times the learning got rougher than he bargained for. When he made mistakes, Cheech would often back-hand him across the face or else would knock him to the floor by throwing a sack of flour at the backs of his legs when he wasn't looking.

As Tony grew into manhood and gained weight and strength, he grew less and less fearful of Cheech. I disliked Cheech because he tormented my brother, and I hoped secretly that Tony would get even with him. He did. After one back-handing too many, Tony tested his newly found strength against the out-of-shape Cheech and sent him reeling into a pile of flour bags. From them on, Cheech's attitude toward his apprentice improved.

As a child I suppose I was like every other little girl in our neighborhood—except for my imagination, which was unusually active. My imagination allowed me to escape the humdrum existence we led as immigrants, and made me notice people and things in a way that my playmates could not. They played hours and hours in a make-believe world, a world I created and governed.

My best friend, oddly enough, was a girl with whom I had very little in common, but whom I liked enormously and envied because of her daredevil ways. Her name was Lena Tamburini; she was a northern Italian whose family traced its roots to a small village near Varese, not far from Milano and Lago di Como. Just after the turn of the century her father built a combined house and saloon next to us on Springdale Avenue, and despite northern-and-

* During my first interview with Tony Ponzillo, conducted when he was eighty-six years old, he told me with a broad grin that he had become a baker "by special request." When I inquired from whom the request had come, he said, "One day when I came home from school, Papa said to me, 'You tell the teach' you no come back there no more. Tomorrow you start with Cheech to bake the bread.'" "That," Tony told me, "is how my father made his 'requests.'" J.A.D.

southern differences our families became quite friendly. In the hot summers it was not uncommon for Mamma and me to slip into the back of the Tamburini saloon and trade a few slices of fresh mozzarella or hard salami for a pail of cold beer. Nor was it unusual for Lena's mother to make an occasional dress for me, knowing that my mother was too occupied with the grocery store to be able to sew for me regularly.

Lena grew up a tomboy, casting aside dolls for baseball; her prowess at bat made her a sought-after player on street teams in our neighborhood. She was fun-loving and adventurous, and when pushed she could be as tough as any boy on our block. My brother, who considered Lena a third sister, liked to tell how she dealt with a local ruffian who had assaulted a young mother one summer afternoon. As the woman was walking with her two children on Lewis Avenue, this particularly troublesome kid had run up to her and had grabbed her breast. Lena happened along just as the woman was regaining her composure, and promised to do her part in hunting down the culprit.

Once she'd gotten a description of him, Lena confidently led the woman and her children to the boy's house. An army of neighborhood kids tagged along just to see what would happen. As usual, Lena gave them quite a show. Spying the brash, tousle-haired boy playing in his yard, she walked up to him and demanded that he apologize to the woman.

"Up your butt!" the boy said defiantly, ordering her out of his yard. Before he could get all the words out, a well-aimed roundhouse bloodied his nose. Lena had slugged him, knocking him flat.

Lena never went looking for trouble. But when it appeared, neither the size nor age of an offender could dissuade her from defending herself, her younger brother, or her friends. In the summertime the horse-drawn ice wagons that wound their way through the West Side were favorite targets of kids who wanted chips of ice to suckle. Rather than ask the drivers for loose chips, it was standard practice to hop on the backs of the wagons and steal them. I was too afraid of being run over or of falling off the wagon to try it, but Lena was always game. One August afternoon she and her brother were hard at work at their ice-pilfering when a driver and his co-worker spied them. Deciding to teach them a lesson, the driver stopped the wagon, reached for his horsewhip, and took off running after them.

Lena's younger brother, named Tranquillo but known as Joe in our neighborhood, was not as daring as his older sister. Fear of the horsewhip quickly overtook him, and he stopped running. While little Joe shuddered at the impending whipping, Lena grabbed a huge rock and reared back to throw it. The driver stopped dead in his tracks.

"If you so much as touch my brother with that whip, I'll bust your head open!" she screamed. Momentarily startled by such bravado, especially from a girl, the driver soon burst into laughter and climbed back on the wagon.

"Hah!" he snorted to his co-worker, pointing back to Lena and her rock. "That little redheaded wop is going to crack *my* head open!"

While Lena was busy rounding the bases in sandlot games, I could be found wheeling around a china doll in a baby carriage. In my imaginary world I was a beautiful young mother, and my whole life was to be spent looking after my doll. I washed her face, ironed her clothes (she had two little dresses that Mrs. Tamburini had sewn for me), and fed her from a makeshift bottle. I even saved enough money to buy a glass-and-tin "wedding ring" from a dime store. I wore it everywhere, telling anyone who cared to listen that I was a wife and mother, and that Tony was my husband. I was far too young for boyfriends as yet, although both Lena and I found ourselves attracted to some of the workers who lived in our neighborhood. Most were handsome, in their mid-twenties, and unmarried as yet. A few of them sensed our attraction for them and played along, giving us nicknames and paying us compliments. Most were German or Irish, and their light-colored skin and fine features captivated me.

When I wasn't playing with my doll, I could be found running errands for Mamma or, more often than not, I'd be reaching into our grocery's endless supply of cheeses and cured meats.

"You eat up all the profits," Mamma would tell me whenever she caught me snacking.

When my errands were finished, or when wheeling around my doll might get boring, I could be found playing games like follow-the-leader and hide-and-seek with Lena, Joe, and some of the other neighborhood children. I was incalculably gullible, and was often the victim of their practical jokes. Lena stood by me, protecting me or, when necessary, rescuing me. Not all of these pranks were harmless, though, and one in particular almost ended tragically.

Those were the days before indoor plumbing, when backyard outhouses still served a household's needs. Outhouses had to be moved periodically, since new holes had to be dug when old ones became unpleasantly full. Ordinarily, the new hole's dirt would be set aside for use in filling over the old one; the job was usually completed by boarding over or else roping off the abandoned spot.

Two lots up the street from us there lived a crew of southern Italian laborers. They were slovenly and never bothered to finish the job of boarding up their waste-filled outhouse hole. Instead, they left an unsightly pit. One spring afternoon when I was twelve, several of us grew tired of playing follow-the-leader and decided to pick some flowers for our teachers. I had been side-tracked by a spray of flowers that caught my attention, when I heard Lena calling to me. They had found several clumps of tiger lilies growing near the outhouse hole, she yelled, asking me to help pick them. Testing my gullibility (although I didn't know it, of course), Lena and the other kids balanced themselves on a wooden plank lying to one side of the gaping pit. I though they were walking *on* it, as I couldn't see the board from where I was standing. They suggested that we resume the follow-the-leader game, and informed me that it was my turn to cross the pit.

I took them seriously.

Seconds afterward I sank neck-deep into the abandoned hole. I let out a shriek that could have been heard in New Haven! At first the other kids were startled, then they began to laugh, each extending a hand to try to pull me out. They stopped laughing and began to panic when they couldn't reach me without falling in themselves. I was screaming wildly by this time, and my shrieking roused a Calabrese shoe cobbler who lived next door. Shirtless and groggy from an interrupted nap, the stout old fellow managed to get a firm grip on me and soon extricated me from the pit. Needless to say, a long, hot bath followed.

Forty years after that god-awful incident, my husband, Carle Jackson, and I were in the midst of an argument; this was after World War II, not long before we finally parted company after years of troubles. Carle was a veteran argument-winner (he'd been married twice before me) and could toss around big words and impassioned phrases with the best of them. I was different—I sometimes threw *things,* not words. This particular time Carle was losing ground to me and, lacking something else clever to say, he threw his head back and said, exasperatedly, "Rosa, you're so damned clever, you could dive into an outhouse and come up smelling like a flower!"

To this day I'm sure he wonders why, instead of lobbing a vase at him, I laughed till my sides hurt.*

I was five years old when music entered our family life for the first time. I had nothing to do with it, being so young. It was my sister's doing, and because she chose to learn music, eventually I became what I did. It happened in 1902; Carmela was fifteen, my idol, the idol of every young girl in our neighborhood. If some of the other teenage girls in our area were thought pretty for their age, Carmela was, in everyone's judgment, absolutely *beautiful.* Other fifteen-year-old girls, teenage boys talked about; but *men* talked about Carmela. Our grandmother used to say that Carmela, except for her Ponzillo (rather than Conti) face structure, was as beautiful as Mamma had been at the same age.

She stood five feet four inches tall, and had an infectious smile that immediately showed itself in her dark eyes when she flashed it. Her breasts and hips, ample and rounded in classical proportions, were separated by a thin waist that enabled her to wear the simplest dress and make it look elegant. For all her

---

* *Thirty years later, when her Carmen was the focus of much controversy in the national press, Ponselle was to make mention of this incident in a way that eluded her interviewer, actress-columnist Jane Cowl. A rabid defender of Ponselle's gypsy creation, Miss Cowl told the singer that, independent of what any reviewers had to say about her Carmen, the Ponselle career had blossomed almost as no other's had, save Caruso's. Had there always been roses along the path to success? Miss Cowl inquired, knowing nothing of her subject's childhood. "Oh yes, lots of roses—and only a couple of thorns, really," Ponselle replied. Miss Cowl noticed a faraway look in the singer's eyes, a look that soon gave way to a knowing smile as Ponselle added an afterthought: "Yes, roses, a few thorns, and, when I was a kid, a touch of the stuff that helps flowers grow." Mistakenly, Miss Cowl thought she was referring to sunshine. J.A.D.*

bodily and facial beauty, though, it was her hair that made her distinctive; it was rich brown, like Mamma's had been, and was so long that it completely covered her hips. Its length became a girlish eccentricity that she kept well into her thirties.

Carmela had been active in the girls' choir of our parish church, Our Lady of Mount Carmel, and had a distinctive enough voice to enable her to sing occasional solos during the Sunday Mass. The church's organist, a chestnut-haired Irish spinster named Anna Ryan, took increasing notice of Carmela's darkly colored voice and instinctive musicianship, and eventually asked her if she'd be interested in studying music. Carmela always deferred to Mamma's judgment in everything, and though Miss Ryan was an outsider to the Italian community because of her Irish roots, Mamma respected her and said she would pay for Carmela's lessons. Miss Ryan explained to Mamma that she only taught piano and organ, and knew nothing about the singing voice. Yet that didn't deter her.

"Your daughter *already* knows how to sing," she told Mamma, "so I don't think I'll have to do anything but show her how to read music, how to play her own accompaniment, and just let her go ahead and sing."

In retrospect, the strategy couldn't have been better. Although Carmela never became the pianist Miss Ryan would have liked, her voice grew in range and expressiveness until, by the time she reached twenty in 1907, Miss Ryan was sure she would have a chance at a professional career. Adding up Carmela's assets, one could easily understand her teacher's confidence in her chance for genuine recognition. First, there was her voice—it was essentially a dramatic soprano, which, in her youth, could extend from the depths of the contralto range on through the soprano's high C. Yet her voice wasn't her only asset, important as it was. There were her striking looks, her bubbly personality, and her womanly poise—all of which she had been displaying regularly at a popular millinery shop called Hurley's, where she had become a model at the age of seventeen.

One of my earliest, strongest memories is of Carmela's weekly piano lesson with Miss Ryan, an event that I looked forward to even more than she. I would sit quitely, my eyes big as saucers, watching Miss Ryan's delicate fingers fly across the keyboard as she showed Carmela the way she wanted a passage played. I wanted to be like Carmela in every way, and after we returned home I would spend hours running my pudgy fingers up and down a windowsill in our living room, imagining it to be an upright's keyboard. Mamma would pat me on the head, encouraging me in my "playing," often singing a song or two with me as her "accompanist."

My eagerness didn't go unrewarded. Before long, I was seated next to Miss Ryan on the rickety bench of the church's upright, learning how to translate the mysterious-looking characters of the musical staff into harmonic tones of the piano. Happily, I learned very fast and played quite well. Miss Ryan used to tell me that I had even more instinctive musical ability than Carmela—a compliment that wasn't lost on my confidence-building, to say the least! I will say that the piano and I seemed made for one another; I knew how to position my hands and wrists instinctively, and never had to be reprimanded for using my wrists and forearms, rather than the simple motions of my fingers, to depress the keys. That already put me several cuts above most other piano students, and by the time I was seven I could play rather complicated pieces without any trouble. In fact, I progressed so rapidly that Papa gave up his miserly ways long enough to buy me a secondhand Huntington upright. From then on, Miss Ryan gave me lessons at home, arriving at eleven every Saturday morning and staying for lunch afterward.

It took me five years to win the small medallion that Meriden's music teachers jointly awarded to the best piano student in the city; I won it playing a Schubert transcription, and afterward Miss Ryan had me show off by giving me a Chopin waltz and having me play it, sight unseen. I was a very good sight reader but could play equally well by ear, an ability that saved me a few times when I strayed from the printed score.

Good as I became at the keyboard, there was one part of my playing that Miss Ryan never liked—my fascination for the string of piano "rags" that Scott Joplin had written, and that were making their way across the country in those days. Because I could improvise well I could play those intriguing tunes with the grace and feeling that Joplin seemed to want. "The Maple Leaf Rag," "The Entertainer"—they were the stock-in-trade of every good piano student (and you had to be really *good* to play them), much to the chagrin of their teachers. I never lost my love for ragtime, and used to delight in making up "rag" versions of great opera arias. I recall several occasions when my Joplinesque version of the "O terra, addio!" from *Aida* regaled both Caruso and Gatti-Casazza at Metropolitan rehearsals.

School often disrupted my love for the piano. Carmela had liked school, to Mamma's delight, but I simply *hated* it. School and I were as ships passing in the night—and, for that matter, if school had been in session at night, rather than in the morning, I might have stayed in it longer. For my part, I wasn't worth two cents in the morning, and didn't begin to wake up fully until noon. It was all I could do to stay awake, especially between nine and ten-thirty, when we had spelling lessons, some geography, and a sort of science course. About ten-thirty we had a short recess, which allowed me to wake up long enough to hold out till noon, when we could eat lunch.

Only twice do I remember being stimulated by anything at school. Once was when I saw a picture of the larynx, which, I was told, was where the singing voice came from. What with Carmela being a singer, and I learning to sing scales and mimic her exercises, *that* fascinated me. Otherwise, the only time I enjoyed myself in school was when we studied music, which was once every week. We had a middle-aged man whom the school system paid to teach music at a different school each weekday. At the Columbia Street school I attended, Tuesday was our "music day" and I always looked forward to it. Each Tuesday I became someone special in my school; the music teacher carried me with him from classroom to classroom, asking me to demonstrate notes on the little reed organ the school owned. At times he even let me teach a class or two on my own—partly because I could sight-read and play better than he could.

If Tuesdays were high points for me, the rest of the school week was sheer torture. I couldn't stay awake, and when I could I was bored. I couldn't make heads or tails out of any of the subjects I was taking, and I could never understand what they were supposed to do for me. When I'd ask Mamma, she'd simply say, "You should know them because they are good for you. You're in another country and you have to learn how to live here." Still, I couldn't see why I had to learn about spelling rules, the American Revolution, the capital of China, and the rest of what passed as "the curriculum"; after all, I wanted to be a concert pianist, and to me anything but music was irrelevant.

My performance in school was as irregular as the winter weather in Meriden. I got good grades on my homework assignments—sometimes even a gold star or two. But on the in-class examinations, I was a disaster; either I flunked or barely got through them. Invariably, I would be called to the principal's office and would hear the same lecture, over and over: "Rosa, you do *so* well on your homework, and then you come to take a test and you can't seem to figure out which end of the pencil to write with!" I couldn't tell them that my friend Lena did all my homework for me. Without her, I'd have been Meriden's oldest living seventh-grader!

Once the school year was over—an event I looked forward to even more than Christmas—I could eat, sleep, and drink nothing but music. To my great surprise, I found that I could learn to play almost any instrument in a relatively short time. In the spring and summer months, my brother Tony played in a street band and for a time used our house to store the group's instruments in; his bedroom was the magic place where they were kept, and while he was working in the bakery in back of the house I would sneak in and pick up a cornet, a clarinet, anything I could find. I could usually manage a scale on them before Tony caught me and ran me out.*

I learned the rudiments of the violin courtesy of Lena. Her parents had coerced her into seven years of lessons, thinking that it would be a ladylike thing to do. I used to hear her squeaking her way through her fingering exercises, and used to kid her about it. For a while Tony and I named her "Maudie Pow-

---

* *Tony, to whom she was close as a youngster, was generally very kind to her, and once paid her a supreme compliment on her musical ability. For some time he had had to endure the tortured accordion-playing of a neighbor, only to hear the instrument finally yield some real music one summer morning. Later in the afternoon when he and Cheech had shut down the bakery, he saw Rosa playing in the yard and nonchalantly asked whether the neighbor had finally hired a teacher. When she asked what he meant, he told her that a "real pro" had been playing the instrument that morning. When he told her what piece he had heard performed so beautifully, she beamed and said that it was she who had been playing.* J.A.D.

ell, Junior," after the great violinist whose picture appeared now and then in our newspaper. One day, after my kidding got to her a bit, she handed the instrument to me and said, "Okay, if you think this is so easy, *you* learn to play the stupid thing." Within three days I could play better than she, even with my unorthodox fingering. From then on my brother referred to us, in mock deference, as "Maudie Powell and her partner, Fritzi Kreisler."

I learned the rudiments of the cornet in a similar way. A member of one of our neighborhood families, the Di Persios, was a fine cornetist who played in the band concerts that Meriden's parks hosted on Sunday afternoons. I was fascinated by the power and the rounded quality of the cornet's tone, and finally I got up enough courage to ask Mr. Di Persio if he would mind letting me watch him practice. He invited me to his house and, quite to his surprise, I was able to play a C-scale from memory just by watching him do it twice. My tone was rough, to be sure, but it got smoother and mellower each time I tried. After a couple of weeks, I asked Mr. Di Persio if Mamma could pay him to teach me cornet.

"*Bambina,* I wouldn't bother with it if I were you," he told me, putting his arm around me. "Twice now I've heard you singing while you help your mother hang up the laundry. What I heard tells me that you have a cornet of your own, right there in your throat. Be thankful that you and your sister are blessed."

I knew I had a voice for one simple reason: I could sing virtually anything that my sister could sing. Often, I could sing louder, longer, and higher than she, even though I never tried to compete with her. Carmela would be the singer, and I the pianist; at most I would accompany her in a few of her practice sessions, though occasionally we would sing Neapolitan songs in *mezza di voce,* or half voice, while doing housework or helping Mamma darn Papa's stockings.

No one, including me, took my singing very seriously until Miss Ryan chanced to hear me singing in full voice. It happened on a spring afternoon in 1908, on a day just warm enough for house windows to be open. Miss Ryan was walking up Springdale Avenue on her way to our bakery, intending to buy several loaves of bread. She had to pass beneath our house's second-story windows to get to the bakery, and when she did she heard what she thought was Carmela's singing; the music she heard was Di Capua's familiar "O sole mio." Later, she told me that she hadn't given the incident much thought, except for the fine quality of the *crescendi* and *diminuendi* she had heard in certain parts of the refrain. It wasn't until my next piano lesson that she told me to congratulate Carmela on how nicely the "O sole mio" had sounded.

Imagine her surprise when I told her that it was *my* singing, not Carmela's, that she'd heard! From then on Miss Ryan had me concentrate on my singing as much as my piano-playing, and my life began to take a different direction.

Mamma helped by robbing Papa's till so that she could buy tickets to see

15

some of the great artists who periodically stopped in Meriden. Five times, thanks to her generosity, I was treated to a glimpse of what true musical art was about. The first was during a concert of the famed pianist Ignace Jan Paderewski—a lion of a man whose handsome face was framed by an unruly mane of hair, and whose playing struck fire in the hearts of everyone who heard him. As with Artur Rubinstein's playing, no one remained untouched by Paderewski's art; he dominated his audience, like every great performer, and made up in his magnetism what he lacked as a keyboard master. For at least a month after I had seen him perform, I drove my family crazy by mimicking his gestures and dynamics at the piano.

Then came my first exposure to opera singing—in the form of the fiery Emma Calvé, the greatest Carmen of her era and one of the greatest actress-singers of operatic history. I remember little of her program, except that she included the "Habanera" as an encore; otherwise, what struck me was the phenomenal range of her voice, both at the bottom and the top. Several times she plumbed the depths of the contralto range and, good ear that I had, I knew that at least three or four times she sang well beyond the high C. Miss Ryan told me afterward that in music circles Calvé was said to be able to sing the F above high C, having a range that encompassed almost four octaves. Whether it was true or not, she was one of the most dynamic performers I have ever seen—so much so that the stage seemed hardly big enough to contain her. She was a rather large woman whose movements were extraordinarily graceful (something I learned to appreciate even more when I took on Carmen myself), and who refused to confine herself to the piano's cradle on the concert stage. Instead, she moved freely about the stage, pausing here, rushing there, singing to every sector of the audience by the end of her program.

Luisa Tetrazzini entered my young life next. Mamma took me to see her when I was about twelve, after I had heard Calvé. At first, my young ears refused to make an adjustment to the florid, birdlike sound that seemed so different from Calvé's larger, more dramatic timbre. But as I grew accustomed to the distinctive Tetrazzini timbre, I quickly began to appreciate her uniqueness. Where I took notice especially was in her high notes; they were broad, finely focused, and wonderfully sparkling. They were produced naturally and therefore easily—there was no sign of any physical effort on Tetrazzini's part as she passed the high C.

Thinking back to Luisa Tetrazzini's singing, having heard most of the great coloraturas who inherited her repertoire, I think it's fair to classify her as a dramatic coloratura. But let me be very specific about this, because the term "dramatic coloratura" admits to at least two meanings. On the one hand, there have been dramatic sopranos with coloratura capabilities; in my time I was considered one, as was my Polish-born colleague Rosa Raisa. On the other hand, there have been coloraturas whose voices have been of greater size and weightier timbre than most others. Joan Sutherland is a contemporary example. So was Luisa Tetrazzini in the 1910s. I am proud to be able to say that I heard her in her prime.

The same held for the imperious Melba—Dame Nellie Melba, *née* Helen Mitchell of Melbourne (and hence the name Melba), Australia. Miss Ryan took me to hear this silver-voiced legend when I was thirteen, and assured me in advance that I would be hearing a voice second only to Adelina Patti's in its prime. We saw Melba at the Poli Theatre in Meriden, where she sang to a capacity house; she sang only routinely heard songs and arias, none of which was especially challenging. Nevertheless, the perfection of her technique was everything that Miss Ryan had claimed it to be. The voice had a quality all its own—a sparkling, shimmering, silvery timbre that showed no tonal differences from its lowest to highest reaches. Its seamless quality and purity of texture were what set apart the Melba voice from others in its day; except for the beautiful Emma Eames, whose voice was said to equal Melba's (though I never heard Eames myself), the simple perfection of the Melba organ was unrivaled in its time. Her other assets were proportionately few; she was a static performer and an indifferent interpreter. And while I was indeed impressed with her as a young girl, especially by her easy production, her singing lacked the drive and Latin warmth I prefer.

I tried to honor her reputation by taking her last name when I was confirmed in 1911. The ritual of confirmation in the Catholic Church called for each young person to take the name of a religious figure whose achievements would be an inspiration throughout life. I could think of no one more inspiring than Melba, at least for my purposes, so I announced on Confirmation Day that I wanted to be called Rosa Melba Ponzillo. Our parish priest, an ill-humored, crass, corrupt man who was cordially hated by most of his congregation, stared at me and in a heated voice informed the congregation that the Holy See recognized no "Saint Melba." My confirmation name would be Rosa *Maria* Ponzillo, after the Virgin. When it came time to administer the ceremonial slap to exorcise the influences of Satan, the priest hit me with a blow that left me dizzy for the rest of the Mass. So much for Saint Melba!

Marvelous as Calvé, Tetrazzini, and Melba were, they were eventually displaced in my memory by the fourth and last of the opera singers I was to hear in my childhood. This lady was neither as beautiful facially as Emma Calvé nor as stately (or, some might say, as haughty) as Nellie Melba, nor as bubbly onstage as Luisa Tetrazzini. She was Ernestine Schumann-Heink, one of the grandest of all Wagnerian artists, a lady whom I heard when she was middle-aged and who at seventy would still boast more voice than many of her youthful contemporaries.

If it seems odd that a Germanic contralto should have registered more favorably with me than Melba, whose voice was considered a miracle, and Calvé and Tetrazzini, whose bloodlines paralleled my own, there is an easy explanation: Mme. Schumann-Heink embodied the highest ideals of musical art.

There was an understated elegance about her that made it unnecessary for her to rely on anything but her perfect technique. Her voice was marvelous—a true contralto, Teutonic in timbre but large, ringing, and nearly seamless from top to bottom. And unlike many German singers I've heard, her voice had no "still tones" in it—and by that I mean whistle-like, so-called "white" tones that have almost no vibrato. Hers had a rich, lovely quality that shimmered like a Latin voice. And she was *involved* in what she was singing; it was not in her nature to be anything but a serious artist, a communicator, a disciplined medium between the composer and the audience.

My brief adolescent encounters with Ernestine Schumann-Heink and Luisa Tetrazzini were to have interesting footnotes later in my life. Two decades after I heard Tetrazzini, when I was singing Violetta in *Traviata* in London, she came backstage at Covent Garden to congratulate me. Though she was no longer at her peak, vocally, she was still performing at the time. I especially appreciated her coming backstage, not only because she afforded me the chance to tell her how much I had enjoyed her concert as a young girl, but also because the role of Violetta had been one of her best parts. She had had a moment of glory in *Traviata* at Covent Garden, but her career in London had ended abruptly; petty jealousy on Melba's part, it was hinted, had driven Tetrazzini away from England's best-known opera company. If so, that was all ancient history by then, and I thoroughly enjoyed being with her backstage. The exquisite dancer La Argentina, with whom I shared Libbie Miller as manager, was also backstage and was photographed with Tetrazzini and me. I treasure both the photographs and the memories they bring back to me.

I saw Mme. Schumann-Heink in a less happy circumstance. I was in Hollywood reviewing negotiations for a film contract when Libbie took a phone call for me; the call was from New York, from NBC's executive offices. Mme. Schumann-Heink was then playing out her last years in San Diego, and was about to celebrate what would prove to be her last birthday. At General Sarnoff's urging, the NBC executives had wanted to do something special for her, knowing that she was not in the best of health. When they asked her what she wanted most, she had said, "I'd like Rosa Ponselle to come and sing for me." We arranged for Jimmy Melton, whom she was also fond of, to join me, and together we gave her a marvelous birthday party. She died not long afterward, in December 1936.

If Calvé, Melba, Tetrazzini, and Schumann-Heink were my first in-the-flesh encounters with the world of opera singing, it was my sister Carmela who remained my inspiration. It was she who took the first bold step to an independent life, she who first aspired to become a part of the world that we saw from afar in the likes of Schumann-Heink and the others.

In June 1908, on her twenty-first birthday, Carmela approached Papa with a plan that she, Mamma, and Miss Ryan had been refining discreetly for several months. If he would allow her, Carmela told Papa, she would take a train to

New York City, get a room there, and study singing until she could somehow break into the music world. Miss Ryan, Mamma said, knew the proprietress of the Euclid Hotel on West Sixty-fifth Street in Manhattan, where Carmela could rent a room and be properly looked after. Mamma went on to say that Miss Ryan had contacted a Manhattan voice teacher, a Signor Martino, who was willing to take on Carmela as a pupil once she arrived in the city.

Papa's reaction was direct and simple: Carmela would continue to live under his roof, would take a husband in the near future, and would then have babies, as women everywhere were accustomed to doing. Mamma pleaded with him to reconsider, to no avail; he had already considered the matter once, and had said all he intended to say. Soon, Carmela was in tears; Mamma cried, and so did I, even though I was too young to fully understand what was going on.

I had seen Mamma cry before, but this time it was different. Her tears were deep and searing, as if she, rather than Carmela, was being held back. Thinking back to that moment, perhaps that was exactly how she felt, and why she cried so hard. All her life Mamma had wanted to do something grand, to *be* somebody. As a young girl in Caserta she had wanted to be a performer, a singer, but had suppressed these desires when marriage to Papa seemed to offer equally satisfying rewards. The comforts of marriage had suited her for a time, but that had been short-lived; eventually, she had had to face the fact that the prospect of living her life on her own terms was all but nonexistent. Now, at the very moment one of her own daughters had a chance to escape the same fate, Papa stood in the way and refused to yield.

This time, Mamma fought back.

As a final and bitter rebellion against the customs of her people, she stood up to Papa and informed him coldly that Carmela was legally an adult and that, as a parent, she was now prepared to stand with her daughter. If that meant standing against her own husband, so be it.

Five days later, without so much as a parting word from Papa, Carmela boarded a train for New York. It would be the loneliest trip of her life.

NEAR THE OLD MET

AT THE RIPE old age of fourteen, Edith Prilik, who was to become my secretary eventually, knew exactly what she wanted to do with her life. She wanted to be a singer. What kind of a singer didn't really matter; she would have been just as happy singing ballads in a cafe as singing operas at the Metropolitan. An older cousin had helped decide things for her. The cousin, a single girl who earned a respectable living as a piano accompanist in several Manhattan supper clubs, had taken Edith to an engagement she was playing at fashionable Reisenweber's Café. Mystified by the surroundings, Edith sat in awe of her cousin as she listened to her play a medley of popular songs before the evening's ballad singer was to be introduced to the patrons.

The singer, unknown to Edith at the time, was Carmela. Reisenweber's billed her as "Miss Operetta," and from the applause that greeted her entrance, Edith judged that she performed there regularly. As male patrons craned their necks to catch a glimpse of her striking looks as she made her way to the restaurant's stage, Edith was transfixed by the statuesque pose she struck. An hour later, when Carmela delivered "Love Me and the World Is Mine" as her parting song, the patrons gave her a thunderous ovation. Edith joined in, and was hooked from then on.

Wanting to be like Carmela, Edith responded to an ad she saw in the *Musical Courier;* the floridly worded ad called attention to the "many stars of the world's great opera houses" who "owed their careers" to a certain Signor Martino. Not unexpectedly, the ad declared him "the most acclaimed teacher of voice culture now practicing in the Americas." Such a mighty endorsement was all Edith needed, and when she arrived at his Forty-fourth Street studio for her first lesson, she was awed by the rows of autographed portraits that adorned the studio's anteroom.

When the signor motioned her inside, she introduced herself in Italian—or made a stab at it, anyway, her awkwardness betraying her unfamiliarity with the language. She had wanted to give the impression that she was fluent in it, but now the signor knew otherwise. He essayed a few questions about her background.

"I was born in Russia, in Odessa near the Black Sea," she told him proudly. "My father was a furrier there—we're Jewish, you see, and Jews aren't treated very well in Odessa. My father didn't want my two brothers to be taken into the Czar's army, so he brought us all to America."

Martino nodded his understanding, and then changed the subject to Edith's desire to become a singer. He took a quick inventory of her assets and liabilities as a future performer; she was a bit short for the stage, he told her, but assured her that her slim figure and pretty face would serve her well with audiences. Then he asked her to sing a scale.

"Not bad, not bad," he said, nodding his head in approval. "It's a lyric soprano voice, very, very small and unsteady right now, but with work we might make it into something good." Undaunted, she thanked him for his frankness and signed up to study with him. Her father would pay for the lessons.

A month later, when no amount of work on either's part was yielding any dividends, Martino sat down with her and calmly suggested that she pursue some other career. Never one to take criticism without an explanation, she demanded to know what she lacked as a vocalist. Martino didn't want to offend her with a direct answer. He merely suggested that she return to the studio later that afternoon, so that she could listen to one of his very best students and then judge her own merits for herself.

At four o'clock in the afternoon Edith returned to the studio and was promptly introduced to Carmela; instantly she recognized her as "Miss Operetta," the beautiful soloist who had so impressed her at Reisenweber's. A few minutes into Carmela's lesson, when Martino had her rock the room with a high *fortissimo* and then diminish the tone to near inaudibility, Edith decided that indeed a change of career plans *was* in order.

Carmela sensed that she had just been used as an example by Martino; it had happened a few times before, with other pupils, but never to one so young as the dark-eyed Russian girl whose hopes she had shattered. Trying to salve any hurt feelings, Carmela offered to take Edith shopping; she accepted, and told Carmela that through her cousin she had heard her sing at Reisenweber's. At once a friendship began, and soon the two were making their way along Broadway.

Many years later, when we were reunited for the Christmas holidays at my home, Edith recalled how exquisite Carmela looked that day in 1909. "She was wearing a tailored tweed suit, a suit designed like a man's but cut so that it accentuated the curves of her figure," Edith remembered. "Her hat matched the pale gray of her suit, and she wore it at a rakish angle. Her hair, which reached her thighs when she let it down, had been braided and swirled along the sides and back of her head. She dressed like a model, but gave off a certain aloofness, rather like a Gibson girl."

Modeling, Carmela told her, had become something of a second career for her in Manhattan. Not that she was proud of it; showing off one's body smacked of the sin of pride, an evil compounded when money was involved. As it was, artists and photographers were paying her as much as fifty dollars a sitting to pose with her hair down, wearing the latest in evening gowns. She accepted only as many of these offers as her supper-club singing would accommodate. The money she made from these sittings she sent home to Meriden.

Edith repaid Carmela's friendship in a way that she desperately needed. For all the money and attention Carmela was getting, she was lonesome for family and friends, and was bewildered by New York City's size and raucousness. Edith offered her the friendly comforts of her parents' home, inviting her to their weekly Sabbath eve suppers. There each Friday evening Carmela would sample the riches of the Priliks' home at Madison Avenue and 128th Street, learning to savor gefilte fish, matzoh ball soup, and other kosher delicacies, all the while marveling at the home's ornate marble-paneled bathrooms and its carved walnut woodwork. On Sundays, Edith would visit her in her small apartment at the Euclid Hotel, and would bring pastries that Mrs. Prilik had baked for her. All of these kindnesses helped Carmela through stretches of loneliness and depression, and she returned them by taking Edith to all her singing engagements.

Carmela's first visit home, after nearly a year in the Big City, was an especially happy occasion. At the train station, Papa embraced her and forgave her for disobeying him. He assured her that the money she had sent home had been put to good uses. Though she could sense his injured pride over accepting money from his daughter—and money earned in defiance of him, at that—she treasured Papa's embrace, and took delight in the success of his and Mamma's business enterprises. Cheech, Mamma told her, had gone back to Italy, and now Tony was manning the bakery full time; business had become so good, Papa said, that Tony was delivering bread to Wallingford, Middletown, Westfield, Cheshire, and Southington, beyond Meriden itself. For the time being, at least, luck was favoring the Ponzillos.

Even *I* went to work, thanks mainly to Carmela. After two or three trips home, she decided I was old enough and talented enough to earn my own pocket money; my piano-playing had already earned me a good following in the West Side, so she took me to a dime store on Lewis Avenue and arranged for me to see the manager. In those days, dime stores were the chief distributors of sheet music, and good sight readers were needed to play new tunes for patrons. The man listened to me, said I would do, and offered to pay me five dollars a weekend to demonstrate songs for customers. Until I was fifteen, I worked from five until nine o'clock each Friday night, and then all day Saturday, playing songs on the order of "Down By the Old Mill Stream," "Every Little Movement," and "Let Me Call You Sweetheart" for the store's patrons.

It was Carmela who oversaw my next move upward in what could loosely be called "show business." By 1912, motion pictures were on their way to becoming a national pastime, and small, privately owned neighborhood theaters ("nickelodeons," in the parlance of the times), were sprouting up everywhere. The movies they featured were silent, and depended upon piano accompaniment for their effect. In New York City, Carmela had come to know several nickelodeon pianists and was amazed to learn what they were paid. It wasn't long before she was urging me to audition at the Crystal and Star movie houses, the only two theaters in Meriden at the time.

I went to the Crystal first, and was hired even though the theater already had a regular pianist on tap. I was hired as a substitute, but was retained also because I could sing. At the time, music publishers paid nickelodeons to screen "song slides," or illustrated song lyrics that were projected between features; because I had a voice, the Crystal used me as a singer, much to my delight. They also paid me well; I earned twenty dollars a week, a respectable sum for a grown man, let alone a teenage girl.

I had been at the Crystal less than a month when Mamma got a call from the rival Star theater. The manager, she said, wanted to talk to me about a job there. About noon one Saturday, a Model T touring car chugged up Springdale Avenue and came to a noisy stop in front of our house. Mamma, busy preparing our lunch at the time, rushed downstairs to greet the well-dressed man who was asking for me. He introduced himself as Richard T. Halliwell, the Star's owner.

"I own and manage three picture places," he told Mamma and me. "One is in New Haven, another is in Ansonia, and the other one is here in Meriden." We nodded our understanding and asked what he wanted of me.

"Well, to tell you the truth, my wife finally went over to the Crystal to see why we've been losing business to them, and she came back and told me that it's because you sing there. I told my wife that I guess we'll have to have you on our side, and I'm prepared to pay you a lot more than you're getting over there."

"But I already make twenty dollars a week, and I don't think I'm worth much more than—" Mamma gripped my arm, muttering in Italian that I was talking too much. "How much are you going to offer her, then?" she said, taking over the conversation.

"I'll double her pay—forty dollars a week—if you'll allow her to travel a bit."

"Travel? Travel to where?" Mamma asked.

"We'd start with Ansonia. My wife knows singing, and she says your girl is tops, that she's going to go places. So I'd like to try her in Meriden, and then have her sing a night or two each week at my place in Ansonia. And if the people there like her, I'll try her out in my place in New Haven."

Mamma nodded, wanting to hear more.

"Now, my place in New Haven is a *real* theater. Nothing small like the one here in Meriden. I call it the San Carlino, because some of the Italians in the neighborhood said the front of the place looked like an opera house someplace there in Italy."

"*Sì, come'l Teatro San Carlo 'n Napule,*" Mamma said to me, nodding, explaining that the opera house in Naples was called San Carlo and that Mr. Halliwell's place—Little San Carlo, literally—was named after it.

"These days," he went on, "people like to hear a good singer do song slides. The movies are fine, but a good singer like your daughter can really pack 'em in. That's why I'll go as high as double her salary if you'll let her sing in Ansonia a couple nights a week. She'll be worth it to me, and if she's good I'll put her on in New Haven, too."*

Mamma talked it over with Papa and, to her surprise and mine, he agreed to let me go. Whether it was the money I'd be making, or whether Mamma's and his battles over Carmela's leaving made him think twice when it came to me, I don't know. Nor did I care; I would be singing, and that was all that mattered to me.

Peculiarly, my greatest success was not in Meriden but in Ansonia during my early association with Mr. Halliwell. I had hopes of achieving real recognition in my hometown, but somehow it eluded me. It was one of several hurts that I received as a girl, and I could never understand why it happened. In his fatherly way, Mr. Halliwell used to try to explain it. "Maybe it's because they know you as a baker's daughter," he'd say. "Or maybe it's because the class of people who go to the movies in Meriden don't appreciate good singing. Whatever it is, don't let it get to you."

Singing in Ansonia made up for Meriden's seeming indifference to me. Although Ansonia and Meriden were nearly thirty miles apart, there seemed a world of difference in the way my singing was received. I got thundering ovations in Ansonia—once, the patrons even delayed a Francis X. Bushman-Beverly Bayne movie to hear me sing ballads!—but in Meriden I got the impression that I was merely a stage decoration, something to look at while the reels were changed upstairs in the projection room. I got so that I looked forward to the Meriden-Ansonia junket even in the depths of Connecticut winters, although we made these trips in an open, unheated Model T. I was always fond of cold air, and though Mr. Halliwell and the projectionist who rode with us thought I was crazy, my love for the open air had an explanation: I always got car sick in a closed automobile, and needed the continual rush of fresh air to calm my stomach.†

---

* *A decade after his association with the girl who was to become Rosa Ponselle, Halliwell was commissioned by the Boston* Sunday Post *to write a feature story on his "discovery" of her in Meriden. His version of their introduction is wrongly set, and depicts her as being much more independent and extroverted than she was as a teenager:*

"One day, while I was at the Meriden house, my wife came into the theater and said: 'I guess you'll have to get a singer of illustrated songs for the theater. This afternoon I dropped into the Crystal and Rosa Ponzillo is singing there. She has a wonderful voice, and it's bound to have an effect on your business.'

". . . I appreciated my wife's judgment and, while pondering over the matter that same afternoon, who should walk into the place but Rosa.

"'Say, Mister Halliwell,' she began, 'do you want to engage me to sing here?'"

It was at this point, according to Halliwell, that the two negotiated her pay. Ponselle's own version, which checked out with family and friends' recollections, is far more in keeping with her and her immigrant family's ways. J.A.D.

† *"I've wondered often whether or not Rosa Ponselle, as she now rides to the theater in her limousine, remembers when Rosa Ponzillo used to suffer the intense cold of those re-*

New Haven afforded me my first taste of real success. The reception I got in Ansonia made Mr. Halliwell want to gamble on my drawing power at the San Carlino, and soon I was readied for an official debut there. I remember my first reaction to the San Carlino. Compared to the tiny, dusty, cramped movie houses in Ansonia and Meriden, this was a veritable palace. The seats were upholstered in red velvet, the carpeting in the aisles was a deep gold, and the movie screen was suspended beneath a proscenium arch. It all seemed *so* big!

"C'mon back with me," Mr. Halliwell said, motioning me backstage. Behind the screen, which could be raised and lowered like a theater curtain, was a set of semicircular bleachers. Mr. Halliwell raised the screen, pushed the bleachers to the front of the stage, and then lowered the screen.

"See that?" he said. "Here you sing with a twenty-piece orchestra. No more pianos! Everything's first class here, and I'm giving you the very best."

My debut was scheduled for a Saturday night, the night the theater was usually filled with two distinct audiences—Italian-Americans and a few hundred Yale students. With all the energy of a Metropolitan impresario, Mr. Halliwell arranged the details of my San Carlino opening. I would sing Ethelbert Nevin's popular "The Rosary," and the orchestra accompanying me would be made up entirely of women. As I would walk onstage, a special slide would be projected, identifying me simply as "Rosa Ponzillo, *Soprano.*" I would make my way to the center of the stage, with the orchestra behind me, and the slide would change. Suddenly, the entire screen would turn a soft, pale rose color, and my face and body would appear silhouetted against an oval picture of an American beauty rose, bordered by a string of ruby-colored rosary beads. My face would be lighted by a makeshift spotlight—actually another slide projector that Mr. Halliwell had modified for the occasion.

The debut itself went wonderfully. The special rosary-bordered slide had just the effect Mr. Halliwell hoped for, and my singing of "The Rosary" went splendidly. The song was in no way demanding—it was a sort of drawing-room ballad, and it hardly extended beyond a single octave, making it almost a vocalise for an experienced singer. But its lyrics were deeply communicative, a cut or so above the love ballads of the day; in its lines, which began, "The hours I spend with thee, Dear Heart/Are as a string of pearls to me," an unrequited love was contrasted with the peace that only prayer could bring. I wrote the orchestral score we used at my debut; in my inexperience I peppered it with strings, harmonic chimes, and other effects, all of which seem embarrassingly dated now. By slowing down its tempo, and by using a long, sustained *diminuendo* at the climax of the song, I was able to wring every ounce of emotion from its lyrics. The effect was magical with the audience, and I

turn trips [*from Ansonia*] *at night," Halliwell wrote in his Boston* Sunday Globe *feature. Alluding to Meriden's indifference to her, he said, "Not long ago . . . a public reception was tendered her in the [Meriden] City Hall, and her admirers presented her with a beautiful chest of Meriden's own silver. Only a few years ago, when these people could have heard her for five cents, they didn't care to."* J.A.D.

repeated it six Saturday nights in a row.* Thereafter, I sang almost entirely in New Haven.

As word of my singing spread through the community, the Italian-Americans began to outnumber the Yalies and I amplified my program accordingly. Soon I included "Maria, Mari'," "Mamma mia, che vo' sapé?," "Ideale," "O sole mio,"† and other gems dear to the hearts of newly settled Italians. After one of my solos, an elderly Neapolitan woman gave Mr. Halliwell a package for me; in it was a well-worn copy of the score to Mascagni's *Cavalleria rusticana* with the pages of the character Santuzza's dramatic moment, "Voi lo sapete, o Mamma!," carefully encircled. It was the first opera score I had ever seen, and the very first opera aria I was to learn. When I sang it, I felt the full size of my voice open up, in ways so different from what I had experienced in popular-music performing. I had always suspected that my voice was bigger than average, but Miss Ryan, afraid that I might damage my voice if I sang very loudly, never allowed me to approach full volume. Mascagni's powerful *Cavalleria* made me aware of the true size of my singing and, to Mr. Halliwell's chagrin, I soon found that I had no trouble dwarfing the twenty-piece orchestra that accompanied me.

I had sung barely six months at the San Carlino when another offer came my way. My benefactor this time was James G. ("Jimmy") Ceriani, a Neapolitan-born opera lover and *bon vivant* who, unlike Mr. Halliwell, knew a great deal about singing and was a Metropolitan regular. He owned a restaurant, the Cafe Mellone, one of the most popular in New Haven and a particular favorite with Yalies. After hearing me at the San Carlino, he invited me for lunch at his cafe; he flattered me by telling me that I could be the equal of Emmy Destinn, the great Slavic soprano then at the peak of her career. I was skeptical, as I had often been told that I was in league with the truly great singers; but this time I was being told by someone who really knew opera, someone who had heard Emmy Destinn and was therefore in a position to compare my voice to hers. Eventually, Jimmy got around to telling me why he had wanted to meet privately with me: he wanted to offer me a steady, five-nights-a-week engagement at Mellone's. To lure me away from Mr. Halliwell, he proposed doubling my salary, paying me the grand sum of eighty dollars a week to do something I loved.

Accepting his terms meant that I would have to live permanently in New Haven; I told Jimmy that I would accept only if he went to Meriden and got Papa's approval. He agreed and, to my astonishment, found Papa generally unopposed to his plans, so long as Jimmy himself would take full responsibility for supervising me. He said he would. In a few days, Mamma had arranged

* *Halliwell's recollections in the* Sunday Globe *closely parallel Ponselle's:* "Rosa stood in the center of the [San Carlino] stage, dressed in a simple white gown, and with this slide on the screen, the beads on the canvas encircling her, she sang 'The Rosary' . . . As she came from the stage the audience almost roared its applause and a few minutes later she came to me and said, 'Oh, Mr. Halliwell, I think I have been successful at last!'" J.A.D.
† *The Neapolitan title is* "Lo sole mio," *abbreviated as* "'O sole mio." J.A.D.

my housing—I would stay with one of her cousins for a while, then I would move in with Margaret Da Vino, a young married woman whom Carmela knew—and before I realized it, I was packed and on my way to New Haven in Jimmy's big Buick sedan.

News of my engagement at Mellone's was soon overshadowed by even bigger news from New York City: Carmela had been awarded the lead in a new musical called *The Girl from Brighton Beach,* soon to open at the Fox Theater on Fourteenth Street. It was to be her first theatrical success, and critics warmed especially to her singing in one of the show's production numbers, a piece titled "Good-bye, Rose." Soon Carmela was sending home envelopes stuffed with favorable reviews and with increasingly large checks from her Broadway appearances.

Everyone was happy but Tony, it seemed. Week after week he donned his baker's cap, stoked the wood-fired oven, and mixed the dough from which some five hundred loaves of bread would be baked and packaged each day. On weekends Papa expected him to help with deliveries, and whatever free time was left he was expected to spend cutting and delivering firewood to Meriden customers. For all of this work, from the time he was thirteen until he was nearly twenty-three, he was paid ninety dollars a month at most. By the time he reached manhood, it was not the salary that bothered him, even though I, his youngest sister, earned nearly as much in a week as he did in an entire month. What bothered him was having to live under Papa's thumb, and having to face the prospect of standing in front of a bakery oven for the rest of his life.

Tony had good business ideas for streamlining the bakery's production, none of which Papa cared to hear about. In place of them Papa substituted ideas of his own. He would buy the cheapest grade of flour on the market; he would bake smaller loaves to conserve what was already inferior dough; he would raise prices gradually to net him more money. Eventually, he decided to add an extra oven to step up production. As usual, Tony was expected to man the second oven at no extra pay.

One day, Tony finally demanded a raise. If he could not have more money, then at least he wanted Saturdays and Sundays off, he told Papa. To his amazement, Papa swore at him and slapped him across the face—a kind of treatment all too reminiscent of the "training" he had received under Cheech. At the end of the day Tony went to his room, packed his belongings, told Mamma what had happened, kissed her goodbye, and left home. He wired Carmela from the train station and asked if she would put him up until he could find a room of his own. By the time he got to New York, she had already rented a small room for him in the West Sixty-fifth Street hotel where she was living. She helped support him until he got his first steady job—as a salesman at Macy's.

For a time, Tony shared Carmela's ambition of becoming a Broadway singer. He had a pleasant *lirico-spinto* tenor voice that, like mine and my sister's, had been cultivated by Miss Ryan's simple instruction.* Had he been more disciplined, and more instinctively musical than he was, he might have had a fine career. As it was, he did manage to get an audition with the Metropolitan about 1914, and was given General Manager Giulio Gatti-Casazza's stock advice to beginners with promising voices. "Get yourself a good coach and learn the minor roles first," Gatti told him. "Then go to Italy and begin your career there. Then if you are good, you should come back to us."†

Life opened several new doors to me in New Haven. It was there that I fell in love, for the first time in my young life. My beau was a young Yale student named Frederick Stimson, whom I fell for at age sixteen. Fred had come to hear me regularly at Mellone's, and with Jimmy Ceriani's permission I went on several dates with him. He was from a well-to-do family, to whom my dark features, Mediterranean roots, and cafe-singing were completely alien. Fred became serious enough, despite their initial objections, to want to go to Meriden to ask Papa for my hand. It never got that far: Fred's parents, as often happened in those days, sent him on a "study abroad" year to Europe—long enough to forget about me, they thought. Although he respected his parents' wishes, Fred never forgot me, and our story had an intriguing sequel. He married a socialite whose bloodlines were more suitable to his family's tastes. From about 1922 onward, he brought her with him to my Metropolitan performances, whenever his business involvements would permit.

One evening he brought his parents, to whom the Diamond Horseshoe had always seemed the essence of culture and class. I was singing a *Trovatore* with Giovanni Martinelli. Fred told me later that his mother had been moved to tears by my singing and acting in Leonora's death scene.

"What a perfectly beautiful voice!" she had exclaimed to her son. "And she's an American, too!"

"Not only that," Fred said with a twist of irony in his voice, "she's also the cafe singer you and Dad forbade me to marry!"

Life has its ironic twists and turns.

---

* *Writing of Tony Ponzillo in the wake of Rosa's Metropolitan success, Richard T. Halliwell, in the same Boston* Sunday Post *feature in which he reminisced about Rosa's San Carlino days, said this:*

"There is another!"

"Rosa has a brother Anthony . . . the possessor of an unusual tenor voice. He has never taken a lesson and until he does, we'll not know, perhaps, what he may one day become in the world of music." J.A.D.

† *However awesome it is to contemplate all three children of nonmusical, immigrant Neapolitan parents having exceptional singing voices, in the case of the Ponzillos it was true. As Ponselle states near the end of this book, rumor had it that a relative on her father's side of the family—a monsignor, supposedly—had a magnificent baritone voice. There is no objective evidence of any sort to support the claim. Essentially, then, the Ponzillo and Conti heritages were devoid of any musical talent.* J.A.D.

New Haven was also my introduction to a seamier side of life. An incident happened to me there which, had I been a different kind of person, might have affected me for life. It happened on the last day of May in the year 1915, when I was eighteen years old. I had been at Mellone's about two years, and was accustomed to keeping late hours—especially on weekends, when Yale students kept tavernkeepers on the job well past midnight. This evening, an unseasonably warm one, saw us closing the cafe at two in the morning. Jimmy was locking the back doors as I awaited him in front of the building, near his car. Two men came along, both of them "in their cups." As they noticed me, they began walking toward me.

The look on their faces was unlike any I had ever seen and I got frightened. As I stood wondering where Jimmy could be when I needed him, I found myself looking into their faces. One was bleary-eyed, unshaven, and flushed-looking; a trickle of tobacco spittle oozed from the side of his mouth. The other was taller, stronger-looking, and eager for a kind of pleasure that I would have been the last to provide. The other man called him Harry. His full name, I learned later, was Harry A. Maxwell, a laborer from nearby Winsted, Connecticut.

I grew numb as they drew closer. I was so scared I thought I would pass out. *Pop-pop-pop,* I heard next—the sound of my blouse's buttons hitting the pavement, torn off by the brute whose hands were now pawing at me.

"Jimmy! HELP, JIMMY!" I screamed.

"Shut your mouth, you little wop!" the one called Harry muttered as he slapped my face. The sting of his blows made my ears ring.

The next thing I knew, the man was being pulled away from me. Jimmy was behind him, his massive arm locked around the man's throat. As the second man stumbled around, too drunk to fight, my assailant freed himself from Jimmy's stranglehold and threw a punch at him. The punch missed its mark. As the man reared back to throw another, Jimmy kicked him in the stomach and slugged him as he went down.

"You and your jerk friend had better get out of my sight or I'll beat your brains out!" Jimmy bellowed, his face flame-red in anger. "Pick him out of the gutter and never come back here again!"

"C'mon, Harry, he's too much for us," the shabby little one mumbled as he reached a hand to his prostrate friend.

The man lay there, completely motionless.

Soon the other man tried to rouse him. He lifted his head and recoiled at the sight of blood on his hand. When the man had gone down from Jimmy's blows, his head had struck the stone curb, fracturing his skull. Three hours later, he lay on a marble slab in the county morgue. Jimmy, who had saved me from being molested, was arrested and jailed for manslaughter.

Margaret Da Vino put me on a train to Meriden the next morning, where, to my surprise, there were newspaper reporters waiting outside our house. One of them, the Meriden *Journal,* wanted a story but I was far too upset to accommodate the reporter. By coincidence, Carmela was home and met the newspapers in my place.* Later in the day, Jimmy called me and said that he'd been released on a thousand-dollar bond and that the county coroner would hold a hearing to determine whether the killing had been justifiable. Tearfully, I promised to do whatever I could to help him.

Papa and Mamma went with me to the hearing. It was pure torture for me, although the coroner and the others present treated me very gently, explaining that my recollections might clear Jimmy once and for all. I cried several times during my testimony but told everything I could remember under the circumstances. Papa was interrogated next, because the coroner needed to establish that Jimmy had acted as my guardian.

In the midst of the questioning the coroner asked Papa whether he would have reacted the same way Ceriani had. A distinct chill came over the room when he answered. "The man would have died much sooner," Papa said in a monotone. Soon afterward the hearing ended, and Jimmy Ceriani was exonerated.

A few months after the incident, Carmela paid me a surprise visit in New Haven. She was making great strides in her career and was now appearing in vaudeville as a member of one of the smaller circuits. When she came to Mellone's to hear me, it had been some time since she had listened to me critically; too, she had never heard me use my full voice, at least the way I used it in the opera arias. Later she admitted to me that as she sat in a remote corner of the cafe, listening to me sing the big arias from *Cavalleria rusticana* and *Madama Butterfly* without any difficulty (I can honestly say, in retrospect, that I simply didn't know they were supposed to be hard to sing), she was forced to conclude that I was a better singer than she. She accepted my superiority in good sisterly fashion. Rather than resenting me, she wanted to help promote me.

As she heard me that evening at Mellone's, she thought back to a conversation she had had with Gene Hughes, her New York manager. Sister acts, Hughes told her, were becoming increasingly popular on vaudeville bills. He went on to suggest that Carmela take advantage of the trend and persuade some other singer to pose as her sister in a vaudeville routine. After hearing me in New Haven she began to see the makings of a publicity man's dream story, and was sure that Hughes would find me easy to work with.

Jimmy Ceriani drove me to New York for my audition with Gene Hughes, and while I was there he treated me to my first Metropolitan opera—a Valen-

---

* *The Meriden* Journal *of June 1, 1915, quotes Carmela as follows: "My sister is entirely unable to come downstairs or even to leave her bed. . . . The incident is closed as far as we go. Rose has given her testimony, and it is now up to the coroner." Actually, the hearing had not yet taken place, hence Carmela's allusion to Rosa's having "given her testimony" was merely a reference to what she had told the New Haven police when they had arrested James Ceriani the night before.* J.A.D.

tine's Day 1916 performance of Puccini's *Tosca,* starring Geraldine Farrar as the title heroine and Caruso as Mario Cavaradossi. I'll never forget the first impressions I had of the Metropolitan Opera House—the "Old Met," as it's now called, to distinguish it from the new theater at Lincoln Center. Its mawkish exterior, a solid yellow-tinted brick, led the press to dub it the "yellow brewery"; but the splendor of its red and gold interior richly offset its mundane-looking facing. The proscenium arch and the enormous gold curtain that hung beneath it were an awesome sight for a Connecticut girl to behold. And the fabled Diamond Horseshoe was every bit as glittering as historians of the old house have written. In those days the Metropolitan had two rows of boxes (a later renovation reduced the boxes to a single row), and in those boxes the cream of New York society displayed their upper Fifth Avenue riches.

After the curtain had rung down on the *Tosca* that Jimmy had treated me to, we made our way through the crowd leaving the galleries. I felt uneasy amid the well-dressed and seemingly important people we soon mixed with in the lobby areas. "I feel like an outsider among these people," I said to myself—and the thought must have shown on my face. As we left the theater, Jimmy put his arm around me and said, "Kid, you belong up there onstage with Caruso, not in the audience with me." I looked at him in disbelief, even though I appreciated his confidence.*

Carmela took me to Gene Hughes's home a few days after the *Tosca* performance. As soon as he saw me, his spirits ebbed; later, Carmela told me that he had pulled her aside and had said, "Who the hell are you kidding? Why, she must tip the scales at two hundred pounds. She's too big for the vaudeville stage." Although his guess at my weight was off the mark (I weighed just over one eighty at the time), there was no concealing my size. I sensed immediately that he held little hope for me, although Carmela kept after him. "Just wait till you hear her sing," she kept saying, reassuring him that I was everything she had said I was.

"Okay, let's hear you, kid," he said, showing me into his spacious parlor. "Your sister says you play your own accompaniment, so go to it."

I took my place at the piano, which dominated the room, and sang the verse and chorus to the charming "Kiss Me Again," from Victor Herbert's operetta *Mlle. Modiste.* Fritzi Scheff, one of Broadway's biggest stars at the time, had popularized a coloratura-like version of the song, and I performed it the way she did. Several moments of absolute silence were all it earned me until, all of a sudden, Mr. Hughes leaped from his chair.

* *In early interviews Ponselle cited* Tosca *as her first experience at the Metroplitan. In later years, however, she told interviewers that a Caruso-Farrar* Butterfly *had been the first Met performance she had ever seen, an event which she placed either in 1915 or 1916. The Metropolitan annals show that Farrar sang a number of* Butterfly *performances with a series of tenors in those two seasons (chiefly Giovanni Martinelli), though never with Caruso. In any case, the Valentine's Day* Tosca *and a performance of Montemezzi's* L'Amore dei tre re *two seasons later (March 22, 1918, with Caruso, Claudia Muzio, and José Mardones as the cast's principals) marked the only times she had seen any Metropolitan performances before starring in* La Forza del destino *herself.* J.A.D.

"I don't give a goddam *how* fat she is," he exclaimed to Carmela. "When can she open with you?"

My audition with Gene Hughes had taken place on a Sunday. The following Thursday at the Star Theatre in the Bronx, a fleabag of a place whose top-priced tickets were a quarter, Carmela and I made our vaudeville debut as "Those Tailored Italian Girls." It took us less than a day to "program" our act, and I worked day and night on the orchestrations we would need. We would begin with the "Barcarolle" from *Les Contes d'Hoffmann,* which we would sing as a duet. Then Carmela would solo in "Musetta's Waltz" from *La Bohème,* singing it to my accompaniment, during which I would cue the orchestra to join my piano-playing.* Together we would sing next "Comin' Thro' the Rye," whose melodic line I altered to include several measures of intricately harmonized runs, trills, and other bits of *fioritura.* Afterward I would take a solo—the "Kiss Me Again," à la Fritzi Scheff. Then would come "O sole mio," which we would sing in Neapolitan dialect, and last a rousing duet version of the well-known measures of the Prison Scene trio from *Faust.* Sung in unison, that would be our finale.

A few days before our opening at the Star, we tried out part of our act at Lorber's Restaurant near the Old Met, where Carmela was singing at the time. Mr. Hughes oversaw this tryout and had us stage "O sole mio" by having Carmela sing the verse from a balcony-like stage, with me "answering" her in the refrain; I would be seated alone at one of the restaurant's tables. "O sole mio" had always been a favorite of ours, and the effect of our arrangement at Lorber's gave us an important vote of confidence.

How well our act was received by the New York public is, I am proud to say, a matter of record in the annals of vaudeville. The fact that we played and eventually became headliners at that Mecca of Vaudeville, the Palace Theatre, speaks authoritatively on our behalf. Located about ten squares from the Metropolitan Opera House, the Palace stood at Forty-seventh and Broadway and was arguably the most beautiful vaudeville theater in America. The theater was all of four years old when Carmela and I arrived there in 1917, and its inner beauty was absolutely breathtaking. Exquisite Italian marble dominated the interior, and even the immense rail that circled the rear of the auditorium was solid marble.

Eight hundred delicately upholstered, flower-imprinted seats filled the theater. Suspended above them were two enormous crystal chandeliers. The orchestra pit was as large as an opera house's, and the acoustics at the Palace were so perfect that they spoiled performers for any other theater. So did the audiences—especially on Mondays, when most of the auditorium was filled by

---

* *It is interesting to note, as Rosa often took care to point out in interviews, that during their vaudeville days Carmela sang as a soprano and not a mezzo-soprano. Thus, her singing of Musetta's waltz was in the key in which Puccini had written it. Only under William Thorner's influence in 1919–20 did Carmela begin to be billed as a mezzo.* J.A.D.

other show people, following a tradition that had grown up about 1915–16. When an act got thunderous applause on a Monday at the Palace, the act had reached the pinnacle of success in vaudeville.

For Carmela and me—or, as we were variously billed, "Those Italian Sisters," "Those Italian Girls," or our original billing in the Bronx, "Those Tailored Italian Girls"—our contract with the Palace organization came a mere sixteen months after we had made our vaudeville debut. Very few entertainers equaled our track record, and we were justly proud of what we had accomplished.

What were we like onstage?

Irving Caesar, the fine lyricist whose collaborations with George Gershwin and Vincent Youmans produced such popular tunes as "Swanee," "I Want to Be Happy," and "Tea for Two," caught our act at the Palace—once in Victor Herbert's company—and remembered it this way:

"To get a sense of the impact these two young girls had, you must first have a sense of the times, of the musical theater in New York just before our country entered the World War. Ballads were the rage of the day and Ernest Ball, Oley Speaks, Albert and Harry von Tilzer, and a covey of others were writing them. Operetta was the 'in' form of music and Victor Herbert, to whom I was very close as a young man, was the greatest composer in that genre. Around 1915 his *Mlle. Modiste* was revived. Victor had written it in 1904 and it had been a big hit during the 1905 theater season. Then, as in 1915, Fritzi Scheff scored a great success with her singing of 'Kiss Me Again.'

"Fritzi, whom I knew, had a very light soprano voice and she could do all sorts of coloratura runs and trills with it. She used to give 'Kiss Me Again' her full bag of tricks, and she was so vivacious onstage, so pretty, that it became a high point in all her vaudeville appearances.

"Picture, now, two Italian-American girls opening at the Palace Theatre, the last word in vaudeville houses. We in the industry knew about the girls because they had a good manager, and because they had become part of the Keith Circuit. They hadn't been with the Keith organization long—not old-timers in vaudeville like Fritzi Scheff, Nora Bayes, or Eva Tanguay—but they'd been knocking other acts into a cocked hat ever since they'd opened at the Star in the Bronx.

"When the curtain went up on their vaudeville act at the Palace, they created a visual effect even before they made a move onstage. Rosa was seated at a grand piano at stage-center, and Carmela stood next to her. Everything around them was a cool, limpid shade of blue—the backdrop, their skirts, everything except their white blouses was blue. The color of the lighting created a soothing effect and gave their act just the right sort of mood with the audience. The visual theme of the act was simplicity itself; everything was kept simple onstage so that nothing would distract the audience from their singing. Even their dress was simple—skirts and blouses, nothing fancy, nothing weighted down by clusters of diamonds or endless strands of pearls, à la Florenz Ziegfeld.

"As they acknowledged their applause, Carmela would make her way to the bend of the piano and Rosa would play a long *arpeggio* in preparation for the 'Barcarolle' duet. The 'Barcarolle,' with its graceful melody and rather slow tempo, kept the audience in a comfortable mood and at the same time showed off how easily the girls sang.

"Then Carmela would sing something popular, something pretty challenging—no orchestra, mind you, just with Rosa accompanying her at the piano. Usually she'd sing 'Musetta's Waltz,' and would show off her even, well-balanced voice and her fine diction. She was very attractive-looking, and the audience would applaud her generously. Then she and Rosa would do 'Comin' Thro' the Rye,' and from the audience it was almost impossible to tell which one was singing the melody and which one the harmony. Their voices sounded so much alike that many suspected that Carmela, whom they'd just heard in a solo, was doing the melody and that Rosa was carrying the harmony.

"That was very effective, you see, in building an element of surprise into their act. By then the audience was beginning to wonder how Rosa would sound in a solo. Their curiosity was piqued.

"At that moment Rosa would get up from the piano bench, and the orchestra would begin playing the opening measures of the verse to 'Kiss Me Again.' Now, remember, this was always associated with Fritzi Scheff, and so you can imagine what went through the audience's minds between the time the orchestra started playing the verse and she began singing her first line. Everyone would be thinking, 'Well, this spunky girl has guts. Let's cross our fingers and hope that she gets through this without falling on her face.'

"First would come the opening couplets of the verse, which aren't too demanding. Yet here the audience got its first surprise; it was Rosa who had the higher voice of the two sisters. Then she'd launch into those sacred Fritzi Scheff coloratura passages, with the near-octave drops down into the lower voice. That's when the hammer hit, right there. People would suddenly straighten up in their seats and there would be looks of astonishment exchanged.

"Then she'd come to the refrain, and she'd invariably take that last note in the verse and diminish it to almost nothing. Then would come that first line of the refrain—'Sweet summer breeze, whispering trees'—which lies very low for a soprano, so low that Fritzi Scheff and others had trouble singing the line audibly. But when Rosa sang it, it was as if someone had welded Tetrazzini's upper voice and Schumann-Heink's lower one. This was the most gorgeous sound ever heard in vaudeville, and it made Fritzi Scheff's voice sound like a schoolgirl's.

"You never heard such applause when Rosa would sing that final phrase, 'kiss me . . . kiss me again!'—holding that high note and giving it that tremendous rounded quality. Why, the audience would be on its feet before she let go of the note!

"Carmela would be back onstage immediately after Rosa's solo and would enter the stage while the applause was still at its peak. As soon as it began to fade they'd launch into 'O sole mio,' and there again Rosa captured the spotlight: she'd take the first note of the refrain slowly, softly, and would swell it until you thought the rafters would split—and then she'd take it down to nothing again.

"By the time their finale came, the audience would be so electrified that they'd want encore after encore. Between the two sisters, and especially Rosa, what with her tremendous musicianship, they could sing and play just about anything written."*

Vaudeville was a world all its own. A network of theater chains and management companies, or "circuits," vaudeville spawned many of the talents who were to become, in films, radio, and television, what today we call "superstars." The list includes Eddie Cantor, the Marx Brothers, Sophie Tucker, Jimmy Durante, George Burns and Gracie Allen, Jack Benny ("Ben K. Benny" in his vaudeville days), and a bit later, Phil Silvers, Milton Berle, and Bob Hope. Except for Eddie Cantor (whose early career was made by the posh *Ziegfeld Follies* where he shared the comic stage with W. C. Fields, Will Rogers, and the black comic-genius Bert Williams), the others were just beginning their empire-like careers when Carmela and I were playing the Palace. Although she and I were rather young (George Burns, Jack Benny, and I were roughly the same age, though Carmela was ten years older), as "Those Tailored Italian Girls" we became young stars in a galaxy that included, in those days, Blanche Ring, Sir Harry Lauder, Elsie Janis, Nora Bayes, Nat Wills, Walter C. Kelly ("The Virginian Judge"), Eva Tanguay, and other great stars, many of whose careers vanished with vaudeville itself.

The big-paying circuits for which we performed—Keith, Pantages, Fox, Poli, Loew, Orpheum—were to vaudeville what M-G-M, Paramount, and United Artists were to Hollywood. These were the circuits whose theaters, bookings, and pay schedules were the best, and whose founders—B. F. Keith, Alexander Pantages, Sylvester Poli, Marcus Loew—were among the giants of the entertainment industry. Theirs were national circuits, stretching coast-to-

---

* *The way the Ponzillo Sisters' act registered with the critics can be gleaned from reviews during their Eastern, Midwestern, and Southern tours in 1916–17. Topeka, Kansas, hailed them as "lovely ladies whose charm and poise on the stage bespeak far more training and experience than they have truthfully had, and whose musicianship is letter-perfect at all times." In Grand Rapids, where they sang the "Duet of the Flowers" from* Madama Butterfly *dressed in geisha costumes, the reviewer declared that "the costumes were mandarin, the voices golden." In Pittsburgh they merited these comments: "These Ponzillo Sisters are—or were—strangers to Pittsburgh. They possess voices of wonderful tone-sweetness, unusual range and flexibility, sufficient power for even a vaudeville stage [!], and the ability to handle them in a manner that left nothing to be desired." Their act, said the reviewer, comprised "a song repertoire combining operatic arias, ballads, and even a syncopation or two of the better sort." J.A.D.*

coast. Others were regional circuits, sometimes taking in only a single state. Texas had its "Interstate Vaudeville Circuit," binding together theaters and acts in Fort Worth, Galveston, Houston, Austin, Waco, Dallas, and San Antonio. On the West Coast there was the Ackerman & Harris Hippodrome Circuit, a network of theaters that ran from the Dakotas to the Pacific Ocean, from Vancouver, British Columbia in the north to as far south as San Diego. The theaters it took in—the Babcock in Billings, Montana, the Grand in Wallace, Idaho, the Liberty in Walla Walla, Washington, the Columbia in Provo, Utah, the Princess in Cheyenne, Wyoming, the Tabor Grand in Denver —are by now faded memories or else renovated movie theaters. In their day they were television's precursor, yesterday's most popular form of entertainment.

For those of us who worked the various circuits (we chose to call ourselves "artists" at the drop of a hat), vaudeville was a circus-like world—a world of impermanence, of living day to day and week to week, of carrying everything one owned in trunks and suitcases, of planning train schedules, of places to eat, sleep, and relax between engagements. Except for the biggest of stars, a vaudevillian's manager merely made bookings and laid out the most profitable routes for his "acts." From there on it was the performer's responsibility to get there, get fed, get lodged, and get back.

From New York west to Chicago, or south to Atlanta, trains were plentiful and travel was easy. But from Chicago westward it was a different story. Acts usually traveled one of two routes—either south to New Orleans by way of St. Louis and Memphis and then on to Los Angeles and the California coast, or else north to Minneapolis-St. Paul and then on to Spokane, Seattle, Portland, and down the California coast. Neither route was foolproof, travelwise, yet the unknowns along the way—plus, of course, the marvelous scenery—made the trips a great adventure.

Carmela and I often played the southern route, a route I retraced later during my early concert tours as a Met star. In our vaudeville days, Gene Hughes, our manager, would prepare us for the southwestern tour by doing what every other manager did for his acts—sending sets of publicity photos ahead to newspapers in towns along the way, forwarding our "bios" and press material to booking exchanges, which would arrange newspaper interviews for us, and notifying theater managers what props we might need. Often we made our way to Chicago by playing theaters in and around the big cities in New York, Pennsylvania, Ohio, and Michigan (typically Syracuse, Rochester, Buffalo, Erie, Columbus, Cleveland, and Detroit). Once in Chicago we would play either the Majestic Theater or the Palace Music Hall, and then we would be on our way south, where the fun would begin.

From the Dearborn Station in Chicago we would take a night train on the Chicago & Alton line, arriving in St. Louis at breakfast time the next morning. Carmela would be her usual wide-awake self, while I would be half asleep, as we would make our way by streetcar to the States Booking Exchange, where, we hoped, a list of appointments for newspaper interviews would await us. Our engagement, or "run," at the Columbia Theater would last a full week, requiring us to do one show a day and two on Saturday and Sunday. We were paid in cash Sunday afternoon and were on our way to Memphis that night, a distance of three hundred and twenty miles on the Illinois Central Railroad. Once in Memphis, we would play the Orpheum Theater, a spacious vaudeville house at the intersection of Beal and Main streets.

Fabulous New Orleans was our next stop—then as now an exciting place, a great city where, in its forbidden red-light district, jazz poured from battered cornets as freely as rum poured in the Creole cafes. That was a side of New Orleans we only heard about, mainly from some of the men who, like Al Bernard and Monroe Silver, both comedians with a taste for gambling, frequented them. Our knowledge of New Orleans was limited to the Lafayette Square district, where, a block or so away on St. Charles Street, we played the massive Orpheum Theater for a week. From there we would make our way to California, often playing either Fort Worth or one of the other towns along the Interstate Circuit, and eventually reaching Los Angeles. Through the northern routes we would make our way back to New York, arriving exhausted and ready for a restful vacation, able to take one because of the money we had earned.

It was money, ironically, that made us leave vaudeville and gamble on opera careers. On the face of things, the odds favored us; after headlining on the Keith Circuit and then playing the Palace in what was basically an operatic act, many thought we were sure bets for a contract with a major opera company. Just *which* company was the real question—and, frankly, not many thought we would make the Metropolitan because we hadn't sung opera before, and we had never even been to Europe, let alone to have sung there.

Romano Romani held out for the Metropolitan all along, even when we would shake our heads in disbelief. "Nino," as we came to call him, had a certain authority we couldn't deny. He had come to America with a formidable record in Italy, and numbered both Puccini and Mascagni among his mentors. Nino's first opera, *Zulma,* had had Puccini's blessing, and was given in Rome with soprano Eugenia Burzio and baritone Cesare Formichi in the cast. The Teatro Costanzi, then under Emma Carelli's management in Rome, had been the scene of the premiere of his second opera, *Fedra,* in 1915, with Formichi, tenor Hipólito Lázaro, and the incomparable Rosa Raisa in the leading roles. *Fedra* earned Nino the first prize from the Casa Sonzogno, the music publishing house that had awarded the young Mascagni the same prize for *Cavalleria rusticana.* While in Italy, recording had attracted Nino's attention and, as a studio conductor for an Italian company, he had conducted recording sessions for Titta Ruffo, Riccardo Stracciari, Celestina Boninsegna, Maria Barrientos, Nazzareno de Angelis, and others.

It was after a Raisa concert in New York that Carmela and I first met Nino. Though we were vaudevillians, we made every attempt to hear the great opera singers of the time, and among them Rosa Raisa was a "name among names." Born into an Orthodox Jewish family in Poland, she and her people had been forced out of their country during a pogrom and had settled in Italy. Her phenomenal voice was apparent in her teens, and Eva Tetrazzini, the sister of Luisa and herself a great soprano, took her on as a pupil. She made her debut in Parma in 1913, exchanging her given name, Burstein, for a Slavic word for "red," *raisa.* Conductor Cleofonte Campanini, husband of Eva Tetrazzini, immediately engaged her at the Chicago Opera, which he eventually managed. She became his brightest star, and even after his death in 1919 she remained Chicago's *prima diva,* making a success of nearly every role she touched. She and I were destined to become great rivals, though we remained fast friends offstage; to my fans, she was the "Chicago Ponselle," and to hers I was the "Metropolitan's Raisa."

Nino Romani introduced me to Rosa and afterward said to me, quite to my surprise, "I've heard you at the Riverside and your voice is even better than hers." I accepted this as a high compliment, rather than factual judgment-making, despite Nino's insistence that he was merely being truthful; like Emmy Destinn and Claudia Muzio, Raisa was something of a goddess to me and I refused to believe that I was in her league as a soprano. (To this day, despite what opera historians have written, I still tend to dismiss it.) Nino was so sure of himself that he took us to William Thorner, a top-flight New York manager who was then negotiating Amelita Galli-Curci's recording contracts.

Thorner auditioned us, but at first he was more impressed with Carmela than me. He lavished all his attention upon her, treating me as something of a nice afterthought. His opinion changed when, one afternoon, a retired baritone who frequently played cards with him stopped by his studio. The distinguished-looking man asked Carmela and me to sing for him. Thorner again heaped his praises on Carmela.

"Can't you hear the difference?" the guest asked Thorner incredulously. "It's the other one whom the gods have smiled upon."

This retired baritone, by the way, was Victor Maurel—the elegant Frenchman whose extraordinary dramatic abilities made him Verdi's choice for Iago in *Otello* and the title role in *Falstaff,* both of which he created. Though he was no longer performing when I met him, he was living in New York City, teaching voice and drama, designing sets, and having a sort of second career as a painter.* One of his young models, whom he coached in exchange for her posing, also befriended me at the time. When we met, she was already on her way to stardom with her equally beautiful sister. I speak of Lillian Gish, whose friendship I have treasured ever since.

Thorner replaced Gene Hughes as our manager in December 1917, at a time

* *Victor Maurel was, at the time Ponselle met him, already at work on the set designs for the production of Gounod's* Mireille, *which the Metropolitan mounted in 1919. He had appeared on the legitimate stage before beginning his operatic career in Paris in 1868. His wife also achieved a footnote in history, by virtue of having visited Dreyfus during his confinement on Devil's Island.* J.A.D.

when we were earning seven hundred dollars a week on the Keith Circuit. His first advice to us was to demand at least twice the money we were getting—not exactly a realistic suggestion, since we were already near the top in vaudeville salaries. We compromised at a thousand a week, a figure more in line with what we were worth as headliners. Our worth was rather clear by this time; we played on bills with the biggest of stars (Eva Tanguay and Nora Bayes were but two who come to mind) and we invariably stopped the show.

We were offered eight hundred, then eight fifty, but we said no each time. The longer we held out, the more some of our friends and colleagues began to wonder about our sanity. One was Eddie Dowling, the actor-producer who was married to comedienne Ray Dooley. When Eddie began telling us that we were being foolish holding out for more money, I said to him, "Mark my words, someday you're going to have to pay *ten dollars* just to hear us sing!" At the time I had nothing to back up my show of confidence, except Nino's and Thorner's predictions. The Keith management wouldn't give in, and so, in effect, Carmela and I went on strike.

For a while it seemed that Eddie Dowling would be proven right. Our names were dropped from vaudeville bills, and we spent most of our time singing limited engagements at Lorber's and other fashionable spots. Our income dropped dramatically, and some weekends we took the train home to Meriden because we had no place to sing. There we took part in local War Bond rallies, and were especially proud because our brother Tony had enlisted in the 145th Infantry. He was stationed at Kelly Field in San Antonio throughout the war and was spared the agonies of trench warfare in France. His singing career progressed thanks to a few engagements with the San Antonio symphony orchestra, earning him the moniker "Caruso in Khaki" in the local press. Carmela and I wrote to him regularly and kidded him that growing up as Ben Ponzillo's son had given him unique qualifications for fighting the Kaiser.

Our brief string of bad luck was broken late in the spring of 1918. It was then that Thorner's long list of Metropolitan and Chicago contacts began to pay dividends. Through Bruno Zirato, secretary to Caruso, he had gotten a message to the great tenor that he had "an answer to a problem." Only later did I learn that the problem was one of casting the role of Leonora in the Met premiere of Verdi's *La Forza del destino*—a problem that had been caused by the departure of several Met sopranos during the World War, a problem that was now causing Giulio Gatti-Casazza, the Met's general manager, regular attacks of anxiety. It was already May, and the premiere was to occur in mid-November. And while the rest of the principals had been cast (Caruso would sing Alvaro, Giuseppe de Luca the role of Carlo, and basso José Mardones the part of the monk, Padre Guardiano), there was still no Leonora. Caruso was in the mood to listen to anyone, as was Gatti-Casazza, and an informal audition was arranged at Thorner's studio. Caruso would make no advance promises to us, his secretary told Thorner, but would at least hear us. All we wanted was a chance—even though I, as Victor Maurel's choice of the Ponzillo Sisters, would be the focus of Caruso's attention for the moment. We were sure that Carmela's chance would come the first time the Metropolitan needed a dramatic voice similar to mine.

Caruso arrived punctually the afternoon of our audition. For the first time, I saw him up close; he was slightly above average in height, a bit overweight, blessed with a sunny disposition and a face to match, and disarmingly charming in a boyish sort of way. His clothes were as much a trademark as his unique voice; the afternoon he came to audition us he was wearing a lemon-yellow suit, with spats and a Panama hat to match.

"Hey, *scugnizz'*," he called to me as he entered the studio. "Do you know you look like me?"

He spoke in Neapolitan, which of course I understood. A *scugnizza*, I knew, was a ragamuffin, a sort of street urchin—an affectionate tag that immediately put me at ease. When he said I looked like him I knew that he meant that my features, like his, were distinctly Neapolitan.

"I don't mind *looking* like you," I said, joining in the banter, "if only I could *sing* like you!"

He laughed at my comeback, and I could sense him thinking to himself, "Well, now, she's certainly smart and brazen enough . . . maybe she'll make a good counterpart to me."

Once the pleasantries were exchanged with Thorner, Carmela, and Romani, we got down to business and I sang "Pace, pace mio Dio." Caruso gave me a hint of what was to come when, at the end of the session, he said to me, "You'll sing with me, you'll see."

"I'll sing with *you*? Where? In what?" That was all I could manage to say.

"We'll see, we'll see," he said reassuringly. "Maybe next year, maybe two years, maybe more. But you'll sing with me."

At that moment he put his arm around me in a fatherly way and, letting his hand brush my throat, he said to me, "You see, you have it there." Next he pointed to my heart and said with a warm smile, "And you have it there, too." Lastly, he put his fingers to my temples and said, "Whether you have it up there, only time will tell." It was the finest appraisal any young singer could have been given.

Two days later, Thorner got a phone call from Gatti-Casazza's office, asking him to bring both of us to the Metropolitan for a formal audition. We came and, in the presence of such luminaries as Caruso, Giovanni Martinelli, Frieda Hempel, Margarete Matzenauer, Adamo Didur, and Pasquale Amato, we sang our entire repertoires. I say "entire repertoires" a bit jokingly. At the time mine was limited to the "Tacea la notte placida" and "D'amor sull' ali rosee" from *Trovatore*, the "Suicidio!" from *Gioconda*, "Un bel dì" from *Butterfly*, "Voi lo sapete" from *Cavalleria*, and finally the "O patria mia" and "Ritorna vincitor" from *Aida*. Carmela's included the "Stride la vampa" from *Trovatore*, "Che farò senza Euridice?" from *Orfeo*, and the "Voce di donna" and "Stella del marinar" from *Gioconda*. Though we both sang well, it was clear that there was a growing favoritism toward me—understandable in light of the need to cast Leonora.

As Nino had been coaching me at Thorner's request, Gatti-Casazza asked to meet privately with the two of us after the audition.

"How long will it take you to prepare her in the 'Casta Diva' from *Norma?*" he asked Nino. Two weeks should do it, Nino answered. I nodded my approval, though at the time I had no idea what the aria involved; I'd never even heard it. Eight years later, when Gatti revived *Norma* for me, I thought back to that moment. Always thinking ahead, he had heard dramatic-coloratura abilities in my "Tacea la notte placida" from *Trovatore*. It led him to want to hear me try the "Casta Diva."

A third audition was scheduled, this one for June 4. Carmela was also invited but wasn't given anything new to prepare. Except for the duet from the second act of *Gioconda,* which we sang that afternoon, I commanded Gatti's attention exclusively. I was nervous as I began the "Casta Diva." Though it lay easily for my voice, it was surely a challenging aria. I felt my singing deteriorate as I went on—so much so that about three measures before the end, I had to stop. Suddenly I felt the room swaying; the next thing I knew, everyone was trying to revive me. I had fainted. Not gracefully, as in one of prolonged swoons once popular in the movies, but practically flat on my face with almost no warning.

Embarrassing as this was for me, it was even worse for Nino Romani. A few weeks before he had brought another protégé to Gatti—Icilio Calleja, a thirty-six-year-old dramatic tenor from Corfu, a promising singer whom Toscanini had presented in *La Wally* at La Scala a few years earlier. Calleja had sung in the premiere of Nino's *Zulma* and had been studying with him ever since. Nino got him an audition with Gatti—in this very same room—only to have his would-be star faint dead away in the middle of an aria! It must have seemed *déjà vu* to Gatti and Nino as they tried to revive me. Fortunately, Gatti saw some humor in it and even remarked to Nino, "Do you have any pupils who can stand and sing at the same time?"

Thinking back, I was nervous to begin with, and probably paced my breathing wrongly and just ran out of air. Whatever it was, when Gatti took me to his office I was sure he was going to tell me that my singing was not up to Metropolitan standards. I started to apologize for such a poor job with the "Casta Diva," but he quickly interrupted.

"You're not being asked to sing *Norma,* so don't give the incident another thought. Just sing the 'Casta Diva' for exercise now and then, much as you would sing any difficult vocalise."

With that he handed me a contract and asked me to read and sign it. It called for me to prepare a number of roles. The first and most important was Leonora in *Forza,* which was to premiere on November 15, 1918. I was also given Rezia in Weber's *Oberon,* an opera I had never even heard of; I was told to prepare it in English, the language in which its libretto had been written. The third role was Santuzza in *Cavalleria,* a part I had longed to sing ever since the elderly Neapolitan woman had given me a copy of the score at the San Carlino in New Haven. Gatti knew that I wanted Santuzza and promised it to me on tour in Atlanta, provided I sang *Forza* and *Oberon* well. I vowed not to disappoint him, and signed the contract after Thorner had examined its contents.

Caruso, I learned later, had stayed behind after I left Gatti's office. He had paced the room nervously while Gatti sat quietly behind his desk, staring aimlessly into space. Caruso's words broke the uneasy silence.

"I know what you're thinking, but I *know* she'll do all right. I'm willing to take full responsibility for her."

"You can't," Gatti said matter-of-factly. "I, not you, am the manager of this company, and the critics and public will hold *me* accountable if this girl fails. This won't be an ordinary debut, and you know it. Because she is an American, and because she has never sung in opera at all, the critics will make it a black-and-white matter. Either she will succeed magnificently, or she will fail abysmally. If she is a success, the doors of the Metropolitan will be opened to other American singers because she will have made it possible. She'll be a heroine to them, and rightly so."

"And if she fails?" Caruso asked. "What then?"

"Then Signor Gatti will be on the first ship back to Italy, and America will never see my face again."

HERE WAS A TENOR

I BECAME ROSA PONSELLE in mid-July 1918. Changing my name was Mr. Gatti's doing. It wasn't much of a change, he said when he gave it to me. He thought it would make me seem more "international"; *Ponselle* sounded vaguely French, but could also pass for an English or even American name. If nothing else, it was easier to say than Ponzillo.

Carmela's awkward situation was Gatti's main reason for making the change. She and I had taken a gamble when we went on strike in vaudeville. We banked on our ability to get opera contracts before our money ran out—a gamble that I had taken and won, but that Carmela had lost, at least for the moment. Although the Met passed her by at first, I felt sure that she would get a contract a season or so later; after all, if I were to prove myself at the Metropolitan, her debut would only make more headlines, I thought.

Thorner, knowing much more about the opera world than I, sensed that despite his confidence in her an offer might never come her way. To be sure, Gatti and his inner circle of advisers liked Carmela's singing. But they saw no reason to give her a contract, because of the wealth of mezzos and contraltos the Met boasted in those days. Margarete Matzenauer and Louise Homer—the one the possessor of the greatest mezzo-soprano voice of my day and the other, Louise Homer, an indescribably pure contralto, that rarest of all singing voices —had established themselves long ago with the critics and public. The more I heard of Matzenauer, especially, the more I began to yield to Thorner's uneasiness. Still, I had faith that Carmela would somehow win them over.

With Carmela having to go back into vaudeville, the Met thought it best to distinguish between us by name. It made us feel awkward for the first time in our lives. Not that we ever discussed it openly. We didn't have to. It was self-evident that we were now living in different spheres.

In one respect the name change meant little to me. Whether as Rosa Ponselle or Rosa Ponzillo, it was I who literally had to face the music on November 15. To begin preparing for it, I allowed myself the luxury of a new apartment, a two-bedroom affair on Ninety-seventh Street near Riverside Drive. Carmela and I continued to live together, despite our different situations; she took the apartment's second bedroom. In the living room we made room for another luxury, a six-foot grand piano. Soon we added a folding bed for Edith Prilik, who often stayed with us.

We weren't in the place long before we found that we had another guest—a fat little mouse that roamed the kitchen at night. I was already a confirmed animal lover (Mamma and Papa never had fewer than two dogs and a cat around our home in Meriden), so I wanted to make a pet of it. Carmela had other plans for the mouse: she wanted the poor thing's head in a trap. She spent at least one sleepless night a week chasing after it, but the mouse always stayed a broom's length ahead of her.

I'm afraid I added insult to injury by cheering it on—and, worse, after Carmela would give up the chase, I would feed it so much mozzarella that it would waddle back to its hole. One night Carmela found me out and threatened to send to Meriden for Robin, a tomcat that Papa had trained to hunt rats in the bakery's flour bins. Thank God she never made good her threat. If she had, I'd have had to feed the cat to save the mouse!

Mouse or no mouse, I quickly discovered that a two-bedroom apartment in New York City was not an ideal place to learn opera scores. There were too many distractions—the phone rang too often, the traffic outside was too noisy, the apartment wasn't soundproof enough—and the summer heat was positively oppressive in Manhattan. Nino Romani, who coached me daily (as he would for nearly twenty more seasons), grew increasingly impatient, and finally made clear that we'd have to find a more secluded place to work. Thinking back to my Connecticut days, I remembered Pine Orchard, a picturesque resort near New Haven, a lovely place that had its own golf course and a meticulously kept beach. I loved the beach because swimming was such good exercise, and I needed to trim off thirty-five pounds for my debut. I was rapidly becoming addicted to golf, too, and found it a good way to rid myself of the tensions of studying.

Nino, Carmela, Edith, and a cook I hired moved to a beach house at Pine Orchard near the Fourth of July, 1918. I invited Edith because she had become one of the family by this time, even though technically she had nothing to do. We found something, though: Nino suggested that I'd soon need a secretary, so Edith inherited a title. While Nino and I went through the *Forza, Oberon,* and *Cavalleria* scores, she taught herself to type on a borrowed Underwood. By summer's end she was managing about twenty words a minute.

When she wasn't typing, Edith would go to the beach with Carmela. The two of them favored a more sedentary life than I, preferring the beach to the golf course and tennis courts. Carmela, especially, did a lot of socializing at the beach; she would sit for two or three hours at a stretch, taking in the morning sun while brushing and combing her beautiful hair. By the time she folded up her chair and came back to the house, she would be surrounded by a covey of eligible young men, none of whom she ever seemed interested in.

She made an exception for Henry Giamarino, a young, good-looking New Haven surgeon whom our own doctor, Bill Verdi, introduced to her. Henry was as much attracted to Carmela as she was to him, and they spent as much time together as his medical practice allowed. Eventually they married—

secretly, because his mother and father, who thought all show-business women were tramps, refused to take part in a church wedding. The marriage lasted less than a year. When the divorce papers were filed, Carmela confided to me that Henry had insisted she give up singing and become a housewife. Remembering Mamma's plight, she had refused to "retire." Whether there were other, more deeply rooted problems that drove them apart, she never said. She spent the rest of her life as a single woman, only occasionally taking an interest in another man.

Preparing my first roles with Nino Romani was one of the great pleasures of my young life. I don't know who was more fascinated with whom; I was captivated by him, and he was by me. That summer, as July blended into August, he became more and more intrigued by my singing, so much so that by September he told me that I was destined for an even greater career than he and Gatti had imagined.

The chemistry of our working relationship was amazing. Especially with *La Forza del destino,* on which we concentrated the hardest, my musical insights into Verdi's score were, he said, well beyond my years and experience. I needed relatively little guidance in shaping phrases and understanding Leonora's personality; every bar of music, every line I sang, guided me intuitively to what I was sure Verdi wanted. But never before had I had someone to verify my intuitions, especially someone like Nino. Here was a man on whom both Puccini and Mascagni—each a god to me!—had bestowed their blessings, and whose classical education gave him literary and philosophical insights far beyond me.

Nino and I came to enjoy one of the closest of relationships, from my debut on through the early 1930s, and again much later in our lives. Even when others shaped my artistry for specific roles—Tullio Serafin for *La Vestale, Norma,* and *Don Giovanni,* Albert Carré for *Carmen,* Wilfred Pelletier in *La Juive,* and others along the way—every score but *Carmen* I prepared with Nino.

There are two parts of our relationship which, now that he is gone, deserve my firsthand comment. One concerns our personal relationship. Throughout my early career, backstage gossip had it that we were lovers, that we essentially lived together. It wasn't true. Neither of us had any reason to cover up a love affair, if one had ever existed; I wasn't married at the time and neither was he, so it would have been perfectly legitimate. I don't mean to say we weren't attracted to each other—I was a reasonably attractive girl of twenty-one, and Nino was a very handsome Latin who simply commanded women's attention. Still, the kind of intimacy we shared was more brotherly-and-sisterly than anything else, and was always grounded on our working relationship.

I should point out, both about my relationship with Nino and about my romantic life in general, that I couldn't have had a deep involvement—or even a casual one—if I had wanted. For one thing, Carmela and Edith lived with me. So did our teacher, Anna Ryan, whom we supported when she grew old. For another, Mamma frequently stayed with us on Riverside Drive, sometimes for several weeks. Even on tour, everyone but Miss Ryan went along—including Mamma—in those early years. If Nino's and my personal relationship was misread in those early years, so was our professional one—and it was partly my fault. For several years I agreed to let Nino advertise himself as "the teacher of Rosa Ponselle." It began as a harmless practice in the early 1920s; he was conducting studio-recording sessions for the Columbia record company at the time, and was supplementing his income by teaching voice. But factually, Nino never taught me to sing. Nobody did, not even Miss Ryan. I was one of those fortunate few who are, I guess, just "born to sing."

Perhaps the geneticists can explain it; I know I can't. All I know is that from about age fourteen I had a fully rounded, opera-like dramatic voice. As far back as I can remember, I never had what I would call a "girl's voice"—the light, breathy-sounding, high-pitched voice we normally associate with young children. My singing voice was always big and round, and even as a teenager I could sing almost three octaves. I never recall the slightest trouble swelling or diminishing a tone anywhere in those octaves.

But I wasn't a *perfect* singer—and this is where I learned a great deal from Nino Romani. Even though I was what you might call a "natural," I had a tendency to sing very high notes (say, the B natural, the high C, and the high D flat) incorrectly. Because I was essentially untrained (I had never had an actual voice lesson in my life), I tended to sing high tones a bit too brightly, not knowing how to "cover" them.*

Nino, who had worked in Europe with Riccardo Stracciari and Titta Ruffo, and who understood voice thoroughly, devised a simple set of exercises that helped me "cover" my high tones. He would ask me to sing a note in the middle of my voice, and then would have me sing the nonsense-syllables *ma-me-mi-mo-mu* while I held the note. These vowel sounds, he explained, were the ones that helped "focus" the voice. Then he would have me sing phrases like *deh vieni,* or maybe single words like *amore,* in progressive tonal steps, ultimately taking me all over the scale. Nino, great teacher that he was, never made much of these exercises. Often I did them in the shower, sometimes on the golf course, or even while swimming at the beach. By the end of the sum-

---

* *The distinction between* covered *and* open *tones is predicated upon the complex physiology of the singing voice, and is one of those distinctions that are more easily heard than explained. One widely circulated reference book defines* covered *tone* as follows: *"The tone-quality produced when the singer's voice is pitched in the soft palate. It is gentler, more veiled in timbre, than [an] open tone."* (The Concise Oxford Dictionary of Opera, *1978 ed., p. 88.*) *Voice teachers often substitute the expression "singing in the mask" for the phrase "pitched in the soft palate," referring to the sensation of a tone's emanating from the area between the roof of the mouth and the cheekbones—an area likened to "wearing a mask" by many voice teachers. As to the exercises Ponselle describes as having learned from Romani, these varied slightly over the years, although she adhered to the same basic vocalises. In warming up, she would always proceed from what might be called a "head-tone hum"—a hummed tone because the* m *sound would help "place" the tone "in a point"—and would then proceed to an actual vowel form. Hence, the* ma-me-mi-mo-mu *beginning exercises.* J.A.D.

mer of 1918, the top of my voice sounded exactly like the middle and bottom, and I was ready for the challenges of my first roles.*

A big bear hug from Mr. Gatti awaited me when I returned to New York in mid-September 1918. I was in excellent shape vocally, mentally, and physically. I was thirty-five pounds thinner, which immediately endeared me to Gatti, who preferred (but rarely got) his sopranos lean.

"You don't need to talk," he interrupted when I began emphasizing my weight loss. "I may be an old man," he said jokingly, "but my eyesight is still very good. My eyes tell me that you have been a good girl all summer, and I am very proud of you."

It took a couple of moments for him to realize that my thinner waist wasn't the only accomplishment of the summer. When I greeted him I spoke to him in Italian—a major accomplishment to me, because I had never been fluent before, except in my parents' dialect, *Napuletan'*. Thanks to Nino, I now spoke the more formal Tuscan Italian, the language of many of the great Italian composers. When Mr. Gatti realized what he was hearing, he gave me another bear hug and welcomed me to the Metropolitan as a bona fide *Italiana*.

His shrewdness as general manager had kept the Met's publicity wing from making me an overnight celebrity. Though I was unaware of it at first, my contract had caused a good bit of disagreement within the Met administration, mainly over how I was going to be "marketed." One camp within Gatti's inner circle was led by W. J. "Billy" Guard, the hawk-nosed public relations wizard the Met had enlisted after its forces bought out Oscar Hammerstein's Manhattan Opera Company. Billy wanted my every move captured in the view finders of the press corps's Graflexes.

Edward Ziegler, Gatti's chief assistant, opted for a different strategy. Rather than let the press "create" a new opera star, Mr. Ziegler wanted the critics and public to "discover" me when I made my debut in *Forza del destino*. Before that magical date of November 15, 1918, he wanted my name kept out of the newspapers except for a handful of unavoidable interviews.

Gatti had weighed both strategies and ultimately went along with Ziegler's. In retrospect, it was the safer of the two plans—safer for me and, just as important, safer for the Metropolitan. Gatti explained it to me this way:

"Caruso believes you will sing beautifully, I believe you will sing beautifully, and so do you. But suppose something happens and you don't. Then what? If we have promoted you too much, your career will be over before it has time to get on its feet. We will have invited the critics to make headlines of a young girl's opening-night difficulties.

"But suppose the critics come to the opera house without knowing very much about you, and suppose you sing the way we all know that you can. Do

* *Philadelphia critic Max de Schauensee maintained that the sheer size of Ponselle's top tones, circa 1918–19, had to be heard to be believed. In later seasons, he always held, she deliberately lightened her entire range for the sake of the* bel canto *roles she undertook.* J.A.D.

47

you see what happens then? They, not we, will make you a star. They will have come with few expectations, but will have left with a new name to write about."

There was more to the Ziegler strategy than this, as Thorner eventually explained to me. Gatti knew only too well that most of Broadway would be suspicious of any large-scale publicity that Billy Guard might mount on my behalf. After all, this was wartime and the Met had willingly enlisted in a patriotic anti-German campaign, divesting itself of several of its best artists in the process. Either because their roots or their sentiments were Germanic, Otto Goritz, Margarete Ober, Melanie Kurt, and Carl Braun had found themselves without renewed contracts during the previous two seasons. In 1917 they were joined by Johanna Gadski, the stately German soprano who had been one of the Met's most popular dramatic singers.*

With such losses as Johanna Gadski and the others behind them, Gatti and Ziegler knew that any attempt to heavily promote an unknown American singer—and, at that, one who had just played the Palace—would be viewed along Broadway as a poor attempt to minimize these losses. Then, too, if I were to fail at my debut, I might be able to negotiate a second, even a third chance with the critics and public, by which time I should be up to par. Gatti was sure this strategy was right—and, naturally, his wisdom prevailed.

I had hardly returned from Pine Orchard when our first rehearsals for *Forza* began. For a time, we in the cast rehearsed individually, then in small groups with a *répétiteur,* and finally in complete ensembles. Nino was unabashedly proud of the way I handled myself in all these sessions. My first triumph came at an ensemble rehearsal with Gennaro Papi, the conductor. We were having coffee during a break in a Convent Scene rehearsal, and I nonchalantly picked up his orchestral score and began thumbing through it.

"Nice section for the brass here, don't you agree, Maestro?" I said in a matter-of-fact way.

"*You* read scores?" he said in disbelief.

"Sure. I play them, too."

With that I walked over to the rehearsal piano, sat down, and sight-played several pages of the score. I could see Papi's surprise as I played.

"Too bad the *others* don't read!" he said as he cast his eyes about the room.

Although Nino had hinted at it, I found out that all but a handful of Met artists were unable to sight-read the clef in which they sang. Of the few who could, only two or three could play the piano. (A notable exception was Margarete Matzenauer, whose great technique and phenomenal memory for scores

---

* *Gadski, in fact, might have been the choice for Leonora in the* Forza *premiere had wartime sentiments not intervened. She had sung an array of Italian dramaitc roles (often with Caruso as a partner) before her marriage to Hans Tauscher, a captain in the German army reserves, began to create suspicions about her loyalties. Tauscher was deported as an undesirable alien.* J.A.D.

much outdistanced everyone else's.) While I was no Marcella Sembrich,* I was certainly good enough to win Gennaro Papi's confidence and to make some of my new colleagues take notice of me.

Heaven knows, I took notice of them!

Especially the incomparable Caruso—the most famous singer of his time, the most universally admired among all the tenors of that incomparable era, the most golden of all the voices in that Golden Age. Watching and listening to him rehearse the magical tenor moments in *Forza del destino,* especially the highly dramatic "O tu che in seno agli angeli," made me want to kneel at his feet. Here was a voice that *loved* you. His singing was purely and simply unbelievable, both in its dramatic and soft *legato* moments, as well as the intuitive musicianship behind it.

What was his singing like?

First, and most important, it was *natural.* When he sang, it seemed as if he was speaking—he merely opened his mouth and out poured those ringing burnished tones that one hears traces of in his phonograph records. Was his voice exactly like it seems on recordings? I would have to say no; I made my first recordings about the same time he made his last ones, so I know how limited the old recording process was. When I listen to his records, and I suppose I have listened to almost all of them by this time, I miss the rich baritonal quality of his voice—and I shudder at the fast tempos he was forced to take on records. Unfortunately, much of his artistry and even a good deal of his voice are probably lost to future generations on those old recordings.

What made the Caruso voice unique were its timbre, or sound quality, and its range. It combined the ease of a lyric tenor and the power of a dramatic baritone. (In fact, he could have passed for a baritone anytime and no one would have been the wiser.) He could so darken his voice that once he even went so far as to record, privately, the bass aria from the last act of *La Bohème.* Because of his unique voice, he could sing a pleading lyrical aria like "Una furtiva lagrima," from *L'Elisir d'amore,* then toss off the "La donna è mobile" from *Rigoletto,* and yet have the sheer power needed for such dramatic roles as Samson or as Eléazar in *La Juive.* Except possibly for certain of the early *bel canto* and Mozartean roles, to which the color and size of his voice, as I heard it, would have been unsuited, Caruso could have sung nearly anything.

I have often been asked how his singing compared with some of the other tenors of his day. I had the privilege of hearing two of his best-known contemporaries, Alessandro Bonci and Giovanni Zenatello. Great as they were, I can attest to his superiority over both of them. Of the two, Bonci was the finer artist, and struck me as being a worthy second to Caruso. For the most part,

---

* *Marcella Sembrich (1858–1935), who sang at the Metropolitan from 1898 to 1909, having sung also in the company's opening season (1883–84), was so proficient a pianist, violinist, and singer that she occasionally gave concerts in which she did all three—almost always to favorable reviews.* J.A.D.

though, it was impossible to compare them because they were markedly different in a number of respects.

Bonci, for instance, was at his best in some of the older classical operas like Bellini's *I Puritani* or Donizetti's *La Favorita.* There, his easy singing at the very top of the tenor voice (including the high D that he was rumored to have had) earned him plaudits; Caruso, on the other hand, would have been less at ease in these roles. Caruso's forte was the Verdi-Puccini-Mascagni roles and, as his career progressed, some of the more difficult French roles; too, he did very well in Donizetti's *Lucia di Lammermoor* and *L'Elisir d'amore,* roles he shared in common with Bonci. But in the *verismo* operas, Bonci couldn't convey the passion, the melodrama, that Caruso did. Bonci could convey sentiment but not outright passion; hence, he would have been miscast in the *verismo* operas.

Giovanni Zenatello was a *verismo* tenor who sometimes approached Caruso as an actor but never as a voice. Where Caruso's was rounded and plummy, Zenatello's voice was wiry and penetrating, with a tendency to become shrill the louder he sang. His greatest success was as Otello, a role that Caruso would have sung brilliantly had he lived—and as evidence I offer his and Titta Ruffo's singular recording of the climactic "Sì, pel ciel marmoreo giuro!," one of the finest phonograph records ever made.

Caruso was an interesting study at rehearsals. He was always punctual, and only did a few vocalises to warm up his voice. To conserve his resources, unless it was a dress rehearsal, he would sing in half voice, occasionally showing off his full volume if he felt disposed to. During most of the rehearsals he would sing high notes in a cantor-like falsetto, an eerie sound compared to what his voice sounded like at full volume.

What I remember best about our *Forza* rehearsals is the way he took care of me, especially as the date of the premiere approached. A natural clown, he often broke up our rehearsals by taking me in his arms, waltzing me to the nearest piano, and asking me to play anything from Neapolitan folk songs to Joplin rags. I often wondered why Papi never objected to such an apparent waste of rehearsal time. Years afterward he told me why; he sensed the wisdom of these spontaneous gestures on Caruso's part, knowing that they were calculated to keep my nerves under control.

The opening night of the 1918–19 season fell, ironically, on what proved to be the happiest day of the year—November 11, 1918, the day World War I officially ended. It was a Monday, and at the Metropolitan the day began with the usual nervous anticipation surrounding an opening night. Stage director Richard Ordynski, who was working with us on *Forza,* spent the morning reviewing the placement and sequence of the sets, to be sure that everything would be in its proper place before the curtain rose on Saint-Saëns's *Samson et Dalila.* Caruso and Louise Homer were to sing the title roles, and Robert Couzinou was to make his debut as the High Priest. Pierre Monteux would conduct.

The entire first act went without a flaw—from Caruso's heroic singing at the gates of the Temple of Dagon and the duet with Homer, "Je viens célébrer la victoire," to the "Spring Song," with which Homer, as Dalila, ended the act. Between Acts I and II, Edward Seidle, the company's technical director, received a note from Mr. Gatti asking him to lower the lights for the rest of the performance. This was a signal to the audience that something unusual was about to take place.

The final curtain had hardly come to a rest on the floor of the stage when it was raised again, showing the cast still in their costumes, but carrying the flags of the Allies. A deafening applause greeted the very sight of Caruso, Homer, Couzinou, Léon Rothier, and Albert Reiss (so short he looked like a little boy surrounded by adults), each in Old Testament garb and carrying the flags of Italy, Great Britain, France, and the United States. Monteux struck up "The Star-Spangled Banner," "La Marseillaise," the "Inno di Garibaldi," and finally "God Save the King." With the vocal strength of a real-life Samson, Caruso led the cast in singing the praises of the countries whose youth had made possible the armistice that concluded "The War to End All Wars."

New York City was still celebrating on Tuesday, the day after the Armistice —a day I spent attending to costume fittings and other details that had to be handled before my debut that Friday evening. I slept late on Wednesday, the day on which the general rehearsal for *Forza* was scheduled. I wanted to be at my peak that day, so I decided to walk rather than ride to the Metropolitan.

When I arrived at the opera house I wrote a "good luck" note to Giulio Crimi, the Italian tenor who was to make his debut in *Aida* that night. Already a seasoned performer by the time he reached the Metropolitan, Crimi had been on the stage eight years and was well known in Chicago, where he had been favorably received by the critics. Though he never pretended to have Caruso's voice, he had a fine *spinto* instrument that everyone at the opera liked. His stage presence and artistic integrity made him a solid performer, and there was little doubt that his debut would be anything less than successful. Still, I wanted to wish him luck.

After I left a note in his box, I got into my first-act costume and vocalized enough to assure myself that I was in good voice. Later I was glad I made these preparations, because I found out that the general rehearsal had been covered by several critics. One of them, Pierre V. R. Key, had this to say:

> Mr. Caruso . . . is an attraction by himself . . . [But] on this occasion . . . out of a seemingly-placid operatic sky, there flashed a newcomer who by her voice, her technique, her art and her buoyant youth, commanded instantly such exceptional approval that finicky opera patrons opened their eyes and ears and allowed themselves significant nods. The young woman responsible is Rosa Ponselle, an American, barely twenty-two years old. [Well, not *yet* twenty-two, anyway.]

. . . In a role of first importance, and singing opposite no less an artist than Enrico Caruso himself, Miss Ponselle stamped her quality and her individuality so firmly that it seemed no hazardous assumption to predict for her a career such as the Elect alone may achieve. Her voice disclosed a tonal beauty such as has not been surpassed by another soprano within memory. It is a big, luscious voice with a texture like a piece of velvet . . . [a voice] so extraordinary that experts present became almost lavish in their praise.

Feelings ran especially higher after the rehearsal, which Gatti celebrated by ordering a late-afternoon party at Lorber's. Though technically I was the guest of honor, another debutante graced our table—lovely Alice Gentle, our Preziosilla in *Forza,* who would also be making her debut that evening. After the last courses were served, and amid toasts from Caruso and other "veterans" in the cast, Gatti hired a cab to take Nino and me back to my apartment. As the driver pulled away from the curb, Gatti said to Caruso, "It's all going like clockwork. She isn't a bit afraid."

Unfortunately, he spoke too soon. The next day, Thursday, my bubble burst.

The day began quite normally; I awoke about eleven and ate a heavy breakfast while still in bed. After my shower I decided to go bicycling, and rode all the way to Grant's Tomb and back. I sang a vocalise or two after I came home, and while I was waiting for Nino, Edith handed me the afternoon newspapers. In one of them I saw a review of Giulio Crimi's debut.

That's all I remember.

Later, Edith told me that she assumed I had fallen asleep. She had been passing the time talking with Carmela, and no longer heard me stirring around the apartment. Eventually she walked by my bedroom and saw me sitting in a chair, clutching the newspaper. My eyes were locked in a stare and my face was as white as a bed sheet.

"Are you sick, Rosa?" Edith asked alarmedly. "What's the matter?"

"What's the matter!" I shrieked at her. "Have you read this review? Did you see what they did to poor Crimi? The critic panned him. He actually *panned* him!"

"Well, maybe it just wasn't his night," Edith said nonchalantly. "He'll have another chance and he'll probably be fine."

*"He'*ll have another chance! What about *me?"* I shot back. "Crimi is a veteran, a pro—and look what's been done to him! Why, when those critics get their pens trained on me, they'll grind me into sausage! I'm a complete nobody compared to Crimi—why, he's sung all over the place, and I just got out of vaudeville! The criticis are going to kill me!"

"No, they won't," Edith said, trying her best to calm me down. "Gatti knows you're good, Caruso knows you're good, and you know you're good. Now, everything will be all right."

"Like hell it will! What in the name of God have I gotten myself into! I don't belong at the Met. I tell you, they're going to butcher me Friday night!"

I was a basket case by late afternoon. Nino found me so nervous that I couldn't remember half the score. Later I tried to take a long walk, but got so upset that I gave up after only a few blocks. Finally, Edith called a doctor; he gave me a strong sedative and I slept most of the day. I awakened in the middle of the night, about 3 A.M., and had to be given another sedative before I went back to sleep.

Friday morning I was wide awake, uncontrollably nervous, and unable to eat anything. All I could think was, *Just what have I gotten myself into?* Edith had to call the doctor again; this time even heavier sedatives were prescribed. I slept uneasily for a few hours, until it was time to go to the opera house and get into costume. I arrived early and was so nervous that I couldn't go in. I actually prayed that a car would run over me so that I wouldn't have to die onstage—a prayer I was to repeat before every performance for the next twenty years. All I could do was walk around and around the building. Finally, some purple-colored bunting caught my eye in the street; purple was my lucky color, so I tried to convince myself that this was a good sign.

By the time I got to my dressing room I was in such bad shape that Edith and the makeup attendants had to do everything for me. I was trembling so badly when they put my costume on that Edith had to steady me. The worst was yet to come. Exactly twenty minutes before curtain time, Thorner showed up—not exactly a welcome guest, as I had hardly seen him since the day my contract was signed. I was hardly in any mood to see him now. At first he told me that he had merely come to offer me an *in bocca al lupo,* the backstage Italian equivalent of "Break a leg!" Unfortunately, that wasn't enough—he wanted me to vocalize for him.

"I vocalized at home," I protested. "My voice was all right a half hour ago, and I don't want to sing until I go onstage."

"I insist," he said in his unyielding way. "Just a couple of phrases to let me know that you're ready for the break I created for you."

By then I was frustrated, on top of being utterly scared. All I could think was, *You call this slow death of mine a* break? *Then why don't* you *put on this costume and go out there?* Finally I sang a couple vocalises just to please him.

"Oh, God—now I've *really* done it!" I screamed. "I've completely lost my voice!"

What I heard when I vocalized scared the life out of me—my voice was small and earthbound, completely devoid of its usual resonance. What I didn't realize was that the heavy carpets and draperies (which my maid had put in my dressing room that afternoon) had absorbed most of the sound, robbing my voice of its usual fullness. I didn't know enough to vocalize in the corridor, where the voice could resonate freely. I didn't know about such things—but Thorner should have. All he did was make things worse for me.

I'll never forget the first moments of the overture to *Forza*. Three brass chords, each sounding like the chimes of a gigantic clock in the middle of the night. I stood waiting in the wings, tears streaming down my face, my heart pounding so loudly that I was afraid I couldn't follow Papi's beat. Over and over I said to myself, *I'll walk out there, have a heart attack, and die right in front of them!* I could already see the *Times* headline in my mind—VAUDEVILLE SINGER DIES AT MET DEBUT.

What a way to make history! I thought.

As my cue approached, Edith handed me a brown leather wallet I treasured. In it were prayer cards and some miniatures of Christ and the Virgin. As I kissed them my makeup and lipstick left their colors on the wallet's glassine pages. *Jesus, Mary, and Joseph. Jesus, Mary, and Joseph.* One after the other I said aloud every little prayer I could think of!

"O, angoscia!"

Those were the first words I sang—and how prophetic they were! There I stood, as Verdi's hapless Leonora, singing to myself about my own anguish! *This isn't acting,* I thought. *This is the real thing!*

"Ah! per sempre, o mio bell' angiol!"

There he was—Caruso as Don Alvaro, his voice like a trumpet! How ironic was one of the first lines he sang to me—*"Ciel, che t'agita?,"* "Heavens, why are you so agitated?" I felt a boyish pinch as he sang the line.

"I'm dying! I'm dying!" I whispered between phrases. *"Coraggio, cara! Io ti sustengo,"* he whispered as I sang my lines—"Courage, dear one! I'll sustain you!"

Somehow I finished the first act. Caruso had saved me, both by his affection and his rock-like security onstage—a security that belied his shattered nerves before the curtain went up. He used to say to us, "To be a great artist one has to have suffered." By his own criterion, he was a great artist. Except for myself and maybe Lily Pons, who was in misery before each of her performances, I know of no singer who suffered like Caruso did whenever he had to sing a new role. He looked like a child awaiting an angry father's wrath.

Forza's second act had made me uneasy during rehearsals. Except for the gypsy Preziosilla's aria near the end of the first scene (which, incidentally, Alice Gentle sang beautifully that night), as Leonora I was onstage singing constantly for nearly an hour.

The first extended solo I had was the "Madre, pietosa Vergine," a prayer-like aria sung to the Blessed Virgin. Midway through it I got the horrible feeling that my voice was going to crack—a sensation that every experienced singer has had at least once, an utterly frightening feeling of impending doom. Somehow my voice held together. The problem was that my throat was parched. Later, I learned to remedy it by drinking pineapple juice between scenes.

In the final part of the first act I experienced something that made me forget myself momentarily. It was the "Maledizione" section preceding the magnificent "La Vergine degli angeli," a moment that belonged to basso José Mardones as the kindly Padre Guardiano. Mardones was one of those singers who hold back everything until the night of a performance—even in the general rehearsal he had sung in half voice. Consequently, I had never heard him sing at a full volume until that magic moment in the second act. Never was there a sound like this! I can only describe Mardones' voice by calling to mind the lowest pedal note of a cathedral pipe organ. None of the basses who came after him (and he died far too young) ever managed to approach, to my ears, the richness, the range, or the sheer volume of his voice. Here was a bass who could sing as high as a tenor, in full voice; for fun, Wilfred Pelletier once accompanied him in the tenor aria "Celeste Aida," at the end of which he sang a ringing B natural! Marcel Journet may have been a more refined artist, and Pinza a more striking figure—but none could match the voice of José Mardones. With Caruso and Titta Ruffo he remains without peers.

"*La Vergine degli angeli . . . vi copra del suo manto*"—here was one of the unforgettable moments of my debut, one of the most beautiful moments in all of opera. It was here that I realized my debut was a success. As the final tones of the orchestra died away, the house erupted and I was recalled a dozen times before the curtain.

After the second act my nervousness began to subside. The curtain calls assured me that I had scored with the audience, that I had survived my fifty-five minutes of Verdian hell. I had nothing more to sing until the last act, so I had the luxury of sitting in the wings and listening to Caruso bring down the house with his "O tu che in seno agli angeli." Again the house went wild when he and Giuseppe de Luca (who was rivaled only by Giuseppe Danise for elegance as a baritone) sang an incomparable "Solenne in quest' ora." By the time the curtain rose on the last act's opening scene, where Caruso and de Luca gave every ounce of themselves to the "Invano, Alvaro" and "Le Minaccie i fieri acenti" duet, I was actually eager to go onstage again. When I did it was to sing the "Pace, pace mio Dio"—an aria that, more than any other, came to be associated with me from then on.

After the final curtain, quite to my surprise, I received almost as many curtain calls as Caruso—a sure sign of my success.*

* *Few debutantes in the history of opera received such splendid reviews as did Ponselle in her first performance. William J. Henderson and James G. Huneker, two of the most exacting and uncompromising of the major New York critics, were quick to praise the magnificence of her voice. "The newcomer is an American, born of Italian parentage," Huneker wrote. "She is young, she is comely, she is tall and solidly-built . . . Added to her personal attractiveness, she possesses a voice of natural beauty that may prove a gold mine. It is a vocal gold, anyhow, dark, rich, and ductile; brilliant and flexible in the upper register. . . ." "Opera has in Rosa Ponselle a dramatic soprano of splendid potentialities," said Henderson, judging hers "one of the most voluptuous dramatic soprano voices" he had ever heard—a list that included Amalie Materna, Emmy Fursch-Madi, Lillian Nordica, Olive Fremstad, and Lilli Lehmann.*

The prestigious Musical Courier was unrestrained in its praise, declaring in headlines that she "upset all traditions by assuming a leading role at the Metropolitan, and without previous operatic experience, carrying it to triumphant success. It is no exaggeration to say

My clearest memories of my debut are of the events backstage, after the final curtain had rung down, after our last curtain calls. When I finally reached my dressing room, Mamma, Carmela, and Jimmy Ceriani were waiting with Edith. I burst into tears at the sight of Mamma and Jimmy— Mamma, who had lived all her life for the moment I now had, and Jimmy, who had boosted my confidence when I desperately needed it and who—God knows!—had probably saved my life that ghastly night in 1915.

Many of my friends from Meriden were there too—especially Lena Tamburini and Giulietta Dondero, my childhood chums. Lena, who had long ago matured into a striking-looking woman, was now married and no longer lived in Meriden. With Mamma and Carmela they read to me a wire from Tony, a telegram sent earlier in the day from the army post in San Antonio. *"A mia cara sorella, un' in bocca al lupo"* it said—"To my dear sister, a good luck wish."

Apart from my family, the first person to enter my dressing room was, interestingly, Eva Tanguay. Because of her vaudeville fame, she made quite a stir backstage as she made her way to call on me. She was radiant and full of compliments. While I accepted them gratefully, I couldn't help thinking how pleased she must be that I was now singing at the Met and not at the Palace! After all, a vaudeville reviewer had once written of us, "Tanguay gets the money, and the Ponzillo Sisters get the applause." Whether she knew that she had been one of the driving reasons behind our going on strike in vaudeville, I can't say. In any case, all rivalries were forgotten in the wake of her presence, her compliments, and the immense floral display she had sent for my debut.

Soon, Caruso, de Luca, and Mardones came to congratulate me. Still in costume, Caruso introduced me to his young bride, Dorothy, who had been watching the performance with his secretary's fiancée, coloratura Nina Morgana; it was Nina's birthday, Caruso announced, adding another reason for all of us to celebrate. Elegant Otto Kahn, one of the richest men in New York and the largest supporter of the Old Met, entered after Caruso and whispered in my ear. "A little memento for you," he said, handing me a plain white envelope; in it was a crisp new thousand-dollar bill.

As the long line of well-wishers gradually thinned, I recognized two familiar faces outside the dressing room. Ray Dooley and Eddie Dowling, with whom Carmela and I had performed at the Palace, greeted us like long-lost friends. Seeing Eddie, I remembered his face when I had said to him, "Mark my words, someday you're going to have to pay *ten dollars* just to hear us sing!" Before I had time to remind him about it, he reached into his pocket and slapped a worn ten-dollar bill on my dressing table.

"Kid," he said laughingly, "you won your bet!"

---

that she made a sensational impression and was sensationally received." *The reviewer for* Musical America *concurred. Upon noting his reservations about several of the other performers, and about the musical structure of Forza itself, the reviewer declared that "the production would have been worthwhile anyway because it brought forward Rosa Ponselle, [whose] incomparable charm, dramatic ability . . . voice of considerable power, and fine musical quality, absolutely captured the audience."* J.A.D.

NOT SINCE THE DAYS OF PATTI

"ROSA, YOU LOOK like hell!"

Not exactly flattering words for the Metropolitan Opera's newest star. But they were true. They were spoken by Bill Verdi, my physician and friend, who had watched the strain of my debut gnaw at me until I looked like a madwoman. The morning after my debut Bill made me board a train to New Haven, to check into a private clinic. There, he could look after me properly. I knew I needed a rest, so I went.

In my hospital room, Edith, Carmela, Miss Ryan, and Mamma took turns keeping me company until Bill pronounced me well enough to go back to New York. He made me promise that I wouldn't overdo anything, for fear I'd totally exhaust myself. Since I had nothing new to sing until *Oberon* on December 28, I limited myself as Bill suggested. I planned a quiet Thanksgiving with Edith and Carmela in our apartment.

Two more performances of *Forza* preceded *Oberon*. Both were with Caruso, one of them a Christmas-week matinee. "Caruso was again colossal," said the New York *Times* the next day, "and Miss Ponselle repeated the admirable impressions made at her two previous appearances." Such flattering comments from the newspapers made it easier to face *Oberon*'s weighty demands.

Oberon marked the first pairing of Giovanni Martinelli and me at the Metropolitan. It was the beginning of a nineteen-year artistic partnership that ultimately encompassed over one hundred appearances together. Giovanni Martinelli was still in his thirties when Mr. Gatti assigned him the role of Huon in *Oberon*. It was one of many dramatic roles in which his manliness and clarion voice served him well.

Giovanni had come to the Met in the 1913–14 season, fresh from a series of European triumphs that included the La Scala premiere of Puccini's *Fanciulla del West,* under Toscanini. By the time he and I sang together in *Oberon,* he was considered a worthy second to Caruso, especially in *Aida, Tosca,* and *Pagliacci.* Caruso, in fact, was so impressed by Giovanni's Canio that he gave him one of his own *Pagliacci* costumes. To be sure, no other tenor could erase the memory of Caruso's pathetic "Ridi, Pagliaccio!" or fearsome "No, Pagliaccio non son!" But Giovanni's portrayal of Leoncavallo's tragic clown, especially in the early and middle 1920s, left no member of an audience unmoved.

To have known Giovanni Martinelli was to have known one of the finest men God ever created. I know of no better way to say it. He was, first of all, an extraordinary physical specimen: he was broad-shouldered, massively built (he had been a blacksmith's apprentice as a young man), and his smile instantly revealed his sunny disposition. His face, crowned by an unruly mane of auburn hair, had a rugged handsomeness rarely seen among tenors. His voice and his physique were a perfect match.

The inner man was every bit as attractive. He was perhaps the least temperamental of any tenor I have known, and was in many ways the most consistent. Conductors could always count on Giovanni to act and sing a role just as the composer would have wanted; he allowed himself few liberties within a score. It was for this reason that despite his limited vocal abilities, compared to some of his contemporaries, he often outshone them. His voice was not what one would call intrinsically beautiful, nor his method entirely flawless; but the *effect* of his singing was never less than magical.

While his range was considerable (I rarely recall his having trouble with the high C), he was at his best in rapidly sung dramatic arias, where his voice could cut through a Verdi orchestra and chorus with little difficulty. Yet in soft, slow, *legato* moments he became so preoccupied with his technique that he would perspire profusely and would begin to oversalivate. Only those who knew him well and sang often with him were aware of his uncertainties. What offset them were his fine acting, sensitive musicianship, and complete identification with the characters he sang. In later years these qualities made him one of opera's finest Otellos, after the bloom of his youthful voice was gone.

Oberon required not one but two lead tenors, one to sing Huon (Martinelli) and the other to sing the title role. This Gatti assigned to Paul Althouse, the American tenor whose Met debut as Dimitri in *Boris Godunov* had earned the critics' praises before the outbreak of the World War. Paul was a life-loving country boy, born and raised among the Pennsylvania Dutch, a good artist whose dramatic tenor voice ultimately became a *heldentenor;* it was Paul, in fact, who first partnered Kirsten Flagstad when she made her Metropolitan debut as Sieglinde. Although no match for Giovanni Martinelli with the public, Paul sang very well in *Oberon*. Later in life he would be remembered for his teaching and coaching, both of which were evident in the careers of two of his many pupils, Eleanor Steber and Richard Tucker.*

By all rights, *Oberon* had a lot going for it. With Martinelli, Paul Althouse and Marie Sundelius in the cast, and with Joseph Urban's brilliantly designed sets, it did well at the box office. It should have done as well with the critics—but didn't. My big moment came in the dramatic aria "Ocean, thou mighty

---

* As with Ponselle, Paul Althouse was entirely American-trained and had never sung in Europe prior to his Metropolitan debut in 1913. Why he was not accorded the same publicity at his debut as was Ponselle at hers is partly explainable by his not having sung a starring role, and partly by the wartime press's attitude toward his Germanic roots. Althouse's "voice, tastes, and temperament," critic Max de Schauensee has written, "were always strongly Teutonic." Had his lineage been different, or had his career begun after the war and not before it, perhaps he would have been treated differently by the press. J.A.D.

monster!" (The performance was sung in English, the language of the original libretto, because of the wartime antagonism toward German.) I carried it off well enough to earn more than a little praise from two leading critics, James G. Huneker and William J. Henderson. Huneker expressed his "hearty admiration for [my] work" in the aria,* and Henderson, though he declared that my technique was not yet perfect, said I had "the voice, the feeling, and the dramatic instinct" to become "one of the greatest singers of our time."

It's hard for today's operagoers to realize how demanding the New York critics of the 1910s and 1920s were. W. J. Henderson affords an interesting example. Born in New Jersey in 1855, he was already an old man by the time he began reviewing me; he had done his first major reviewing for the *Times* in 1883, and had moved to the New York *Sun* in time to watch the tenor mantle pass from Jean de Reszke to Caruso in 1902–3. Here was a critic who spared no one's feelings when a performance was bad—not the singers', the conductor's, nor the management's. He was never quick to praise anyone, and often reserved his harshest criticism for the best-known performers. He had collaborated with Walter Damrosch on the latter's *Cyrano de Bergerac*, which had premiered in the 1912–13 season at the Met, and was the author of several books on musical subjects. A self-described "sea dog," he had also written extensively on sailing and navigation, two of his passionate interests. He was perhaps the toughest of the New York critics, and one praiseworthy phrase from his typewriter tended to make great artists feel worth their salt—at least for that particular performance. The next time, if the artists were inconsistent, Henderson might behead them with hatchet-like phrases in the *Sun*'s columns.

Because he devoted more space to Ponselle's singing in Oberon *in his New York* Times *column than did Henderson in the* Sun, *Huneker's review is worth quoting at some length. Though given to some questionable stylistic references as regards composers (of* Oberon's *he made reference to "old daddy Weber," and was given to calling* Forza's, Aida's, *and* Trovatore's *"Joe Verdi, late of La Bella Italia"), Huneker's musical insights were indisputably keen. Noting, first, that the general rehearsal a few days before the performance had been unrealistically smooth, perhaps causing the performance itself to be just the opposite, he had this to say of Ponselle's singing:*

"Remains Miss Rosa Ponselle, upon whose broad shoulders rested the hapless heroine Rezia. To say that she has grown in artistic stature would only be the truth. Singing Verdi, especially with Italian blood in her veins, is not the same as delivering the majestic and tragic music of Weber. Miss Ponselle is too young, has had too little experience to sound the heights and depths of the mighty 'Ocean' aria—itself at times too grandiloquent, not to say stilted; but with her dramatic temperament, musical intelligence, above all, with her beautiful, natural voice and its remarkable range, from a rich, velvety contralto to a vibrating, silvery soprano—well, for a newcomer on the operatic boards a few months ago, and with her artistic training and antecedents, we confess our hearty admiration for her work and high hopes for her brilliant future. Her scale is seamless, so equal are her tones from top to bottom. Her personality is pleasing, her acting immature.

"She has a buxom, well-proportioned figure, and in Turkish trousers she was fascinating . . . In excellent voice, she sang not only the big aria with better effect than at rehearsal—rhythmically she has gained, while the plaintive cantilena in the last act caught the fancy of the audience and the applause was spontaneous. In one costume, and she wore several gorgeously barbaric, she resembled Henri Reginault's Salome. Her features seemed more Moorish than Italian. That she won her hearers there can be no possibility of doubt; to alter slightly a colloquialism, she 'has arrived with both lungs.'" J.A.D.

Many of his colleagues, if not as uncompromising as he, boasted similar accomplishments. Lawrence Gilman was one. Completely self-taught in music, he became chief critic for the *Herald Tribune* after writing for the *North American Review* and, in the first years of the new century, serving as music reviewer and then managing editor of *Harper's Weekly*. Like his colleague Henderson, Lawrence Gilman wrote books on biographical as well as musicological topics. He was among the most respected critics of his time.

So was Henry Krehbiel—to whom, I suppose, the title "Dean of the New York Critics" could have been applied without much debate. Born in Michigan in the early 1850s, he was the eldest of the Manhattan critics; he had reviewed almost every important opera production in Manhattan from 1880 onward. That year he was appointed music critic for the New York *Tribune,* a post he held until his death in the spring of 1923. Before joining the *Tribune,* he had studied law in Cincinnati but had changed careers by becoming a reviewer for the Cincinnati *Gazette.* From then until the end of his long career, he contributed richly to musical scholarship while serving as one of the two or three top critics in New York. An early supporter of Wagner, Tchaikovsky, and Dvořák, he championed the cause of what was then contemporary music. He was also vitally interested in Negro folk songs, many of which he scored. His many books—including a three-volume translation of the life of Beethoven and a two-volume history of music in New York—and his prestige as a critic earned him, in 1901, the Cross of the French Legion of Honor.

Samuel Chotzinoff and Pitts Sanborn were among the others on whose words in the daily newspapers our careers seemingly hung. Chotzinoff was the more musical of the two; he had been accompanist to a number of artists including violinist Efrem Zimbalist and, for a time, Alma Gluck (then Mrs. Zimbalist). He was an excellent pianist and accompanist, and thoroughly understood what singing was about. So did Pitts Sanborn, but from the vantage point of a scholar rather than performer. Born and raised in the Midwest, Sanborn studied at Harvard, intending to be a musical scholar. He changed career directions in the early 1900s when the New York *Globe* made him senior music critic, a position he held until the mid-1920s.

Two weeks before Christmas, 1918, each of these critics had his way with one of the most important premieres in the Met's history, Puccini's *Trittico—Gianni Schicchi, Il Tabarro,* and *Suor Angelica.* Though I had already been assigned *Oberon,* I had wanted to be part of that premiere. By the end of the summer of 1918, Gatti had assigned Geraldine Farrar the title role in *Suor Angelica,* and Florence Easton the part of Lauretta in *Gianni Schicchi.* Rumor had it that Claudia Muzio would sing Giorgietta in *Il Tabarro;* I assumed this was true, until Gatti telephoned me at my apartment the Monday after Thanksgiving. He asked me to learn *Tabarro* as an urgent personal favor to him; he said nothing more than that. Nino Romani and I worked seven days and nights on it, until I could have sung it in my sleep. By the time I sang *Oberon,* the effort had proved needless; Gatti telephoned me again, and told me that Muzio would sing Giorgietta at the premiere. He said nothing more on the subject, except that I could sing it as part of my repertoire if it became successful. Whether it was because he felt he had asked too much of me, what with *Oberon* looming ever larger in my immediate future, or whether Muzio's seniority and proven box office power held sway with him (as well it should have), I can't say. It may have been that Muzio's availability suddenly became questionable but was soon guaranteed.

Though the *Trittico* passed me by, I did get a chance for a Metropolitan premiere during my first season. I was ecstatic until Mr. Gatti told me what the opera would be: *The Legend,* by Joseph Breil. I said I'd never heard of Joseph Breil. All I could gather from Mr. Gatti was that he, Ziegler, and Earle Lewis, his box-office manager and right-hand man, considered Breil's work to be worth a Metropolitan premiere. In any case, the Met's administration had decided, after a competition for young American composers, to produce two new works. *The Legend* was one, and *The Temple Dancer,* written by John Adam Hugo, was the other.

Nino Romani's lack of enthusiasm, when I told him the news, quickly betrayed his disagreement with the management. I wasn't exactly heartened by his lukewarm attitude, though I decided to give Breil and his new opera a fair hearing. After all, I told myself, every new composer has to start somewhere— and surely the Metropolitan wouldn't have accorded a premiere to an unworthy score, especially with a Puccini premiere so close at hand. I realized I was wrong when I read the plot summary that Breil had forwarded through Nino Romani. It was a patchwork of borrowed librettos from some painfully obvious sources.

The summary spoke of a mythical country called Muscodavia, in the Balkans. The setting was the mid-nineteenth century. One of the major characters was a Count Stackareff, who has a double identity. By day he is a titled but penniless nobleman, but by night he is Black Lorenzo the Bandit. As these twin selves he lives at a hunting lodge in the mountains of Muscodavia, sharing the lodge with his daughter Carmelita. I was to play his daughter—a sort of naïve, pie-eyed girl whose greatest fear is that someone will discover her father's double identity. She's particularly worried that her lover, a Cossack-type named Stefan Pauloff, will do the discovering.

In the end, her lover is sent by the local villagers to capture the bandit, Black Lorenzo, either dead or alive. In the midst of a love scene, her father, a.k.a. Black Lorenzo, overhears Pauloff telling Carmelita about his dangerous assignment. In a moment of unexplainable bravado, the father gives away his real identity and Pauloff prepares to give chase. Carmelita, after praying to no avail, stabs Pauloff to save her father—proving, I suppose, that blood is thicker than water. In any event, when local soldiers come looking for Black Lorenzo, having also discovered his real identity, they see Carmelita standing over Pauloff's dead body—so they shoot her, thereby ringing down the curtain on this hapless libretto.

If the text of the opera was a patchwork of borrowed themes—a bit of Verdi in the father-daughter relationship, a hint of Puccini's *Fanciulla* in the Black-Lorenzo-the-Bandit theme, and such other assorted borrowings as a dual identity—the score was a labyrinth of simple melodies grafted to some unwieldly minor chords. At times the music and plot took some comical turns. At one point the daughter, worried about Pauloff's discovering who her father really is, sings an aria in front of the Virgin. At the end of the aria an old servant enters the scene and tells her that the Devil stalks the area at midnight. The Devil, says the servant, has a penchant for knocking on doors—and he (or she) who answers the knocks will die within one year.

Carmelita, too enlightened for this kind of superstition, laughs at the old woman, dismissing her Satanic fixations. Instead of accepting the rebuff, the weatherbeaten old lady offers to tell Carmelita's fortune by means of a deck of cards. The ace of spades turns up every time the cards are cut, sealing Carmelita's fate. This quiltwork of a scene also sealed Breil's fate; it illustrated how, in the space of fifteen minutes of music, he had stitched together moments from *Forza del destino* (the prayer before the Virgin), *Ballo in maschera* (the superstitious meanderings of the old woman), *Faust* (the Devil's intrusion into the plot), and *Carmen* (the fortune-telling episode).

I would have given anything to get out of this lamentable premiere. But, I kept telling myself, Gatti had asked me to do it and I could never let him down. As it was, Breil's composing let him down. W. J. Henderson endured his feeble score long enough to write that it had caused him "some sad moments" as a critic. Huneker recounted the first-performance disaster in blunt prose:

> It would be idle to deny after a first hearing that "The Legend" was not legendary, but as heavy as unleavened dough; [and] that "The Temple Dancer" was more viable both vocally and musically . . . Candor—which is the short, ugly word in criticism—compels us to state that [these] works would shine to advantage across the street from the Metropolitan Opera House; in a word, at the Casino, the home of light operatic entertainment. . . .
>
> The stories of the two novelties have been related in these columns. We refuse to repeat them, except to say that they are neither better nor worse than the average. Sung in the vernacular, they might as well have been sung in Choctaw. The words for the most part were unsingable. Ponselle and Easton [with Morgan Kingston and Carl Shlegel, the star of "The Temple Dancer"] disguised the horror of the dentals, sibilants and gutturals, lending emphasis to the labials . . . By all means let us have opera in English, but let us have English that is singable.
>
> It is not necessary to dwell at length upon the merits of the new music. The Breil score is melodious and commonplace. It ambles along and chokes the action whenever it can . . . Miss Ponselle had to perform a lot of vocal stunts and only her extraordinary voice en-

abled her to compass some of the long-breathed phrases. She possesses a magnificent bellows . . . [and] deserves praise for her mimique. This young woman is striding to her goal with seven-league boots. She is the only satisfactory "find" of the present opera season. . . .

The reception of the two novelties was hearty. Mr. Breil and Mr. Hugo were called before the curtain with the singers and [conductor] Mr. Moranzoni . . . The lobbyists decided that the Hugo work had better chances for life than "The Legend." But we resent a "certain critical condescension" among our own when such expressions were often heard like this: "Surprisingly good for an American composer, isn't it?" . . . Either the music is good or it is bad! When that is settled then the patriotic motive may be blared on the trombones of America. No taint, however, of "modernism" was to be detected in these native compositions; all was safe, sane, and—soporific.

As for Joseph Breil, eventually he contented himself with writing for radio, where among other things, he contributed the theme song to *Amos 'n' Andy*.

With *Forza* and *Oberon* in my command, and with *The Legend* behind me, it was time, my manager told me, to capitalize on the publicity I had received at my debut. That meant two things, Thorner said: making phonograph records and going on a national concert tour. Record-making came first. I had no recording contract when I was in vaudeville, and was free to accept the best one that came my way. In those days, the best was epitomized by the Victor Talking Machine Company, whose high-priced "Red Seal" opera records were the *crème de la crème* in the phonograph industry. Caruso had become an exclusive Red Seal artist shortly after he arrived in New York, and had led the way for every other Metropolitan singer of his stature. Naturally, I wanted a Victor recording contract, if only to be able to record with Caruso.

What I got, thanks largely to Thorner, was a contract with the Columbia Graphophone Company, predecessor of today's gigantic CBS/Columbia interests. Columbia was a distant Number Two in those days, although it had been the pioneer in celebrity recording; in 1903 its red-label "Grand Opera Series" had sported the names of Scotti, Schumann-Heink, and the legendary Polish bass Edouard de Reszke, among others. A number of singers recorded for both Victor and Columbia, and this would also have appealed to me. But a different set of circumstances intervened. Because Nino Romani was a studio conductor for Columbia, he had a vested interest in steering me there; and Thorner, who was rapidly proving himself a selfish manager, may have been in line for an under-the-table payoff if I signed with Columbia rather than Victor.* Knowing nothing of these machinations, and feeling that Victor must have thought

---

* *Although such a payoff was never directly known to Ponselle, at least at the time, it was rumored and, to be accurate, was by no means an unheard-of affair in the highly competitive recording industry. The late Gustave Haenschen (1890–1980), a respected radio conductor who had served the infant Brunswick company as director of popular releases from*

me unworthy because no one had approached me, I signed on the dotted line and made my first Columbia discs.

Between my debut in November 1918 and the premiere of *The Legend* the next March, I crowded in eight sessions at Columbia, recording the "Ave Maria" from *Cavalleria rusticana* (adapted from its "Intermezzo"), "D'amor sull' ali rosee" from *Trovatore*, "Vissi d'arte" from *Tosca*, "Un bel dì vedremo" from *Madama Butterfly*, "Voi lo sapete" from *Cavalleria*, "O patria mia" from *Aida*, Paolo Tosti's popular "Addio" (recorded in English as "Good-Bye," as Melba, Eames, McCormack, and others had), and the lovely "La Vergine degli angeli" from *Forza*.

My last session of the regular opera season occurred on March 1, 1919, and in it I recorded a duet arrangement of the sacred song "Whispering Hope." Alma Gluck and Louise Homer had made a best-selling record of it for Victor, and Columbia wanted a competing version in its catalogues. My partner was not my sister Carmela, but rather an American mezzo named Barbara Maurel, who was then singing with the Boston Opera Company and whose last name she had borrowed from Victor Maurel, her teacher. I didn't think much of her voice and protested to Nino that Carmela could outsing her anytime. Soon Thorner made his authority felt and told me not to argue with Columbia's wisdom. When I pressed him, he told me that Barbara was a "favorite" of one of the company's executives. I backed off and bided time until Carmela got a Columbia contract. Soon after, we began recording many of the arias and duets we had sung in vaudeville. Among the best were "O sole mio," the "Barcarolle" from *Tales of Hoffmann,* and our intricately harmonized variations on "Comin' Thro' the Rye."

The Columbia Graphophone Company announced my first recordings in a press release from Meriden, where a banquet and reception were given me just after I had recorded the *Butterfly* and *Cavalleria* arias. Columbia's advertising men, never short on superlatives, opined that "the Columbia recordings of Ponselle are unquestionably the sensation of the musical world." Only a few years earlier they had used nearly the same line to characterize Emmy Destinn's records.

The Metropolitan Opera House, fittingly, was the site of my first concert appearance—a Verdi gala on February 9, 1919. I sang three times in a program that claimed the talents of Frieda Hempel, José Mardones, Luigi Montesanto, Sophie Braslau, Giulio Rossi, and the British tenor Morgan Kingston. Except for Kingston, these were all gifted artists. Frieda Hempel, though middle-aged

---

1919 to 1929, had heard rumors of the Thorner payoff through Walter Rogers, Brunswick's director of classical releases. Rogers, a pioneer recording artist himself and a studio conductor at Victor before being lured away by the Brunswick interests, had attempted to bid on the Ponselle Sisters in 1919, but had been politely rebuffed by Thorner. Eventually, Rogers would have under contract Elisabeth Rethberg, Sigrid Onegin, Giacomo Lauri-Volpi, and other European stars who made celebrated Metropolitan debuts in the 1920s.
J.A.D.

then, had one of the most beautiful faces I had ever seen; her voice had a beauty all its own, a smooth, lovely coloratura that shone particularly in the great *bel canto* roles. Sophie Braslau, then very much in love with impresario Arthur Judson, was a fine contralto whose career on Victor records mirrored her reputation as a concert and opera singer. And Mardones—what more needs to be said about him? That night, after singing the "Miserere" from *Trovatore* with Kingston, I sang the Finale to the second act of *Aida* with Mardones and the others. Much as I respected Braslau, Luigi Montesanto, and Giulio Rossi, at that moment I identified purely with the awesome splendor of José Mardones' voice.

April 1919 was a magic time for me. On April 6, in a Sunday-evening concert at the Metropolitan, I sang my first Verdi *Requiem;* I shared honors with Margarete Matzenauer, Charles Hackett, and Mardones, under Giulio Setti's baton. This was the second I had sung of the well-known sacred words by opera composers. The first, a performance of Rossini's *Stabat Mater* with Hackett, Mardones, and Gabriella Besanzoni (again with Setti conducting), had taken place on January 20; I loved the *Stabat Mater,* though not as much as I did the Verdi *Requiem.* As with any other performer's preferences, mine had to do with my own conception of what my voice was best suited for. Even without the great "Inflammatus," Verdi's more sophisticated, more emotional style held greater appeal for me.*

In mid-April, Edith and I readied ourselves for the train trip to Atlanta, to open the week-long Metropolitan season there. She had never been south before but had been told by Bruno Zirato, Caruso's secretary, that Atlantans took Southern hospitality very seriously. The fine basso Adamo Didur told us about the lavish parties at the Atlanta Biltmore, the traditional barbecue at the Druid Hills Golf Club (which, with its twofold promise of eating and playing golf, instantly appealed to me), and the splendor of the opening nights in the city's Auditorium.

Opening night went to Caruso and me in *Forza del destino.* Just as important, so far as I was concerned, I got to sing my first *Cavalleria rusticana* there. When I saw the playbill I could hardly contain myself; I would sing Santuzza to Paul Althouse's Turiddu, after which Caruso, Antonio Scotti, and Frieda Hempel would sing *Pagliacci.* Although I would not be singing opposite Caruso in *Cavalleria,* our double-bill performances would close the week, just as the two of us would open it.

On the train ride south I spent most of my time sitting on a folding chair between cars, taking in as much fresh air as I could. My old foe, motion sickness, kept me from spending as much time with my colleagues as I would

---

* *Many years later, in recalling the 1919 Requiem, Matzenauer told Hugh Johns, a mutual friend of Ponselle's and hers, that no dramatic soprano voice had blended so perfectly with her own as had Rosa Ponselle's. Using the intricate give-and-take of the "Dies Irae" as an example, Matzenauer said that their musicanship and approaches were so strikingly similar that they could anticipate and respond to each other's embellishments with complete security.* J.A.D.

have liked. I did get to know a few of them in the special club cars we used. I spent a fair amount of time with the lovely Spanish coloratura Maria Barrientos, who was to sing a performance of *Martha* with Caruso; she was an elegant woman whose ringing upper voice was a staple of the Columbia record catalogues. Too, I came to know Claudia Muzio for the first time. I had always been in awe of her, and refused to believe critics and colleagues who claimed that I was her equal.* While the size, color, and timbre of my voice may have afforded me opportunities that hers didn't, there was an unforgettable throb in her voice that wrung tears from the stoniest of listeners. As to personality, she wore about her a detectable sadness, an impression of being unfulfilled in some important sense. So far as I know, she allowed herself only a few diversions, one of which was the movies; especially on tour, she would eagerly make her way to the nearest movie house, often with her mother at her side. Perhaps the plots of those melodramatic films offered an escape from the tension of performing.

One colleague I came to know better during that train ride to Atlanta was Enrico Caruso. During one of my infrequent stays in my car I noticed him standing in the aisle near my door, taking in the scenery from a window. I was still unsure of myself around him and was surprised when he asked if I might like to sit and talk.

"Talk with you? It would be a privilege!"

Because my relationship with him had been an entirely musical one, I expected him to talk about singing. Instead, the conversation quickly turned to his private life, and in particular to his lost love, Ada Giachetti. At the very mention of her name I saw his eyes puddle up; he had loved this errant soprano very much, and could never understand why she had abandoned him after a decade of living together. Despite his newly found happiness with Dorothy Park Benjamin, who became his wife, it was clear to me that the intervening years hadn't lessened the hurt of his rejection by the woman who had borne him two sons.

The Caruso biographers' words to the contrary, that single conversation was the only real exchange I ever had with the great tenor. Over the years, I have been wrongly accorded a place in his life, an error first committed by Dorothy, his wife, in her first book about him. According to her, while Enrico was recuperating from the lung illness that kept him away from the Met in the winter of 1921, two of his "most intimate friends"—Antonio Scotti and I—were ushered into his sickroom, at which point I knelt by his bedside and wept. The story is untrue. Although I sang with him twenty-nine times, I hardly knew Enrico Caruso beyond what I saw and heard of him as a performer—except for what he chose to tell me about himself during that Atlanta train ride. I was never once invited to his apartment, and certainly not when he was seriously ill.

* *Muzio herself had an even stronger opinion, according to the late May Higgins, her personal secretary. "There is only one soprano who can sing better than I," Miss Higgins quotes Muzio as saying. "That soprano is Rosa Ponselle."* J.A.D.

A few opera *savants* who make backstage gossip their stock-in-trade have gone so far as to suggest that Caruso and I had an affair. This, too, is utter nonsense, as those who were close to both of us know. At best, I was like a niece to him—a spunky Neapolitan kid, a bit earthy, full of raw energy, but possessed of the same musical instincts that he had. Geraldine Farrar was much more his idea of a woman—indescribably beautiful, the epitome of high fashion, Everyman's Dream Girl. No, Caruso's and my common ground was music, and our working relationship flowered because of his warmth as a person. I loved and worshiped him as an artist—and in that I was hardly alone.

From the moment the special Metropolitan Opera train pulled into the Atlanta station, Caruso and I were front-page news. All three of the city's newspapers carried photographs and stories about us. (In one Atlanta photo, tall and lean Bruno Zirato stood between Edith and me, looking rather like the Empire State Building surrounding two much smaller structures.) In one of the dozen or so interviews I gave during the week, a reporter reminded me that only a season ago Carmela and I had sung at the Forsyth Theatre on a vaudeville bill. The reporter asked me whether I wanted to forget about my vaudeville days, now that I was a Met star; I told him frankly that I wasn't a bit ashamed of my Keith Circuit performing because if it hadn't been for vaudeville I wouldn't have come to the Metropolitan's attention.

More than six thousand people heard Caruso and me in *Forza* in a splashy opening-night performance in Atlanta. By my standards I sang even better than I had in New York; I was relaxed, for one thing, and was no longer under the duress of having to prove myself. I thought back to Jimmy Ceriani when I read the critics' reviews the next day; they called me "a delight to the eyes as well as the ears," and declared me "the finest artist the city has known since Emmy Destinn first delighted us some years ago."

Between opening and closing the Atlanta week I got to see a *Faust* with Martinelli, Léon Rothier, and Frances Alda; an *Aida* with Muzio, Margarete Matzenauer, and the Spanish tenor Hipólito Lázaro ("The greatest tenor since Rubini," according to the Barcelona critics); a Caruso-Barrientos *Martha,* with Adamo Didur and Kathleen Howard completing the cast's principals; a performance of *Bohème* with Alda, Martinelli, and Antonio Scotti; and a matinee performance of Bellini's *I Puritani* (a production that the Met would later mount in New York for Giacomo Lauri-Volpi), in which Hipólito Lázaro polished off the high D in the aria "A te, o cara, amor talora" with almost no effort.* When my turn again came, at the close of the week, I sang a

---

*Although Ponselle did not make a habit of listening to recordings, even her own, various situations could trigger her interest in them. Hugh Johns occasioned one such situation when, in talking about Lázaro with her, he produced several copies of Lázaro's many commercial acoustical recordings. On listening to them Ponselle became noticeably distressed at what seemed to her, at least on record, his irregular intonation, stylistic lapses, and forced high notes. Whether charitably or accurately, she left open the possibility that such errors may have owed more to primitive record-making than to Hipólito Lázaro. When, in 1979, the tenor's daughter attended a Peabody Conservatory tribute to Ponselle, the singer referred to Lázaro as "one of the great tenors, and great stars, of my day." J.A.D.

Cavalleria that moved Claudia Muzio enough to hug me backstage until I could hardly breathe. Afterward, the critics wrote that "no one could possibly sing or act more finely than Rosa Ponselle the fiery music of Mascagni's troubled heroine." Santuzza, unlike Breil's hapless Carmelita, was a troubled heroine with something to sing!

At the close of the Atlanta tour I began an extended series of Southern concerts, appearing first in Norfolk, then in Charlotte, and on to New Orleans. The best of my concerts was the one in Charlotte, because I shared the stage with one of the greatest of all baritones, the legendary Riccardo Stracciari. We had been engaged to close the Charlotte Music Festival, and had never met before then. I knew his reputation, of course, owing to his prominence as a Verdi baritone throughout Italy; I also knew of him through Nino Romani, with whom he prepared a number of his roles. Peculiarly, he had left the Met a decade before I had arrived, and was then singing in Chicago and San Francisco. He was a man of Caruso's age, approximately, rather handsome and physically well suited to the opera stage. His voice sparkled like a shower of diamonds, brilliant and penetrating, alternately dark and light depending on the mood he wished to create.

While Titta Ruffo boasted the most singular baritone voice I ever heard (Giuseppe de Luca appropriately called it "a miracle, not a voice"), Stracciari's was an easy candidate for the most beautiful (along with Pasquale Amato's, which many thought Stracciari's superior), and certainly one of the most durable. Long after Ruffo's voice had lost its core, and after the richness of Amato's had left him, Stracciari was still wowing the Italian critics with his Figaros and Rigolettos—roles that he sang, it is estimated, nine hundred and eleven hundred times, respectively. Happily, Columbia saw to it that he and I were recorded together, in the "Mira d'acerbe lagrime" and "Vivrà! contende il giubilo" sections from *Il Trovatore*.

After my Southern tour I went to the Midwest, to sing a joint concert with Paul Althouse at the Evanston (Illinois) Music Festival. The festival had engaged six artists that year—John McCormack, Frieda Hempel, Reinald Werrenwrath, Mabel Garrison, Paul, and myself. The biggest draw (as he was everywhere) was McCormack; he so packed them in that bleachers had to be set up onstage to accommodate all the ticket holders. Frieda Hempel drew well, both because of her Metropolitan reputation and the popularity of her Victor Red Seal recordings. Reinald Werrenwrath, one of the finest of all concert artists and a master of the art song, had a great following on records and, like Baltimore-born Mabel Garrison, a coloratura of flawless technique and exquisite tone, was also well received at the festival.

Considering the great artists whose company I shared, I was both flattered and surprised by one of the reviews I received. The Evanston *Evening News Index* reviewer had this to say about my singing: "Not since the days of Patti have I heard such perfection of the female voice; purity, warmth, ease, dignity, breadth, volume and sweetness! A voice combining a young girl's exquisite clarity, naturalness and tenderness with the poise, authority and ripeness of an artist of experience." I have read other flattering reviews about my New York performances. But to read them about my concert singing, especially from critics who knew me only from my recordings, was very heartening.

It's important to realize how much a part of American cultural life concert-going was—and, by extension, how important an opera singer was in the first decades of our century. Those were well before the days when a person in, say, Zanesville, Ohio, or Keokuk, Iowa, could flick a switch and hear a Metropolitan Opera broadcast or telecast. Radio was still in its experimental stage, so, other than through recordings, no one had steady access to opera and opera singers unless they happened to live in New York or Chicago. In the melting pot society that America had become, largely through the influx of immigrants like my mother and father, music and art earned high priorities with the public. At first, through a long line of great singers beginning with Jenny Lind and ending, in a way, with Adelina Patti and her successors, Melba, Eames, and Sembrich, opera had been identified with the rich. Caruso changed all that. By appearing in person in concerts, and by making Red Seal records almost as fast as the Victor Company could press them, Caruso brought grand opera to the masses.

The public demand for concerts and recitals made them lucrative "second careers" for many singers—especially those whose billings identified them as members of the Metropolitan Opera Company. Then even more than now the imprimatur of the Metropolitan, coupled with the importance of opera itself, helped guarantee an artist a successful concert career. But the closely packed dates and the taxing travel schedules sometimes created problems. Most travel was done by train in those days, and great care had to be taken to allow a performer enough rest between appearances. This was an ideal that occasionally eluded our managers' best efforts. Sometimes we had to board trains in the middle of the night, causing us to arrive in anything but a relaxed condition.

With travel time varying from as little as three or four hours to as much as two or three days, it was all but impossible to sleep regularly. Boredom only added to our restlessness. One way I tried to combat it was by having Edith read to me. It was something she loved doing, and I thoroughly enjoyed it. With few exceptions I've always preferred to hear something aloud, rather than to read it myself. So, on those long train rides, I tried to make up for the formal education I'd never been able to complete. My method, though hit-and-miss, at least gave me some needed enrichment. Edith's and my tastes ran to novels and plays whose stories resembled opera plots. They ranged from Shakespeare to Ibsen and Balzac to Dickens, though without Nino Romani's guidance I had no way of telling the literary quality of what I was reading. Only later did I learn to discern the ephemeral from the timeless in literature.

A novel I grew fond of—enough to want to read it myself, several times over—will illustrate what I mean. It was called *The Gadfly* and was written by

E. L. Vonynich. When I first read it I thought it was brilliantly conceived, and I spent hours talking about it with Nino. He thought it interesting, but, measured against his standards of great literature—Mussato, Malespini, Dino Compagni, Dante, Petrarch, and the other heroes of Italian verse and prose—Vonynich's sense of language and style were commonplace and would have to stand the test of time. Not long ago, someone sent me a copy of *The Gadfly*, and I couldn't wait to reacquaint myself with it. My eagerness soon gave way to disappointment; too many years had passed, and the plot now seemed overly melodramatic and contrived. I put it away as a once-pleasant memory.

When we grew tired of reading, Edith and I would crochet or do needlepoint. If Mamma or Carmela joined us during the longer stretches between my appearances (and they often did, especially during the early years of my concertizing), they would join in. We made lots of linen pieces and accent items for my Riverside Drive home. I still have a number of them; they now adorn some of the rooms in Villa Pace.

For a number of us, the response to our concerts and recitals was great enough, especially in large cities, to enable us to appear as many as three or four times a year in the same place. In my case, I might appear once in recital, twice in concerts with a city's symphony, and, if the Metropolitan visited there, once more on tour with the company. In smaller cities, where people's access to opera was rather limited despite the many touring companies then in existence, I would appear only once a season—almost always to full houses, thankfully. Sometimes I would go two seasons without performing in one or another locale, depending upon the schedules my manager could arrange.

What I sang varied from region to region, although I adhered to the same basic format. I always began my program with a well-known aria, usually from a Verdi opera; this, after all, was what I was best known for, until *La Gioconda, Vestale, Norma,* and *Don Giovanni* entered my repertoire in the mid- and late-1920s. Often I began with the "Ernani, involami," "Pace, pace mio Dio," or "Ah! fors' è lui!" Then I would sing a group of classical songs, perhaps three or four of them, by Beethoven, Handel, Pergolesi, Donaudy, Giordani, or Scarlatti. My accompanist would then have a solo spot on the program, playing three or four short compositions (usually romantic pieces), while I would be offstage resting. I would return for a final song before intermission—usually a popular piece of the type I would do for encores, such as Farley's "The Night Wind," Chadwick's "He Loves Me," or possibly older gems like "Danny Boy," "Annie Laurie," or "Beautiful Dreamer."

The second half of my program would begin with another aria—often the "Tu che invoco" from *Vestale* or the "Suicidio!" from *Gioconda,* but occasionally something outside my repertoire, such as the "Vissi d'arte" or "Un bel dì." My accompanist—William Tyroler in the early days, and Stuart Ross later—would then have a long solo, after which I would sing a group of four or five songs. Most of these were reasonably contemporary, at least compared to the group in the program's first part. These might be French art songs, or a series of lieder selections, or a mixture of songs by such composers as Faure, Delibes, Sadero, Buzzi-Peccia, Respighi, Schumann, Richard Strauss, Giordano, Grieg, or Wagner. My encores depended mainly on where I was singing, though I always tried to include popular songs like Tosti's "Good-Bye" and "Home, Sweet Home."

I made some adjustments to this format simply because people in different parts of the country had different tastes. In the Northeast, and especially in the eastern parts of Canada, I included more French songs. In St. Louis and various parts of the Midwest, lieder were quite popular and I would adjust my programs accordingly. Grieg songs were well received farther north, and Stephen Foster or James Bland songs, especially as encores, were invariably requested in the Southeast. Certain cities wanted Italian folk songs (Philadelphia, Boston, and Toronto loved Tosti and di Capua), so when I sang there I added gems like "Ideale," " 'A vucchella," "Santa Lucia Luntana," or the buoyant "Luna d'estate." (Bostonians also liked their Handel, and I did my best to accommodate them.)

I also made adjustments when I sang in San Juan or Havana, both of which were ports of call for concert singers. One season I learned several groups of Spanish songs for Puerto Rican and Cuban audiences. Eventually, I was able to weave some of them into my Texas and New Mexico appearances.

Because I wasn't known principally as a concert singer (as were John McCormack, Julia Culp, Reinald Werrenwrath, and Alma Gluck, for example), I never gave a true "recital" in New York City. Nor did I ever sing what I would call a "New York program"—the highbrow, rather cerebral program that heavily emphasizes esoteric musical literature. I suppose I could have brought my type of program to Carnegie Hall or Town Hall—many other opera singers did—but somehow it seemed quite out of place there.

I don't mean to imply that New York had a restrictive idea of what recitals and concerts should be. On the contrary, there were purely Spanish concerts, German concerts, folk concerts, Stephen Foster concerts, and even "costume concerts." (Frieda Hempel all but had a patent on her "Jenny Lind" recitals, in which she was costumed like her great predecessor and sang from her repertoire.) To my way of thinking, many of these seemed either gimmicky or outdated; in any case, they held no appeal for me. As it was, the only recitals I gave in Manhattan were purely charity events, like the annual Bagby Foundation concerts at the Waldorf-Astoria.

The same held for the occasional concerts and recitals I gave in Europe; they too were for charity. Except when I sang at Covent Garden or, in 1933, at the first *Maggio Musicale* in Florence, my stays in Europe were always in the summer months and were taken up with learning new roles. Typically, then, I would sing a charity recital wherever I might be staying. The Grand Hotel in St. Moritz was a favorite site from the late-1920s onward, and on one of the hotel's foyer walls there is a plaque noting that I once sang there.

One of those recitals became part of a tragic page in the history of European royalty between the world wars. On August 29, 1935, as she was being driven to one of my Grand Hotel concerts, Queen Astrid of Belgium was killed in an auto accident. She was only thirty years old. Her husband, Leopold III, later became a prisoner of war when the Nazis overran Belgium.

From 1924 onward I made a point of spending at least two weeks in Italy during my summer abroad. While there I was often the guest of Princess Mafalda, who was not only a dear friend but a member of one of the most musical royal families in modern history. Staying at the palace as their honored guest became less a matter of royal pomp and more one of endless informal fun. Our evenings were invariably filled with music-making. (Princess Mafalda, beyond entertaining me lavishly, was always looking out for art songs that she thought might suit my singing. It was she who discovered and presented to me in manuscript form two songs that I came to love—de Fontenailles' "A l'aimé" and Tosti's "Si tu le voulais.") At the end of my stay each year I gave a charity concert at the palace, once with Tito Schipa as my partner in duets from *La Traviata*.

In America I did my share of appearances with the major symphony orchestras, though it wasn't my favorite concert format. Not that the enhanced musical effect that the orchestra provided wasn't attractive. Rather, it was the proverbial strings attached to symphony contracts that often made me shy away from them. Singing with the National Symphony in Washington, then under the direction of Dr. Hans Kindler, was somewhat typical of the strategic problems involved: to sing with the National was also to commit oneself to a "sister performance" in Baltimore. (Washington and Baltimore were by no means the only cities to make this part of an artist's contract.) Not only did this sort of an arrangement tie up one's schedule, but indirectly it cost money—performing with symphonies required one to spend a day or two in rehearsal, with no income to show for those extra days. With such congenial, highly professional conductors as Otto Klemperer, however, these obstacles were quickly overcome. Working with men like Maestro Klemperer was a privilege as well as a pleasure.

In my orchestral concerts I sang operatic arias, among which the "Divinités du Styx," "Bel raggio," "Mariettas Lied" from *Die tote Stadt,* the "Divina Afrodite" from *Fedra,* and "Pleurez, pleurez mes yeux" from *Le Cid* were my favorite war-horses. These are very demanding arias and the requirements of each are somewhat different. "Mariettas Lied," for instance, is especially difficult, because one must be in top form to be able to spin out the long phrases that its composer, Erich Korngold, wove into it.

I loved singing it and for quite a while amused myself by playing my own highly improvised accompaniment. One evening at a party in Hollywood (Italo Montemezzi, the composer of *L'amore dei tre re,* gave the party for Korngold and other musical celebrities), I played my improvised version for the composer. To my delight, he commended and sanctioned it. About fifteen years later, when he telephoned me at Villa Pace, I learned that his earlier reaction had been more than simple flattery. This time he wanted me to record it with the Baltimore Symphony, with my own arrangement, for use in one of the film scores he was then working on. It was all very flattering, but inwardly I felt that it would be a mistake; I had been retired for a dozen years or more, so I decided to decline his offer. Still, the memory is comforting in retrospect.

Older generations will remember the grand opera concerts the Metropolitan used to offer every Sunday evening. They featured interesting and varied programs, always at popular prices, with the Metropolitan's orchestra, chorus, and soloists. During my nineteen seasons I sang fifty-four Sunday night concerts and enjoyed every one of them. With few exceptions, these were serious affairs at which it was possible to hear, from time to time, singers like Kirsten Flagstad, Lauritz Melchior, Lucrezia Bori, Lawrence Tibbett, Elisabeth Rethberg, Lily Pons, Giovanni Martinelli, Léon Rothier, and me—sometimes with two or three of us on the same program. The few exceptions, however, were notable. In one of them Gladys Swarthout, Frederick Jagel, Virgilio Lazzari, and I sang the "Spinning Wheel Quartet" from *Martha,* dressed in Victorian clothes and riding bicycles around the stage. In another my dog Whiskers, whom I taught to sing with me in "thirds," competed with me in a mock audition. Whiskers got the Met contract. I lost. It was all in good fun.

The Sunday night concerts gave me the opportunity to sing sacred works (my *Stabat Mater* and Verdi *Requiem* performances were Sunday events), select operatic scenes (the Triumphal Scene from *Aida* and the Convent Scene from *Forza* were favorites), well-known ensembles (I recall doing the duets from *Aida, Norma,* and *Gioconda* with Carmela), and also the popular trio "Qual voluttà" from Verdi's *I Lombardi,* either with Beniamino Gigli, Orville Harrold, or Armand Tokatyan (tenors), and José Mardones or Ezio Pinza (basses), and every once in a while a complete opera (I sang both *Cavalleria* and *Trovatore* in concert form at Sunday night performances). In solo moments I might sing arias from the operas in my repertoire, as well as from *Semiramide, Alceste, I Vespri siciliani, Tosca, Otello, Butterfly,* and *Giovanna d'Arco*. My songs usually paralleled what I sang in regular concerts and recitals.

Throughout my career, Edith kept detailed written records of the programs I sang in each city. She would note which songs or arias got the most applause, which ones the audience shouted for encores, and which ones the local critics seemed to favor. (She would also note which gowns, jewelry, and accessories I wore, so that I would never repeat an ensemble.) Within a year or two I would be singing in the same city and would plan my program according to Edith's notes.

Though I was used to traveling and tight scheduling from vaudeville days, my first concert tours in 1919 and 1920 were learning experiences. Compared to the well-organized world of vaudeville, concertizing was often a do-it-yourself business. There were no circuits, no theater chains, to see to it that one's needs were met—not even rudimentary needs, at times. For instance, I found that many halls and auditoriums weren't equipped with adequate stage lights. Because a recitalist must make a visual as well as musical impression upon an audience, proper stage lighting is essential so that each facial expression and gesture can be seen easily. I spent a whole season struggling with lighting problems, and finally solved them on my own. I looked up an electrician I had worked with on the Keith Circuit and paid him to make me a folding set of footlights. Wherever I sang, those folding footlights went with me.

The summer of 1919 was special to me. It began with a joint concert that Carmela and I gave in Meriden, an event modestly billed by the Poli Theatre as "The Ponselle Concert Sensation." It seemed as if everyone in the city turned out for the concert; that alone compelled me to give my best effort, although the gap between Meriden and me was widening, owing to my fame. The newspaper comments underscored why. "Meriden knows that Rosa Ponselle is one of America's greatest artists," the *Journal* commented, "and she knows, too, that Meriden rejoices with her that she has achieved such a triumph, for musical history will class her with the greatest of all singers." This was all very flattering, but I couldn't help asking myself at what price success had come. After all, I was still the same girl who had sung in Meriden's movie houses, but now I had become a "star." Ironically, I had once craved Meriden's attention in a deep, almost desperate way. Now Meriden openly craved mine.

Our block on Springdale Avenue had hardly changed since I left it. Virtually nothing had changed so far as Mamma's and Papa's life-styles went; although Carmela and I had sent them several thousand dollars from our vaudeville earnings, they lived quite as they had before we became successful. They had saved some of the money, but Mamma, saint that she was, had given hundred of dollars to less fortunate families in the neighborhood. Tony was due home from the Army soon, and had already conceived a plan to combine Papa's wood deliveries with a coal-hauling business. Mamma's little grocery store was still thriving, and our backyard at 159 Springdale was now a maze of grape arbors; Papa was making and selling his own wine, a "business" he kept going long after Prohibition went into effect.

The bakery had steadily declined since Tony had gone into the Army. Papa, true to his past, had so cheapened the quality of his bread that most of his steady customers eventually refused to buy from him. Papa never knew when to leave well enough alone.

Meriden was still home to me and, out of a respect for my need to rest, the people there left me alone except when I was scheduled to sing a concert. Otherwise, I felt free to walk the streets of the West Side, or browse in downtown shops, without being hounded by reporters and photographers. On Sundays, as I had done as a girl, I sang in the choir loft of the Mount Carmel Church, singing an impromptu "Ave Maria" or, sometimes, a "Panis Angelicus" with Carmela. Mamma always sat next to us in the loft and more than once we heard her soft lyric voice join ours. It touched me that the career she had wanted as a young woman was now mine. I owed her my sense of independence and never let her forget it.

When Nino, Edith, and I took a cottage at Lake Placid in the summer of 1919, our work was cut out for us: I had been given two new roles for my second season, Aida and Rachel in Halévy's *La Juive*. *Aida* was familiar territory to me and neither Nino nor Mr. Gatti thought that I would be anything less than happy in the role. *La Juive,* on the other hand, was entirely new to me. It was scheduled as the sixth performance of the new season (*Tosca, Aida, Bohème, Faust,* and a gala for the Prince of Wales preceded it), and Caruso would sing Eléazar, the father of Rachel.

La Juive had an interesting history to it. Written by Jacques Halévy in the early 1830s, its text (by playwright Eugène Scribe) was an eloquent statement against religious prejudice. Rossini is said to have rejected the libretto, though it isn't conclusively known why; in any case, Halévy, who had been raised in an Orthodox Jewish family, found it a great challenge and was able to infuse into his score the Jewish-Christian conflicts that its theme hinged upon.

The Scribe libretto centered on the conflict between a Catholic cardinal, Brogny, and a Jewish goldsmith, Eléazar, whose daughter, Rachel, falls in love with a Catholic prince, Léopold. At first Léopold disguises himself as a Jewish painter, but during a Passover celebration—a secret celebration, because of the Catholics' intolerance of the Jews and their religious ceremonies—his unfamiliarity with the ritual leads him to confess to Rachel his true identity. Her love is too deep, too passionate, to allow her to abandon him—even at the price of incurring her father's wrath.

The relationship between Eléazar and Cardinal Brogny has a prior history to it, as the text makes clear in the first act: in Rome, before he had entered the seminary, Brogny had launched a pogrom in which two of Eléazar's sons had been killed. Not long afterward, Brogny's wife and only daughter had disappeared when his family's home had mysteriously burned to the ground. In encountering Eléazar again, the Cardinal's memory of his lost daughter is sharpened—as is Eléazar's abject hatred of everything the Cardinal stands for, both as a man and as a cleric. Ultimately, Brogny learns of the relationship between the Catholic prince, Léopold, and the Jewess Rachel; he calls upon Heaven to curse all Jews, and orders the death of Eléazar and Rachel by having them boiled in oil.

Sensing that Eléazar holds the answer to Brogny's daughter's fate in Rome, the Cardinal offers to spare Rachel's life if she will convert to Christianity. She refuses and is thrown into the seething caldron. Eléazar is next—but, in the tension of the moment, Brogny shouts that he will spare him if he will tell him where his daughter is.

"*There* rests your daughter!" Eléazar retorts with all the venom he can muster, pointing to Rachel's body in the caldron.

La Juive was my first excursion into the French repertoire, and to help me master the language and text I chose Canadian-born Wilfred Pelletier, who had been one of Caruso's coaches in *Samson et Dalila*. Pelletier, or "Pellie," as we always called him, was married to lyric soprano Queena Mario at the time;

eventually, he would marry tall, statuesque Rose Bampton, with whom he shared the rest of his life. Both as a Metropolitan coach and conductor, Pellie was to work with me again in the coming seasons in opera and in Sunday evening concerts at the Metropolitan. Like everyone else who worked with him, I admired his musical insights into the difficult French repertoire, and treasured his affectionate, easygoing ways.

Word reached me early on that Caruso was investing more of himself in this role than in any other since he had taken on Samson several seasons earlier. A perfectionist, musically as well as dramatically, he was coaching the opera's Passover Scene with New York rabbis and cantors to be sure that he would be faithful to Jewish tradition. The fact that Eléazar became a tenor role had to do with another great tenor, the Frenchman Adolphe Nourrit, who, it is said, asked Halévy to make a dramatic character out of the persecuted goldsmith. Nourrit was tired of the rather stereotyped tenor roles, in which flashy movements, love interests, and swordsmanship counted more heavily than great acting. In the end, Halévy made room for many kinds of voice and characterization in his score. There were dramatic and lyric soprano roles (Rachel and Eudoxie, respectively), as there were with the two tenor ones, Eléazar requiring a dramatic tenor voice and Léopold a *lirico-spinto* tenor.

When the curtain rose on *La Juive* on November 22, 1919, it was Caruso who commanded the spotlight. Nothing showed this more than W. J. Henderson's review in the *Sun:*

> No one who is familiar with the achievements of the most popular tenor of this time would expect to be told that he met all the requirements of such a role as Eleazar. Nor would any of the millions of devoted admirers of his voice care. Probably no one knows this better than Mr. Caruso himself. All he has to do to evoke thunderous applause is to linger on a high note and to emit a final phrase at the full power of his voice. Therefore he commands the respect and admiration of all who regard operatic creations as of more import in art than their interpreters, for he has again and again shown himself a sincere seeker after genuine dramatic results. He had conceived the part in earnest study and he sang and acted it with an art as far removed as possible from that of his more familiar Italian roles. There was dignity in his declamation and beauty in his cantilena. His chanting in the second act was a lyric utterance of exquisite character, while his delivery of the pealing air of the fourth act ["Rachel! quand du Seigneur"] might have excited the envy of Nourrit himself.

How well I sang Rachel's music is as debatable now as it was then. I thought I did it well, especially considering that it was my first French role.

Critical opinion was evenly divided, as is clear from two of the more detailed reviews I received. First, W. J. Henderson's:

> . . . Miss Ponselle did not fulfill the promise of last season. Her voice sounded much more constrained and less noble in tone, while her action was primitive indeed.

Next, James G. Huneker's judgment:

> . . . Rosa Ponselle's artistic development grows apace. Her singing and acting are surer, better coordinated than even last season. The role of Rachel is wholly conventional, one of the "O, ciel!" kind, but she easily compassed it . . . If the present recrudescence of the work proves successful it will be entirely due to the magnificent singing of Caruso, Rosa Ponselle, and the magnetic conducting of Artur Bodanzky . . . As for Caruso and his impersonation of the old Jew, Eleazar, we may say that he has seldom demonstrated his vocal artistry or his dramatic gifts in such a striking manner.

Huneker liked me, Henderson did not; it became a familiar pattern for my first two seasons at the Met. Somewhere between the former's praise and the latter's criticism lay, I suspect, the real assessment of my performance as Rachel. Huneker, at least, paid me an enormous compliment at the end of his review. "There are only two beautiful voices in the Metropolitan Company," he wrote, implying a reference to Caruso. "Rosa Ponselle's is the other one."

I can't leave *La Juive* without paying tribute to the finest Cardinal of them all, Léon Rothier. By the time he undertook the role in the Metropolitan's production, he had been onstage twenty years and the quality of his voice had grown a trifle fuzzy. But it was such an *expressive* voice! Léon had great warmth and sincerity as an artist, and in retrospect I can't imagine any finer Brogny than he. His depiction of the Cardinal's complicated, twisted character was literally overpowering. We sang together a total of seventy-eight times, and each time I learned something new from him.

The reviews were hardly in for *La Juive* when another Ponselle made headlines across the country. Not Carmela, but Tony: the New York *Globe* had discovered in October 1919 that he could sing. The *Advertiser,* a Boston newspaper, picked up the story during the first week of November and included news photos of Tony vocalizing at the piano; there was also a picture of him seated next to Papa in a delivery wagon. The whole affair made for a nice story—except when Tony was quoted on his opinion of opera singers in general, and tenors in particular. Here is the way the story read:

> Caruso is the most famous—and richest—of tenors. His income from his voice runs into the hundreds of thousands of dollars each year.

He is courted and feted wherever he goes, receiving often indeed—
though he began his life as a butcher's boy—the honors of royalty.

Hundreds of thousands of his countrymen look upon Caruso with
eyes of admiring envy.

Is there, in fact, one who doesn't?

There certainly is! Tony Ponzillo, brother of Rosa Ponselle, prima
donna of the great Metropolitan Opera Company does not. Further-
more, much as he admire's Caruso's voice, he admits he wouldn't
be a Caruso!

The amazing proof of Tony Ponzillo's sincerity is that while
shoveling coal in Connecticut there came to him expert emissaries of
that same Metropolitan grand opera on the word of his famous
sister. Hearing him sing, they declared his voice as great as Caruso's
in his youth. But Tony does not care to be the second Caruso.

"I don't want to be a slave," he said. "Nobody who is on the
grand opera stage is anything else. When I want to sing, I sing.
When I don't want to sing, I don't sing. That's the life."

"I am a businessman and my own boss. Sometimes, when I can
get him, I have a man work for me. I am boss; I am not bossed.
The grand opera tenor—he sings when he's told and rests when he's
told. He goes to bed late and gets up late."

Tony should've quit while he was ahead—but didn't. Here was his parting
comment: "No real man respects a tenor. I'd rather be a real man. I don't want
my life to be one long gargle!"

Although it earned my brother headline coverage, most of the story was
liberally embellished by imaginative copywriters. It was true that Tony had
auditioned at the Met and had been told to learn a repertoire and then come
back for another audition session; all this happened long before anyone had
heard of me. This, of course, wasn't good enough for the newspapers, so they
alluded to certain "expert emissaries of that same Metropolitan" who had come
all the way to Meriden to audition him. The impression was that he had
hardly laid down his coal shovel when the Met offered him a long-term contract. It was all nonsense.

Tony embellished a bit himself when he said confidently that he was "a
businessman and my own boss." The first part was true, but not the last; he
was still very much under Papa's thumb, even at twenty-nine. Papa still
regarded him as an errant, strong-headed boy and thought nothing of inter-
fering in his dealings with coal brokers and customers. So long as the business
was quartered in our house on Springdale Avenue, Papa had easy access to records and conversations. In desperation Tony moved the business to an office at
353 West Main Street in Meriden, where for the first time since his Army days
he began to feel like his "own boss."

THE TWO-WORD HEADLINE

AIDA WAS TO have been the proverbial piece of cake for me. I barely had to study the score; from the prelude and "Celeste Aida" through the final "Pace!" of the Tomb Scene, I knew and loved every bar of it. My first *Aida* wasn't sung at the Met; Gatti, as part of his arrangement with the Brooklyn Academy, asked me to sing it there. The performance was scheduled for the first week of March 1920. Ten days before, I got the flu—a rarity for me, as I seldom got sick. I thought I was over it but faltered once during the general rehearsal. Two days later, on the day of the performance, I felt fine. I even managed to keep my nerves in check while waiting backstage for my entrance cue.

Giulio Crimi sang Radames that night. I remember listening to him spin out the final phrase of "Celeste Aida," taking the high note effortlessly, swelling the tone until he seemed to overpower the orchestra. I felt so good I could hardly wait to go onstage. I remember the ovation that followed "Ritorna vincitor!," the long *scena* in which the slave-princess Aida pours out the conflicting emotions of love for Radames, the chosen commander of the army that will wage war against her father and her people. I had always found the "Ritorna vincitor!" an easy aria, and the Brooklyn audience responded with prolonged applause.

It's interesting how singers often divide on their preferences for certain arias. Take, for instance, "Ritorna vincitor!" and "O patria mia," Aida's two greatest solo moments. On different occasions I remember talking with three great Aidas—Rosa Raisa, Claudia Muzio, and Elisabeth Rethberg—about these two arias. Muzio, like me, preferred "Ritorna vincitor!" because it was a dramatic as well as vocal feat, and because it lay better for her voice. Rethberg and Raisa felt equally comfortable in both arias, and each enjoyed the challenge of the finely spun high C in "O patria mia."

Aida so fascinated me that I occasionally made overtures to Raisa and Rethberg about it. One proposal to Rosa Raisa was seriously meant: I wanted to sing Amneris to her Aida. Though Rosa wasn't under contract to the Met, my offer wasn't as farfetched as it might seem. Amneris lay perfectly for me; it presented no problems where the vocal registers naturally break, and I could color my voice to contrast with Raisa's brilliant timbre. All in all, I thought a Raisa-Ponselle *Aida* would have been intriguing—in concert form, if necessary, to avoid contractual difficulties between the Metropolitan and Chicago companies. Neither of our managers concurred, despite our confidence in the basic idea.

On another occasion, jokingly this time, I made a pact with Rethberg that I would sing a dual *Aida* with her, so long as I got to sing "Ritorna vincitor!" and she took "O patria mia." When we kiddingly bargained over the Tomb Scene, she stopped me and said, "There isn't a singer on earth who could match your 'O terra, addio!' and there never will be." For all her flattery, hers was the Metropolitan's definitive Aida in my time.

I could have used Elisabeth Rethberg that night in Brooklyn. During the second scene of Act II, shortly after the famous "Triumphal March," I noticed an uncomfortable dryness in my throat. Between the second and third acts, Edith kept me supplied with pineapple juice; usually, a few sips would work magic for me. This time, nothing seemed to help. Knowing what I was about to face in the Nile Scene, I got panicky and felt sick to my stomach. To get in control, I let myself become engrossed in Amneris' little prayer, which my friend Jeanne Gordon, a stunning-looking American mezzo with an outstanding voice, sang wonderfully that night.

I followed with "O patria mia"—but not very successfully. Whether the last stages of the flu made my throat dry or something else came into play, I barely negotiated the high C. I got on the note all right; it came just as it always had, whether on the concert stage or in the recording studio. But after a couple of beats I got the sinking feeling that I was losing the tone. So I cut it short.

Only Edith and Nino Romani noticed it. The local critic, Edward Cushing, gave me a surprising review in the Brooklyn *Eagle,* and focused his comments on the Nile Scene in particular. "With the consummate singing of Mr. [Pasquale] Amato pleading, as Amonasro, for her to save her people," he wrote, "Miss Ponselle sang and acted her 'Nile River Scene' with a pathos and realism unapproachable in our judgment."

For reasons I've never really understood, that incident left me with an ungodly fear of singing *Aida* at the Met, where a missed high C would have been unthinkable. As a result, I sang *Aida* chiefly on tour—twelve times, to be exact —though I ventured it only twice in Manhattan. Of all the operas I've sung or heard, I consider it the greatest ever written.

When I think of *Aida,* I naturally think of the exquisite casts in which I was fortunate to have sung, and the conductors who brought this masterwork to life in those performances. Overall, I sang the majority of my Aidas to Giovanni Martinelli's Radames, Giuseppe Danise's or Giuseppe de Luca's Amonasro, Julia Claussen's Amneris, and Ezio Pinza's or, earlier, José Mardones' Ramfis. (The list, of course, is much longer for each role. My Amonasros, for instance, included not only Danise and de Luca but also Pasquale Amato, Michael Bohnen, Mario Basiola, Titta Ruffo, Riccardo Stracciari, and Lawrence Tibbett. The majority of my Aidas, however, were with de Luca and

Danise—three and four times each, respectively.) Exactly half of my fourteen Aidas were sung under Tullio Serafin's baton.

Although my Amnerises included Jeanne Gordon, Margarete Matzenauer, Marion Telva, and Ina Bourskaya, invariably I think of Julia Claussen, the statuesque Swedish mezzo-soprano, whenever I think of the ideal Amneris. Julia's voice, it is fair to say, was impressive rather than beautiful. Its carrying quality was something to behold, and enabled her to rise above other singers in ensembles. She sang all the popular mezzo-soprano roles, and also sang Brünnhilde to fine critical acclaim. In the Italian repertoire she achieved a more Latin style than Matzenauer (whose voice, however, was beautiful *and* impressive). Julia's Amneris was so dramatically conceived that it was almost frightening.

When we toured I discovered something about her voice that I never would have suspected. While touring we usually stayed in the same hotel, and because of her voice's power we could all hear her warm-up exercises when she began them. Early on the day of a performance she would sound as if she had almost no voice at all. Only by the most patient, torturous effort, a little bit at a time, would she transform her voice into the lustrous instrument we were accustomed to hearing. Later, when the curtain would rise and Julia would hurl those huge tones into the dark theater like so many brilliant light rays . . . well, all one could do was marvel!

It's a bit hard to imagine a Verdi opera being poorly received by the critics fifty years after its premiere. Such was the fate of *Don Carlos* when the Met offered it for the first time in December 1920. Nearly a half century had passed since its last New York production had been mounted, at the old Academy of Music in 1877. For the Met premiere I was assigned the part of Elizabeth de Valois. Martinelli sang the title role; Margarete Matzenauer sang Princess Eboli, Giuseppe de Luca sang Rodrigo, and Adamo Didur the role of Philip II of Spain.

Based on a Schiller tragedy, *Don Carlos* loosely follows the lives of generations of Spanish rulers—King Charles V, his son, Philip II, and his son, Carlos, the opera's title character. Elizabeth, whom I portrayed, marries Philip but is actually in love with his son, Carlos. Their secret relationship is eventually given away by Eboli, a princess who is herself in love with Carlos but whose affections he does not care to return. When his father learns of the relationship, he consigns Carlos to the officers of the Inquisition. In the end, none other than Charles V himself—not dead, as presumed by his family and subjects, but living secretly as a monk—saves Carlos' life.*

---

* *Originally conceived and performed in five acts, the somewhat cumbersome libretto of* Don Carlos *led Verdi to revise the opera some seventeen years after its Paris premiere in March 1867. The Fontainebleau Scene, with which the original version opened, was dropped, and the score revised accordingly. At the Metropolitan premiere in 1920, however, the Fontainebleau Scene was restored.* J.A.D.

As with any masterwork, especially a Verdi one, the public came in droves —and, just as predictably, the critics sharpened their pencils for opening-night reviews. W. J. Henderson, in his inimitable way, reduced *Don Carlos* and everyone associated with it to putty. The score, he said, was "machine made from beginning to end," constructed in such a way that it was "tuneless and unvocal" for the singers. Offering the tenor sections as examples, he declared that "Mr. Martinelli probably sang more high notes than he ever sang before in a single role. . . ." As for me, he said flatly, "it can be noted that Miss Ponselle was neither queenly nor tear-compelling, neither most musical nor most melancholy. . . ."

Fortunately for me, the rest of the major critics thought I'd sung well. James G. Huneker wrote that in me he found a "native richness of vocal and dramatic endowments" to which "plenty of temperament, latent as yet," had been coupled. Then he coined a phrase that stuck with me ever since. "A Caruso in petticoats?" he ventured. "Who knows what she may achieve with her labor rightfully directed." Henry T. Finck, then writing for the New York *Post,* chose a singer of my own sex for comparison. ". . . If she sang everything as well as she does some of the [*Don Carlos*] numbers she would be a second Nordica [and] under proper guidance she might become one."

Whatever the critics' final verdict, Elizabeth caused me some mixed memories—many of them visual. While preparing the role (and Elizabeth, I should add, was not musically difficult for me), I gained a great deal of weight and went onstage the heaviest I had ever been. Though I lost the weight next season, my appearance and my costuming made for some lamentable studio photographs. The costumes, made by a Metropolitan designer, were glitteringly overdone but were probably as flattering as my shape would allow. The makeup for Margarete Matzenauer and me was something else—heavy mascara around the eyes, with waxed and beaded lashes to complete the "effect." Whatever the effect was supposed to be, the studio photographs show a different one. What with our naturally large, dark eyes and all that makeup, we look like two bejeweled raccoons.

Adamo Didur, whose once beautiful voice had become unsteady by 1920, sang Philip II. Whatever the state of his voice, in this and every role he was a fascinating actor and a reliable vocalist. (As Fiora in *L'Amore dei tre re,* which was one of my favorite roles, I never sang with or ever heard a finer Archibaldo than he.) Didur had been the Met's first Boris, although Feodor Chaliapin had an exclusive stamp on the character. Chaliapin also sang Philip to my Elizabeth, and his conception of the King was an absolute masterpiece. As a stage partner, he was something else: if a colleague gave him an inch he would steal an entire scene. He was so artful about it that one wouldn't realize what was going on till it was too late.

Assessing my progress after *Don Carlos,* I was aware that my Leonora in *Forza del destino* was still my best accomplishment to date. Everyone had praised my Santuzza, to be sure, but *Cavalleria* didn't make the exacting demands of *Oberon, La Juive, Don Carlos,* or *Aida.* The reviews I received (even from the hard-to-please Henderson) made me aware that I had, modestly or immodestly, a great voice, but that my artistic growth was still something of a question mark.

Verdi's *Ernani,* which I sang after *Don Carlos* and *Andrea Chénier,* gave me the perfect opportunity to prove myself. Here was a soprano role that had given nearly everyone else problems. The best-known piece of music in the score, "Ernani, involami," illustrates why: the vocal line lies extremely high one moment, then drops impossibly low the next. In between are passages that require total security of technique. Some consider it the most difficult soprano aria Verdi ever wrote. I found it less so; it almost seemed written for my particular voice.

It afforded me a wonderful opportunity to cap a dramatic-coloratura performance with a prolonged, full-voice trill near the end of the aria. It's one of those Verdi moments where the time value of the trill can be almost as long or short as the performer wishes. Gennaro Papi, who had conducted my *Forza* debut, was at the podium in my first *Ernani* and gave me all the time I wanted with that rich trill. As a playful comment, he would rest the baton in his hands, until I indicated I was coming out of the trill. Then his baton would be in the air again. For me it was a moment of victory because, after the "Ernani, involami," my hardest work in the score was done. From then on it was a pleasant downhill coast till the final curtain.

Titta Ruffo had just joined the Metropolitan and was to have made his debut singing Carlos to my Elvira in *Ernani.* His name added considerable luster to a cast that included Giovanni Martinelli and José Mardones as, respectively, Ernani and Don Ruy Gomez. Unfortunately, Ruffo became ill a day or two before the performance and had to be replaced at the last minute. Luckily, Giuseppe Danise stepped into the part and brought to it an elegance that few baritones could have matched. Richard Aldrich paid him a high compliment in his *Times* review the next day, declaring that "he gave a dignified and suitable impersonation and sang with finish."

Aldrich was considerably less generous with me. "As to the [Verdi] style," he judged, "it was perhaps least in evidence in Mme. Rosa Ponselle's singing as Elvira. She sang, of course, with great volume, but she sacrificed quality to power; and had little conception of the claims of legato, such as should be exemplified, for instance, in 'Ernani, involami.'" This, he claimed, I "dismembered in an apparent attempt at dramatic expression." Giovanni Martinelli incurred his displeasure on the same grounds, despite a performance that Aldrich judged "sufficiently picturesque and romantic in action"; still, in his view Martinelli "had not the clearest conception of the style of the work."

Fortunately for both of us, two of Aldrich's colleagues thought otherwise. Pitts Sanborn admitted to participating in the standing ovation we received at the end of the performance. My Elvira, he wrote, "was nothing short of glorious. Hers is a voice that has both the low range and the high range for this exacting role, and she seems to have made distinct progress as a singer." Deems Taylor, then writing for the *World* and already a successful composer, heard things in my voice that he had never heard before. "Her upper voice was lovely," he judged, but "her lower tones were so extraordinarily broad and dark that they aroused a suspicion that her true voice might be a mezzo-contralto." His comments, like Sanborn's, were a welcome counterbalance to Aldrich's.

Sadness, it seems, hits us when we least need it. The first intrusion of unhappiness into my adult life came in the summer of 1921. The date was August 2. I was at a party given me by Rocco Di Orio, a New Haven restaurateur; it was a lovely occasion, full of warmth and friendship, everyone celebrating and wishing me great success in my next season. Some of the guests had arrived late because of previous commitments; the last to arrive entered the room ashen-looking, carrying with them a copy of a newspaper extra.

"CARUSO DEAD!"

The two-word headline absolutely paralyzed me.

There was complete silence for a few moments, and then a rush to learn what had happened. He had died in Naples, the paper said; he had suffered a relapse of the illness that had kept him away from the Met since Christmas. As I listened I thought back to opening night, nine months earlier, when he and I had sung *La Juive*. I had sung with him again before *Don Carlos*—two performances of *Forza del destino,* our mainstay. I remembered standing next to him backstage during opening week, when he had drawn a sketch of Rigoletto as a good-luck charm for Nina Morgana; that night she was to make her debut as Gilda opposite Giuseppe de Luca and Mario Chamlee. Ironically, it was Nina, I learned later, who first received news of Caruso's death. She and her new husband, Bruno Zirato, were spending part of their honeymoon in the Caruso penthouse at the Vanderbilt Hotel. It was there that the fateful message was relayed by telephone, and Nina had answered.

The burden of informing the newspapers and wire services fell to Zirato as his secretary. On the day of Caruso's funeral in Naples, oddly, a postcard bearing his familiar handwriting reached the Vanderbilt, addressed to the Ziratos. Caruso had urged them not to worry about him; he was recuperating nicely, he wrote.

As his body lay in state a continent away, the New York newspapers lamented his passing, at the same time praising what he had done for the cause of opera both here and abroad. I could only put his loss in personal terms; he had helped make my career possible, and had defended me to Mr. Gatti when he had nothing to go on but a hunch that I would do well in *Forza*. I tried never to disappoint him.

Sixty years after his death I remain convinced that he stood without peers among the great tenors of our century. I am not alone in my opinion. One of my colleagues provided the best testament I've ever heard. Asked whether Caruso was, in fact, the greatest tenor of the century, this colleague said calmly, "If you were to put together the voices and talents of Gigli, Pertile, Martinelli, Lauri-Volpi, Schipa, and the rest, their combination still wouldn't be fit to kiss Enrico Caruso's shoes." The silver-haired man who spoke these words knew his subject well. He was Giovanni Martinelli.

Strangely, my grief over Caruso's death only got worse when, in my own small way, I tried to honor him. Twenty-four years old, I was still dependent upon my family, and especially my mother, for emotional support. Naturally, my first reaction to the news of Caruso's death was to go home to Meriden. As soon as I arrived I asked Tony to phone the rectory of the little Mount Carmel Church; I wanted him to ask the pastor, Father Ricci, to offer a memorial Mass in Caruso's honor. I said I would make a suitable donation to the church, and would sing three sacred pieces during the Mass. Word was to be circulated quickly so that as many people as possible could attend.

At nine-thirty on the morning of the Mass I awoke to see Mamma, Edith, and Tranquillo Tamburini standing at the foot of my bed. I was startled, to say the least, and wanted to know what was the matter. Tranquillo was direct with me, as he had always been.

"Rosa," he asked abruptly, "are you trying to make money out of Caruso's death?"

"Of course not!" I said, still only partially awake. "What are you getting at, anyhow?"

"Well, I just came back from early Mass and—"

"—and Father Ricci," Mamma interrupted, "is selling tickets to the Caruso Mass for two dollars apiece!"

I blew up. I bounded out of bed, threw on a robe, and horrified Mamma by calling the priest anything but holy names. Soon Tony was in the room; I asked him to call the rectory and to tell the priest to be at our house in no more than ten minutes. I was ready for blood and neither Tony nor Mamma could calm me down.

Soon Father Ricci made his entrance and demanded an explanation for being called on such short notice. I gave him one.

"What do you mean charging two dollars for a memorial Mass that *I* already paid you for! When I sing in concerts I wouldn't think of asking more than a fifty-cent admission. But this is no concert, this is a Mass! Where do you get off with this ticket-selling, anyway?"

Now the priest had his turn.

"Your vanity may be inflated by those writers in New York," he said angrily, "but when you address me you'll do well to remember that you're addressing your parish priest!" In stilted Italian, he chose his words carefully; the essence of what he said was that as our parish priest he could do anything he wanted to raise money.

"Don't you suppose *I* should be asked whether *I* want to participate in your moneymaking ploy before you go ahead and sell tickets in my name?" I managed half the response in Italian, then switched to English as I got madder.

"I tolerate less impudence from children!" he shouted at me, turning on his heels to leave the room. With that, the last length of a very short fuse burned within me.

"Get out! Get out of here, Pop! Don't you ever show your face here again, do you hear?"

In my anger I'd mixed up English with Italian and had mistakenly called the priest "Pop," unable to grasp the Italian word for "Father."

Needless to say, I canceled the Mount Carmel Mass. I sang it the next Sunday at St. Joseph's, a larger, Irish-dominated parish near the courthouse in Meriden. There, free of charge, nearly eight hundred people came to join a young soprano in worship and in memory of the tenor W. J. Henderson called "the peer of any singer in history."

Caruso had been dead a month when I returned to New York. A letter awaited me from President Harding, asking me to sing at the memorial services surrounding the burial of the Unknown Soldier on Armistice Day. Because the President had asked, I accepted immediately but was barely able to perform on the day of the ceremony.

The World War had hardly touched my life, save for the depressing news that appeared in the newspapers on the battles and gassings. Few men I had been close to had served, and the two who had—Jimmy Ceriani and my brother—had come home safely. Tony had never left the States during the war; Jimmy had gone overseas but had not seen extensive combat duty. But now, on Armistice Day, 1921, the suffering and death that had scarred so many others' lives now had their effect on mine as America buried its Unknown Soldier at Arlington Cemetery.

Earlier that month a body had been exhumed from each of the four burial grounds in France—Belleau, Thiaucourt, Romagne, and Bony—where so many Americans had lost their lives. On the day of the ceremony, the four coffins containing the disfigured corpses of the now unidentifiable men were placed in a small, flag-draped room. A sergeant of the 59th Infantry was ushered into the room, carrying with him a spray of white roses. When the young sergeant left the room, the crowd knew that America's Unknown Soldier had been chosen. A few minutes later, honor guards carried out the wooden coffin on which the sergeant had laid the roses.

Midway through the ceremony, flanked by Louise Homer, Kingston, and Didur, I sang to the crowd. It was all I could do to maintain my composure. I remember most the pathetic wails of mothers who broke down when the coffin was carried to its resting place. The solemn piece I sang, "I Know That My Redeemer Liveth," from the *Messiah,* was almost impossible for me to sing that day.

Sad as the closing months of 1921 were, the string of happy events that came my way in the new year were some compensation for them. Five days into the year I sang Margared in the Metropolitan's first offering of Edouard Lalo's *Le Roi d'Ys*. It was written in the late 1880s, and its plot centers on the jealousy between two sisters for the love of a man. I played the jealous sister, and Frances Alda the sister loved by the tenor character, Mylio.

Like many other dramatic-soprano roles in the French repertoire, Margared in *Le Roi d'Ys* made heavy demands on the middle and lower ranges of the voice. Though not a sympathetic role, it afforded dramatical possibilities within a limited framework. Musically, though I had a long solo aria and a duet with Alda, I didn't find the score very memorable.

To the newly arrived Beniamino Gigli went the honor of creating Mylio at the Met, and of endearing to everyone who heard him the lovely aria "Vainement, ma bien aimée!" Here was a tenor to whom the gods had been particularly generous. His was one of the most perfectly produced, most uniform lyrical voices ever heard. It was not a large voice, but the freedom with which it was produced gave it a carrying quality that counted far more than sheer volume. And the sound of it—so utterly lyrical in *L'Elisir d'amore,* so youthful in *La Bohème,* and yet so manly in *Andrea Chénier* and *La Gioconda.* Gigli had such a profound impact on his colleagues, especially other tenors, that he nearly crowded them out of the limelight. I remember seeing Martinelli after Gigli's debut and hearing him say, "After he sang his first three phrases, I could see my whole career going right out the window!" Happily, the two remained colleagues and friends—the one the essence of manliness and a seeker after dramatic perfection, and the other sheer voice wedded to instinct.

Lalo's score was by no means universally applauded by Henderson, Finck, and the other reviewers, although they expressed a high regard for the cast—despite the fact, as most of them knew, there had been considerable friction among us at rehearsals. The source of virtually all of it was Frances Alda, who used her legal name (Mrs. Giulio Gatti-Casazza) as a mandate to order around the stage director and to offer unwanted advice to the conductor, Albert Wolff. Gigli had an interesting way of handling her; he simply smiled politely and made his way about the stage to sing his arias, disregarding most everything she said.

Frances Alda was uncompromisingly blunt in her dealings, and though she had kind things to say about me on many occasions, I admit I was uneasy around her. I found my own way of dealing with her—a calm, reasoned, yet firm way. At the general rehearsal for instance, she gave me directions that ran counter to the stage director's. "Over *there,* Ponselle! Watch what the hell you're doing!" That was Alda's idea of how to get a person to "cooperate."

I put my strategy to the test.

"May I ask who's in charge of this production—is it you, or is it Madame

Alda?" I said calmly to the director. "I'd like to know only because I can't quite follow two sets of directions, and I haven't yet mastered how to be in two places at the same moment." Sensing that she would meet her match if she wanted to pursue the issue, Alda left me alone. Eventually I learned that she handled everyone this way. It was as if she had to tangle with them to accord them any real respect.

Any mixed feelings toward Frances Alda were quickly forgotten in the wake of next month's activities. The high point came on February 22, when my brother Tony married Lydia Babuscio, his fiancée since the previous spring. I took some credit for playing matchmaker. I had met Lydia's father, a wholesale grocer and produce dealer named Angelo Babuscio, when he had paid an unexpected call at my Riverside Drive apartment. Edith had met him when she was shopping for wholesale prices on party-sized orders of imported canned goods. She and Carmela and I had grown fond of him but had never spent much time with him. One evening he came by during an informal dinner party we were giving for Tony, Lena (Tamburini) Angle, Sperando Ciotti, and other friends from Meriden. Because we were all having fun we asked him to stay for a while.

We could see that he was reluctant for some reason. Carmela kept reassuring him that any other plans he had could be taken care of by a simple phone call, but still he felt reticent about staying. Finally, we coaxed the reason out of him: his daughter was waiting outside in the car, all alone.

"Well, we'll just take care of that," I told him as I opened one of the dining-room windows facing the drive. "What's your daughter's name?"

"Lydia," he answered, just in time for me to lean out the window and sing out her name. I imagined her to be a schoolgirl until, a moment later, I saw a womanly face appear from the window of one of the cars below. When I sang out her name again and pointed to her, she nodded her head. I motioned for her to join us. As soon as she got out of the car I could see how striking-looking she was. I turned to my brother and to Sperando Ciotti and said with a wink, "You boys are in for a surprise!"

Quickly, Tony claimed a brother's privileges in his sister's house and answered the door. From the moment he laid eyes on the beautiful young woman whose deep brown eyes and warm smile greeted him, he couldn't concentrate on anything or anyone else. At first she seemed uneasy around me, until she realized that I didn't fancy myself some "star." Though she could hardly avoid noticing Tony's immediate fondness for her, she tried to remain aloof from him—at least until Carmela and I asked him to sing. After that, Lydia was his; and from that autumn evening in 1920 until their wedding day two years later, they met in New York as often as Tony's business schedule permitted.

They were married in the Church of St. Thomas, at 118th Street and St. Nicholas Avenue in Manhattan. I was maid of honor, and Carmela sang during the ceremony. Because of our prominence, the wedding became a national news story. The New York *Times* related one detail that hurt all of us. "The bridegroom's mother, Mrs. Benjamin Ponselle of Meriden, was present for the wedding, but his father was unable to leave for it." At least Papa was consistent in his anti-social ways. He came neither to my debut nor to any of my Metropolitan performances, and even stayed away from his only son's wedding.

Though estranged from Papa, Tony and Lydia moved into the Springdale Avenue house where we grew up. Because Mamma took to Lydia so quickly, they lived rather harmoniously. They became even closer when, in mid-April 1922, Lydia learned that she was expecting. Carmela, Edith, and I could hardly contain ourselves at having a *bambino* to look after. Mamma, who had given up any thought of grandchildren in the wake of Carmela's and my career, was even harder to contain.

I couldn't see Tony starting a family and living under Papa's thumb, so I told him to build any house he wanted at my expense. He agreed, a bit reluctantly, and soon bought a sizable lot on Bradley Boulevard in Meriden. He commissioned our friend Sperando Ciotti to build a home on it. Lydia did some of the designing, and I offered to help locate whatever furnishings she and Tony might want.

As a sort of "extra honeymoon," I took Tony and Lydia with me to Atlanta when the annual Metropolitan tour began in April. I rented a suite for them at the Piedmont Hotel while I prepared for my first Atlanta *Ernani*. I opened the Atlanta run and, as with my first *Forza* three years before, it scored well with the critics.

From Atlanta, Tony, Lydia, Carmela, Edith, and I went to Meriden, where "Rosa Ponselle Day" was held on Monday, May 8, 1922. Although my hometown had honored me before, the mayor and city officials outdid themselves this time. I felt like the Queen of England. The newspapers made much of it. One of them, the Meriden *Daily Journal,* featured a full-page set of ads paid for by friends and prominent people in the Italian community. Some were unintentionally comical—there was one from L. S. Mullon, a local chiropodist, who proclaimed, while commending me, that "corns, warts and moles can be removed successfully"—but all were sincerely meant. One stood out prominently, near the middle of the page. Under the title "A. P. Ponzillo Coal Company" there was a photograph of Tony, below which one of Papa's gauche sayings was printed: "Our Business Is Black, But We Treat You White!"

I had a bad run of publicity, both personally and professionally, in the winter and spring of 1923. One came out of the blue and showed me what gossip columnists could do when they targeted someone. The Washington, D.C., *Herald* ran a headline that read "Opera Stars Deny Separation Rumor"—a fabricated story suggesting that the bewitching soprano Lina Cavalieri and her singer-husband, Lucien Muratore, were splitting up because he and I were having an affair. Lucien, whom I respected enormously as a singer, unloaded on the press in a subsequent interview. "A shamefully ridiculous story!" he said contemptibly, adding that he loved Cavalieri "better than my own life." My only comment to the press was that I failed to understand how any man married to Lina Cavalieri, one of the dozen or so most beautiful women on two continents, would even want to *look* at another woman. The story died rather quickly.

Professionally that year I got into a squabble with a critic—something that Nino Romani and others had always warned against. It began over a concert I gave in Columbus, Ohio, an event well attended and well reviewed by the city's largest newspaper, the *Dispatch*. The critic for the morning newspaper, the *Ohio State Journal,* liked my voice but took me to task for gesturing too much. The reviewer, a woman named Daisy Krier, had said that "the Metropolitan Opera Company has not purged [me] entirely of the vaudeville spirit."

At first I let the comment pass, but soon the *Musical Leader* got hold of the incident and asked me for a comment. "I do not believe that any composer wants an artist merely to stand on a platform like a wooden image and emit a series of sounds, no matter how perfect the technique and tone, without an effort through gestures to convey the meaning of the aria and the feeling with which he himself has endowed it," I said. "Nor do I believe that ninety-nine percent of the average audience wants it. If one wants sound only, why not stay at home and wind up the phonograph and save the admission price?"

So much for criticizing a critic. It's something every singer has wanted to do at least once—though it's a dangerous practice.

The big news of the 1922–23 season was twofold—incredible profits for the Metropolitan and an exceptional list of new singers. The New York *Telegram* dubbed it the "Best Opera Season Since the World War"; the ledgers showed that the Met would register more than $2,000,000 in income, and more than $100,000 in clear profit. Peculiarly, the nation's economy was rocky that year. What had made a difference to the Metropolitan, the critics ventured, was a combination of ingredients that included proven productions (including the Wagnerian ones, now back on the rosters in their original language), a collection of first-rate singers equal to the best of any previous age, and a string of newcomers who gathered immediate shares of the spotlight.

Since the fateful season when Caruso had fallen ill, three sopranos had joined the ranks, each destined to become a legend in the annals of singing. The first was Amelita Galli-Curci, whose bell-like coloratura voice set the standards for her competitors in the 1920s. She was the heir to Tetrazzini's roles and, by my standards at least, outdistanced every other coloratura of her era.

Maria Jeritza, the blond Moravian-born soprano who made press history by singing the "Vissi d'arte" from *Tosca* in a prone position, arrived at the Metropolitan in 1921 and was an immediate sensation. I cannot write truthfully about Jeritza without acknowledging that a great rivalry came between us in the 1920s. On one occasion—fortunately a backstage incident witnessed only by stagehands—our uneasiness boiled over. We shared one of the large dressing rooms reserved for prima divas, which meant that our maids and attendants were to remove our belongings and decorative touches as soon as we were finished rehearsing or performing. That way, the room would be ready for the other's immediate use.

On this particular occasion I had to dress for *Norma,* which I was scheduled to sing that evening. Jeritza was also in the house, going over a few staging details for *Cavalleria rusticana.* Given the monumental demands of *Norma,* and my well-known nerves, I had hoped to have the dressing room to myself. Before I arrived Edith and my maid found the dressing room locked; Jeritza, they were told, had the key but was too busy to come and open it. When Edith told me about it, my temper flared; the stagehands, in a moment of mischief, saw that I was mad and egged me on. Finally, I ordered them to force the door open—which they did, revealing Jeritza's belongings inside. I promptly threw them into the hallway and closed the door behind me.

Meantime, someone told her what I was doing. She stormed down the hallway, barely able to contain herself. As if to threaten me, she barked that she would "tell Gatti" and that *he* would see to it that I was properly dealt with.

Like a schoolgirl threatened with talk of the principal's wrath, I had a comeback already prepared.

"Tell him anything you want," I said threateningly. "And while you're at it, why don't you tell him that *you* will be singing *Norma* tonight!"

The incident passed, and we made up. Our rivalry ended with our careers, and in retirement we became good, if not close, friends. On two occasions, once in Hollywood and again in New York, she made me guest of honor at lavish parties. I reciprocated at Villa Pace.

Our rivalry aside, Maria Jeritza was without question one of the greatest stage personalities in the Metropolitan's history. Although I never felt that she understood the Italian tradition (which, to be fair, was only a part of her expansive repertoire), she was a clever and resourceful actress, especially in Korngold's *Die tote Stadt.* In the Wagnerian repertoire, her Elsa and Elisabeth were equally marvelous. Her voice, though not always as warm as I might have preferred, was inarguably God-given, and had a distinctive beauty to its timbre.

There was no rivalry between Elisabeth Rethberg and me, though perhaps there could have been. Our repertoires overlapped much more than Jeritza's and mine, though Elisabeth (as with Jeritza) sang a number of Wagnerian roles well. Of the voice of Elisabeth Rethberg it can be said, as no less a judge than Toscanini remarked, that hers was perhaps the most perfect *lirico-spinto* soprano voice ever heard. Those who experienced in subsequent years the fluid quality of Renata Tebaldi's voice, and the marvelous *pianissimi* of Zinka Milanov's, would have found both qualities in Rethberg's shimmering, limpid singing. Her arrival at the Metropolitan in the 1922–23 season advanced immeasurably the art of *bel canto.*

Among the male ranks of the Met rosters many names were added, some already well known to the critics and public. The first was Feodor Chaliapin, a giant (literally and figuratively) among basses, a "great blond cherub of a man" in the words of Geraldine Farrar. As noted earlier, I had the privilege of singing with him in *Don Carlos,* and can only underscore what the historians have said of him—that he was unrivaled as a singing actor, in his age or any subsequent one. Neither Ezio Pinza nor Alexander Kipnis, who had once sung Varlaam to Chaliapin's Boris, equaled his acting triumphs despite the marvelous (and totally different) quality of their voices.

Titta Ruffo, who joined the Metropolitan that same season, was also without rivals among baritones. I sang with him frequently, and his singing was as unique as Caruso's. Sadly, the sheer volume of his voice often overshadowed its intrinsic beauty and the exquisite *mezza voce* possibilities it afforded. One of his long-standing complaints was that the public never accepted his *mezza voce* singing; they expected him to sing at full volume, especially in the familiar arias. It was an unreasonable expectation, since a singer contours his tones and phrases by these contrasts in volume, and helps take the drama to a proper climax. Although in Titta Ruffo's case the splendor of his voice lay more in his middle and top tones than the lower ones, his basic technique and, of course, the quality and size of his voice, made his singing a once-in-a-lifetime rarity. I was fortunate to have sung with him nineteen times, in *Aida, Andrea Chénier, Ernani,* and *La Gioconda.*

Giuseppe Danise and Michael Bohnen, artists of entirely different voices and temperaments, were also newcomers to the Met. Bohnen earned nearly everyone's respect but mine; I sang with him once, in *Aida,* and found him lacking as a vocalist and a stylist. Giuseppe Danise was much more to my liking—elegant, intelligent, musically sensitive, possessed of a uniquely colored voice, a fine and consistent actor. He was a real "singer's singer," and I was privileged to have sung with him on more than ninety occasions, in ten operas. He was a superb performer and a true gentleman. Eventually, he would marry lovely Bidú Sayão, a woman of exquisite charm whose exceptional career he helped shepherd.

Aureliano Pertile and Giacomo Lauri-Volpi, two of the great names in the annals of tenor singing, arrived within a couple of seasons of each other, each with the same struggle ahead of him—namely, to carve a niche with a public dominated by Martinelli and Gigli. Because of Pertile's immense reputation in Europe, the odds favored his having a brilliant Metropolitan career. As it was, New York hardly responded to him. It fell to the critics to underscore the great worth of this fine actor and interpreter. Strangely, his Metropolitan contract omitted most of the great roles he was famous for in Europe. A few years later, when I sang with him in London (four performances in all, in *Forza* and *Gioconda*), I saw firsthand what an ideal partner he was. To all of his roles he brought an incredible dramatic tension. After Giovanni Martinelli (and beyond Caruso), he was my favorite tenor colleague for dramatic works. His tenure with the Met was lamentably brief.

For the mercurial Giacomo Lauri-Volpi, a case could be made that his voice

A publicity portrait for vaudeville, 1917,
near the time Carmela and I reached top-billing status at the Palace.

My brother Tony,
when he went into vaudeville in 1922.

An informal
taken by an itinerant photographe
spring of 1907. Papa managed a smile
baker's hat; Carmela had been helpir
come form a piano lesson. O

Carmela, about 1912,
early in her career in vaudeville.
Her singing was providing a steady income,
and *The Girl From Brighton Beach* would
soon launch her on Broadway.

My mother, Mad
to whom Carmela and I owed everyth
of Mamma, this has always been my fa
summer of 1918, while I was pre
approaching fifty, her comp

amily,
rd of our home in Meriden, in the
n bearing. Tony hadn't taken off his
a kept right on knitting. I had just
ted our family.

One of my first professional photographs,
1915. The carefully pinned drape that served
as my dress helped hide my plump figure.

onzillo,
blished. Of all the casual photos
aken at Pine Orchard in the
debut. Though she was
uthful and unlined.

With Nino Romani at Pine Orchard,
Connecticut, where we prepared my roles in
Forza, Oberon, and others after I signed
my Metropolitan contract
in the summer of 1918.

As Leonora in *La Forza del destino,* Act II, during rehearsal on November 13, 1918. My cloak was a deep red, matching the cross along the front of the white dress.

As Rezia in *Oberon,* December 1918, my second role at the Metropolitan.

My first Santuzza in *Cavalleria rusticana,*
tlanta, 1919. The costume was improvised.
My hair, which I wore rather long, became
demark because of the way I tucked it under.
The press dubbed it "The Ponselle Bob."

As the mad Margared in Lalo's *Le roi d'Ys,*
January 1922, which Frances Alda (Rozenn),
Beniamino Gigli (Mylio), and I created at the
Metropolitan, under Albert Wolff's baton.

Mathilde in Rossini's *Guillaume Tell,* 1923. ▷
ne Renaissance flavor of the costume and its
arl cap are reminiscent of DaVinci's portrait
f Beatrice d'Este. Without cuts, its six-hour
th explains why *Tell* isn't produced very often.

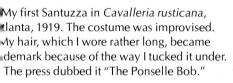

1 "Relaxing" on the afternoon of my debut,
h in the cramped living room of Carmela's and
y apartment at 307 West Ninety-seventh in
hattan. The news photographer arrived about
our in the afternoon, and despite the terror
s feeling inside, I tried to accommodate him.
n always amused by the dime-store pillows
ewn on the floor. The photographer thought
they would add "life" to the scene.

With Caruso in Halévy's
More than sixty years later, t
quand du Seigneu

Carmela as she appeared in concerts
in the early 1920s.

Joseph Breil's not so l
(left) and Louis d'Angelo. The
remnant from a Mack Sennett
with a fur collar—were

ng rehearsal November 20, 1919.
Caruso infused into "Rachel,
aire!" is still vivid in my memory.

gend; 1919, with Paul Althouse
designed for us—mine like a
uis d'Angelo's like an Indian rug
work as the libretto.

With Giovanni Martinelli in *Ernani*,
during a rehearsal in 1921. The dress was a pale green
silk; the long cloak was trimmed in emeralds and pearls.
Occasionally I wore this same dress, but without the cloak,
in the third act of *La Gioconda*.

◁ As Selika in *L'Africaine*, 1923. My costume in *Aida* borrowed liberally f[...] my Selika, which has often caused this st[...] portrait to be identified incorrectly.

▽ As Maddalena in *Andrea Chénier*, 19[...] I kept the role in my repertoire till 1932, sir[...] it thirteen times at the Metropolitan and three on tour.

◁ In my fourth-act costume as Selika i[...] *L'Africaine*, with the dancer La Argentina[...] left, in my dressing room at the Metropoli[...] She and I became friends through Libbie M[...] whom we shared as a manager.

—or, at least, his high notes—had no equal in his day. It was not a singularly beautiful voice, especially, although his *mezza voce* singing could be ravishing. Although his acting could be fiery, Lauri-Volpi was not an exacting musician, and could often be counted on to alter the time values of high notes. At times, he made a musical score seem more an athletic than an artistic feat.

Nevertheless, his high notes were phenomenal. As anyone who sang with him will underscore, the high C was nothing for him. In studio settings he could sing a ringing E flat above the top C. And though his voice was quite lyrical when he made it so, it could cut through an orchestra and a chorus because of its penetrating timbre.

Moody and distant, he had few friends at the Met, especially other tenors. He is said to have hated Gigli in particular—ostensibly because he considered him a lower-class Italian, but more probably because the timbre of Gigli's voice was more beautiful and compelling than his. In such lyrical roles as Rodolfo in *Bohème* or Nemorino in *Elisir d'amore,* there was little room for Lauri-Volpi with the critics and public so long as Gigli was at the Metropolitan. But in *Trovatore, Aida, Puritani,* and *Turandot* (this last created by him at the Metropolitan opposite Jeritza in the title role), Lauri-Volpi's clarion voice made him a formidable competitor, even for Martinelli. His popularity also made it difficult for Edward Johnson—a far more sensitive artist, although less gifted vocally than Lauri-Volpi—to be ranked as a *primo tenore* during his first season at the Metropolitan.

Gigli, Martinelli, and I shared honors in two revivals in the 1922–23 season. The first was Rossini's *Guillaume Tell,* which Gatti revived for Martinelli after an absence of three decades from the Met rosters; I was chosen to sing the role of Mathilde opposite Giovanni's Arnold. Then, with Gigli, as Vasco da Gama, I revived Giacomo Meyerbeer's melodious *L'Africaine,* which hadn't been heard since Caruso, Olive Fremstad, and Riccardo Stracciari had sung it in the 1906–7 season. Fortunately for me, both revivals went well; the critics liked the way I sang Mathilde and went so far as to say that my portrayal of Selika in *L'Africaine* was one of my greatest accomplishments.

Of the two, to be honest, I vastly preferred Mathilde's role and music. For several reasons, I never really enjoyed singing Selika, even though the *tessitura* was congenial to me; I liked only one or two of her solo moments—mainly the long, unaccompanied cadenza in "In grembo a me," which challenged one's sense of pitch but which I found rather easy. The costuming, because of the wide-ranging geography of the libretto (the scenes extend from the court of Spain to the heart of an African jungle), afforded all sorts of variety, from a queen's robes to a tiger skin in the dungeon scenes. But musically, the melodies seemed largely contrived, causing the singers to have to work for every dramatic effect instead of their coming naturally and spontaneously.

In retrospect, I think the popularity of *L'Africaine* owes almost entirely to one ensemble, to the tenor aria, "O Paradiso," and to the elaborate ballet. Though I shared the role with Rethberg, I managed to sing it twenty-six times in New York and nine on tour. It became a matter of self-discipline for me to like performing it.

I was faring reasonably well in my efforts to like it by the end of the season, when Gigli and I sang it as a matinee performance on the season's last day. Perceptive audience members might have noticed a certain urgency in the last act; they would have noticed that we were hurrying tempos a bit, as if trying to rush the closing of the curtain. In fact, we were: we had a train to catch to Atlanta, and the rest of the touring company's singers were at Pennsylvania Station waiting for us.

Gatti left midway through the fourth act. Because I sang the final scene of *L'Africaine* alone, Gigli had a chance to duck out before the end of the performance; he left the theater in full costume as Vasco da Gama, wading through a throng of reporters and photographers as his wife and little son awaited him in a limousine. Gatti had a special cab waiting for Edith and me and we made it to the station just five minutes before departure time. As we rushed to our train, the New Orleans Limited, we were given a chorus of "Andiamo" by Gigli, Martinelli, Antonio Scotti, Lucrezia Bori, and Queena Mario.

The train had just begun to move when we approached the main car. Edith jumped aboard as it crawled ahead. I stood on the steps behind her. Suddenly I felt myself being hoisted into the car in one long motion. Feodor Chaliapin had plucked my five-foot-seven-inch, one-hundred-and-sixty-pound self from the steps to the seating area, hardly exerting himself in the process.

A moment later, when he swept down the aisle, I made a *sotto voce* comment to Queena Mario about his awesome strength, and what intimacy with him might be like. Queena made a priceless comment. "If you really want to know, just go to Russia or to France and ask any good-looking woman you meet. Chances are, she'll be able to tell you!"

Had he overheard the remark, he would have been delighted. With the possible exception of Ezio Pinza, no one worked harder at a Casanova image than Feodor Chaliapin.

A TELEGRAM FROM VIAREGGIO

LACKING NOTHING in the way of comforts, and wanting little more out of life than I already had, I turned twenty-seven in January 1924. Edith planned an elaborate party, and the New York *World* sent a reporter to cover it. The youthful reviewer—Prosper Buranelli, a young Italian-American who would later be associated with Lowell Thomas' broadcasts—got an earful from the likes of our guests. Conductors Giuseppe Bamboschek and Gennaro Papi were there, as were José Mardones, Frances Peralta, tenor Mario Chamlee, and other Met colleagues. Prosper Buranelli's review showed graphically that opera singers can have fun biting the hand that feeds them:

> The climax came at two a.m. when six famous artists, headed by Ponselle herself and accompanied by a pianist and a couple of fiddlers, sang the 'Lucia Sextette' off-key. Maestro Papi conducted. Metropolitan singers have been known to sing off-key before, but the devoted six quite excelled themselves in this extraordinarily-un-welcomed art. Tenor Chamlee sang in a glorious voice, a half-tone flat. Mme. Peralta was half a tone sharp. Mardones chanted an extraordinary succession of dour bass notes. And Rosa herself went from flat to sharp in a bewildering fashion.

My brother Tony, who supervised the cooking for the party, took off his apron and joined us in the sextet, following my lead by singing flat and sharp as the mood struck him.

"The final chord, *fortissimo*," wrote Prosper Buranelli, "curdled the juices of the ears!"

Tony, Carmela, and I were rarely closer as adults than when I was in my late twenties. Our closeness stemmed from our youthful visions of unbridled success for each other, underscored by our accomplishments to date. They were different kinds of accomplishments, to be sure, but they were nevertheless real. Unfortunately, my brother's were short-lived.

Tony made easy adjustments to marriage and fatherhood. The birth of his and Lydia's only child—a boy, Anthony Gerard, christened on my birthday in

1923—gave him a drive to make something of himself, more so than any of us would have imagined. He got up the courage to try out for small-time vaudeville and appeared briefly at the Riverside, where Carmela and I had once been headliners. For his debut he prepared a program of familiar songs made popular by Caruso and John McCormack—"O sole mio," "Santa Lucia," "I Hear You Calling Me," "Just a-Wearyin' for You," "Oh, Dry Those Tears," and a little gem that Caruso recorded called "Your Eyes Have Told Me What I Did Not Know." He complemented them by singing two arias, "Celeste Aida" and "Vesti la giubba."

He had hoped the reviewers would take notice of the arias and make much of the way he sang them. As it was, only one critic covered his debut and accorded him all of two or three lines. After identifying him as my brother (Tony changed his last name to Ponselle to be sure the family connection would register), the reviewer wrote, "He is credited with making a somewhat trembling curtain speech in which he tells his audience that this is his first professional appearance." Nothing was said of his voice except that it was "reliable."

It was sad that Tony's performing career never got off the ground. He toured in vaudeville for about seven months, but gave up and went back to Meriden. Certainly, he had a great deal going for him—a basically good *lirico-spinto* voice, a loving and supportive young wife, and two sisters who had already made names for themselves. Yet he lacked the discipline that serious singing demands. Eventually, his sense of pitch was affected by an ear problem that had developed when he was in the Army; from then on, any semblance of a career eluded him.

Carmela's career began to blossom when, in 1922, she signed with theater manager Maurice Frank. A hard-driving "idea man," Frank devised a three-step plan to get her into the Metropolitan. The first step came in November 1922, when, on Armistice Day, she was a principal in the first complete opera broadcast in radio's brief history. It was an oratorio version of *Aida,* originating over WEAF, Western Electric's early station. The New York *Herald* estimated that nearly six hundred thousand people had heard Carmela's Amneris, which she sang to Anna Roselle's Aida, Dimitri Dobkin's Radames, and Léon Rothier's Ramfis. The performance was broadcast from the Kingsbridge Armory in the Bronx.

Frank's next step was to book her into Carnegie Hall for a concert appearance in mid-April 1923. Although his shrewd publicity enabled her to fill the hall, Frank wasn't able to attract the Hendersons, Gilmans, and other major critics to the event. As a result, she didn't receive the kind of coverage she needed to make a serious bid for the Metropolitan.*

---

* *Maurice Frank's attempts to secure a Metropolitan contract for Camela often resulted in rewriting her and Rosa's early lives and vaudeville careers. In 1923 he offered this imaginative account of the sisters' budding years: "Denied the privilege of musical practice at home, the Ponselle Sisters at a tender age entered the choir of the Catholic church of Our Lady of Mount Carmel in Meriden. On their way to and from Sunday school they prac-*

Late in 1924 I began to notice a change in Carmela—a change especially in the way she viewed me. Word came back to me from mutual friends that she had begun to claim most of the responsibility for my career. I was largely her creation, she said: it was she who had taken me to Miss Ryan, she who had pushed me into the silent-movie houses, she who had interceded with Gene Hughes so that I could sing with her in vaudeville.

The list went on and on and most of it, on the surface at least, was true. I had always credited Carmela with being the ambitious one. I merely tagged along. But the fact remained that in the eyes of the Metropolitan management my natural gifts as a singer and musician were greater than hers. In our vaudeville days, when she thought we had an even chance for success, she freely admitted that mine was the better voice and that I was an instinctive but well-trained musician where she was not. As my star ascended at the Metropolitan, she began to downplay our inherent differences and, in the process, began to resent that her career had not equaled mine. For the time, at least, Maurice Frank's campaign to get her into the Metropolitan kept her worst feelings in check. I did what I could to keep things that way.

Hollywood provided a much-needed change of scenery for me late in 1923. I stayed two weeks there, capping a series of West Coast concerts that proved to be very successful. Arriving in Hollywood, quite to my surprise I soon found the movie colony as much in awe of me as I was of it. Later, I learned why. Hollywood's glory lay solely in its films and stars; otherwise, it was culturally desolate. There were no concert halls, no opera houses, no museums, no smatterings of what the film makers had left behind in New York and Chicago. Hence, whenever a musical celebrity came to town, he or she received the red-carpet treatment.

Mary Pickford and Douglas Fairbanks made a point of inviting me to their celebrated estate, Pickfair, the center of Hollywood's social life. That evening Doug Fairbanks reminisced about his acting days in Boston and New York; he asked about Carmela, whom he had known in New York when she was modeling clothes there. Mary had just come from a self-described bad experience working with the director Ernst Lubitsch on a film called *Rosita;* during

---

ticed hymns and attracted the neighbors by the quality of their voices." Unfortunately for accuracy, however, Carmela was nearly twenty years old when Rosa was in Sunday school—a fact that Frank rectified by listing Carmela's birth as occurring in 1895 rather than 1887.

Frank's acumen again showed itself when it fell to him to explain why his client had been largely absent from the stage since 1918. Carefully skirting the fact that the sisters had gambled on their future in vaudeville by demanding a massive salary increase—a gamble Carmela had lost when the Metropolitan failed to offer her a contract—Frank told the New York Times and other papers that "she long delayed her own studies to aid [her] younger sister's career." Readers with nominally good memories may have noticed, at the time, that this new account of Carmela's absence from the stage contradicted one that Frank had given several newspapers prior to her Armistice Day Aida broadcast, where she was said to have given up the stage "to entertain the soldiers and disabled men in Army camps." J.A.D.

my stay she contented herself with her performance in a new picture, *Dorothy Vernon of Haddon Hall.* As with her other releases, this one was made under the banner of United Artists, the film corporation that she, Doug, the film director D. W. Griffith, and Charlie Chaplin had formed in 1919.

I met Charlie Chaplin during my Hollywood stay and found him an enigma. He wore the expression of creative genius about him constantly and, like the handful who shared his great ability, his moods and behavior admitted to extremes. He and I communicated through music, as I had little else to talk with him about. But in music, because he was an inspired artist himself and because he was enormously sensitive to shades of nuance among tones, he came alive with me. I remember particularly an afternoon at the United Artists studios where I sang part of Massenet's "Elégie" to his unorthodox violin accompaniment.

The greatest friend I made during that first visit to Hollywood was a divine lady whose career outlasted almost all her contemporaries' because of her great acting ability and singular beauty. I speak of Gloria Swanson, whom I met while she was working on a picture called *Manhandled.* Hardly five feet tall in her bare feet, she had the personality of a giantess. The founder and director of the Keystone Comedies, Mack Sennett, had first employed her as a teenager, and by 1923 she was already one of the most popular screen stars in America. Gloria and I saw a lot of each other when she left Hollywood to make films in New York, where her career had begun. She was a regular at my Metropolitan performances, and I went to see every new film she made.

I also met the saturnine Pola Negri, whose reported difficulties with Gloria were reminiscent of mine with Maria Jeritza. I tried my best to give Miss Negri a fair shake, even though I was clearly in Gloria's camp; later, Gloria told me that the "feud" between them was a concoction of the press. But, as it was, this dark-haired beauty remained too aloof to give much to others (to me, anyway), and I found her too temperamental to be a good friend. My acquaintance with Lillian Gish—whose name, like Gloria Swanson's, continues to rank with the greatest in the history of film-making—more than made up for anything I missed in Pola Negri. To my pleasant surprise, Lillian told me that she had often stood in the back of the Metropolitan to hear Caruso and me in *Forza del destino* and *La Juive.* Lillian and I have remained friends throughout the years.

One of the clearest memories I have of my Hollywood stay is of a party given for me and other New York notables by the Howard Verbecks in their spacious home at 2319 Wilshire Boulevard. At least the party *began* on Wilshire Boulevard—and where it ended made it a full-page story all over the country. Verbeck, a prominent California artist, had so loved his Wilshire home, one of the oldest residences in the city, that when he and his wife bought acreage on Lucerne Boulevard, one and a half miles away, he decided to have the house at 2319 Wilshire moved to the new location.

But in arranging for the intricate house-moving, he had failed to consult his wife's social calendar—only to discover, after all the contracts were signed and the arrangements with the city made, that his wife had scheduled a dinner party that evening. Realizing that they stood to lose a great deal of money by canceling either event, they opted to do both at the same time. The result, as the newspaper accounts showed, was a party to end all parties:

> At midnight, along fashionable Wilshire Boulevard, past the sleeping homes of Los Angeles' society, rolled a three-story mansion, mounted on roller and hauled by heavy motor trucks to which huge cables were hitched. At the shouts of workmen and the sputter of engines, sleepers awoke and rushed to the windows. They stared, they marvelled, they chuckled. But what amused them was not merely the spectacle of a house on wheels; it was what was going on inside the house while it slowly sailed past, like a big ship.

In the Verbecks' gigantic living room the Paul Whiteman Band played while guests danced by lantern light and were fed from special battery-powered grills. Even in a town known for its eccentricities, then as well as now, this was unusual enough to warrant headline coverage in Hollywood. There the story was titled, "Joy Riding in a Three-Story Mansion."

Italy beckoned in 1924—not to sing there, but merely to live and breathe it for a summer. Though my roots were Italian and my operatic roles were mainly Italian ones, I had never been to Italy and had never seen my parents' birthplace. It was a situation I decided to remedy in my twenty-seventh year, although I chose not to sing there until much later. Frankly, I was terrified of Italian audiences and imagined myself having to go through the same kind of nervous strain I endured at my Metropolitan debut. Once had been enough, so I contented myself with taking a boat to Italy and spending the summer there studying.

At sea on the S.S. *Leviathan* those of us who were first-class passengers entertained one another lavishly, delved into each other's livelihoods and pastimes, and took turns dining at the captain's table. The first-class passenger list was rather impressive—the Reginald Vanderbilts, U. S. Consul Roger C. Treadwell, railroad magnate H. E. Farrell, and several foreign ambassadors. Also on board were some Olympic long-distance runners and the Cuban welterweight champion, H. Ponce de León. Sol Hurok, then a budding impresario, traveled with one of his new clients, our old friend Adamo Didur.

As usual, Edith and Nino Romani went with me. Edith spent most of her time getting my ledgers in order, painstakingly entering every piece of clothing and every jar of makeup I bought. By 1924 my personal staff had grown large enough to talk about our having a "payroll" to meet. I had a theater maid, a wardrobe mistress, three household maids, a live-in cook, a chauffeur, and, when Edith needed it, part-time secretarial help.

Edith inherited another responsibility that summer—overseeing my diet so that I would come back to the States slimmer than when I left. Then, as now, luxury liners pacified their passengers with ample food and drink, but I was already past a need for either when I got on the *Leviathan*. I had learned a hard lesson about keeping weight off during my study of *Don Carlos* at Lake Placid and Silver Lakes. That summer I had hired an Italian couple to do my cooking, and I was hardly out of my bathing suit for seven or eight weeks. Throughout June and July I renewed my acquaintance with heavy courses of pasta, but paid the price the first time I tried on a new dress. Mad at myself, I blamed it all on the cooks; it was easy to hold them accountable for the forty extra pounds my overactive fork had deposited on me. Thin again, but fearing the same set of circumstances in Italy, the Home of Pasta, I delegated responsibility for my diet to Edith.

Once the *Leviathan* entered port at Southampton, Edith, Nino, and I took a chartered boat across the English Channel to Le Havre, where we were to board a train to Paris. By the time we got there I was pale and utterly drained, thanks to the combination of a rough Channel crossing and an uncommonly jerky train ride. A week in Paris did wonders for my spirits—and, in retrospect, for the ledgers of jewelry stores and clothiers.

Smoother trains took us to Lyon and then to Turin, where for the first time I set foot in my parents' homeland. From Genoa we followed the coastline to Livorno (where Nino had a large villa overlooking the sea), then to Grosseto and Rome; there we toured Vatican City, and I had my first papal audience. From Rome we journeyed to Naples, first to pay our respects at Caruso's tomb, and then to visit Mamma's sister in Caserta.

Seeing Caruso's crypt was not something I looked forward to in any sense. I dreaded it because I had seen photographs of his body lying in state, encased in glass just as it had been on the eve of his funeral three years earlier. The prospect of having to look at the corpse of a man whose importance to me had been incredible totally unnerved me and made me afraid that I would never be able to erase that image from my memory. I stood outside the mausoleum and said a silent prayer for him. Mercifully, as a concession to his widow, his body was later entombed in marble.

Our trip to Caserta was to have been a special one to me. I allowed myself to play the role of the opera diva there, at least the way I made my entrance. Mamma would have been proud of me. All of the town's notables were on hand when my two limousines—one for Nino, Edith, and me, and the other one for our luggage—made their way around the picturesque town square. There were many on hand who had known Mamma and Papa before they had married; naturally they wanted full details about their present lives and their reactions to my success. Most of the Casertans imagined them living in some sort of a castle—which was hardly what one could call our Springdale Avenue home in Meriden.

After the informal welcoming ceremonies were over, I asked for directions to the outlying area where my aunt was living. Directions in hand, I continued playing the diva and ordered my drivers to take me there immediately. I had changed clothing and makeup so that I would look my best for my aunt, a lady whom I had never seen. To avoid another bout with motion sickness I had had the canvas top taken off our car.

As we pulled out of town I tried to imagine what kind of home my aunt would have. I wondered what her reaction would be when she saw me. I knew she had lived in Schenectady for a time, and that she read and spoke English passably. I also knew that Mamma had sent her several of my reviews, beginning with Caruso's and my *Forza* performances.

By the time we reached our destination, we and our cars were covered with dust and thistle; we looked nothing like we had when we had entered Caserta several hours earlier. Not far outside of town, evenly graded dirt roads had given way to deeply rutted cattle trails. In the hot sun, one of our radiators had boiled over. When our hapless caravan at last pulled up in front of my aunt's house, I was sick to my stomach and perspiring profusely. Angry at arriving in such condition, I took one look at the place I was visiting and saw that it didn't matter what I looked like. What I had imagined to be a well-kept but simple home turned out to be a two-room shack built partly on stilts. Under the stilts was a pigpen. In the middle of it, slopping her hogs, stood my aunt. She was a rugged, rotund, middle-aged woman who looked vaguely like Mamma but to whom the years had been far less kind.

She was mystified at seeing me; she hadn't gotten Mamma's letter telling her I'd be visiting her. She embraced me nevertheless and asked to see photos of Mamma, Papa, Carmela, Tony, and me. I had had several made for her, and she took them with a nod of approval. After a while she asked if any of us would like something to eat; neither Edith nor I was in any condition to eat solid food, but Nino and our drivers were hungry. Edith wanted to lie down and was shown into the house; later she told me she nearly retched as the scents of the pigpen wafted through the crude flooring. When she finally lay down she used up her last bit of energy swishing away flies—until she noticed bedbugs crisscrossing her underclothing. A minute later she was dressed and back outside with the rest of us.

The high point of the visit was yet to come. During dinner I asked one of the drivers to get a small box from one of my trunks. Proudly, I told my aunt that I'd brought her a gift. She seemed moderately interested and laid aside her fork long enough to eye the package with some curiosity before tearing it open. When she finally parted the layers of cotton hiding its contents, she exclaimed in a huff, "What do I need with this?"

It was a bottle of French perfume.

While sightseeing in Montecatini in July, I received a telegram from Viareggio, an answer to one Nino had sent a few days earlier. The wire was from Puccini, to whom Nino had wanted to pay his respects and, at the same time, introduce me. The telegram couldn't have been more heartening: Puccini would see us in three weeks and would spend as much time with us as his health would allow.

Nino had warned me that the great composer's health was a question mark, and that Signora Puccini, an incredibly jealous woman (not without reason, according to some who knew their situation), still hovered over him, watching his every move and insisting that he stay within the confines of their lodge at Viareggio. None of it made any difference to me; meeting the great Puccini would be an unforgettable moment in my life.

The moment finally came on a hot, muggy August afternoon. At half-past one, a servant ushered us into Puccini's study, telling us that the Maestro would join us in a few minutes. My heart raced as my eyes took in every detail of the room. A two-tier chandelier hung in one corner, casting its light over the Maestro's upright piano and scoring desk. It intrigued me how he apparently wrote. He would sit at the keyboard on a padded swivel chair, next to which, on the left, was his working desk; this arrangement allowed him to turn quickly from the keys to the score with an economy of movement. His writing desk, which sported a statue of Verdi, stood in another part of the room. Across from it was a visiting area with several armchairs and a small table.

It was in a similar room at the composer's villa at Torre del Lago, Nino reminded me, that a very young Enrico Caruso had been introduced to Puccini three decades before. After hearing this ebullient young Neapolitan sing several measures of "Che gelida manina," from *Bohème,* Puccini had exclaimed, "Who sent you? God?"

Once the usual greetings were exchanged, Puccini asked me to sing, offering to accompany me in anything of his I wished to perform. I chose the "Vissi d'arte" from *Tosca.* Minutes later, as my voice throbbed with emotion at Floria Tosca's phrase, *"Nell'ora del dolor perchè, perchè Signore, ah . . . perchè me ne rimuneri così?"*—"In my hour of misery why, why, O Lord, why do you repay me like this?"—Puccini let his hands lay still on the keys, saying nothing. In the moments that passed between the last echoes of the piano chords and the words he finally said to me, *"Che peccato . . . che peccato non ho sentito questa voce primo!"*—"What a pity that I never heard this voice before!"— the words of that final phrase from "Vissi d'arte" must have haunted him. He was at the end of his life, dying by inches from cancer of the throat, having "lived for art and love" just as Floria Tosca had.

During the course of the afternoon I sang "Vissi d'arte" several times for him, lingering on certain phrases more than others, trying this or that shading on various notes, all the while asking the great man which way he preferred the aria sung. He paid me a rich compliment when he said, *"Cara,* I prefer any way *you* interpret my music!" Later in the day, before we were served dinner, we posed with the Maestro for informal photos on his villa's tiled veranda. Edith took them with a Kodak I had bought for the trip. They were among the very last photographs ever taken of Puccini; three months later, a heart attack ended his misery.

Several weeks after his funeral, I received a letter from Signora Puccini asking if she and her family might have prints of some of the snapshots. In return, she enclosed an unfinished manuscript bearing the Maestro's familiar notation. It was an art song, untitled as yet. At the top of the manuscript, in his unmistakable longhand, he had written, *"Dedico all bellissima voce di Rosa Ponselle"*—"Dedicated to the beautiful voice of Rosa Ponselle."

Two highly demanding roles—the title role in Amilcare Ponchielli's *La Gioconda* and the part of Giulia in Gasparo Spontini's *La Vestale*—were turning points in my career. Each came my way in the space of a year, from December 1924 to November 1925. *Il Trovatore,* as with *Aida,* preceded them, each one a step toward the mastery of the Verdi dramatic-soprano roles and each, I am happy to say, a success for me. Leonora in *Trovatore* is usually listed by critics and historians as being one of my best achievements as an artist, even though I sang the role only seventeen times in my career—eight at the Metropolitan, and nine on tour.

For all its demands—and they were many—Leonora gave me no trouble, no anxiety, even with its challenging high Cs and D flats. Whether it was the D flat in "D'amor sull' ali rosee" or the D flat in the trio involving Count di Luna, Manrico, and Leonora, none of the high notes gave me any pause; on tour I often encored the "Miserere" and would add the optional high C in the scene's second part. Unlike, say, Aida's high C in "O patria mia," these notes lay more easily for my voice because of the way Verdi placed them.

Leonora's character, as with her music, afforded different approaches that some other roles couldn't. I varied my costuming, even down to the color of my hair. Sometimes I played her as a blond, and others as a deep brunette. Either is defensible since "pure-blooded" Spaniards can be either light- or dark-haired. All in all, I liked singing Leonora a great deal—particularly opposite Giovanni Martinelli as Manrico, a role that his artistry and voice fit like a glove.

Gioconda, which Beniamino Gigli, Titta Ruffo, José Mardones, and I sang to much acclaim in the 1924–25 season, opened the next season in grand style, even for the Metropolitan. Nearly two thousand people had to be turned away at the doors opening night; the evening's box office receipts proved a record breaker, totaling some sixteen thousand dollars. Except for Gigli, most of the rest of us singing that night were American-born; Merle Alcock and Jeanne Gordon were to sing La Cieca and Laura to my Gioconda. This enabled the publicity wing to announce an "All-American Cast," which played some part in the high box office tally.

The star-studded events onstage were practically outshone by the brilliance of the Diamond Horseshoe and the Gold Coast crowd that filled it. Seated in the splendor of "Vanderbilt Row," beginning with Box 1 (Mrs. Ogden

Goelet's) were Mrs. Whitney Warren and Miss Grace Vanderbilt. Mrs. Cornelius Vanderbilt was in Box 3, and the Charles Dana Gibsons (of "Gibson girl" fame) were the guests of Mrs. William K. Vanderbilt in Box 6.*

Box 15, Edith told me after the performance, became the center of everyone's attention when the Clarence Mackay family made their entrance. Their eldest daughter, Katherine Mackay O'Brien, had been called "the most charming and unaffected social registerite in the Diamond Horseshoe," and her sharp intellect and personal charm had made her a favorite of the press. But this evening her younger sister, Ellin, was the center of attention. Rumors continued to circulate that she, a Catholic socialite, would soon marry songwriter Irving Berlin, a widower and a Jew.

La Gioconda, because of its weighty score and the demands of volume, range, and endurance it makes on the title character, puts it in a Wagnerian league as an opera. The fact that the 1924–25 revival featured principals with sizable voices only underscored the taxing nature of Ponchielli's score. Tullio Serafin's genius had most to do with the success of the revival. This was his first season with the Metropolitan, and *Aida* (first with Rethberg and subsequently with me) had been his vehicle for winning the critics. W. J. Henderson, hardly one to mete out praise to lesser talents, wrote that Serafin's first Metropolitan *Aida* was the most vital performance since Toscanini's last appearances a decade earlier. It was a high compliment, richly deserved.

What separated Tullio Serafin from every other opera conductor of his era (and I must exclude Toscanini from my observations, because I never accepted an invitation to sing under him†) were his vast musical knowledge and sensitivity, both of which were wedded to a total understanding of the art and science of singing. His understanding of the voice was almost unrivaled. I remember watching my friend Jeanne Gordon rehearsing for the Verdi *Requiem* under Serafin's baton. She was having trouble with her high notes, and was getting more and more frustrated because she couldn't figure out what was going wrong. Seated at the piano, Serafin led her through several troublesome pages of the score, all the while fixing his eyes on her neck and shoulders.

"Do you sense that you're doing something differently?" he asked.

She said no.

"It's your shoulders and neck muscles," he told her. "That's where the trouble is."

* The society columns listed a young Vanderbilt descendant identified as John Hays Hammond, Jr., among the occupants of Box 6. This same John Hammond became one of the most important figures in the history of recording—especially in jazz, with which his name and career have long been linked. J.A.D.

† On several occasions Toscanini had his friend and confidant Bruno Zirato approach Ponselle about European operatic and American engagements, each of which she tactfully refused. She remained, in her words, "scared to death of him," despite Zirato's repeated assurances that her flawless musicianship would have precluded any significant clashes between them. J.A.D.

When she asked him to explain, he told her that she was tensing the muscles along the front of her neck; she was holding her shoulders in an unnatural position, which further complicated things. The result was that her tones were being forced, causing her to have particular trouble at the top of her range.

"What am I supposed to do to correct it?" Jeanne asked.

"Think of your knees," he told her smilingly.

"My *knees?* What do my knees have to do with anything?"

"Nothing at all. Which is precisely why I'm asking you to concentrate on them. Just try it."

She did—and had no more trouble with her high notes during the rehearsal. Later she asked him why his simple remedy had worked.

"You see," he said, "by making you concentrate on a part of your anatomy which doesn't directly affect your singing, I got you to relax the muscles of your shoulders, and the ones along the back and sides of your neck. That made your tone freer, and your tendency to constrict your high tones disappeared."

This was but a small example of the kinds of hints and remedies he had amassed over the years. Later, they were key ingredients in the early bloom of Maria Callas' artistry.

Any singer who worked with Serafin will agree that he was a "total" conductor. He didn't merely coach the principals and let others prepare the rest of the cast. He viewed each opera, each performance, as a unity between the orchestra and the singers, a unity flowing from his own concepts of dramatic and musical effectiveness. This approach left no room for assistants to work out details; he prepared everyone, down to the smallest *comprimario.** His personality was, at least for me, a key ingredient in what made his method work. Though he could be a stern taskmaster, his direction was done *con amore*. No threats, no temper tantrums, just constant encouragement.

As a conductor he made the orchestra "breathe" with the performers. In rehearsals, he would make mental notes on a singer's breathing patterns, particularly on exposed high tones, by scrutinizing their attacks and approaches. He would practice breathing with them, and would pace the orchestra accordingly. This allowed him to give each singer maximum rein where a score might afford some flexibility with time values.

In the first act of *Gioconda,* for example, Gioconda has a prolonged high B flat that is to be sung *pianissimo*. The moment occurs just after the mother's prayer, "Voci di donna." Instead of confining me to a precise time value for the B flat (which is the last thing a performer can be thinking about, if her performance is to be dramatically convincing), he would practice breathing with me, listening to my attack and gauging how long I normally held the note. This particular moment was doubly difficult because Gioconda, Enzo,

---

* A comprimario *singer is a performer whose role is a minor one, viewed in the context of an entire opera. Literally translated from the Italian, the term means "with the principal," referring to a performer whose role or music complements the text sung by the principal singers.* J.A.D.

and La Cieca must all exit together while Gioconda holds the prolonged B flat. By studying my breathing and by concentrating on my attack, Serafin kept the orchestra with me throughout that difficult-to-coordinate march offstage.

Serafin had suggested, when I was preparing *Gioconda* in Italy, that we all visit Venice so that I could see many of the sites that would have been familiar to Gioconda. Venice was still the beautiful, romantic city it had always seemed in songs and storybooks. Motorboats hadn't yet invaded the canals, and the gondolas were still decorated in highly personalized ways, with family crests, mascot colors, and colorful banners and flags, instead of advertisements for soft drinks and cigarettes. In a small band of gondolas, each with its own gondolier, our small party—Serafin, his wife Elena Rakowska, Nino Romani, and a few Italian friends—made our way through the city.

We drifted along, taking in the sight and sounds of Venice at dusk. I was dressed in a full-length ermine coat, as we had just been to a formal dinner. In the gondola I was relaxed, letting my gaze fall on the beautiful buildings and the bright stars of the early evening sky. Everywhere, street musicians played and sang—and, of course, the gondoliers sang, too. Feeling completely relaxed, I joined the singing and marveled at how perfectly the water and the high walls of the buildings conducted the sound. It was a heavenly sensation!

Almost at once we attracted a crowd of passersby, who ran along both sides of the canal shouting, "Who are you? Where are you from? Tell us who you are!" The larger the crowd got, the more I sang—and finally Elena Rakowska raised her voice with mine. It was all so much fun, and so outrageous! I don't know how many songs we actually sang, but by the time we reached our destination the crowd was so large that we couldn't get out of the gondolas safely. There was nothing for us to do but sail back to the lagoon till the crowd went away. It was an anticlimactic way to end such a spontaneous round of singing, and pretty soon we were all grumbling and complaining about not being able to get out of the gondola.

We had gotten so disgruntled by the time we sailed back to our destination that no one was saying anything to anyone. The men got out first and huffily offered us their assistance. I assumed a similar air of annoyance at the whole affair, and confidently put my foot on the edge of the dock.

Unfortunately, I missed.

I fell right into the murky waters of the canal, white ermine coat and all! Luckily I had the unusual ability to buoy myself, bobber-like, in any depth of water, so I wasn't in any danger. It happened so quickly I couldn't even get mad. I just broke out laughing. It was an unplanned bit of slapstick that put a disintegrating evening back together.

La Vestale, by Gasparo Spontini, came my way on November 12, 1925, ten days into the new season. In retrospect, its classically structured music—the music of a transitional composer, music sometimes reminiscent of Mozart or Gluck but at other times suggestive of what was to come in Wagner—was entirely new to New York audiences. Its only American performance of any real note had taken place nearly seventy years earlier when a French opera company quartered in New Orleans had mounted a production in Philadelphia. *La Vestale*'s libretto centers on two main characters—the vestal virgin Giulia and the Roman warrior Licinio. During the course of the opera, Licinio, about to be honored for his victory in battle, learns that Giulia, whom he loves, has become a vestal virgin. After the fashion of all operatic heroes, especially those portrayed by tenors, he resolves to make her his own—even if it means abducting her. She, in the meantime, has been chosen by the High Priestess of the Temple of Vesta to guard its sacred flame; if it goes out, the penalty is death.

The night of her vigil begins with a prayer sung in front of the temple's massive altar. There Giulia implores the goddess Vesta to calm the passion she feels for Licinio. But when he makes his entrance, she gives up all hope of controlling her feelings. In the midst of their passion, the sacred flame dies. So must Giulia die—but just as her execution is about to take place, a bolt of lightning, *deus ex machina,* rekindles the sacred flame, sparing her from death. The opera ends happily as the two lovers oversee a festival honoring Venus.

Edward Johnson sang Licinio to my Giulia that first performance; this was his fourth season at the Met and the first classical revival in which he was to participate. Giuseppe de Luca, José Mardones, and Margarete Matzenauer completed the cast, and Serafin conducted. Critical acclaim was almost unprecedented. "We have little doubt," Lawrence Gilman wrote, "that Spontini would have been delighted with the Metropolitan's production of 'La Vestale' . . . Its splendor and massiveness would have rejoiced his megalomaniac soul." Gilman, as with the other critics, went on to compliment me in ways that I had never before experienced.* But to me W. J. Henderson's simple assessment made me feel a worthy exponent of the much-talked-about "Metropolitan standard." He wrote that I had "ceased to content [myself] with splitting the ears . . . and has gone in for real singing." Here again, Serafin's wisdom had prevailed and Henderson's casual comment, made possible by his anything-but-casual musical judgment, revealed it. Very artfully, Serafin had suggested that I keep my voice light throughout *Vestale*—even in its very dramatic moments, where my natural tendency might be to exploit the sort of volume and intensity I was used to in *Gioconda*.

By this time—although I was the last to know it—Gatti had brought Serafin into his plans to revive *Norma* for me. *La Vestale,* as I'll explain a bit later, had a logical place in this scenario. So did the necessity for me to lighten my voice for the kind of classical singing both roles demanded. Nino Romani helped me accomplish this, mainly by using sections of *Vestale* which Serafin

---

* *Ponselle hardly overestimates critics' reactions here. "Here was a singer," wrote Gilman, "who could sing Spontini's long, gravely-sculptured melodies with the required sense of line and dignity of style, and with the formal and somewhat stilted pathos that is their quaint and special mark—as in her second-act aria, 'Tu che invoco con orrore'; for Miss Ponselle sang these passages of cantilena with admirable phrasing, with loveliness of tone, and severity of style, and she was no less admirable in those moments of true dramatic expression with which the score abounds."*J.A.D.

had prescribed as vocalises for me. Henderson had sensed this immediately, though most of the other critics let it pass unnoticed. He went on to declare that mine was "one of the most beautiful organs of tone that the Metropolitan has ever known"—a declaration that practically made my whole year.

If *La Vestale* took my career to a higher plateau, Carmela's Metropolitan debut as Amneris in *Aida* in December 1925 gave her operatic career a long-overdue start. As it was, her first Amneris was not really a success. She sang it opposite Rethberg's Aida and Martinelli's Radames, and there had been trouble between Martinelli and her throughout the rehearsals.

"Your sister needs her head examined!" he told me angrily one afternoon after he had left a rehearsal.

Looking back on her debut, I think that Carmela must have unduly felt the weight of my presence and reputation. Not that she couldn't have equalled my reputation; had her life gone differently, I sincerely believe that she would have rivaled my reviews, even though she sang as a mezzo and I a dramatic soprano. As it was, my reputation had been made long before she came to the Met. I know it made her feel insecure.

Poor Martinelli bore the brunt of it—and why, I don't know. There was no one nicer or more tolerant than he. But poor Carmela, in her insecure way, pushed him beyond his endurance.

From what I could piece together, she had gone through several rehearsals ordering Giovanni around the stage, endlessly changing her stage actions, and constantly arguing with him about his approach to their fourth-act duet. Finally, during the ante-general rehearsal, he lost his temper and threatened to walk offstage if she made one more comment to him.

Her debut performance, unfortunately, was one of the least successful of her career. The New York *Evening Post* was the only paper to give her singing any real space, and what the critic wrote hardly bolstered her confidence:

> . . . It would be manifestly unfair to pass final judgment upon the singing of Carmela Ponselle, for her nerves were unstrung and she did not do herself justice. She was, however, most impressive in her opulent beauty and fitted well into the picture. It seemed at times as if she would have been more satisfactory had she not forced her tones, but that fault . . . will probably be overcome. It seemed a pity that she had to be pitted against that glorious-voiced singer, Elisabeth Rethberg, whose Aida was what it always has been, and against Martinelli, who was in fine voice and spirits. . . .

Had the reviewer stopped with saying "her nerves were unstrung," her reaction would have been understandably better. But to have judged that her tones were "forced"—and to suggest that she had somehow been "pitted against" Rethberg and Martinelli—was simply too much for her. When she found that

Edith had pasted the review in her scrapbook, she took a thick black pencil and obliterated what it said.*

Early on, W. J. Henderson had predicted that *La Vestale,* despite its being "a very brilliant production," would "probably soon pass again into history." After a mere nine performances—eight at the Metropolitan, and one on tour in Philadelphia—his prediction was met. It was one of those productions that became an immense critical success, but a box office failure. Yet for me and, in a way, the Metropolitan itself, it helped pave the way for *Norma.*

Critic Oscar Thompson, writing in *Musical America* shortly after my first *Norma* in November 1927, speculated on the front office's doings. "After *La Vestale,*" he ventured, "it was a foregone conclusion that *Norma* was in store for Miss Ponselle. Miss Raisa's exploitation of the part in Chicago performances had caused rumors to be floated as far back as 1920 that Mr. Gatti was considering it."

Actually, Thompson's guesses were somewhat off the mark.

Undeniably, Raisa's Chicago *Norma* was a factor in Gatti's decision-making. But it wasn't *because* of her success that he opted to revive the opera for me. (Too, the fact that he had asked me to prepare the "Casta Diva" for my final audition in 1918 showed that he was thinking of *Norma* before 1920.) Rather, Raisa's superlative performances merely underscored that the operagoing public would support such a revival, and, just as important, that the critics would make a major event of it because of the difficulty of Bellini's score.

(While on the subject of *Norma*'s difficulties, I can't resist commenting on the cavalier treatment that this most demanding of all classical roles is accorded today. Much to my chagrin, Bellini's masterpiece is viewed as something no more unusual in an opera-company repertory than a Verdi work. It's no longer seen as the culmination of a *bel canto* career, as a work demanding

---

* *Carmela's Metropolitan debut has always been the source of controversy among those close to the Ponselles. The public account of how she came to the Met was another instance of fiction supplanting fact, thanks to Maurice Frank's inventiveness. According to one United Press account, Carmela had sung "Annie Laurie" and a number of other ballads at a meeting of the Catholic Writers' Guild in New York; there Otto Kahn happened to hear her and engaged her for the Metropolitan's Sunday Night Concert series. This was an especially amusing story, since Kahn had been present during two of the three auditions she and Rosa had been given by Gatti-Casazza in 1918. Kahn had found nothing in her singing to warrant voting her a contract then—nor did he try to use his influence in such artistic decisions.*

Edith Prilik, who was not always reliable as a source but who was closer to the situation than anyone else, provided an entirely different account, according to which Carmela did everything in her power to force Rosa to ask for a contract on her behalf. On Christmas Eve, 1924, Carmela had even threatened to commit suicide if Rosa would not intercede with Gatti-Casazza for her. Miss Prilik (later Mrs. Albert Sania) recalled this scene:

"Nino Romani, Rosa, Carmela and I were decorating the tree and preparing for Christmas Day when Carmela let out a shriek and ran toward the living room windows. She flung them open and screamed. 'This is the end! If I don't sing at the Met, I refuse to go on living!' This was about the tenth time this scene had been played out, and Rosa was accustomed to it by now. 'Go ahead and jump,' she told her matter-of-factly. 'Just don't bloody up the sidewalk—I can't stand messes!' Meantime, Nino and I finished decorating the tree." J.A.D.

strict and long-term preparation to be able to master. What disturbs me especially is that *Norma* is now being sung in regional companies where, at best, youthful and ill-prepared sopranos make mockery of the "classical line" that Bellini's writing epitomizes. This is manifestly unfair to the singers, to the work, and also to the audience. Even among the major opera companies, inexperienced or else miscast sopranos are given *Norma* to prepare—despite the fact that, after Maria Callas, only Joan Sutherland, Montserrat Caballé, and a few others have had any business singing it.)

Gatti first approached me about *Norma* in 1925, when the combination of *Gioconda* and *Vestale*—the one Wagnerian in its demands and the other a formal vocal showpiece—lay ahead of me. Serafin had already assured him that I was ready for *Norma*—and to Gatti, Serafin's word was law. In a far more limited sense, so were the major critics' words law; and after my *Gioconda* and *Vestale,* when even W. J. Henderson was saying that I was one of the Met's finest assets, it seemed clear to Gatti that the time for *Norma* had arrived.

Because the revival would be built around me, I was privy to most of the inner-circle discussions about the rest of the cast. There were four principal and two secondary parts that had to be filled. All that was assured, as of late 1926, was that I would sing the title role; the rest of the cast was as yet a question mark. Eventually, Gatti, Edward Ziegler, and Earle Lewis shared the final casting list with me.

"We want to give Clotilde and Flavio to Minnie Egener and Giordano Paltrinieri," Gatti said, "and I think Pinza is just right for Oroveso."

I couldn't help but smile. Minnie Egener, like Thelma Votipka in a later day, was one of the finest and most consistent *comprimario* artists the Metropolitan had; she was a superb musician and an exemplary colleague who, like the tenor Paltrinieri, could always be counted on to make the most of a minor role—in her case, the part of Norma's confidante, and his part of one of Pollione's centurions.

Pinza was a logical choice to sing Oroveso, the arch-Druid father of Norma, to whom the opera's first aria ("Ite sul colle, O Druidi!," a call to worship for the assembled Druids) would fall. Vocally, José Mardones would have been everyone's first choice, as this was a role tailor-made for him—a "toga role," a part demanding a sonorous bass voice, superior technique, and almost no acting. But health problems and a disrupted personal life took Mardones away from the Met, back to his native Spain. Pinza, who had replaced him as the High Priest in *Vestale,* became the final choice in *Norma.*

Gatti assigned the role of Adalgisa, one of the most demanding in all of mezzo-soprano literature, to a young American singer, Marion Telva. Here, the fit of the voice to the character and the blend of Norma's voice with Adalgisa's were the deciding factors in Gatti's casting. Adalgisa was originally written as a soprano role, which meant that to cast it properly one had to take into account the blend of Norma's and her timbres. Because my voice was dark-colored and had a mezzo-soprano quality to it, Marion's mezzo timbre suited mine perfectly. This would not necessarily have been the case with other mezzos.

(For instance, Ebe Stignani, with whom I sang *Vestale* in Florence in 1933, was an ideal vocal match for me in that opera—so much so that it would have been hard to better our great scene together, in my judgment. But in *Norma* I don't think our voices would have blended like Marion Telva's and mine—nor, for that matter, would Gabriella Besanzoni's, Sigrid Onegin's, or even Margarete Matzenauer's, because of the deeper, more dramatic timbres of their voices.)

I bridled only once during our discussions of the cast. That was when Gatti told me that he had given Lauri-Volpi the role of Pollione, Norma's faithless husband.

"I thought you'd give it to Martinelli," I told him, my face giving away my disappointment at his having chosen Volpi.

Gatti then explained why, in his judgment, Lauri-Volpi would be best for the part. He began with Gigli, which he needn't have; great tenor that he was, Gigli hardly looked the part of a Roman proconsul, though in Europe it became part of his repertoire. Martinelli, Gatti agreed, would certainly have looked the part and would have been better suited musically and stylistically than Gigli; but, as it was, Giovanni was experiencing trouble in his personal life and did not want to take on the role.

"But I still don't see why Volpi is best," I confessed.

I could concede him several important assets in *Norma*. Volpi was a fiery performer and, though a smaller man than Martinelli, he certainly looked the part of a proconsul. Pollione's music demanded a high C in the tenor's first aria, "Meco all' altar di Venere," and if there was one thing Giacomo Lauri-Volpi had, it was a ringing high C. But, to me, the role demanded much more than easy high notes; it called for a mastery of classical style, and also a well-projecting middle range to the voice, both of which I felt Lauri-Volpi lacked.

Only later did I see a deeper reason for Gatti's having chosen him. The reason had nothing per se to do with his singing. (That, Gatti assured me, Serafin would take care of.) It had to do with Lauri-Volpi's and my relationship as colleagues. Gatti knew that Volpi and I kept a certain distance between us; there was none of the fondness that I found in my relations with Gigli, Martinelli, Edward Johnson, or most of the other tenors at the Met. Lauri-Volpi was a difficult person, and his hair-trigger temper made me wary of him. In the end, this kind of uneasiness between us proved just right for *Norma*'s libretto: his offstage personality fit Pollione ideally and, as Norma, I found it easier to revile him than I might have Martinelli's or Johnson's Pollione.

Preparing *Norma* involved two different stages. The first one had to do with my imagination, rather than my singing. I relied on Nino Romani, whose command of history was formidable, to teach me about Druid tradition, and about Gaul during its period of Roman occupation—the period in which the libretto to *Norma* (by Felice Romani) was set. Then I began to fantasize how I would look onstage as Norma—how I would move, what my costume would look like, what different moods and emotions I would convey in each of the opera's key moments. Late at night I would allow myself the luxury of taking the score to bed with me and letting my imagination run free as I would mentally sing the music. In the early hours of the morning—two, three o'clock, maybe four—the silence of my bedroom enabled me actually to envision myself onstage. It was as if I were watching my own performance from somewhere in the middle of a theater.

The second stage of my preparation was the hard-work one. I rented a house at Lake Placid early in June of 1927, and from then until mid-September I let the music settle into my voice.* In July, Marion Telva came for five weeks' work on our duets. We began our day at ten and broke for lunch at noon; then we'd be back at the piano from two until four, and would again rehearse from seven until ten or eleven at night. The only respite we allowed ourselves was an occasional swim before lunch.

By the middle of August our senses of each other's musicianship were so well honed that we were able to carry off the harmonies of our scenes with unerring precision. By the time orchestral rehearsals came about, Serafin was astounded at the perfection of our timing, particularly in the difficult "Mira, o Norma!" Those familiar with Bellini's score will recall that Norma and Adalgisa are required to sing intricately woven coloratura passages written mainly in "thirds"—that is, the melodic and harmonic notes being set apart by one intervening tone.

Because of the *rubato* Bellini allowed, Marion and I couldn't rely on our individual responses to Serafin's baton to keep ourselves together. Finally, we worked out a way to keep our intonation synchronized. We would take each other's hand, as two troubled friends would; but, unknown to the audience, I would squeeze hers a fraction of a second before I would begin a note. If it fell to Marion to lead in a certain measure, she would squeeze my hand the same way. We were never out of time once.

Before Gatti had proceeded with the revival, *Norma* had last been heard at the Met in the 1889–90 season. The legendary Lilli Lehmann had sung it under Walter Damrosch's baton, with her husband, tenor Paul Kalisch, as Pollione. Thirty-seven seasons had passed between Lehmann's and my Normas, and there were few who could remember hers well enough to compare us intelligently.

Except, that is, for W. J. Henderson, who, I am proud to say, gave me one of the finest reviews I ever received and, in all likelihood, one of the most gen-

---

* *Ponselle took a full two years to prepare* Norma, *though the "hard-work" phase she alludes to came in the second year, 1927. Her reference to letting the music "settle into" her voice is her way of distinguishing between memorizing a score, which she found very easy, and actually "living with" the music over a period of time. Merely memorizing a score and singing through it are mechanical rather than dramatic achievements. Only when the music and text had become part of her did she feel prepared for a new role.* J.A.D.

erous ones he ever wrote. Not that he was very generous with the rest of the cast. He dismissed Pinza's Oroveso with one sentence ("There is only one other principal in the opera . . . the High Priest, which Mr. Pinza sang indifferently"), and undermined all of Marion Telva's hard work by saying that she "was in deep water and her conscientious efforts to keep her head above it commanded sympathy rather than enthusiasm."

Neither assessment, in my opinion, was deserved. Nor, especially, was the scathing paragraph he accorded Lauri-Volpi's Pollione:

> . . . [Of this] idol of all upstanding Italians . . . little commentary can be said. He is not given to lyric legato such as Brignole [a great nineteenth-century Pollione] poured into this music in the ante-Metropolitan days, nor has he anything approaching subtlety of nuance. Bellini's music requires style which is entirely foreign to Mr. Lauri-Volpi's art. His Pollione was less like a Roman patrician, but rather like a challenger of Bully-Bottom, who wishes to roar like the lion.

Knowing something of Lauri-Volpi's legendary temper, I was happy for Henderson that he was then an old man. Otherwise, his well-being might have been in jeopardy.

For all of his dissatisfaction with the other principals, Henderson heaped praise on my Norma. In discussing me he began with a quote from La Rousse, an admonition that *Norma* demands flawless technique blended with "the qualities of the tragedienne and the passionate accent of the artist." I had added to my repertoire, he said, "an embodiment which will increase her fame and which deepens the impression created in recent seasons that the ripening of her talent has been the result of a growing sincerity of purpose and earnest study." My "Casta Diva," he declared, was "a genuinely beautiful piece of singing."

Of all the reviews I had yet received, this one mattered the most. After that first *Norma*, Perle Mesta gave a party for me that cost twenty-five thousand dollars. I was so emotionally spent that friends had to urge me to go to it. During the evening I was paid every possible tribute, by every conceivable musical celebrity, to what seemed an endless round of toasts. All night the champagne flowed like the Hudson; it was an event that only Perle could have conceived. The next day, all that mattered to me was Henderson's review.

"A growing sincerity of purpose and earnest study . . ."

"A genuinely beautiful piece of singing . . ."

At last I felt I'd made the transition from a singer to an artist.

LONDON WAS MY CHOICE

LIBBIE MILLER came into my life when I needed her most. Hardly twenty-five when she was introduced to me in 1922, she was already on her way to a fine career in the concert-booking business. Warm, charming, and as shrewd as she was bright (a Hunter College graduate, she was the only woman among my inner circle who had gone to college), she was the consummate agent, adviser, and friend. A *yiddische momme* who would drop everything to fix me chicken soup (her panacea for all ailments) if it would help my mood, Libbie became, with Edith and Lena Angle, a *sorella di latta* to me. Her ability as an agent made me question why I needed William Thorner any longer.

I had grown weary of Thorner when I saw how he conducted himself with Amelita Galli-Curci, who eventually took him to court for breach of contract. Galli-Curci was as sincere a person as she was an artist, and over the years she had grown uncomfortable at Thorner's billing himself as her teacher. It made her even more uncomfortable to see her artistic stature used as a lure for young, inexperienced singers whom Thorner, if they seemed promising, would then try to sign to long-term exclusive contracts.

Several times Galli-Curci and her astute husband, Homer Samuels, had sent sternly worded requests that Thorner not bill himself as her teacher. Each time, Thorner ignored them. Finally, Homer Samuels took out space in several New York City papers, declaring that Thorner had "never taught the Madame a note." The wire services, always looking for something controversial, made a sizable news item out of Homer's notice. The publicity prompted Thorner to sue Galli-Curci for fifty thousand dollars in damages. Wanting to get back at her in print, he went so far as to take out full-page ads in the *Musical Courier* and the professional magazines, showing photographs of Anna Roselle, Yvonne d'Arle, Galli-Curci, and me. Under Amelita's photograph he printed the caption "Teacher of Galli-Curci (At Her Best)."

These ads carried excerpts from two letters, one dated 1913 and the other 1916, supposedly written by Galli-Curci; in them she declared that Thorner, and no one else, had been her teacher. Late in August 1923, when his campaign against Galli-Curci was in high gear, he wrote a self-serving press release in which he depicted himself as "the man who lifted Rosa Ponselle out of vaudeville and the cabarets and made a prima donna of her almost overnight."

For all of that, however, the press release said that he had "always felt the greatest pride in pointing to the great Galli-Curci as one of his former pupils."

This time his claims went beyond Amelita's being one of his pupils. "Not only does Mr. Thorner claim to have discovered her voice and taught her how to use it," his self-authored releases said, "but he declares he fed and clothed her and gave her shelter while she was . . . preparing for her swift climb up fame's ladder." This was nonsense—although Galli-Curci saved her counterpoints for the courtroom. There, and also in the newspapers, she told the real story of her phenomenal development: she had decided to pursue a career as a concert pianist until Pietro Mascagni, a friend of her family's, heard her sing and suggested otherwise. "From there on," she said proudly, "I relied on myself, in the main."

Eventually, she and Thorner settled out of court. A master manipulator of the press, he had cast a pall over her reputation, portraying her as an ungrateful student who had forgotten her teacher as soon as she got to the top. To a small segment of the public, he made her seem an ingrate. No one noticed at the box office: there her reputation was always secure.

Thorner's treatment of Galli-Curci both hurt and angered me. It hurt me because, in a sense, he had used me as ammunition against her in the press. Of all his so-called "pupils," she and I were the most acclaimed in our day; so, by depicting her as an ingrate while claiming that he had made me "a prima donna almost overnight," there was the implication that I was somehow grateful to him. And what angered me was that he had never once given me a voice lesson! In all my years with him he had done but one thing for me: he had made the right contacts with Gatti and Caruso so that I would be given an audition. Other than that, he had only collected his share of my paychecks.

Seeing his darker side displayed against Galli-Curci, I wanted out of my contract with him. Libbie found a quick way for me to do it. My original contract with him was for four years, extending through 1922. As it was, 1922 had come and gone; it was now 1924. So I went to him and explained that I wanted Libbie to take over my bookings.

I showed him a copy of the contract we had signed in September 1918. It said very plainly that I could permit him to be my "exclusive manager and representative for a term of four years." My understanding, I told him, was that he and I had ceased to be manager and client as of September 30, 1922, and that I merely wanted to talk this over so that there would be no hurt feelings on either side.

"It's not a matter of hurt feelings," he said sternly. "It's a matter of a contract that's now in force."

"I'm sorry but there *is* no contract anymore," I said.

"Well, then, why have you let me keep doing some of your bookings during the last two years?"

"Because Libbie's been doing all my concerts, and the agreements with the

Metropolitan were the only things left for someone to handle. Those I left to you because you had always done them."

"That's the only reason you've let me negotiate your contracts for the last two seasons, then?"

I hesitated. "Well, I'll always be grateful to you for what you did for Carmela and me after we left the Keith Circuit. But I still think that—"

He cut me off.

"You're beginning to sound like Galli-Curci," he said angrily. "I gave you everything, you admit it, and now you want some little Jewish princess to take over your career!"

Now *I* got mad.

"I never admitted any such thing! If it weren't for Nino Romani, you wouldn't have known who the Ponzillo Sisters were! And another thing—you know damn well you never gave me any singing lessons, so you can just stop saying you did!"

"My, my," he said mockingly. "You're all alike!"

The next time I saw him was in court, two years later. Meantime, he had continued to collect ten percent of my earnings by way of an escrow account he had arranged with the Met in 1918. At Otto Kahn's suggestion, I retained Nathan Burkan as my lawyer. Burkan represented Victor Herbert and other musical celebrities, and his legal wisdom had been one of ASCAP's early assets. Thorner's lawyer was James T. Schiller, an expert at putting words into witnesses' mouths, against whose tactics Burkan coached me heavily.

In court, through Schiller, Thorner tried to argue that he and I had made verbal contracts that extended our original four-year association into an agreement that would last as long as my career. I couldn't believe my ears—yet I had no real defense because it was his word against mine. Lacking any witnesses, Schiller tried to convince the jury that our written contract of September 1918 left wide room for interpretation—so much, in fact, that it could be construed as a career-long contract. After listening to this for several hours, the judge grew weary of it and said to him pointedly, "I have the contract before me, Mr. Schiller, and it's as plain as the nose on your face!"

The jury sided with me, which led Thorner to appeal the verdict. Meantime, he replaced Schiller with Charles C. Pearce, a well-respected trial lawyer. The case went to the Appellate Division of the New York State Supreme Court in February 1928. It took Nathan Burkan a mere five legal points to defeat Thorner a second time. I left the courtroom free to retain Libbie Miller as my exclusive manager.

The success of *Norma,* both with the critics and at the box office, put my career at a crossroads. It was the kind of role that had capped a career, at least in the past; Lilli Lehmann had sung it at the zenith of her American career, near the end of the most celebrated reign among Wagnerian singers in her day. In my case, *Norma* entered my repertoire when I was only thirty. Naturally, then, I had to ask myself what I was going to do next.

Nino Romani and Libbie laid out the possibilities. On the one hand, I could content myself with the eighteen roles I had sung. On the other, I could search the *bel canto* literature for other classical heroines of the *Vestale* and *Norma* type. Then, too, I could undertake several of the familiar Italian roles I hadn't yet sung; like Raisa I could sing Alice in *Falstaff*, and since I had not sung a Puccini role yet there remained the challenges of *Tosca, Manon Lescaut,* and others. Or I could venture into totally different territory—Strauss, Wagner (*Lohengrin* and *Tannhäuser*, at least), Mozart, and others whose works were as yet foreign to me.

There were pros and cons for each of these. Except for *Tosca,* I had reservations about most of the Puccini roles; either my physique was too out of character (at five foot seven, weighing one forty, I would hardly have been a credible Cio-Cio-San!), or, more to the point, my voice was both too large and too dark-colored for most of his heroines. Natural as *Tosca* might have been, it would have been very hard to keep my emotions in check, especially during the second act—and it was a role so thoroughly associated with Jeritza at the Metropolitan that it would have been hard to establish myself in it.

The more lyrical Wagner roles of Elsa and Elisabeth were other options, and were attractive to me because of the caressing quality of their music. (I mean "caressing" in rather a Latin musical sense, as opposed to the intensely dramatic Teutonic quality of, say, Brünnhilde's music.) It's clearly arguable whether I could have sung the heavier Wagnerian roles creditably; I had the range, the power, and the stamina they required, but my Italian timbre and temperament would probably not have suited them. As it was, I went so far as to buy a costume for *Lohengrin;* it had belonged to the legendary soprano Salomea Kruceniski, who sold it at auction during a benefit for the poor people of Viareggio, near the time I visited Puccini there. But, as matters proved, I never sang Elsa.

Gatti-Casazza resolved my dilemma temporarily by assigning me the Metropolitan premiere of Verdi's *Luisa Miller,* and by bringing back into the repertory, after twenty-one years' absence, Mozart's *Don Giovanni. Luisa Miller,* which I created for the Metropolitan with de Luca, Lauri-Volpi, and Tancredi Pasero, was one of Verdi's "middle period" operas and was, for me, a safe extension of what I had been doing. *Don Giovanni* was another matter entirely. Gigli would sing Ottavio, Pinza the malevolent Don, Editha Fleischer (whose lovely lyric voice had first been heard at the Met in 1926) would portray Zerlina, and Elisabeth Rethberg would sing Donna Elvira. Donna Anna, a part that Emma Eames had sung definitively when the Metropolitan had last given the opera, went to me. Serafin would conduct.

At no earlier point in my career could I have agreed to singing Donna Anna with the full confidence that I could sing whatever Mozart had written for her. With *Norma* behind me, I felt sure I could sing anything, no matter how difficult. Considering the demands inherent in Mozart's music, I needed that kind of self-confidence. Unlike Verdi, whose scores made room for (and sometimes encouraged) unwritten high notes, altered time values, and a number of other excesses, the beauty inherent in Mozart's work depended on a strict adherence to the written score. To sing what he had written demanded solid technique and total musical preparation. A lack of either would show up quickly in a performance.

Of the principals in the cast Gigli and Pinza, in that order, commanded most of Serafin's time during coaching sessions. Each had the requisite voice and technique, but neither could read music; consequently, Serafin had to work with them line by line, often note by note, and had to temper their tendency to embellish the score.

Opening night for *Giovanni,* November 29, 1929, was star-crossed for me. I got the flu and had to cancel, forcing Gatti to put on my understudy, Leonora Corona, in my place. Her uncertainties in the role—occasioned by her not having even one rehearsal owing to scheduling problems—undermined the cohesion of the ensembles. The next day, Lawrence Gilman wrote in the *Herald Tribune,* "It will perhaps be sufficient to say that she made Miss Ponselle's indisposition seem a costly thing indeed for the Metropolitan." Gigli had a moderate success opening night with his Ottavio (his "Dalla sua pace," Gilman commented, was "one of the happier events of the evening"), but Elisabeth was apparently not at her best. Editha Fleischer met everyone's expectations as an ideal Zerlina and pleased even Henderson. Not so with Pinza's Don: Henderson thought him miscast, and Gilman said plainly that he lacked "the elegance, the grace, the adroitness [and] the magnetic charm" that the part necessitated.

I was credited, rightly or wrongly, with giving *Don Giovanni* a new lease on life when I joined the cast the day after New Year's, 1930. If I did so it was mainly because Gigli, Pinza, Fleischer, Rethberg, and I were so used to each other, given Serafin's marvelous preparation, that we jelled when we sang together. Late in life, Serafin declared that the blend of Rethberg's, Gigli's and my voices in the so-called Masked Trio was the most beautiful he'd ever heard in an ensemble. Happily, the critics were generous to me, some even suggesting that my Donna Anna had surpassed my Norma.*

* *Olin Downes's review in the New York* Times *echoed fellow critics' sympathies when he declared that Ponselle "roused her audience to demonstrations of enthusiasm which recalled the legendary days of the opera gods of a past generation. Such singing as she accomplished in a role far removed from the vocal and dramatic style to which she is accustomed was something of a revelation even to her most ardent admirers . . . Last night she consecrated herself wholeheartedly to the essence of the Mozartean tradition, never projecting herself out of the picture, always maintaining an aristocratic elegance of line, and aloof distinction, and a careful coordination of vocal and dramatic elements with the performances of her associates." Even Serafin—not always given to superlatives about performances he conducted—left the podium, as Ponselle relates, with some indelible memories of the quality of singing evident in the revival.* J.A.D.

Memories of my first Donna Anna, thanks to Ezio Pinza, are not entirely musical. The popular press helped "create" Ezio Pinza—or, at least, his romantic facsimile. He was always depicted as courtly, irresistibly charming, utterly confident, and incredibly handsome. He was all of that—onstage. Offstage only the handsomeness applied; otherwise, the rest of these qualities belonged more to a man like Giovanni Martinelli.

Elisabeth Rethberg, who was almost everything Ezio wasn't, fell victim to his charms shortly after he arrived at the Metropolitan. Their relationship caused several difficulties during *Don Giovanni*. At first, Elisabeth forgave (or else refused to face) his errant ways; it wasn't unusual for him to keep her waiting while he was supposedly "rehearsing" at some or other hotel. Only Serafin seemed able to keep him collared.

During my first *Giovanni* I remember standing backstage, my eyes and ears glued to Elisabeth's performance. Several times earlier Pinza had made passes at me but each time I had rebuffed him with a laugh; I wasn't attracted to him, and I found it hard to take him seriously.

Odd as it may seem to today's operagoers, who are accustomed to following their favorite singers' careers from continent to continent, I had spent a decade singing opera nowhere but in the United States. As early as 1919, offers had come from London, Paris, Milan, and Buenos Aires, but, inwardly fearing foreign audiences (especially Latin ones), I had declined all of them.

Tullio Serafin finally persuaded me, in 1927, to sing Norma in London at Covent Garden. He and others told me that Londoners were as avid as their Italian counterparts in Milan, Florence, and Naples, but were far less harsh on newly arrived talent. Martinelli, who had sung often at Covent Garden, painted a marvelous picture for me of the life of an opera star in London—formal parties at the Savoy, Claridge's, and other landmarks, elegant dinners at the estates of London's aristocrats, and lectures and public appearances on the art of singing. Though I led a restricted social life when I sang, it all sounded wonderfully compelling. Eventually, my resistance fell and I signed a contract with Lieutenant-Colonel Eustace Blois, Covent Garden's impresario. No sooner had I signed than the usual doubts and fears began to have their way.

Colonel Blois became director of Covent Garden in 1928, at a time when the company's German wing was perhaps the strongest in the world. His appointment signaled a return to a balance in which Italian and German works would be given equal status in the repertoire. My Norma and Gioconda would be, I was told, the keystone of his plans for the 1929 season. My debut was scheduled for May 28, and I allowed myself most of the month to get a feel for London and its people. I wanted and needed a lot of support, so I asked those closest to me to make the crossing with me. Edith and Libbie made the trip, as did the elegant dancer La Argentina, whom Libbie also represented. I invited Natalie Townsend, a longtime friend, to help oversee the social aspects of my stay; the wife of Lawrence Townsend, well known in Washington circles,

Natalie knew London society from the inside and would be a great help to me. For additional reassurance, I called up my childhood chum Lena and asked her to go along. Being with Lena always enabled me to keep my feet on the ground; she was bright, witty, earthy when the occasion arose, and always kept me laughing. Perle Mesta, who always liked to be where things were happening, also traveled with us.

The Covent Garden theater, which I surveyed as soon as I arrived in London, was at least twenty-five years older than the Metropolitan, dating back to the mid-nineteenth century. Like its Manhattan counterpart, it was ungainly on the outside but had an inner warmth that wholly enveloped both performers and audiences. The architecture was predominantly Mediterranean—a handsome portico with Corinthian columns, a magnificent grand staircase, three tiers of richly decorated boxes, an interior bathed in hues of crimson, rose, ivory, and gold. Behind the curtain everything was drab, dusty, and cramped, quite as backstage areas are everywhere.

I had been told that Covent Garden's acoustics ranked with the best in the world. I found out for myself a week or so after I arrived. I tried a verse from "Annie Laurie" as I walked from one part of the stage to another; I sang with only nominal volume, but heard my voice resounding through every part of the auditorium. Even the most delicately spun *pianissimo* made its way to every row, giving me the range of sensations every singer needs to gauge how well the voice is projecting. I felt perfectly at home at Covent Garden.

While I prepared for my debut, I sampled as much of London as time allowed. I stayed at the Savoy, one of the finest luxury hotels in the world. Being near the river, it afforded me the long walks I was used to in New York; often I would walk alone near the river, mentally reviewing *Norma* while getting a bit of exercise. Had it not been for a strictly enforced quarantine on animals, I would have taken my pets with me when I walked; as it was, Argentina took care of them so I wouldn't worry about them.

My old friend Vincenzo Bellezza, who had conducted the London premiere of *Turandot* two seasons earlier, was to conduct *Norma*. He and I had known each other since 1918, when Caruso's influence had enabled him to make the transition from accompanist to conductor; since then, he had distinguished himself in Buenos Aires, Colón, New York, and, as of 1926, in London as well. Although the London cast—Irene Maghini-Cattaneo as Adalgisa, Nicola Fusati as Pollione, and Luigi Manfreni as Oroveso—was not the equal of the Met's Telva, Lauri-Volpi, and Pinza, Bellezza's conducting brought unity and authority to the production. Rehearsals progressed well, and everyone associated with the theater made me feel welcome and secure—except Maghini-Cattaneo, who lost my trust when she created a childish scene at the general rehearsal.

Every seasoned performer knows how much he or she depends upon other cast members—particularly in moments of unexpected trouble. Nothing is ever guaranteed in a performance; one learns to expect an occasional mishap or momentary indisposition, and during those moments supportive colleagues can help or hinder the situation. Especially in an opera like *Norma,* where intricate ensemble singing is demanded, a sense of oneness and trust among the principals allows each one to sing with total confidence. My Metropolitan Adalgisas —Marion Telva, Gladys Swarthout, and Elda Vettori—always gave me that confidence, just as I did them. Once, Telva was gripped by a momentary loss of voice and whispered that she couldn't sing a cadenza only a few measures ahead. I told her to mouth the words and I would sing for her; I turned my back to the audience, and no one was the wiser. Afterward, she cleared her throat and was able to continue. She would have done the same for me, as would Claussen, Homer, Matzenauer, or any others who truly understood the communal essence of performing. Yet in Maghini-Cattaneo, despite the rich, mellow timbre of her dramatic voice, I never felt real confidence.

At the general rehearsal I was attired in a simple dress, as I was saving my delicate, heavily beaded costume for the night of my debut. The costume was very difficult to clean, so I got Colonel Blois's permission to wear a dress during the rehearsal. The rest of the principals, including Maghini-Cattaneo, were in full costume. When she saw that I wasn't, she lost her temper and demanded to know what "right" I had to be exempted from Covent Garden rules. Before I or anyone else could explain things to her, she made a direct accusation that my "exemption" had come as a result of an affair I was supposedly having with poor Colonel Blois—a man I hardly knew! I forgave her the accusation, but never fully trusted her again.

Two social events, for vastly different reasons, remain with me of my Covent Garden debut. One was an elaborate party I was given at the Savoy in June 1929, just after my *Gioconda;* John McCormack, Antonio Scotti, Vincenzo Bellezza, and Fred Gaisberg, the Gramophone Company's pioneer recording director, had arranged the affair. During the final course, John McCormack talked seriously with me about my future, and pleaded with me to begin studying the Wagnerian literature. I said I would think about it, but that I couldn't make any promises.

John knew, I'm reasonably sure, that Gatti had once asked me to prepare Isolde and the three Brünnhildes. I had felt my temperament more suited to the Italian and French repertoires (Rachel in *La Juive* had just entered my repertoire, and I was looking forward to more French roles), so I politely declined. Until Frida Leider arrived in the early 1930s, Gatti tried a succession of sopranos in the heavy Wagnerian roles. Among them, in addition to Easton and Matzenauer (who sang Kundry in English), were Nanny Larsen-Todsen, Barbara Kemp, and Gertrud Kappel. Each impressed me in different ways— Larsen-Todsen for the dramatic drive that had led Wagnerites to crown her "Queen of Bayreuth," Barbara Kemp for her flawless diction and great acting, Gertrud Kappel for the purity of her soprano sound and the unusual richness of her lower register—yet none seemed to garner the critical praise in New York that Frida Leider would eventually claim.

The other event I most remember happened a few weeks earlier at Claridge's. My friend Natalie Townsend—a pupil of Jean de Reszke, who knew many of the Golden Age singers—arranged a luncheon at which I could meet one of my childhood idols, Dame Nellie Melba. Having taken the great lady's name at my confirmation, only to have the priest change it to "Maria," and having heard Melba's name over and over in my youth, I was naturally excited at the prospect of meeting her.

I couldn't have been more disappointed when I did.

I remember walking across the private dining room to greet her. A bit nervously, I held out my hand.

She looked at me as if I were an impetuous fan about to bother her.

"You must be the new singer from New York," she said tartly, ignoring my hand. "What sort of voice are you supposed to have?"

Caught unaware by her offensiveness, I answered her haltingly.

"I guess it's a dramatic soprano . . . I mean, that's what the critics say."

"I pay little attention to critics," she said in her haughtiest voice. "I shall be my own judge of your voice. What sorts of roles do you sing, anyway?"

"Oh, *Norma, La Vestale, Gioconda,* roles like those."

"Well, whatever you purport to sing here," she said, looking down her nose while trying to make herself my height, "you will have to make an adjustment to Londoners and their reactions."

"An adjustment?" I said, having no idea what she meant.

"In America you've become accustomed to hearing applause after every major aria and scene. Here, the audience will applaud only at the conclusion of an act, as the curtain is being rung down. Londoners applaud *no one* unless at the end of a scene or an act."

"I really needed that," I told Natalie Townsend, who was terribly embarrassed by the scene. I held some hope that Melba would at least attend *Norma,* so that she could hear firsthand what I was like. A few days after the episode at Claridge's, Natalie received this letter from her:

> I am frightfully sad for one of my dearest friends is dying, and I am
> with her a great deal. This evening there is a consultation and I
> must be there. Their [*sic*] very poor and I am calling in a big man;
> but I am afraid there is no hope—will you tell Ponselle how sorry I
> am but I hope to go to her next performance. I have sent flowers—
> tell her I know she will have a big success because she is a very great
> artist—I am sorry but I know you will understand and miss
> me. MELBA.

Dying friend or no dying friend, Melba did attend the performance—incognito. I had my moment of glory in the "Casta Diva." For the first time in anyone's memory, the audience broke precedent; I received a six-minute ovation.*

---

* *In London as in New York, Ponselle's Norma was wildly acclaimed. Said Ernest New-*

If it pleased Melba, so much the better. To a woman who once ordered around John McCormack as if he were an underling, and who is said to have taken Giovanni Martinelli's curtain calls (she claimed the audience was calling for "Nellie" and not "Martinelli"!), it is hard to guess whether I, a newcomer, could ever have pleased her critical ears.

My final verdict on meeting Melba was that the priest who had confirmed me in the little Mount Carmel Church in Meriden had been wiser than I'd thought. In changing my confirmation name to Maria, he had said sternly, "There is no 'St. Melba' in the Church." He was right—there was no St. Melba.

The summer after *Norma* and *Gioconda,* London was my choice for an important first in my career. On Gatti's advice, I sang my very first *Traviata* there. With Donna Anna behind me, I had faced again the dilemma of what to do next. I settled on *La Traviata* because it offered an intriguing set of challenges. First, there were the vocal challenges—so different from those of the other Verdi operas I had sung. Then there were the dramatic challenges. At five feet seven in my bare feet, and weighing nearly one hundred fifty pounds at the time, I didn't especially look like a Violetta.

Initially, Gatti had some reservations about my doing a role on which Lucrezia Bori and Amelita Galli-Curci almost held a patent. In my defense Tullio Serafin pointed out that most of the legendary nineteenth-century sopranos had sung *Traviata,* usually in conjunction with much heavier roles. (It is on record that Lillian Nordica, so secure was her technique, once sang Isolde and Violetta on successive nights.) Serafin also pointed out that the "fragmentation" of the soprano voice into the now standard categories of lyric, *lirico-spinto,* dramatic, and coloratura was purely a twentieth-century convenience. It hardly precluded a dramatic soprano with coloratura capabilities singing a role usually associated with much lighter voices.

I had seen *Traviata* a number of times before studying it. Bori played Violetta as only she could; she was small-framed, moved about daintily, and had a look of innocence about her, even though as Traviata she was to have been a worldly woman. Vocally, she portrayed her lyrically, rather as she would Mimi in *La Bohème.* In all, her Violetta was like a finely etched cameo.

Claudia Muzio, on the other hand, made Violetta a much more dramatic creation. The difference between her and Bori's characterizations was the difference between them as sopranos and, in a sense, as women. Vocally, Muzio's was a darkly colored *spinto* voice that throbbed with feeling. Lauri-

---

man in the London Times, *"Here is that rarity of the operatic stage, an artist who can not only sing but create a character . . . Not only is her voice of great beauty but she also has the art of making it convey every nuance of the mind without its even for a moment losing its pure singing quality. The range of psychological inflection in it seems unlimited." Newman's remarks were echoed in the columns of the* Morning Post, *the* Daily Mail, *the* Evening Standard, *and the* Daily Sketch, *all of which made headlines of it. The* Morning Post's *headline, "Rosa Ponselle's Triumph: London Conquered in Five Minutes," summed up the effect that her "Casta Diva" had on the usually restrained Covent Garden audience.* J.A.D.

Volpi once wrote of the "tears and sighs" inherent in her voice, and of the "restrained interior fire" of her personality. No scene in *Traviata* more embodied these qualities than her Letter Scene, "Addio del passato." Fortunately for posterity, the Columbia company recorded her singing it at the very end of her life. It remains one of the finest of all *Traviata* recordings.

In its dramatic intensity, my Violetta bore a greater resemblance to Muzio's than to Bori's—but with an important difference. Muzio's *Traviata* was laden with sadness, with a deep sense of tragedy, even early in the score; the "Ah! fors' è lui" contained an element of it, and the Death Scene merely carried to a logical conclusion what a member of the audience felt in the opening act. My Violetta, on the other hand, was one of much dramatic contrast: she would live hard, and would give up life unwillingly, not resignedly. To her last breath, she would *fight* for life.

A distinguished Violetta of the last century—Gemma Bellincioni, who at eighteen had sung Gilda in *Rigoletto* at La Scala, and who went on to become the first Santuzza, Fedora, and Salome in Italy—helped me translate this drama into reality on the stage. I studied Violetta with her in Naples. She was long retired by then, so she could give me the uninterrupted time I needed. We had a wonderful give-and-take about each of the important scenes and arias in the opera. Others had taken for granted that the final scene should be done the way Bori and everyone else did it. I opted for something different— something more intense, something that would so captivate the audience that they might believe, if only for a moment, that as Violetta I might actually *defeat* death. I asked Bellincioni to show me exactly how she had done the last scene. The moment I saw her act it in front of me, I was absolutely certain her approach to it was the right one for me. She gave me her blessings and let me appropriate it entirely.

My conception of *Traviata* worked—I quote the *Times* critic, Ernest Newman, very proudly:

> We were told that Madame Ponselle was singing Violetta for the first time on any stage; but one found it difficult to believe it. Nothing finer has been seen or heard at Covent Garden this season . . . Madame Ponselle proves to us once again that the finest singing— given a good voice to begin with—comes from the constant play of a fine mind upon the inner meaning of the music; her Violetta is so exquisitely sung because it is so subtly imagined. Even coloratura, as she sings it, ceases to suggest the aviary and becomes a revelation of human character.

Were Newman's endorsement not enough, his colleague Francis Toye, who was one of the most respected critics in all of Europe and a renowned Verdi specialist, declared flatly, "I do not think that I have ever heard anything to surpass or even equal it."

The success of *Norma* the year before had led Colonel Blois to want to repeat it in 1930. In 1931—my last Covent Garden season because of an augmented concert schedule in the States—he would do the same with *Traviata*. In all, I sang twenty-one performances of six operas in London—*Norma* and *Gioconda* the first season, *Traviata, Norma,* and *L'Amore dei tre re* the second, and *Traviata, Forza del destino,* and Romano Romani's *Fedra* in the final one.

L'Amore dei tre re was especially memorable because its composer, Italo Montemezzi, was present at the first of our two performances. The audience induced him to take a bow after the second act. Though Montemezzi wrote a number of other operas that had their premieres in major houses—among them *Hellera, La Nave, L'Incantesimo,* and *La Notte di Zoraima,* a weak effort that I created at the Metropolitan in 1931—*L'Amore dei tre re* was unquestionably a masterwork. A fast-moving drama based upon a tragedy by Sem Benelli, *L'Amore* can be viewed and appreciated on two levels: as a human drama, based upon the complicated relationship between Fiora, her lover Avito, and the murderous King Archibaldo, or else as a political drama, with Fiora's spirit and power—even in death—representing Italy, and the kings representing potential conquerors. Fiora was one of my favorite roles, as it was for Bori, Rethberg, Muzio, Easton, and many others in my time; yet I sang *L'Amore dei tre re* only six times in my career.

In my Metropolitan performances I had the privilege of being cast with Martinelli, Gigli, and Edward Johnson. Each sang Avito somewhat differently, yet, as one would expect from singers of their caliber, they were superb in the role. In London I had the good fortune to be cast with Francesco Merli, one of the finest tenors then singing in Europe and, like Aureliano Pertile, a standard-bearer of the high quality of Toscanini's direction at La Scala.

Though Merli was about ten years older than I, his career had begun only two seasons before mine, when he made his debut at La Scala in Spontini's *Fernand Cortez.* He arrived at Covent Garden in 1926, creating for the London public the role of Calaf in the British premiere of *Turandot.* His voice, to be fair in describing it, was not a romantic, caressing instrument on the order of Gigli's; though large and rather vibrant, his voice was penetrating and metallic in timbre. Yet he was an absolutely convincing Avito—so much so that during one of our rehearsals I became more involved in the drama than I dared allow.

This particular rehearsal was with piano only, and took place in a small room backstage. We were rehearsing a love scene whose text is so beautiful and moving that to this day, just in thinking about it, it can bring tears to my eyes if I don't keep my emotions in check. During the scene, though it was just a rehearsal, Francesco Merli and I *became* Avito and Fiora: what were supposed to be stage kisses quickly became passionate, real-life embraces. Nothing like this had ever happened to me before—and I viewed it as a danger sign. Although there are moments when it's hard to resist, no singer can ever afford to become a character; if it happens, the most imminent danger is that the emotions will constrict key muscles in the throat, defeating one's technique. Merli, a seasoned performer, was just as aware of this danger as I was. After the rehearsal, we never mentioned the incident, and it never happened again.

Although Nino Romani's *Fedra* did not receive the acclaim in London that it had in Rome when Raisa, Lázaro, and Formichi created it in 1915, the fact that Colonel Blois accorded it a Covent Garden premiere speaks well for its worth. Londoners heard an augmented version of the original score, as Nino decided to add a new aria for me. He had toyed with the idea for quite some time, but didn't firmly decide on it till we were crossing the Atlantic. By the time we docked he had written and orchestrated "O divina Afrodite," probably the opera's best-known piece of music.

Though a one-act opera, *Fedra* is an extremely complex work. Not that its libretto (written by Alfredo Lenzoni, a master at integrating words and music) is difficult in itself; although it is somewhat complex, psychologically, centering on a love triangle between two *sorelle di latte*, Fedra and Carila, their lover Ippolito, and Fedra's husband Tesco, its action can be readily grasped from the text. What made it complex was the absolute correspondence between each measure of music and each phrase of the libretto. Except for "O divina Afrodite" and a brief duet, *Fedra* is an uninterrupted flow of music, perfectly matched with sensitively chosen words. The unity between text and score is complex enough to require at least two or three hearings to be fully grasped.

If the London critics were somewhat lukewarm to Nino's creation, the Covent Garden audience was not: thanks to Tullio Serafin's inimitable preparation and conducting, Nino and the cast merited fifteen curtain calls. Cesare Formichi, who had created the baritone role of Tesco in *Fedra*'s Rome premiere sixteen years earlier, sang the role to my Fedra in London. A well-educated man whose large, dramatically expressive voice earned him much acclaim in Milan, Chicago, and London, Formichi became one of the better-known baritones of his generation although he never sang at the Metropolitan. Stella Wilson, a lyric soprano, sang the role of Carila, and Elvira Casazza, a distant relative of Gatti, sang Natrice, who had raised both Fedra and Carila. Antonio Cortis, the fine Spanish tenor, portrayed Ippolito, although Romani never accorded him the same accolades he bestowed on Hipólito Lázaro, who had created the role in Rome.

Good as my memory may be of my London performances, I cannot personally vouch for the effect they had upon those who heard me. After all, I was onstage singing and could only be conscious of that. Except for the memories of those who might have been in the audience, then, I have only the critics' columns to go on. But fortunately, one lovely woman (a dear friend, although she would not find me out of place if I referred to her as a "devoted fan"), heard virtually all of my London performances and has since written about them. I refer to Ida Cook, the English novelist (under the *nom de plume* Mary

Burchell) and, most recently, Tito Gobbi's collaborator on his autobiography. With her sister, Louise, Ida was in the Covent Garden galleries every time I sang. I have asked her to comment on those performances:

"In order to realize how completely that first *Norma* was an EVENT in capital letters, one has to know how different—how blessedly different—was the musical world then. It was not a period when every Tom, Dick, and Harry felt qualified to undertake the role of Otello. Still less did every Jane, Mary, and Anne imagine she could sing Norma—or Turandot or Salome, possibly alternating those roles as the fancy took her. At that time we waited humbly for the necessary phenomenon to appear, and the last woman to have sung at Covent Garden had been Lilli Lehmann, no more than a legend to almost everyone in the house that night.

"Our hearing and judgment had not been blunted by indifferent radio performances (we called it 'the wireless' then and listened on earphones). Neither had some distorted vision of Bellini's masterpiece been reduced to pocket-sized mediocrity on a screen in our own dining-room while we chewed our way through the evening meal. If I remember rightly, we had not even heard a gramophone record from this unknown work. We were as ignorant—as innocent, if you like—as the audience who waited on that December night in 1831 for Pasta to waft the phrases of "Casta Diva" for the first time upon the world.

"We had come to the opera that night with almost agonizingly eager expectation, and if we sat on a wooden seat in the gallery (for which we had paid three shillings and sixpence—the equivalent of rather less than a dollar then) we were literally a fraction nearer to Heaven than those who sat in the stalls below. We had read of Ponselle's tremendous impact in the role when the work had been revived for her in New York. We had, as we stood in line outside the opera house, incredulously watched the diva herself *walk* along Floral Street and in at the stage door. Now we waited for her to come onto the stage, following in the wake of a rather motley collection of priests and priestesses.

"It is over fifty years ago, but I can see her now—that beautiful, utterly commanding figure, as she took her stand under the dusty cardboard oak—which immediately became the totally realistic tree from which she was to cut the mistletoe. I remember that many years later Maria Callas said to me, 'I think you know, Eeda, that to me Ponselle was probably the greatest singer of us all —but can you tell me how we differed on the stage?'

"I could, I am glad to say. Ponselle was like a goddess. One understood immediately why the tribe practically worshipped her, and one shared the emotion with them. So that when she proved to be an intensely human, fallible woman the shock was almost as great for oneself as for her followers. (Callas —perfectly legitimately and with tremendous effect—played the role as a woman throughout.)

"After the first phrases of anger and reproof to those around her on the stage, Ponselle began the 'Casta Diva'—that perfectly supported *pianissimo*, that rocklike steadiness of tone, that flawless *legato*. It was like someone weaving a spell and, one and all, we succumbed to it—to such a degree that at the end of the aria, in spite of the rule then in operation at Covent Garden forbidding applause during an act, the silence was shattered by a storm of cheering and clapping in which even the orchestra joined.

"Enthralled by the drama, moved to tears by the pathos, wrung by the queenly dignity and the womanly despair which made up the rest of the evening, my sister Louise and I went home that night knowing, in a vague sort of way, that we had heard, seen and felt the ultimate in vocal art. We still think that is the only way to describe the full Ponselle experience.

"There is, of course, something intensely personal about one's reaction to a great singer for, unlike every other musical performer, the singer is his or her own instrument. It is useless to suppose that a mere gramophone record (however good) conveys more than a part of the total impression. The real thing is an indescribably-subtle amalgam in which sound, sight, movement and stillness combine with some sort of almost psychic power. I can perhaps best convey what I mean by saying that I seldom play a Melba record; I find them rather boring. Yet when I recall her in the balcony scene from *Romeo and Juliet* sung at her Covent Garden farewell in 1926, what I remember is not a rather disagreeable, horse-faced woman in her sixties. I only remember Juliet singing of her tragic young love in a way to bring tears to one's eyes. This is why, when I hear confident young men pontificating about performers they have never seen nor heard, I am astounded by their arrogance and their ignorance.

"During that first season Ponselle sang three Normas and two Giocondas, stunning us afresh with her impact in a verismo role following so immediately on the great classic role of Norma. The second season (1930) she had the opening night in the Covent Garden premiere of *La Forza del destino,* with Aureliano Pertile, Benvenuto Franci and Tancredi Pasero. By now she was, as they say, the talk of the town, and the King and Queen (George V and Queen Mary) attended a later performance. As the lights went up in the first interval, we spied the Duke and Duchess of York (later George VI and Queen Elizabeth, now our beloved Queen Mother) in another box. I cannot say whether the King and Queen had alerted the younger couple to the prime necessity of hearing Ponselle or whether it was the other way around, but we had the thrill of seeing the Royal Family greet each other with surprised and congratulatory waves across the house.* Those were the days!

"During that season Ponselle sang her first *Traviata*—the first time she had sung the role anywhere in the world. I have heard many Violettas in my time, naturally. Some were good, three were great and in my opinion Ponselle was the greatest of the three. I remember at the time one of our leading critics wrote, 'It transcended interpretative art and became creative art.' I think per-

---

* *Ponselle was introduced to the King and Queen the day before the* Traviata *performance. The King asked her not to be distressed in any way if he were to leave the theater before the last act, as his duties might make staying impossible. To her surprise, he remained in the royal box until the final curtain. Later, the King and Queen invited her to be their guest at the royal paddock, for the races.* J.A.D.

haps Covent Garden was the ideal house for this extraordinary character study. Large enough to show the full amplitude of the glorious Ponselle voice *per se,* it had miraculous acoustics based on the old wooden-frame building and so one heard every nuance of the musical magic. In addition, it was not so large that any of the infinite variety of subtle dramatic touches were lost.

"The season ended with two performances of *L'Amore dei tre re,* the first one attended by the composer, Montemezzi, himself. I have described in my autobiographical *We Followed Our Stars,* the unforgettable impression on that last night when Pinza, as the old blind king, carried the body of the murdered Fiora from the stage. I can only add that I was so euphorically moved that I actually bestowed a good-night kiss on someone I intensely disliked!

"In the third season, 1931, we had repeats of *Traviata* and *Forza del destino,* and to these was added the London premiere of Romano Romani's *Fedra.* I think I am right in saying these were the only performances ever given of this work in an English opera house. Many years later, in touching recognition of this, Ponselle gave to the Archives of Covent Garden the Fedra costume which she wore on that occasion.

"No one is going to pretend that *Fedra* is a masterpiece. But with Ponselle as the Fedra it was a remarkably effective piece of theatre, with some extremely singable passages, apart from the very dramatic aria which Romani interpolated specially for her. Oddly enough, I remember most vividly the moment when the curtain rose and Ponselle was lying there on a couch, staring into the audience in sullen silence. She neither moved nor uttered a sound but you *knew* that she was set apart from those around her by her own awareness of her guilt. So much for those who parrot, 'But they didn't act much then, did they?'

"She had been announced to sing on the last night of the season in *Forza,* but she cancelled because of illness and her place was filled by the admirable Iva Pacetti. If we were crushed with disappointment it was not Pacetti's fault. She just was not Ponselle."

With such incredible reviews from London, many of which found their way into the New York papers, my *Traviata* created its own stir at the Metropolitan. Lauri-Volpi was Alfredo and Giuseppe de Luca was Germont when I sang my first New York *Traviata* in a benefit performance in mid-January 1931. Unbelievably, considering what the London critics had said, my Violetta was anything but uniformly received in Manhattan.

Critic Oscar Thompson's comment that my Violetta was "one of unusually dark hue and highly emotionalized from the outset," set the stage for the other reviews. W. J. Henderson, perhaps making up for the good things he had said of my Giulia and Norma, said that I had "elected to disregard the fact that Verdi's music is essentially lyric." Consequently, in his view, I had made "every number passionately emotional by introducing methods verging closely on the declamatory." He took particular exception to my "Ah! fors' è lui" and

my part of the "Dite alla giovine." In the former, he charged me with pepper-
ing the lyrical music with what he described as "spasmodic utterances"; in the
latter, he wrote, I had made the music "cold and heavy." Overall, he accused
me of having transformed a "plaintively pathetic conception into hard-breathed
tragedy."

I looked to Pitts Sanborn for support, but found little. "Though Miss Ponselle accomplished some beautiful and moving singing in the course of her first
American 'Traviata,'" he judged, "she will fortify her Violetta in the future,
not through violent onslaughts on Verdi's melodic line, but through the
finished phrasing . . . [and] unblemished elegance his mid-nineteenth century
style demands."

So there it was: Francis Toye, perhaps the greatest Verdi authority then living, said that he had never heard anything to surpass or even equal my
Traviata; but Pitts Sanborn thought much less of my creation and W. J. Henderson charged that I had essentially redesigned the character of Violetta. So
much for two continents' worth of critics!

(Eventually, Henderson's readership in the New York *Sun* demanded to
know whether his remarks about my Violetta weren't a strong indication of a
pro-Bori stance on his part. Pressed for an answer as to which of our *Traviatas*
he preferred, he replied wryly, "Neither. Verdi's.")

Depressed as I was over the strange reception that awaited my Violetta in
New York, the worst was yet to come: Lucrezia Bori, whom I had always
counted as a friend, grew cold to me after *Traviata.* It happened a few days
after that mid-January performance, when I saw her one afternoon at the Metropolitan. Valuing her criticisms and observations as a colleague (and, needless
to say, as one of the greatest of all Traviatas), I had tried to reach her by
phone and had left several messages with her secretary. She had never answered them.

This time, instead of the warm smile and kiss on the cheek with which she
had always greeted me, she walked past me and uttered only a chilly "Good
morning." For quite some time, until Geraldine Farrar helped patch up things
between us, I couldn't reach Bori. It was as if she would come to me with her
arms outstretched, but would never bend them to embrace me. It was all so
strange! Five years before, she and I had shared Fiora, in Montemezzi's
L'Amore dei tre re, and no uneasy feelings had surfaced on either side. This
time, with *Traviata,* I gained a role but almost lost a friend.

Fortune—"luck," "chance," call it what you will—is a vital but unreliable ingredient in life. Often it's like money—it's most abundant when you don't really need it. Until I turned thirty-five I had had enough luck for any ten people. I had made my way from Meriden's West Side to an international opera
career, and not just as a member of the greatest opera company in America,
but, modestly or immodestly, as one of its biggest stars. My voice was known
from one coast to the other through my recordings and concert appearances,

my income was secure even though the Depression was on,* and, just as important, there had been no illnesses or tragedies in my family.

Fortune failed me for the first time in 1932, when Mamma developed pneumonia and had to be hospitalized. At first the prognosis was reasonably good, but Mamma ignored her doctors' warning to stay in bed until she was fully recovered. Soon she fell ill again—this time seriously.

I was on my way to a concert appearance in Hartford when Edith and Libbie received word from Tony that Mamma was growing delirious. Naturally, I felt torn between my concert and the responsibility I felt toward my mother; I couldn't do anything myself, so I got hold of Dr. Bill Verdi and asked him to meet us in Meriden. By the time I got there, Bill had examined Mamma and gave me the bad news: her illness was so advanced that he was sure she wouldn't survive.

Carmela was at Mamma's side when Edith, Libbie, and I were taken into her bedroom. I knew she could make out my face and knew who I was because tears came to her eyes when I took her hand. The sight of her in that bed, helpless, barely conscious, her life slipping away from her, made me cry like a baby.

She turned toward Edith and said to her in a series of pitiful gasps, "Please take care of my little Rosa, won't you?"

I got hold of myself and tried to buoy her spirits.

"Don't worry," I said to her, "you're going to get well and I'll be back to see you real soon." I saw her fix her eyes on my face and again gasp for the breath to speak to me.

"You may see me, Rosina, but I won't be able to see you."

By the time I reached Hartford, I was so emotionally drained that I doubted whether I could sing. Libbie and Edith drummed into me that if only I would try concentrating on the music I would get through the performance. I made a few adjustments to the printed program and got through the first part of the concert. By making myself block out everything but the words and notes I was singing, I managed to get through the rest. I launched into my encores mechanically, as usual saving "Home, Sweet Home" till last.

That was fine—until I reached the second verse, in which there is a couplet that speaks of a mother's love for her child. At that point my voice broke and I ran offstage crying. The audience, not knowing what was happening in Meriden, slowly began stirring until the theater's manager walked onstage. Libbie, always one to think quickly in a crisis, gave him a handwritten note that said, "Miss Ponselle is overcome with sentiment at the thought of being in

* *As of 1928, Ponselle's net worth was estimated to be nearly $4,000,000, a sum she had amassed through stocks-and-bonds investments she had made using her income from the Metropolitan, from her concert appearances, and her recordings. Throughout the mid-1920s her annual income exceeded $120,000, the greatest percentage of which derived from her concert engagements. In mid-1928, conservative advice from the Fifth Avenue Bank in Manhattan, whose president counseled her that her stock should be converted to bonds, led her to be able to retain most of her wealth through the Depression.* J.A.D.

her home state, singing before her own people." Though it wasn't the truth, at least it was better than no explanation at all. A few days later, when the newspapers carried Mamma's obituary, the audience members finally learned what had happened.

Mamma's funeral was the worst ordeal of my life. To this day I can't escape the memory of seeing her lying in state, flowers enshrouding her casket, a pearl and gold rosary entwined in her fingers. Papa, who had shown almost no emotion toward her while she was alive, wept like a child as he bent over her lifeless body, his hands stroking her soft white hair. The scene proved too much for all of us—her children, her neighbors, the downtrodden immigrant families she had helped . . . She had been the focal point of more lives than she ever realized, and now she was gone.

When we buried her at the Sacred Heart cemetery in Meriden, I completely lost my composure. I held up reasonably well until the undertakers lowered her casket into the grave. The eerie sound of shovels of dirt striking her casket made me wail till I nearly passed out. I had to leave the gravesite.

Two weeks later I faced another ordeal. I had to sing a performance of *La Gioconda,* whose story, operagoers know, involves the love between a beautiful young balladeer and her aged, blind mother. It was a touring performance in Philadelphia in November 1932; Rose Bampton, the striking-looking young mezzo who had made her way to the Met by way of Buffalo and Massillon, Ohio, was to make her debut as Laura that night. Most of the audience was aware that I had buried my own mother only two weeks before, and I sensed their compassion. My vivid imagination is what got me through *Gioconda.* I made myself imagine that I was singing only to Mamma.

Mamma's last wish had been that I sing in Italy. "Even if you sing there only once," she would say to me, "your own people will have a chance to hear that you are like Caruso." Out of respect for her memory, I had Libbie finalize a contract that I had been offered for two performances of *La Vestale* at the first *Maggio Musicale* in Florence. The *Musicale,* or "May Musical," was a creation of the Mussolini regime. It was a series of operas and plays organized around an international music congress, and would feature international stars, conductors, and stage directors in spectacular productions.

For this first *Musicale* six operas had been chosen. Verdi's *Nabucco,* whose liberation theme was dear to the *fascisti,* would open the festival on April 22, 1933; Carlo Galeffi, Antonio Melandri, Gina Cigna, Ebe Stignani, and Tancredi Pasero would perform it under the baton of Vittorio Gui. Donizetti's *Lucrezia Borgia* would follow, with Pasero, Gigli, and the soprano Giannina Arangi-Lombardi in the lead roles. Next would come *Vestale,* with Pasero, Stignani, and the Italian tenor Alessandro Dolci singing with me. *Falstaff,* with Ernesto Badini, Dino Borgioli, Rosa Raisa and her husband, Giacomo Rimini, would follow; Victor de Sabata would conduct.

Pinza and the mezzo-soprano Conchita Supervia would then join Badini and Borgioli in performances of Rossini's *La Cenerentola,* to be sung under Tullio Serafin's direction. Then, as the festival's last outing, Lauri-Volpi would head a cast in Bellini's *I Puritani* that included Carlo Scattola, Pinza, Mercedes Capsir, and my dear friend Mario Basiola. This, too, Serafin would conduct.

As I hadn't sung *Vestale* for several years, I got in touch with Serafin and asked him to help prepare me. An immensely generous man, he offered me half the villa that he and his wife, the soprano Elena Rakowska, had rented at Boscachiesa Nova, just above Florence. I accepted his offer and arrived in Italy in early April, in time to guarantee both a good rest and several extended coaching sessions. It took very little time to reacquaint myself with the intricacies of the Spontini score.

My only fear was the treatment I might receive at the hands of the Florentines, a notoriously demanding group of self-assured opera lovers. I found out on the evening of May 4, and again three nights later when I repeated my Giulia. Radio had carried the first performance as far south as Naples; critics there, in Rome, and in Florence labeled my voice the peer of any that Italy had produced. With my vivid imagination, I sang the performance to my mother; I imagined it so vividly that wherever my eyes turned in the dark theater, I saw only her face.

That first *Vestale* created such a stir that a crowd had to be turned away for the second one on May 7. My fears behind me, I gave a performance that rivaled the best I had ever sung. Again, Ida Cook's recollections:

"We went on hoping for a long time that another Ponselle London visit might be planned, but 1932 saw a much reduced season and 1933 held out no greater hope. And then, sensationally, it was announced that she was to sing in *La Vestale* in the 1933 Florentine Musical May. I scraped together the few pounds necessary, left the less affluent Louise to listen on 'the wireless' to the one performance to be broadcast, and took myself off to Italy for the first time in my life.

"Nowadays, I never pass the Comunale (then the Politeama) without thinking of that first *La Vestale*. The audience was itself worth a careful study. There was Richard Strauss—the first time I ever saw him in real life. There was also Stravinsky, who left me a little cold, I admit. The place was crowded with celebrities from the musical and social world of Italy, and though I was too ignorant to pick out individuals, the overall effect was magnificent.

"The sensation she caused is difficult to describe. It is not a role of tearing drama. What is required is an almost superhuman degree of vocal control and faultless classical singing. Again and again one could almost sense the audience collectively holding their breath. Then the high point of incredulous appreciation came in the prayer, 'O nume tutelar,' where the most miraculous *pianissimi* are called for. No one, to my knowledge, ever responded to that challenge as Ponselle did. At the end of the aria there was pandemonium and insistent calls for her to sing it again. Vittorio Gui, who was conducting, was determined not to break the no-encore rule and for some moments the opera went on, in competition with vociferous shouts for an encore. Then suddenly and inexplicably he gave way, went back, and allowed her to sing the prayer again.

"Years afterwards—long after the War, in fact—I met Maestro Gui for the first time, in the gardens at Glyndebourne, and I told him I had been present at that famous *La Vestale*. He remembered every detail too and said, with a reminiscent smile, 'Do you know why I finally gave way and let them have that prayer again?' I shook my head and he went on, 'I heard a poor little voice behind me say, "Who knows if we shall ever hear anything like that again?" and I thought, "Who knows?—They shall have it." ' "

Not long after the performance, one of the listeners who had heard the radio broadcast sent word that he wanted to meet me in person. The man involved was not someone to whom an artist said no—Mussolini, *Il Duce* himself. At first, he had mistaken the wild applause for a political disturbance in the theater. I accepted his invitation and made the journey from Florence to Rome in a chauffeur-driven car he had sent for me.

I arrived at his spacious headquarters at the Palazzo Venezia, where I was taken to an immense room on the second floor. The room was richly decorated with fresco walls and ceilings in a Renaissance style. At the opposite end of the impossibly long room sat the balding man at whose feet all of Italy bowed. I must have been visibly nervous as I made the long walk to his desk.

"Come to me . . . you're not afraid of me, are you?" he said, rising from his chair. He gestured for me to sit with him on a sofa in another part of the room. I felt awkward and wondered how I would make conversation with him; after all, I was hardly what one would call an expert on world affairs. Beyond that, I knew almost nothing about the Fascist movement, or even what reforms Mussolini stood for.

As it turned out, I had nothing to worry about.

"Your father is Benardino Ponzillo and he comes from Caserta," he said with a boyish look on his face. "Your papa was a *bersagliere* as a young man. And your mother, may her soul rest in peace, was Maddalena Conti, also from Caserta. So, my American songbird, you come from Neapolitan stock and therefore I think of you as a *sorella*, as one of Italy's own family."

Unknown to me, he had had someone check on my roots. He put me at ease instantly. We talked for the rest of the afternoon, like two long-lost friends.

What with the warmth I was feeling in Italy, I cabled Libbie in New York and authorized her to reopen negotiations with La Scala. My two *Vestales* had been supreme confidence builders, and at last I was ready to consider singing in Milan. I might have done so—if it hadn't been for *I Puritani*, the last opera of the *Maggio Musicale*.

I liked the score of *Puritani* (the Met had given it with Hipólito Lázaro in the difficult role of Arturo) and, delighting in watching Serafin prepare an opera, I attended several of the rehearsals. At all of them, Lauri-Volpi, who was to sing Arturo, had refused Serafin's request to sing in full voice when asked; instead, he sang in a whisper, and sometimes merely hummed along.

When I asked him why, he told me rather haughtily that he had sung Arturo so often he knew it backwards.

He continued to refuse Serafin's requests, until the Maestro finally quipped to the orchestra, "Well, if he makes a mistake, it will be his neck and not mine."

When the performance took place, he did more than that: he missed a note. In the second verse of the taxing "A te, o cara, amor talora"—usually a vocalise for Lauri-Volpi—he cracked the high note, sending his voice into an out-of-tune falsetto.

Before he had time to recover, the audience rose at him, drowning out the orchestra in a rumble of whistles and catcalls. It was a demonstration of rudeness that Lauri-Volpi himself rivaled when, at the end of the act, he lost his temper backstage and smashed props, furniture, and anything else that came between him and his dressing room.

That incident had a shattering effect on me. For the first time I saw what an Italian audience could do to one of its favorite tenors when, in a difficult moment, his technique failed him. The next morning, I cabled my feelings to Libbie in New York. The message was simple:

FORGET MILAN. ONLY IN AMERICA. ROSA.

A SIP OF WINE

FROM THE MID-1920S through the mid-1930s, a new generation of singers prospered at the Metropolitan. It was a decade of memorable debuts and thrilling performances. Happily, many involved American-born, American-trained singers. Their emerging careers led Gatti-Casazza to be sure that his gamble on me was now paying dividends.

Lawrence Tibbett's star stature was a case in point. He had auditioned for me in 1922, while he was studying with Frank La Forge. Hearing the promise in his voice, I encouraged him and put in a favorable word to Gatti. The next season he made his debut as the Monk in *Boris Godunov,* and went on singing small parts of that sort. On January 2, 1925, he went onstage as Ford in Verdi's *Falstaff.* With Gigli, Bori, Antonio Scotti, and Frances Alda in the cast, he had little hope of being noticed. By all rights he should've gotten more notice as Valentin in *Faust* or Silvio in *Pagliacci,* two of the half-dozen roles then in his repertoire. As it was, at the last minute he replaced another newcomer—the lyric baritone Vicente Ballester, a Spaniard—and, in the second act, sang one of the best renditions of the "E sogno?" in memory.

Though Scotti, for whom *Falstaff* had been revived, got most of the applause in the title role, in Tibbett the audience heard and saw a fresh voice and fresh face—a ruggedly handsome American boy whom they crowned with an ovation that "split the roof," as Lawrence Gilman wrote. The next day the wire services had a front-page story on their hands, and a new career was in the making.

But not so with poor Marion Talley, who, for reasons known only to Gatti, was promoted the very way he had opposed in my case seven seasons earlier. Then, he had wanted the critics to do the star-making with little or no advance press; this time, an eighteen-year-old girl who had never sung except in her native Kansas City was promoted as a "new star" before she had sung a note in New York.

A *Rigoletto* in February 1925, with Lauri-Volpi, de Luca, Mardones, and Merle Alcock, was to be her debut performance. Her family and friends chartered a train to help pack the audience, and at every stop her father, a telegrapher, tapped out the group's eastward progress. Eventually, the tapping continued from a specially installed telegraph key backstage. When the reviews were all in, the verdict was "too much, too soon." Her "radically incorrect placement," said Henderson, made her seem an amateur in a professional company. A year later her career ended with a telling performance of *Le Coq d'or*. With proper guidance, she might have enjoyed a long and productive career.

Between Lawrence Tibbett and Marion Talley—the one a genuine star and the other a short-lived meteor—there were Grace Moore, Frederick Jagel, Gladys Swarthout, John Charles Thomas, Helen Jepson, Richard Crooks, and Rose Bampton, each a product of the late 1920s or early 1930s.

John Charles Thomas was a contemporary of Tibbett and was well known in and around Broadway before Gatti extended him a contract in 1933. He made his debut opposite me in February of the next year, singing Germont to my Traviata. His voice had a rounder timbre to it than Tibbett's, but his technique did not permit the exquisite softness that (as we all called him) Larry could bring to an aria. Nor could he create a believable character the way Larry could; what he did was simply sing, but with a rich, resonant quality that everyone admired. Eventually, radio and phonograph records, rather than the Metropolitan, made him a household name—or, rather, three names.

In 1932–33 the Met's "Tenor Triumvirate" lost two of its brilliant members: Gigli left in 1932 after refusing to take the same salary cut the rest of us did (from $2,500 to $1,000 per performance, to help stave off shortfalls), and Lauri-Volpi decided to confine his career to Europe the next year. Tito Schipa, one of the Chicago Opera's luminaries, was an early beneficiary of their leaving, and captured most of Gigli's lyrical roles. Though smaller than Gigli's, his voice was velvety and pure, boyish-sounding in its lyricism, but somewhat limited in effective range. We sang together many times, and fragments from one of our *Don Giovanni* performances—an early Saturday matinee radio broadcast, with my friend Milton Cross at the microphone—offers proof of his easy singing of difficult music.

Richard Crooks and Frederick Jagel, each an American, also benefited from Gigli's and Lauri-Volpi's departures. Crooks arrived in the winter of 1932, scoring well with the critics (thanks to Wilfred Pelletier's coaching) in Jules Massenet's *Manon*. Radio and recordings had made him a celebrity by then, and in many circles his warm, lyrical voice was compared, in substance and style, to McCormack's. Though the comparison was probably unfair to both men (John McCormack was too singular a phenomenon to compare to anyone, and to my ears Crooks's voice was more akin to a very lyrical Charles Hackett, another American), Richard was a serious artist whose triumphs in the French repertoire gave him a niche all his own at the Met.

Where Richard Crooks's voice was lyrical, Frederick Jagel's was a voice whose size, texture, and tone made it adaptable to a wide range of roles, from Almaviva to Siegfried and Tristan. Though he never rivaled Martinelli with the critics or the public, he sang everything well and, like Florence Easton among sopranos, was one of the Met's most adaptable assets. He went on to become a fine coach and singing teacher at the New England Conservatory.

Two American women who made their Metropolitan debuts in that same era deserve special comment. One was Rose Bampton, who sang Laura to my Gioconda during that difficult performance a few weeks after Mamma had died. Rose grew up in a houseful of boys in Massillon, Ohio; Paul Brown, the football coach, grew up not far from her family's home. Buffalo eventually claimed her (along with two others, Nina Morgana and Katharine Cornell), and it was there her singing began to draw attention. Wilfred Pelletier and his wife, Queena Mario, oversaw her development in New York, and eventually Rose married Pellie.

Rose had one of the finest mezzo-soprano voices I ever heard—and I say that without any hesitation. Stately and beautiful, she was a gifted actress and was never less than total in her study of a new role. At the Curtis Institute, where she studied, Marcella Sembrich—then teaching many years after her distinguished career had ended—gave her encouragement and guidance. Once in Pellie's hands, her career grew by leaps and bounds. It was he who oversaw the transforming of her voice into a dramatic soprano—a great loss to the mezzo ranks at the Met, but an asset to such roles as Alceste, which she sang with great style.

Grace Moore and Rose Bampton were miles apart, both vocally and personally. Rose's ruby-like mezzo was a phenomenon; Grace's sizable lyric soprano was nice to listen to, but registered mainly because of the body and soul that housed it. Rose, very much a lady in her sunny simplicity, loved only Pellie; Grace, if one could believe her press (and that would be a mistake), never knew what the word "one" meant, at least as it applied to men. She had made her mark initially in popular music (Irving Berlin had given her first crack at "All Alone," "What'll I Do?," and, other waltzes he wrote during his courtship of Ellin Mackay), and, with Otto Kahn's money and help, she sailed into the critics' columns as Mimi in a February 1928 *La Bohème*.

Offstage, Grace was the foodstuff of a gossip columnist's diet. In newsprint she became an earthy woman who sampled love at every table—and rumor had it that the tables were numerous. She wrote a tale-telling autobiography (she titled it *You're Only Human Once*) and alluded to affairs with "three of the richest men in the world," among scores of others.

This was the Grace Moore the public knew—the one Grace herself largely created. The Grace Moore I knew, with whom I shared Libbie as a manager for a while* and with whom I vacationed occasionally at St. Moritz, was too shrewd and too self-aware to live the life of (forgive the phrase) "a Pinza in petticoats." Grace's only failing—if, indeed, she had one—was that she lived and breathed headlines, and was a master at creating them. When describing events to interviewers, she embellished liberally and encouraged others to follow suit. She delighted in the resulting press she got—no matter how outrageous some of it was.

---

* *Miss Moore became acquainted with Libbie Miller near the time of her Metropolitan debut, and remained her client until Libbie's singleminded interest in Ponselle led Miss Moore to others, culminating in Jean Dalrymple's management.* J.A.D.

For my part, I found Grace a fun-loving companion, a girl who was aware of her artistic limitations, a girl capable of much sensitivity toward friends when the chips were down—and, I might add, a girl who took her marriage vows very seriously when she married the Spanish movie star Valentín Parera, with whom she retreated to the privacy of a farm they bought in Connecticut. She lived a full, rich but tragically short life; she died in a plane crash near Copenhagen in 1947, en route to a tour of Sweden.

Gladys Swarthout, whose Carmen eventually succeeded Bruna Castagna's and mine at the Met, was another American whose debut, I'm happy to say, was linked to my career. Where Rose Bampton made her debut as Laura to my Gioconda, Gladys sang La Cieca opposite me in that same opera. While the timbre of her voice was not as singular as Rose's, her technique was secure and her acting quite commendable.

Helen Jepson's schoolgirl looks and fine lyric-soprano voice served her well as Nedda in *Pagliacci,* Giulietta in *Les Contes d'Hoffmann, Louise,* and *Thaïs.* Helen prepared her Thaïs under Mary Garden's direction, and was so effective in the role that Mary herself declared Helen's conception of the converted Thaïs superior even to her own.

For all the glitter that this new generation of Americans occasioned, the Metropolitan debuts of a host of European stars made for even greater headlines. Lily Pons arrived a few days after New Year's Day, 1931, and was immediately ranked with Galli-Curci as a coloratura. She was the essence of composure onstage, but, like me, she was a basket case until the curtain went up.

Lily arrived without much fanfare, except for the fact that Giovanni Zenatello and Maria Gay were her chief promoters; as I was a friend of theirs, I knew about Lily in advance and was present at her debut. She was everything she was touted to be as a singer—the easy high Es and Fs and all—except that, for me at least, she did not erase memories of Galli-Curci. There was something in Lily's method of production, perhaps her way of nearly closing her mouth when she sang those ultrahigh tones, that made me conscious of something more "authentic" in Galli-Curci's production. But as an actress, Lily was in a league of her own. In retrospect, how much of it was traceable to her daintiness is hard to say; whatever the case, she was an exquisite performer.

My clearest memory of Lily is that of an exhausted little French girl, managing a smile while mopping the perspiration from her face after her first Metropolitan *Lucia.* She had made a point of seeking me out when she arrived in the States, as she knew I was a friend of the Zenatellos. Here she was, now a bona fide member of the Metropolitan ranks, her debut a clear success.

"I did well? I sang nice?" she said to me as soon as I came into her dressing room. I could sense that she really wanted to know what I thought.

"Let me put it this way, Lily," I told her as I put my arms around her. "You knocked the 'elle' out of Ponselle!"

"Mais, Rosa," she said, picking up on my word-playing, "a Pons is only half a Ponselle!"

The Zenatellos are owed credit for bringing another great star to the United States: Bruna Castagna, whose voluptuous mezzo voice made her one of the finest Carmens of our century. Tullio Serafin had been one of her earliest mentors, and had negotiated her successful South American tours in the late 1920s. Toscanini intervened next, bringing her to the attention of La Scala. The Zenatellos then took over the direction of her American career, bringing her first to the New York Hippodrome as Carmen just a short time before mine was heard at the Metropolitan. Some critics' intentions to the contrary, we never became rivals in the role; the public seemed equally enthusiastic about both of our Carmens. Though Amneris was her debut role at the Metropolitan in the spring of 1936, her sensuous voice had been heard abroad in such roles as Isabella, Azucena, Laura, Dalila, Dame Quickly, Leonora in *La Favorita*, La Cieca, and Ulrica.

Like me, she had a sister who also sang—Maria Castagna, also a mezzo-soprano, who sometimes sang under the name Maria Falliani. Though I never had the opportunity to sing with Bruna (she would have been a splendid partner for me, had I sung *Adriana Lecouvreur*), I sang with Maria in *Gioconda* during my first Covent Garden season. Later, when I retired and moved to Maryland, I heard Bruna as Carmen, a role she sang in Baltimore a half-dozen times.

I allow myself a small amount of credit for one of the most celebrated Metropolitan debuts of the 1930s—Lotte Lehmann's, as Sieglinde in *Die Walküre* in January 1934. I can take no credit for the role in which she debuted; my influence, rather, was with Gatti over the necessity to engage her. I had come back from London brimming with enthusiasm over Lotte's voice and artistry. I had heard her Marschallin in *Der Rosenkavalier* and had been bowled over by it. Dutifully, I carried all this back to Gatti, and found that he had heard substantially the same thing from a number of sources. It wasn't long until Lotte was engaged.

I had also heard Frida Leider during my Covent Garden seasons, and was fortunate to hear one of her Chicago Opera performances after I returned. She made her Metropolitan debut in January 1933, five seasons after Chicago had first heard her. I admired her enormously and, as with Lotte, I spoke glowingly about her singing every time I could. She became one of the most celebrated Brünnhildes and Isoldes (her debut role, opposite Lauritz Melchior's Tristan) of the century, in England, America, Berlin, and Bayreuth. She was equally acclaimed in Milan, where she sang Wagner in Italian, as was the custom. Performing Isolde and the Brünnhildes in Italian gave her, she often said, a new insight into *legato* singing.

Kirsten Flagstad made her debut the next season after Lotte Lehmann's. From Sieglinde she soon ascended to Isolde and the other roles that brought her such acclaim. Comparisons among the three—Flagstad, Leider, and Lehmann—were inevitable and, having heard and known all of them (though Lotte the best), I formed my own opinions, too. There can be no question that

Dubbed the "Madonna portrait" by Columbia Graphophone, which
commissioned it in 1920, this was frequently used to promote my first recordings.

As Gioconda, in the third-act costume ▷
I purchased from Salomea Kruceniski in
1924. Gioconda was the first heroine
I portrayed as a blonde. Though
its demands are Wagnerian, this
was one of my favorite roles.

△ As Elvira in *Ernani,* which I first sang in
December 1921 to Giovanni Martinelli's
Ernani, José Mardones' Don Ruy Gomez,
and Giuseppe Danise's Don Carlos.
This is the costume I had made when
Elvira came back into my repertoire in 1928.

Concert apparel, 1925 ▷
After *Don Carlos,* I regained control
of my diet and was able to wear
concert dresses that accented my slimmer
waistline. This was one of my favorites.

◁ As Fiora in Montemezzi's L'*Amore dei tre re,* 1926. This was my second-act costume, a gown of delicate pink silk accented by rubies. A wine-red cloak completed the costume. This portrait was taken in my penthouse in Manhattan.

△ Onstage at the Metropolitan as Donna Anna, in front of the curtain Joseph Urban designed for the revival of *Don Giovanni* in 1929.

◁ Another concert gown, this one of red taffeta and black lace, with puffs of feathers for decorative trim. This was taken in the library of my Manhattan penthouse in 1929.

As Norma, November 1927.
I played her with dark red hair to accent the wild, almost unearthly
appearance that marked her as the Druids' high priestess.

A snapshot that Edith took of Puccini and me
at his villa in Viareggio, August 1924. This was
among the last photographs ever taken of him;
he died three months after our visit.

On tour with the Metropolitan in 1925,
with Lucrezia Bori at an Atlanta soiree. Bori h
a cameo-like perfection. No one ever forgo
the artistic impression she made.

for sheer voice Kirsten Flagstad was unique. At her debut W. J. Henderson wrote of her voice as "full-throated, [with] richness, abundant power, and a scale that preserves its quality all the way up." The lyrical timbre of her voice belied its great power. It was not a dark, dramatic voice but its power was immense. Once I remember kidding around with her backstage at the Met, each of us trying to sing louder than the other. I found myself singing a shade or so under her volume. Never before had I known that sensation.

Was Flagstad the greater singer, then, compared to Frida Leider or to Lotte Lehmann?

The question itself is unfair. "Don't make *comparisions*," Gatti used to chide the *cognoscenti* in his peculiar English; "comparisons" came out rhyming with "visions." His point is well taken, though. For me, nevertheless, the totality of Leider's and Lehmann's performing outweighed Flagstad's, despite the incomparable Flagstad voice and technique. Because, to my ears, there was less dramatic urgency in Flagstad's singing, she sometimes made Wagner's music more ethereal than dramatically tense. Although firmer comparisons can be made between Flagstad and Leider because of their similar repertoires, Lotte could (and did) sing everything from lyrical to dramatic roles and classical to contemporary song literature; she was equally at home in all of it, and had a technique unique to her, enabling her to turn any weakness to a dramatic advantage. For me, she remained one of the most interesting and compelling artists of her day.*

Tall, stately Karin Branzell proved an ideal partner to Flagstad, Leider, and Lehmann in the Wagnerian roles. Since her arrival at the Metropolitan in 1924 she had steadily proven herself in the Italian and French repertoires, as Fidès, Dalila, Amneris, La Cieca, and Azucena. Singular as her voice was—velvety, gorgeous, flexible, and yet voluminous enough to put her in a league with Flagstad, Melchior, and Friedrich Schorr—her artistic sincerity was very much a complement to her rich vocalizing. The skill with which she projected a text was of a high order; interestingly, it covered a slight speech impediment that the perceptive listener would have noticed otherwise. As the depth of her artistry increased over the years, she kept her voice largely intact. She made a triumphant comeback at the Met in 1950.

With a new generation of artists prospering in my midst, I was part of the Met's "Old Guard." Though some of the new artists were older than I (Lehmann, for instance, was at least seven years my senior), my career dated back to what was already being painted as "the Age of Caruso." After *Norma* I had arrived at an impasse in my career that *Don Giovanni* and subsequently

---

* *By admission of each, Lehmann and Ponselle were a "mutual admiration society." Lehmann paid Ponselle endless compliments over the years, both as a singer and an actress, and the two remained in contact. Though mutual respect also characterized Ponselle's and Flagstad's relationship, friends recalled that Flagstad seemed uneasy with Ponselle's extroverted ways offstage. Edwin MacArthur, Flagstad's accompanist and eventual biographer, was a link between them.* J.A.D.

Traviata had resolved. But after *Traviata* I was again at an impasse: what would come next?

After much thought, I agreed to do *Carmen*.

It was a complex and by no means hasty decision. Earle Lewis had first suggested it to me in 1932, after several patrons of the Met had brought it up to him. From 1928 on I had been appearing regularly on radio, and had often included the well-known arias from *Carmen* as part of my programs. Whenever I sang the "Habanera," especially, my fan mail was extremely favorable— not merely because of the popularity of the aria, which is timeless, but because of the way the listeners felt my voice fit the music. Since many Metropolitan patrons heard me on radio, talk of my doing Carmen became one of several topics of conversation in the Met's inner circles.

Though Gatti didn't entirely share Earle Lewis's fascination with me as Carmen, he knew why the role would appeal to me. In *Vestale, Norma,* and *Don Giovanni,* according to the critics, I had proven myself as a Classical interpreter. Then came *Traviata* and it ignited a spark within me: here I had the luxury of not only singing a role, but actually creating a flesh-and-blood character. From then on I wanted to do roles that would challenge me as an actress, without the rather confining formality of the classics. To say the least, Carmen would be a challenge.

I was well aware that Bizet's errant gypsy had caused setbacks in a number of otherwise brilliant careers. W. J. Henderson said that Adelina Patti had so robbed Carmen of her fiery intensity that she had "made a kitten" of her. Maria Gay had been fiery enough, but the critics charged her with making Carmen too vulgar. Maria Jeritza had also tried the role, but, said Henderson, "with all her energy she did not seem to get far beneath [its] surface."

Carmen's *tessitura* accounts for many of the problems that various sopranos have had with the role. It particularly affected Geraldine Farrar's and Mary Garden's Carmens. I adored both of these great artists and heard them in almost everything they sang in my time. Their problems with Carmen were similar: despite their impressive middle and lower ranges, they had to adapt the music to their voices, rather than the other way around. Of the two, Farrar's was the more successful, at least to my thinking; her acting was superb, she looked the part, and she colored her voice with tones that were alternately teasing, suggestive, and fiery. Mary Garden, on the other hand, never quite looked the part. Though she always managed to look and move differently in every role she played, her features seemed to resist a gypsy look. Carmen never quite fit her.

At the turn of the century, Emma Calvé had been *the* Carmen. In the generation after her there had been others whose voices and acting met the demands of the role, but even some of them had trouble being accepted in the role. Olive Fremstad was a case in point. Her incredible soprano voice, refined by Lilli Lehmann's teaching, had an exceptionally free middle and lower range. (Though she is best remembered for her Isolde and Brünnhildes, she began her career with Azucena, Amneris, and Fidès.) No less an authority than Maude Adams declared that, as an actress, Fremstad was the greatest of her generation. It was Carmen that first made her a celebrity in Germany, and everyone expected it to work its magic in New York. It did—but only with the critics. The public, for some reason, all but rejected her in the role. Our mutual friend Hugh Johns, who knew Fremstad very well, told me that she never came to grips with this puzzling rejection.

My fascination with doing Carmen had grown by 1933, when I sang at the *Maggio Musicale* in Florence. While preparing *Vestale* I had broached the subject with Serafin. He wasn't as enthusiastic as I'd hoped, though he conceded that I had the voice for Carmen.

Nino Romani, on whom I had always relied for advice, was positively opposed to it.

"It's a mistake," he warned. "At this point in your career, it could be the worst mistake of all."

Naturally, I pressed for an explanation.

"Can you see Muzio as Carmen?" he said.

I admitted I couldn't.

"That's what makes me want to plead with you not to sing it. You know you're more like Muzio than not."

When I queried him he told me that he could only see me as a dramatic heroine in roughly the same tradition as Muzio—a woman of dignity whose constant striving for romantic love was matched by an immense capacity for suffering. That, he claimed, was what had made me an exceptional Violetta— and what might be my undoing as Carmen.

I didn't see it that way at all. I felt I had the voice for *Carmen* (and, to be sure, Nino never suggested otherwise), and I was confident that the right kind of coaching would be the key to everything else. That's where Albert Carré entered my plans.

Former director of the Opéra-Comique in Paris, Carré was said to know more about *Carmen* than any other man living. Independently, Maria Gay and Geraldine Farrar had recommended him, each feeling that he could do for my Carmen what Tullio Serafin had done for my Norma.

His biography was certainly impressive. He was a nephew of the French librettist Michel Carré, whose collaboration with composers yielded, among many other operas, *Faust, Roméo et Juliette, Les Pêcheurs de perles, Hamlet, Mignon,* and *Les Contes d'Hoffmann.* As a young man Albert Carré had worked under Bizet and had been affiliated with the Opéra-Comique when *Carmen* was first produced there in 1875.

I signed a contract with him late in 1934 and paid his and Mme. Carré's expenses for a season's work at St. Moritz.* The ink was hardly dry on our agreement when I received in the mail his first sketches of the stage settings.

* *Carré's wife, whom he had married, divorced, and remarried during a long and stormy involvement that had begun at the Opéra-Comique, was the lyric soprano Marguerite Giraud Carré, who during her career had created fifteen roles in less than two decades. Ponselle respected both her musical judgment and sense of the stage, and was more than eager to have her accompany her husband to St. Moritz.* J.A.D.

These and several pages of suggestions on the costumes and the choreography I turned over to Valentina, who was to design my costumes, and George Balanchine, who would direct the dance sequences.

The costumes are a story in themselves. There were to be four in all, though eventually five were actually made—but not without some spirited exchanges among Valentina, Eddie Johnson, and me. All of the costumes were distinctive—in some cases as much for the colors Valentina used as for their basic style. She had a marvelous—and rare—sense of simplicity in her approach to costuming, and had an uncanny feeling for the drape, fall, and movement of a fabric. At that time she was already established as one of the top designers in Manhattan, and had regularly dressed Garbo, Lynn Fontanne, Katharine Cornell, Grace Moore, Gertrude Lawrence, Gladys Swarthout, Katharine Hepburn, and other notables. Through her husband, George Schlee, a financial wizard who became a "roving ambassador" between big business and the performing arts, she was well known in operatic and theater circles, and had been a dancer before becoming a designer.

The design she created for an optional costume for the last act launched the first of several controversies that were to surround my Carmen. When I went for my initial fittings I was expecting a traditional hoopskirt design for the last act, typical of what most earlier Carmens had worn. She showed me the costume, and though it was not yet at a stage where it had to be fitted, I could see how lovely it would be. When I told her so, she shrugged off my enthusiasm.

"Lovely, maybe. Nice, maybe. Pretty, maybe," she said. "All of that—but very, very boring to look at."

"Boring?" I asked. "What makes you think it's going to be boring to the audience?"

"Because there's no *fire* in it. It's everybody else's Carmen, not *your* Carmen. You sit here and let me show you *your* Carmen."

Moments later, in walked a girl of my proportions, dressed in one of the most striking costumes I had ever seen. It was a black velvet matador design, cinched in at the waist, with a jacket embroidered with gold, and pants tailored to fit me like a glove. There was a matching velvet cape, lined with a blood-red satin.

"You see that lining?" she said as the model swept open the cape. "Red like the meat of a bull! I've designed a matador's cap for you, and I want you to wear a red carnation in one lapel of your jacket. They'll take one look at you and never, ever forget that vision!"

I couldn't help but pick up on her excitement, though even I found it too dramatic, too stark a contrast, for an opera. I told her so.

"No, Rosa, you don't understand. Whether it's opera or not, it's *theater*. You're a singer, and I'm a designer. I know what I'm doing, and the Metropolitan will know what I'm doing. Yes, it's dramatic—but it's so simple, visually. And so effective! Why, that one little red carnation against all that black velvet—they'll see that carnation all the way to Verona!"

It still seemed too much to me, and at the risk of offending her I had to say so.

"Have it your way, then! Go on and wear that hoopskirt! I'll make you look like every other Carmen, if that's what you're going to insist I do!"

She and I had never clashed before—and this was hardly the occasion to start, since we had already invested so much of ourselves in how I was to look. She was angry—and not a little hurt—that I wouldn't go along with her thinking, and she got more insistent as she talked. Finally, she gave me an ultimatum.

"If you insist that I make you look like every other Carmen, then here is my answer to you: After opening night, you just forget that I exist! I'll never do one stitch for you again!"

I wasn't about to let that happen, so we agreed to let the Metropolitan help us decide which costume I would wear. Eventually, it went to Eddie Johnson, who met with us individually to discuss it. He told me that everyone he'd spoken to had been fascinated by such a daring conception of Carmen's appearance. Even in France and Italy, he said, he'd never seen such a design. There was only one reservation on anyone's part: the matador pants.

"We love your designs," Eddie eventually told Valentina, "but there's opposition to having Rosa wear pants instead of a skirt."

This challenged Valentina, who quickly designed a tight-fitting black floor-length skirt—a skirt that from a distance looked as if I was wearing pants. The Met okayed it, and though I was still afraid of the audience's reaction I reluctantly agreed to wear it on opening night.* Meantime, I delighted Valentina by getting my weight down to a trim 134, the slimmest I had ever been during my career.

Albert Carré and I formally began our study sessions during the first week of June 1935 at the Grand Hotel in St. Moritz. Our sessions took in every phase of the production, from its lighting, set designs, and prop placements to the most minute details of the singing, dancing, and acting requirements of the score. Usually, we worked from noon till dinnertime, concentrating heavily on French diction for an hour, following it with two hours of singing and at least three hours of dancing and acting rehearsals. Early in the summer, when we began these sessions, Carré began taking notes on our work. By the time he finished his note-taking in mid-August 1935, his leather-bound notebook encompassed more than three hundred pages of delicately penned drawings and instructions.

---

* *The matador costume figured significantly in the critics' reactions to Ponselle's visual impact in the role, as is evident from several of the reviews she will subsequently quote. Valentina, in a May 1981 interview with discographer Bill Park, remembered that by opening night she, Valentina, had taken on Rosa's fears about the audience—fears which were quickly alleviated when the applause literally erupted. At the post-performance party, Mary Garden, who had been seated in a box just offstage, sought out Valentina and told her, "If only I had known you when I did Carmen! My God, I never once thought of doing her in such a striking way in the last act!"* J.A.D.

During the actual work sessions, we often used one of the Grand's ballrooms as a rehearsal area. Over and over I would walk through the sequence of each act, saying aloud what I would be doing onstage, timing my movements with the piano. Here's how we worked through Carmen's entrance to the "Seguidilla" in Act I:

"I'm coming down the stairs with flowers in my hand," I would say to Carré, descending an imaginary stairway in the Grand's ballroom. "I'm surrounded by a group of young, attractive men."

"You are Carmen, fiery and exotic and sensuous, and you are *always* surrounded by young, attractive men," Carré would speak from his chair, much as a film director would to a leading lady walking through a part.

"I walk downstage, acknowledging with a sensuous movement the groups of admirers who always surround me, and then I throw the flowers on the floor of the stage."

"Now Don José enters," I would hear Carré say from a distance, relaying what José would be doing. "He enters the factory with two soldiers but when he comes out he doesn't touch you. He goes to the center of the stage, then crosses it and stands in front of a chair."

"Now I'm being held by two of the soldiers but I manage to free myself. One of them is a lieutenant, Zuniga, and I walk in front of him. I take the cigarette out of my mouth and blow smoke in his face."

"Remember, now, you're going to be playing with that cigarette while you walk in front of him," Carré would counsel. "The cigarette is going to be your prop for that moment. Keep in mind that the cigarette is small and can't be seen easily from the back of the house. You're going to have to use your gestures wisely. If your hand motions are too confined, the audience won't know what you're doing. If your gestures are too broad, the action will look contrived. So you've got to strike the right balance."

I would go on.

"The Lieutenant yanks the cigarette out of my mouth and throws it on the floor of the stage. At that point I hear one of the factory girls making remarks about me and I get into a fight with her."

"You've got to make the fight look *real*," Carré would stress. "You've got to look like you're kicking her and punching her. You want to pull her hair and scream at her. Make it look real!"

"I keep pulling her hair till one of the officers separates us and the Lieutenant drags me away."

"And fight with *him*," Carré warned. "Fight with him till he forces you into the chair. Only then should you give up the fight."

In our mock-up of the stage the chair would be at stage right. I would time my movements so I would be in the chair by the fourth *la-la-la* I would be singing. That's how precise Carré wanted the pacing. I tried to achieve that precision in every act.

How well this plan worked is a matter of debate—even forty years later.* I wasn't in the best of form when I sang my first *Carmen;* I had had the flu all week, and was sick enough to cancel the midweek dress rehearsal. (Gertrud Wettergren, who had just arrived at the Met from the Stockholm Opera, took my place at the rehearsal, singing Carmen in Swedish.) I knew there would be the usual problems that go with first performances, although this one went well—even without the benefit of my having a dress rehearsal. I knew, too, that as time went on I would make changes in my characterization. Any artist makes such changes through the natural course of sensitive performing. But first, I had to know how the critics reacted.

After *La Vestale,* Edith and Libbie created a ritual for reading my reviews. We would wait till most of them were in, and Libbie would gather them in the order she thought I'd want to hear them. If I seemed apprehensive (as I was when I sang *Norma* for the first time), she would read aloud the best one first, get to the worst in the middle of the session, and end by reading the second most favorable review. She and Edith would alternate reading them to me, but Libbie dictated the order in which they were presented. We usually did this over a glass of red wine.

When the reviews were in for that first *Carmen,* I knew that something was wrong. Libbie and Edith were trying to be too cheery. I took a sip of wine and asked whose review was first. Lawrence Gilman's, they said. Libbie read it aloud:

> It should be noted without further ado that Miss Ponselle in her first engagement with the baffling role achieved an intelligent and work-manlike performance. Rosa-of-the-sumptuous-voice is no sensationalist, no brainless experimenter in the treatment of new roles. She is a serious and thoughtful artist, obviously intent on recreating the character she would bring to life . . . [It] was vividly-conceived, alive at every moment, and moved from point to point in the psychological unfolding of the character . . . [Yet she] should have put less emphasis on Carmen's toughness and more upon making unmistakable her powers of seduction. For a Carmen whose seductiveness is not convincing from the start has either fixed her attention upon an element of secondary importance in the part, or she has undertaken a role for which Nature did not fit her. [Yet] Miss Ponselle and Carmen will grow intimate as times goes on.

I sat quietly and took another swallow of wine. Suddenly, Nino Romani's worries began to haunt me.

* *As a Ponselle "event," Carmen surpassed even Traviata. By the time the curtain rose on Friday, December 27, 1935, tickets were virtually nonexistent. "Nearly a thousand persons were turned away," according to the New York Mirror. The fact that Ponselle's Carmen was broadcast four times in only two seasons by the Metropolitan also attests to its sustained appeal to the public.* J.A.D.

"Who's next?" I asked. B. H. Haggin—a fine critic, though not on a par with Gilman. Edith read his comments:

> It is my impression that Miss Ponselle achieves her characterizations not through dramatic instinct but through study, and that a good deal of study has gone into her Carmen. The method has produced some good results in some instances; in this case, however, it has produced an impersonation of an impersonation—the external characteristics and mannerisms of the conventional operatic Carmen— the head-tossing and shoulder-shrugging and hip-twisting, all not proceeding from any inner reality, and all therefore without external coherence and credibility. The fault with the Card Scene, then, was not its conception—for Carmen is not a hussy, not a philosopher, even here—but in its exaggeration of the conception. The best was the fierce intensity of the last scene with Jose.* And there were other good points: the excellent dancing, the costumes (except possibly that of last act, which one might expect to be less severe and more gaudy), and of course the sumptuous voice.

Although the audience reacted so enthusiastically to the matador costume—so enthusiastically, in fact, that I never wore the hoopskirt once onstage—I wondered what Valentina was thinking as she read Haggin's comments about the last act.

"Now to Chotzinoff," Libbie said as she prepared to read his review:

> Miss Ponselle, looking picturesque and slim, did all the things one expects Carmen to do and she did them with communicative zest. She ogled the soldiers, stuck her elbows in their stomachs, negotiated shimmies, threw missiles, spat out orange peel, fell into tantrums, yawned, giggled derisively, grew seductive and blanched at the thought of approaching death. Yet her actions appeared to be spontaneous rather than studied, and the audience responded to her waywardness as if it comprehended the mainsprings of that fascinating character . . . [Carmen] revealed a volatile side of her temperament, the existence of which we had not suspected before . . .
>
> Public interest in the venture was attested by a house jammed to the doors . . . Vocally, there was much to admire in her vibrant and plenteous lower tones, but I could not help noticing a slow tremolo in her upper register, in forte, especially. [But] at that . . . I can

---

* *With Carré's direction, Ponselle conceived the "fiery intensity" of which Haggin writes. Though Carmen knows that José is destined to kill her, emotionally she refuses to accept it—but, as she dashes past him, he stabs her, fulfilling the prophecy of the cards. Carré's staging had Ponselle stagger to a wall-like wrought-iron grillwork after José stabbed her. As her body slowly slid down the grillwork, she fixed her stare on José's face, still unable to fathom what he had done.* J.A.D.

safely recommend it to opera lovers as well as to students of feminine psychology.*

Beyond the obvious disagreement between Chotzinoff and Haggin—the one judging that I sang it well but acted the role in a stereotyped way, and the other, Chotzinoff, claiming that I had conceived Carmen properly but had had vocal problems along the way—I couldn't find any basis for Chotzinoff's claim that there was a "slow tremolo" evident in my upper register. I was just getting over the flu—granted—but I never had any vocal problems with *Carmen*. Not that *Carmen* can't be risky. It *can* be, but luckily my voice fit her like a glove. As with Santuzza, it was the only role in my repertoire that never caused me to lose any sleep.

Where it can cause problems is in the use of chest tones, where the temptation to carry the chest voice too high into the range can be hard to resist. The temptation stems from wanting to enlarge the volume, or else change the coloration, of the lower middle voice. There are certain passages in a number of opera scores where this use of the chest voice can be especially tempting. In *Andrea Chénier*, for instance, in Maddalena's aria, "La mamma morta," some sopranos (Claudia Muzio was one) would sing the intense passage near the end of the aria in chest tones. The wise singer, like Elisabeth Rethberg, would sing the passage an octave higher, avoiding any potential problems. I, too, transposed that section an octave higher, for the same reason.

As I think my recordings tend to show, my singing was free of problems with chest tones. If one isn't careful, these tones can become focused in the throat rather than the head. When that happens the column-like equalization of the voice can be lost. At first the loss can be momentary, but over a period of time real damage can be done. I was able to avoid these problems because I knew how to keep my chest tones focused in the head. With me, this was both a matter of what came rather naturally (my chest voice had always been rich and well balanced, even when I was very young), and a matter of being conscious and vigilant about tonal focus. In *Carmen*, which abounds in opportunities for chest tones, I knew what the tendencies and temptations were, but I circumvented them by using the chest voice wisely.

By not carrying chest tones too high into my range, I never jeopardized the evenness of my vibrato—which made me wonder why Chotzinoff, of all the critics who reviewed my first *Carmen*, thought he detected a slow tremolo in my upper range.

Pitts Sanborn's review was next. I wondered whether he too had heard a tremolo. He hadn't, it turned out—but when Edith finished reading his review, my heart all but sank:

---

* *Chotzinoff added a tongue-in-cheek sentence to his review, saying, "It was the best sung Carmen since . . . and the most energetic and tantalizing since . . ."—in each place leaving a blank space for his readers to insert the names of whichever previous Carmens most appealed to them. It was another way of calling attention to the extremes of individual preference which surrounded the many conceptions of Carmen, then as now.* J.A.D.

Miss Ponselle in her first public essay depicted the gypsy baggage in terms of a Tough Girl of old-fashioned vaudeville. The brazen air, the killing glances, the arms akimbo, the noisy bravado were all there. And if her dancing seemed only mildly funny, her acrobatics and pugilistics were almost worthy of an eminent predecessor [namely, Maria Jeritza]. If you can lie down on your tummy to sing a prayer, what's to prevent your doing so to read your fortune?

It is altogether likely that the music of *Carmen* lies badly for Miss Ponselle's voice. In any event, her tones last evening were too often thin and brassy. Nor did she seem altogether aware of the vocal requirements and possibilities of the part. Otherwise, a singer of her attainments hardly would make such sad work of the "Seguidilla."

However, she wore some startling costumes, which, whatever their relation to the life of an Andalusian gypsy, are bound to be talked about.

I had another glass of wine, hoping that it would calm me down. Unfortunately, Olin Downes's review in the New York *Times* was read to me next. After that, my spirits hit rock bottom:

We have never heard Miss Ponselle sing so badly, and we have seldom seen the part enacted in such an artificial and generally unconvincing manner.

Her first act was more carefully composed than what followed. It had less exaggeration, fewer mannerisms, some interesting detail, and clean diction. She used a little of the spoken dialogue of the original version of the opera* with good effect, but already showed a cheerful disregard of laws of good singing, for which she has won richly deserved eminence. She also played fast and loose with time and rhythm, and thus to an extent unnecessary for any genuinely expressive purpose. It appeared that Miss Ponselle had determined at any cost to quality of tone, to pitch, to vocal style, to be "dramatic." This unfortunate intention only served, of course, to defeat the very ends it was designed to promote.

Especially from such a voice and such an artist are these methods unnecessary and inadvisable, for Miss Ponselle is primarily a singer and secondarily an actress, and not all her efforts put her in the dramatic frame.

---

* *Carré and Ponselle made what were then standard cuts in the score, opting for a minimum of spoken dialogue. What dialogue there was, Ponselle, at Carré's encouragement, interpolated rather freely, varying it often from one performance to the next. Ponselle had wanted to perform the Opéra-Comique version, with all the dialogue intact, but it had never been done at the Met. At the time there was concern about how much dialogue Metropolitan audiences would accept in an opera, and how well such dialogue might carry in the old house. Hence, the decision to minimize the amount of it.* J.A.D.

Her dancing need not be dwelt upon, although in the Inn Scene it raised the question whether Spanish gypsies preferred the Charleston or the Black Bottom as models for their evolutions. The sum of her acting was affected, overdrawn, often inept. There was bad vocal style, carelessness of execution, inaccurate intonation. The principal virtue of this Carmen was its slimness, for Miss Ponselle has heroically reduced, and is now a tall and personable gypsy. That is her Carmen's principal distinction.

What was there to say to this? All I could remind myself was that this was the same Olin Downes who had nearly exhausted his supply of critical superlatives trying to describe my Norma and Donna Anna.

"You know what might have earned you that review, don't you?" Libbie said in an I-told-you-so tone of voice.

"You mean his Brooklyn series?" I said.

Late in November of 1933 two well-known concert series, the Town Hall Endowment Series and the Olin Downes Series in Brooklyn, had approached Libbie about engaging me. At my instruction Libbie had given both of them a tentative yes, depending on what the fees would be. At the time I was charging a minimum of $2,500, which the Town Hall management was more than happy to pay. Olin Downes wasn't; he wanted to engage me for $2,000, and not a cent more.

He wrote me a couple of letters and appealed to Libbie to get me to change my mind. In January 1934, Libbie wrote back, saying that we couldn't take less than $2,500 unless we could arrange a date that would have a logical place in my concert schedule. Downes wouldn't go along with us, so we let the issue rest.

Word got back to Libbie that Downes regarded me as "uncooperative" and "unprofessional" because I wouldn't reduce my fees the way some other Met artists had. Eventually, I told Libbie to let him know that his criticisms were getting back to me, and that I didn't appreciate them. Libbie, being a manager, was afraid to alienate anyone in the business, so she kept trying to smooth things between Downes and me. For me it was too late—and now, like her, I couldn't help wondering how much of his review stemmed from my unwillingness to sing at his price.

Olin Downes's review helped transform *Carmen* into a genuine controversy. It also helped sell a lot of tickets to my performances. The controversy took on major proportions when a number of other critics took up the gauntlet. In the New York *Journal,* critic Henriette Wicker wrote of the "tremendous applause" and "tumultuous clapping after every act, for many minutes" that greeted what she characterized as "a wild gypsy of abundant vitality." She declared the evening "first-rate entertainment" and made the point, as others would, that there was "no use comparing her Carmen to this or that one of the past." My Carmen, she wrote, was distinctly my own.

Danton Walker, critic for the *Daily News,* wrote in a headline story that my Carmen had risen above its supposed "flaws." In his column he raised a key question, rebutting Downes and Haggin without naming names:

> Miss Ponselle, reading the reviews of her first Carmen last Friday night, must have suffered . . . For the same music critics who praised the shoddiest 'Traviata' that ever opened an opera season [a reference to Bori's, Tibbett's, and Crooks's efforts on opening night], disapproved, denounced, excoriated and otherwise panned the day-lights out of Miss Ponselle for her interpretation of the Bizet opera . . . If Carmen wasn't vulgar, what was she? A factory girl who discovered that sex was her trump card and who played it—to her own destruction—wouldn't be, in the words of Bert Lahr's song, 'too, too refayned.' She was a roughneck first to last, with a bawdy wit and a native gayety which most of the Carmens missed, but which our Rosa has suggested superbly.

Comforting though these words were, Danton Walker's stature among the New York critics was hardly large enough to undermine the influence of Downes's or Haggin's verdicts.

Pierre V. R. Key, writing in the Hartford *Courant,* entered the foray after Paul Bekker, critic for the *Staats-Zeitung* and a respected German reviewer, charged that I had consulted every authority but "the most important one—Georges Bizet." This was an inane comment, and Key's review underscored why. My Carmen, he said, "differed in virtually every respect from the Carmens of Emma Calvé, and Mme. Bressler-Gianoli; from the Carmen Geraldine Farrar gave us, and that of Mary Garden as well. Being so markedly different . . . no comparison with any other interpreter of the part would seem in order."

I was very pleased with the way Key made this point. With so many different Carmens, it made little sense to imply, as Bekker had, that the score would be the final authority to consult in creating the character. Carré, who knew more about preparing a role like Carmen than Paul Bekker, had me begin not with Bizet's score but with Prosper Mérimeé's novel. I had followed this same procedure from *Forza del destino* onward, and it paid dividends with *Carmen.* Mérimeé's Carmen is an amoral, tough, dangerous seductress whose only redeeming quality is that she never lies. This is exactly how I played her.

I held hopes for my second performance, which had to be rescheduled for the first week of January because I was still recuperating from the flu. Haggin judged that this one "had the same general and specific characteristics as the first performance," but was "a little less violently acted and sung." A few news-papers that hadn't covered the first one now got into the act; many of them seemed to want to rival Olin Downes on the use of negatives. "Miss Ponselle's singing," wrote an anonymous critic in the *World Telegram,* "leaving aside the exaggerated antics she so freely dispensed as acting, lacked color, variety and style. Her voice had little of its once lovely quality. In only a few instances . . . did the luscious roundness emerge."

W. J. Henderson, who would have been in an ideal position to speak about *Carmen* because he had heard so many, gave his views in the New York *Sun* after the second performance. "Is this the real Carmen or not?" he asked rhetorically. "There have been Carmens and Carmens," he wrote. He had seen both Lilli Lehmann and Adelina Patti in the role, but neither had come close to the mark. Lehmann's was not well done, he declared, and "it is not of Patti that men speak when they strive to recall the golden age of song at the Metropolitan. They always murmur the magic name of Calve." At that point he attempted a comparison between Calvé's and my acting and dancing:

> There have been derogatory comments on Miss Ponselle's dance. It had been carefully prepared under competent authority. It was correct. That was not the subject of comment. It was not good dance, good posing or good acting. Mme. Calvé's was not good dance either. And when people were shocked by it they were living in the Age of Innocence . . . Whatever [this Carmen] does, she is Rosa Ponselle and she has the world by the ear.

For the first time I could ever remember, the venerable Henderson had failed to make his point. What was he trying to say? That Calvé was *the* Golden Age Carmen—and that I came closer to her in the role, but that she wasn't terribly good either? Especially now, I could have profited from his clarity and insight—but he offered neither. At least he alluded to my condition, saying that I had been "ill and under strain."

Time magazine summed up the *Carmen* controversy in its January 6, 1936, issue. "First impression," the editors said, "was to wonder why anyone so flagrantly sexy as her Carmen should trouble to work for a living in a cigarette factory. She sang the 'Habanera' belligerently, as if defying the world. She turned on bewildered Don Jose like a tigress, sidled up to the captain of the guards like an old-time cinema vamp. The stage scarcely seemed to hold her, [but] the audience appeared to love it." This was less a fresh observation than a summary of what the critics had already said.

Depressed as I was over most of these reviews, I took comfort from those who came to my defense. Because the intensity of my acting had been the subject of part of the controversy, I was overjoyed when four well-known actresses—Jane Cowl, Blanche Yurka, Peggy Wood, and Constance Collier—praised my dramatic interpretation. Blanche Yurka and Peggy Wood had been singers. Years before her Lady Macbeth and Queen Gertrude earned her rave reviews in New York, Blanche Yurka had studied at the Metropolitan Opera School during Heinrich Conried's administration, and had sung small parts for some time afterward. Peggy Wood had been a pupil of Emma Calvé, and had sung leading roles before her Portia established her as one of New York's finest actresses.

Jane Cowl, a famous Juliet in her own right, was interviewed by the Associated Press in January 1937, and was asked to list the greatest artistic achievements of 1936. At the top of her list were John Gielgud's Hamlet, Nazimova's revised interpretation of Ibsen's *Ghosts,* Kirsten Flagstad's Isolde, and my Carmen. "I'm one of the radicals," she told the AP. "Rosa Ponselle's Carmen created an awful blare, but I liked it. Her version was enormously different, but why after all should that role, or any other role, be standardized?"

Constance Collier, who had come to the States from England just before World War I, and whose great acting had won acclaim on both continents, sent me a long letter praising my Carmen. So did my old friend Léon Rothier, who had studied with Jacques Bouhy, Bizet's original Escamillo. Léon had heard every great Carmen since Galli-Marié. Mine, he wrote, was "finely-acted" and "superbly sung."

Three great Carmens of the past helped bolster my spirits with their insightful, supportive comments. One was Maria Gay, who had sat through several of my rehearsals. She too had been charged by the critics with making Carmen "tough." She told me that I had given the role all there was to give.

Geraldine Farrar was dining with friends in Connecticut when Olin Downes's damning comments were brought to her attention. She wrote out a hasty message on index cards and had it hand-delivered to my Riverside Drive penthouse. "Do not let your spirits be dampened by any press comments," she urged. "I found the base of your Carmen well-grounded, full-blooded—and knowing something of nerves, you did it *so* well; time will make all smooth and you will have a *definite* success. Be happy in the result of your study and ambitions."

The day after Farrar's message arrived, another came from Grace Moore, postmarked Chicago. It reassured me immensely. "Ask me if I've heard about last Friday's *Carmen!*" Grace exclaimed in her note. "Mary Garden phoned and told me I just *have* to see your next performance. She says you're the greatest Carmen since Emma Calvé!"

A CANADIAN HONEYMOON

"THE OLD ORDER CHANGETH," says a timeworn maxim. At the Metropolitan, the Old Order changed in the fall of 1934, though only a handful knew it. Giulio Gatti-Casazza, the stalwart hand-at-the-rudder of the Metropolitan for twenty-six years, vacated his position in the midst of the Depression's bleak economics. Otto Kahn, who had been a financial keeper to the Metropolitan, had died that spring, robbing Gatti of a major source of power and creating a void that no one else could fill. Meantime, rumor had it that a young, aggressive appointee to the Board of Directors—RCA's David Sarnoff—had pressured Gatti's staff for audit sheets and other accounting documents that were foreign to the Metropolitan's ways.

"Mr. Witherspoon will be your new *commendatore*," Gatti told me in confidence near Thanksgiving, 1934.

I had known Herbert Witherspoon rather well, and took some comfort in his direction. I told myself that he would be quite like Gatti, and that we would have a fine working relationship. As it was, I never had the chance to find out. On May 10, 1935, less than two weeks after I gave an elaborate goodbye party for Gatti and his past and present artists aboard the S.S. *Rex,* Herbert Witherspoon died suddenly in his office. A week or so later, the order again changed: Edward Johnson, who had made his debut a dozen years earlier and who had sung opposite me in my first *Vestale,* now ascended to the lofty position of general manager.

I can't deny that I was deeply anxious over these changes—especially Gatti's resignation, which triggered the subsequent events. He had been more to me than his title signified. Over the years he had become a surrogate father—a great man whom, unlike my flesh-and-blood father, I could respect and look to for guidance. He was a man of exquisite culture and taste, well educated and at home in several languages, a born leader whose catholic tastes and courageous foresight in music had ensured him a lofty place in modern operatic history. It was he who had first brought *Boris Godunov* and *Pelléas et Mélisande* to La Scala, he who had helped popularize Wagner in Italy. And for more than five thousand performances of an estimated one hundred seventy-seven works between 1908 and 1935, it was he who orchestrated the emergence of the Metropolitan as the greatest opera company in the world.

It was a different Gatti whom I visited at his magnificent villa at Lago Maggiore the summer before my *Carmen*. In place of the man whose awesome energy and certainty of planning had enabled him to work in the present while mapping out productions four, five, or six seasons in the future, I saw instead a man who seemed tired and unwilling to look ahead. Though happily married (so far as any of us singers knew) to ballerina Rosina Galli, whom he wed after he and Frances Alda divorced, his conversations now seemed to focus entirely on the past. At the time I didn't realize that he was thinking about resigning.

Gatti and Herbert Witherspoon, different as they were culturally by virtue of Witherspoon's American roots, were similar in important ways. A Yale graduate who had become a singer through private training, Witherspoon had been one of Gatti's prize acquisitions early in his tenure as general manager. A distinguished artist onstage, on the concert platform, and on Red Seal records, Witherspoon was a warm, affectionate man whose understanding of the singer's psyche had been honed by his own career. He shared with Gatti a formal and disciplined but yet fatherly relationship with his artists. Had he lived, he would have afforded Eddie Johnson the wisdom of a mentor. As it was, Eddie was named general manager when his performing career was still spoken of in the present tense: he was to have sung Pelléas to Bori's Mélisande, but the revival had to be shelved because of his appointment.

Early in his tenure, Eddie Johnson took an unfair rap from the press over contracts for the new season. The newspapers dwelled on the fact that Kirsten Flagstad's contract had been signed but that Johnson had left the "Big Four" (supposedly, Lily Pons, Lawrence Tibbett, Lotte Lehmann, and myself) hanging. I can't speak for the other three, but in Eddie's defense I will say that he called and wired me several times, explaining that he was under enormous pressure as a new administrator and hoped I'd bear with him. It would never have occurred to me to do otherwise.

Eddie and I got off to a very good start because I was cooperative, and because I took public exception to a stand that Larry Tibbett took in the newspapers. When his contract didn't materialize after he thought it should have, he had his managers, Evans & Salter, issue a statement that he would have to abbreviate his Met appearances because he earned much more money singing on radio, in concerts, and on film. This was true of any of us but didn't need to be used as a weapon against Eddie, who was trying to be fair to everyone. I said so in print and underscored that for me neither radio nor Hollywood, regardless of the pay involved, could take the honorific place of the Metropolitan Opera House. My comments made Eddie happy, and I knew it.

I meant what I said—even though I was interested in Hollywood and a film career myself. If anything had come of it, I would have had to thank Larry Tibbett for it. His starring role in the 1930 release *The Rogue Song* had cemented relations between Hollywood and the Metropolitan. The film's success led to speculation that before long several Met stars would be awarded contracts. With the new sound-on-film techniques replacing the Vitaphone process, which Warner Brothers had pioneered in 1927, the problems involved in recording operatic voices—even ones as large as mine—were minimized.

In January 1930, Lawrence Evans, one of Tibbett's managers, wrote to me asking for a testimonial on *The Rogue Song;* Evans was trying to parlay Larry's first film into an even bigger second one, and wanted celebrity testimonials to help his negotiations. I was too busy to screen the film myself and asked Edith and Libbie to do it.

A week or so later, Edith handed me this draft for my signature: *"Bravo! Bravissimo!* Your performance in *The Rogue Song* is most excellent. I was happily surprised at the progress made in talking pictures, especially in the progress of recording the singing voice. My very best wishes for continued success."

Libbie attached a note to the message. "If you want, you can say, 'Your performance is wonderful,' instead of 'most excellent.' Personally, I think it was very good, but no more." Then she explained why she and Edith had mentioned the improvements in sound recording. "I brought in the part about the progress made in the talkies," she said, "because I thought that would be a good hint to all the companies that you might be induced to make one."

Libbie's ploy worked like a charm.

On January 31 I got a telegram from the producer E. V. Darling. "If you will make a test for the talkies either in New York or Hollywood," the wire read, "I feel almost certain a terrific contract will materialize from same. Wire me immediately." As in any business deal I engaged in, I was too shrewd to let my interest show immediately. I waited several days before sending this terse answer: "Thanks for the telegram. Someday I may consider making talking pictures. Regards, Rosa Ponselle."

From then on until 1936, when I went to Hollywood to make a screen test for Metro-Goldwyn-Mayer,* I received a steady stream of inquiries from Darling and other producers. Finally, Irving Thalberg, M-G-M's boy-wonder vice-president, brought Louis B. Mayer and me together. Thalberg, who knew me only by name, wanted to essay my personality himself; with his wife, screen star Norma Shearer, he saw to it that I was invited to a formal dinner party after one of my Hollywood Bowl concerts.

The party was a black-tie affair attended by M-G-M's on- and off-screen notables. A nine-foot Steinway graced one corner of the room, and before long I was asked to sing. My choices ranged from the "Casta Diva" and the "Seguidilla" to "Summertime" from *Porgy and Bess.* I knew from Thalberg's letter of the next day, which arrived with a van load of flowers at the Beverly Hills Hotel, that I had scored with him. "It is impossible to tell you how much

---

* *Based upon a letter sent by Libbie Miller to M-G-M's I. I. Altman, one of the directors of the company's New York City operations, it seems that two other screen tests—both done apparently in 1934—preceded the December 1936 Hollywood test referred to here. From what one can infer, each test was made in New York and comprised five or six segments. Apparently, neither test has survived.* J.A.D.

you contributed to last night's affair," he wrote. "You were warmth, beauty, talent and generosity. You changed a formal affair into an intimate house party and a magnificent concert at one time. Our heartfelt thanks for a glorious memory."

On his own Thalberg decided that *Carmen* would be my best vehicle. With Louis B. Mayer's approval he involved George Cukor in the project. George, whom I adored from the moment I met him (as did everyone else), got the project into gear by hiring a translator to convert the *Carmen* libretto into a first draft of a script. George and I shared a laugh when the finished product arrived: Don José had been left out of the script entirely!

The script turned out to be the smallest problem of the project. Libbie complained, rightly or wrongly, that I was the problem—especially where money was concerned. She had arranged a private meeting with Mr. Mayer after my screen test had met everyone's expectations. Only the three of us would meet, and my salary expectations would be the sole agenda item.

In the confines of his magnificent office, after we exchanged the usual pleasantries over glasses of sherry, Mr. Mayer essayed a feeler question to me. He explained that Hollywood was unaccustomed as yet to dealing with opera stars on my level. He reaffirmed that Thalberg, he, and the rest of M-G-M wanted to do justice to my artistic stature. He asked me what figure I wanted to begin the negotiating.

"A quarter of a million dollars," I said. "I'll want half of it in advance, and the other half, if the picture is good, will be a small part of ticket sales, and you can pay it to me in semiannual sums. Libbie can work out the details with you."

Out of the corner of my eye I saw Libbie turn pale when I gave the quarter-million-dollar figure. She had warned me ahead of time that even very big stars were hardly commanding a hundred thousand dollars and that I should take whatever Mr. Mayer offered for a first film. Right or wrong in principle, I disliked that kind of strategy; I believed firmly in the notion that the higher the price, the greater the demand one created. With that in mind, I excused myself and went back to my hotel suite. It fell to Libbie to do the negotiating, which is what I was paying her to do as my manager.

Later, she described in her sullen way the scene I missed.

"I admire your client," Mr. Mayer had said to her after I left.

"She's a great admirer of yours," Libbie said, continuing the small talk in the hope that if an ax were going to fall, it would fall gently.

"Something about her salary expectations puzzles me," he said, staring off into space. Libbie's reply came nervously.

"These expectations she has—well, these are things I'm sure we can work out, and I think maybe I can talk her into something more—"

"More reasonable? Is that the word you're searching for, Miss Miller?"

"Yes. Something more, uh, reasonable."

"Well, I'm glad you see it that way," Mayer said as he gripped the lapels of his suit coat. "For a while I thought your client had been consulting the pages of the telephone book."

"The telephone book?" she replied, puzzled at the allusion.

"What I mean, Miss Miller, is that the only way your client could have come up with *that* salary would be by adding up the numbers in the Los Angeles telephone book!"

Libbie sputtered and muttered that she could talk me into a lower figure. She tried, but I wouldn't budge. To me it was a matter of principle—and I was reasonably sure that Mayer and I would come to terms in due time. He wouldn't budge either. Through Libbie I agreed to keep in contact with him, as *Carmen* would again be before the public the next season. Maybe then, I thought, M-G-M would come around.

Carmen influenced my life more than professionally. I went on tour in it in the spring of 1936, singing a performance in Baltimore on April 4. The performance was memorable in a number of ways. One involved a brief hospital stay, occasioned by the too realistic acting of my Don José that evening, the gigantic tenor René Maison. René was my favorite José, no doubt partly because he had studied the role with Albert Carré and had, therefore, a complete understanding of my own conception of Carmen. During this particular performance he had thrown me around a bit too realistically, causing a hairline fracture in my forearm. I was treated and released at Johns Hopkins.

The other memorable moment came not as a result of the opera but rather a society party given for Lucrezia Bori two nights earlier. With Nino Martini as Rodolfo, Bori had opened the three-day Baltimore run in *La Bohème*. At that post-opera party I met the man I would marry—Carle A. Jackson, son of the city's mayor, Howard W. Jackson.

Our meeting was purely a matter of chance. His father, who had no interest in opera, had to attend the party because of his political position. At dinner that night he told his athletic-looking eldest son, "If I have to go to this damn thing, you're going too." Carle went, but stayed in the back of the theater as much as he could.

Afterward, at Bori's party, he grew fascinated with me from a distance. He had no idea who I was or what I did.

"Who's the dark-haired dame with the nice-looking tail?" he asked one of his friends over drinks. When the friend gave my name, he said in all honesty, "So who the hell is Rosa Ponselle?"

Two nights later he came to my *Carmen*. This time he stayed in his seat. Afterward, when we met backstage, he admitted that only one scene had really interested him: it was the scene in front of the bullring in the last act where Carmen and Escamillo make their entrance in a carriage. He had helped arrange for the well-groomed horses that drew the carriage onstage.

Horses were one of Carle's chief pastimes, and had been since his boyhood. His mother, Ella Mae Galloway, a free-spirited Irish girl whom his father had met and married near the turn of the century, had taught him to race them. Her family's history was full of the kind of adventure that would have registered favorably with any young boy; they were seafarers, the Galloways, and had lost some of their kin in eighteenth-century shipwrecks on the coasts of South America.

Ella Galloway had inherited her family's adventurous spirit and love of sailing, and had been engaged to a Naval Academy cadet before she and Howard Jackson had met. She loved horses as much as she loved the sea, and kept four driving horses long after carriages had disappeared from American living. One of her horses, a jet-black mare of gargantuan proportions, was her pride and joy; at its best the animal could run a mile in a little over two minutes, pulling its owner in an iron-treaded buggy.

Five days a week, at exactly two each afternoon, the buggy would be waiting in front of the Friends School in Baltimore, a private academy in which Carle spent most of his school years. Although the school day didn't end till half-past two, none of the teachers opposed Mrs. Jackson's requests to have her son excused early. By the time the rest of the schoolboys were packing their books to go home, the Jackson buggy would have won two races in a public park near one of the city's small lakes.

With Mrs. Jackson at the reins and with young Carle at her side cracking the whip, the racing would go on till suppertime. Not even the police were able to halt her racing. The best they could do was to call the mayor and urge him to plead with his remarkably independent wife.

Carle was in awe of his father. Howard Jackson was in his mid-forties when Baltimore first elected him mayor in 1922. Though he lost the next election, he was voted back in office in 1930 and again in 1934. He had two sons by the time he began earning a living as half owner of an insurance business; his youngest boy, Riall, was named for his business partner, Harry Riall. Around City Hall, Jackson earned the reputation of being a stern taskmaster, and during the bottom of the Depression his energy and selflessness had earned him the respect of the electorate. Taking care of his personal needs from his insurance company income, he had spent his annual salary as mayor on food and coal for hard-luck families.

If the mayor was rigid with his sons, especially in their youth, he overcompensated by showering them with gifts. Carle saw it as a reaction to his not being able to spend much time with his boys. "My father had three dinner jackets," Carle used to say. "One hung in his closet at home, another was always in his office closet, and the third one was usually being cleaned and pressed. When he was mayor, most of his life was taken up with official luncheons and dinners, so we became accustomed to seeing him in nothing but dinner dress."

His way of rewarding Carle and Riall was to let them have anything they wanted. If Carle wanted a new horse, all he had to do was ask and name the price. If he wanted a new car, he merely had to charge it to his father's account. The same for Riall—even to the extent of the mayor buying him an airplane when he wanted to learn to fly.

Carle was thirty years old, divorced, and the father of a nine-year-old boy when I met him. He had married the sister of a boyhood friend when he was nineteen, but had left her after three months of marriage. She gave birth to a baby not long after their separation, and he went back to her briefly; they were eventually divorced. Despite his marital history, he was one of Baltimore's most talked about men. He was an expert polo player and was considered one of the best horsemen in the state. At nearly six feet-three, with a two-hundred-pound physique that tapered perfectly from shoulders to waist, he was the incarnation of the All-American Man. My attraction to him was instantaneous, as was his to me.

I had had my share of involvements with men before Carle—after all, I was nearly forty when I met him. In many ways he was the embodiment of the type I had dated all along—tall, athletically built, and fair-skinned as opposed to the olive-skinned men I had grown up with. (This was a physical preference that Edith used to tease me about. "You're going to disappoint your mamma if you ever bring one of those blue-eyed blondes home to Meriden," she would say, never quite understanding the appeal that an entirely different set of features can have to someone unaccustomed to them.)

Edith and I dated a lot of men during my Metropolitan and concert tours. We devised a very effective ploy for choosing our dates. Because I was a "celebrity"—and, at that, a young and single one—I tended to gather a lot of male interest. Some of it was genuine and some of it, as with anyone in the public eye, was based on someone else's desire to be seen in public with a "star." Almost always there would be flowers, notes, and invitations awaiting me backstage, and Edith would very slyly try to find out as much as she could about the men who sent them. She was very attractive herself, and they were often interested in her, so between us we usually had our pick.

Edith would wait until they showed up backstage, and would scrutinize them for both of us. Those who were attractive and who seemed the most "gentlemanly" to her were told that she and I "might be free after the performance," though she would have to speak with me first. This supposed reluctance on my part—"Miss Ponselle is quite tired after singing, and only rarely socializes on tour," she would tell them—would usually make them all the more eager. In short order they would be painting soothing word-pictures of candlelit dinners, and perhaps an afternoon of sailing, tennis, or golf the next day.

Edith would then excuse herself and come into my dressing room to "intercede." Meantime, I would be dying of curiosity.

"Wait till you see *him!*" she would gasp, rolling her eyes as she described one of our latest beaux-for-a-day.

It was all very innocent, like two teenagers going to a prom, but it was great fun and made me look forward to those springtime tours.

When I was in my late twenties I found myself the object of romantic attention from men whose accomplishments would have made any woman take them very seriously. One was a very successful Los Angeles businessman, Richard Wayne, whom I met during my first visit to Hollywood. We met at the United Artists lot, though we really got to know each other at a party given by a mutual friend. Richard was one of Los Angeles' "eligible bachelors," and we saw a lot of each other that summer. He talked of marriage, and the press room got wind of it.* I was too young, I felt, and my career was so all-consuming that I couldn't imagine being a wife, at least the traditional wife my mother had embodied so perfectly. Although Richard and I stayed in contact for some time after I returned to New York, our involvement was rather brief and, in retrospect, not really intense.

Glenn Martin, the aircraft magnate, was another suitor whom I liked a great deal and spent a lot of the time with. Though our relationship never deepened to the point that we would have married, we were quite compatible and shared a number of interests. Glenn was a splendid man and, of course, was very much a celebrity in his own right. He was used to the limelight, and this removed the element of inequality that sometimes characterized other dating relationships I had.

S. Davis Warfield, uncle of the eventual Duchess of Windsor, proposed to me when I was in my mid-twenties, and when he was approaching what for another man would have been retirement age. Not that "retirement" would have been in Davis's vocabulary; he was one of the wealthiest men in the railroad industry, and he played almost as hard as he worked. He had an ornate private car that he would link to the special Metropolitan train that took us on tour, and he entertained us lavishly wherever we went. What initially I took to be a rather fatherly interest in me soon became a romantic one on his part. He told me that he knew a conventional marriage would not interest me because of the extreme difference in our ages; in so many words he told me that he would not mind if I had other relationships, if only I would marry him. Though infidelity in any form would have been repugnant to me, I took his proposal in the pragmatic, unconventional sense in which he made it. He knew I would say no even before he uttered it, but somehow he did so anyway. I told him I was flattered that he should think so much of me that he would want to marry me—and I meant it, because he was a fine person in every sense, even if I never viewed him in any but fatherly terms.

Giuseppe "Pippo" Russo was another story indeed—a charming, passionate,

---

* *Ponselle talked openly about her "romance" with Richard Wayne in an interview she gave to Atlanta columnist Jessie Fulsom Stockbridge, late in 1923. "They danced together in the large studio," she wrote. "The lights were low and the pianist played 'My Hero' from* The Chocolate Soldier. *Miss Ponselle began singing it softly as around they waltzed. The next day they rode to the top of a high hill and Mr. Wayne pointed out a lot of several acres. 'This was mine; it's yours now.'" Though Wayne was sending "a fat letter each week and a night telegram at every stop Rosa makes," the publicity-wise Miss Stockbridge was finally compelled to say in print, "Isn't this a page from Lochinvar out of the West for you?"* J.A.D.

attractive Italian who momentarily made me forget my fondness for blue-eyed Saxons. I fell in love with Pippo in 1932, and had a fiery relationship with him that was rivaled only by my relationship with Carle four years later. Though we never lived together—not so much that we didn't want to, but rather because my career would have suffered in the wake of the bad publicity it would have generated—we talked very seriously of marrying, and to all our friends we seemed a perfect couple.

Pippo was a successful businessman when I met him (he was one of the few automobile importers who marketed the much-admired Isotto Fraschini limousines and touring cars in the U.S.), but when the Depression severely affected his dealings I lent him a lot of money. It was then that our troubles began. Our love affair had reached a peak in 1933 (I even remember writing an intimate letter to him while waiting to go onstage in Florence at the *Maggio Musicale*), and it ended in February 1936. It had begun to come apart a year or so earlier. My lending him money had made him indebted to me in more than the literal sense, and it was the main cause of our breakup. He became indifferent, and I began to feel second-place in his life, so I broke off our involvement. I met Carle not two months afterward.

I got my first insight into Carle's differences from Pippo one month into our relationship. Pippo (and, really, any other man I'd been involved with, even slightly) had spoiled me by following me from city to city during my concert tours, showering me with flowers and gifts at every stop. I mentioned to Carle that I looked forward to his doing the same.

"Sorry, baby, I don't operate that way," he told me. "If you want to see me, you know where I live. If I want to see you, it'll be when *I* want to, and not the other way around."

He floored me—I wasn't used to that kind of independence, but at the same time I was wildly attracted by it. Before long I found myself spending as much time in Baltimore as in New York—so much so that I asked Carle to rent a home for me that summer. Soon we rented, under his name, a lovely Baltimore estate called Finlagen, owned by Charles Morton Stewart. The newspapers were already onto us, so our putting the lease in Carle's name momentarily sidetracked the reporters.

From the middle of June till the following September of 1936, Carle and I were inseparable. I was at his side constantly, meeting his circle of friends, learning about horses and polo, and immersing myself in Baltimore society. My colleagues at the Met soon became aware of our involvement and made me feel very special by their kindnesses. I remember singing a radio concert that September and getting a wire signed by Geraldine Farrar, Marion Telva, Florence Easton, Frederick and Nancy Jagel, Mary Mellish, Charles and Virginia Hackett, and Mario and Ruth (Miller) Chamlee. They wired me from Salem, New York, where they had gathered just to hear my broadcast and to drink toasts to my newfound happiness with Carle. Never had I felt such warmth from friends.

I became Mrs. Carle A. Jackson on Sunday afternoon, December 13, 1936. The simple ceremony took place in the privacy of my penthouse, amid a small group of family and friends. My brother Tony and his wife, Lydia, were there; they had even managed to get Papa to come. Richard Crooks and Carmela provided the music—he sang "Because" and she did "Oh, Promise Me." Valentina designed my dress—a long, clinging, pleated pan-velvet gown, with a matching silver velvet hood, in lieu of a traditional veil.

Our decision to go ahead with the ceremony was rather spur-of-the-moment. I was getting my hair done at a small parlor in Pikesville, a suburb of Baltimore. I was under a dryer when one of the beauticians handed me a slip of paper. It read, "I'm outside in the car. Come out and talk to me." It was Carle's handwriting. I excused myself, left the place, and went to the car.

"They're at it again," he told me as he handed me a copy of *Variety*.

In it was a feature in which a reporter speculated that I was planning a "secret wedding" in a matter of weeks. I was used to newspaper stories by this time, but I knew that this sort of thing bothered Carle terribly. He was a private man, and suddenly felt as if he were courting me in a goldfish bowl.

"Do you want me to issue another denial?" I asked, wanting to please him. He shook his head no.

"Why should we disappoint *Variety*?" he said, taking me in his arms. It was his way of proposing. A month later we were on our way back to Manhattan from a Canadian honeymoon.

My Metropolitan schedule, which would take me through the middle of April, required us to spend our first months together in Manhattan, in my penthouse at 90 Riverside Drive. The problem was that Edith and Carmela lived there too; we even kept a spare room for Anna Ryan.

Carle, wanting our privacy, asked me to have them move out. Carmela was the first to go. He and she never got along; he refused to tolerate her eccentricities. Though I didn't fully understand it at the time, she was beginning to have troubles and was occasionally prone to erratic behavior. Carle's rigid, pragmatic ways left no room for her harmless but sometimes taxing ways.

The older she got, the more pronounced some of her problems became—but not without reason. To understand Carmela's problems was first to understand what it must have been like to have had every ingredient necessary for a brilliant career, only to have that career never materialize—at least, not on the scale it should have. It had taken six years for her to get her first Metropolitan contract. In the nine seasons with the company, she sang a number of Sunday night concerts, but only twenty opera performances—nine as Amneris, five as Santuzza, and six as Laura in *Gioconda*. To say that she was underutilized is an understatement; her Adalgisa, Eboli, Preziosilla, and Azucena were every bit as good as her Amneris and Laura, and she was excellent in the Rossini *Stabat Mater,* the Verdi *Requiem,* and other sacred works. She was also a fine Dalila and a credible Carmen. Looking through her scrapbooks after her death in 1977, I was amazed that almost all of the major New York critics had reviewed her at one time or another and, except for her debut, had praised her performing.

Not only could she have sung far more roles at the Met, but she and I could have sung together more often than we did. Gatti never much encouraged it, even though our *Gioconda* (particularly our second-act duet) had once led W. J. Henderson to write, "Together they made the fire fly." I suppose my well-known stage fright, which had reached alarming proportions by the time Carmela was signed, had something to do with Gatti's not featuring us together more often. I was nervous enough for myself before a performance and, knowing my emotions, I would probably have been even more nervous for her, even if I had no real reasons. It's just the way I was made up.

On her own, Carmela turned down several opportunities because no one would meet her salary demands. This was one of several ways in which her uneasiness with my success showed itself: she felt that because she was a Ponselle she was entitled to the same fee I would get. There was no reasoning with her about this—and over the years it cost her dearly, both in money and prestige.

She and Carle (or, I should say, Carle and I) had it out over her living with us not long after we were married. I sat her down and explained to her, almost in a motherly way, that as newlyweds we needed our privacy. She said she understood and would look for an apartment. By the end of the week she was at a new address, 230 Riverside Drive, in the upper Eighties. The card on the door of her fourth-floor apartment identified her as "Carmela Ponzillo Ponselle, Leading Mezzo-Soprano Opera Star." Every few years for the next four decades she replaced the yellowed card with a fresh one, so that visitors would always know who she was.

Relations with Eddie Johnson began to cool when it came time for Libbie to negotiate the roles I would be singing in the 1937–38 season. The two of them had gone back and forth for a month during the previous season, with Ziegler, Earle Lewis, and Eddie wanting me to keep *Trovatore, Gioconda, Ernani,* and *Traviata* in my repertoire. There was also talk of my singing Desdemona to Giovanni Martinelli's Otello, which the Met was planning to revive for him.

A revival of *Norma* was also discussed, though frankly I was not at all in favor of it. The standards we had set in the 1927–28 revival had been so high that another revival, especially only a few years hence, might not measure up to them—especially without Tullio Serafin, who had left New York for Rome, where he remained from 1934 till the middle of World War Two. Too, *Norma* was being used as a ploy to coax Marion Telva out of retirement; she had married Elmer Jones, an immensely wealthy man, and was enjoying a life of leisure though Eddie wanted her back in the fold. Much as I would have wanted to see Marion at the Metropolitan again (but, I should say, she stayed in retirement despite Eddie's offer of Adalgisa), I felt that using so difficult an opera as *Norma* as a lure—and, with it, a hint that I might partner her again in the title role—was an inappropriate reason to try to mount another revival.

Could I have sung Norma again, particularly after putting so much of myself in such a low-*tessitura* role as Carmen? Could I have equalled my own standards of a decade earlier?

In the end, it was less a matter of whether I could, and more one of why I should. The danger of singing Carmen, everyone told me, was of lowering my voice. Emphasizing the lower register, so the reasoning went, would ultimately take away the flexibility and naturalness of the upper register. Yet I had sung not only Selika and Margared, which are weighty transitional roles, but also Gioconda, which makes uncommon demands upon the lower register. Though I devoted my energies exclusively to *Carmen* for two seasons, I never intended to make a career of it, and I kept up my vocalises and re-studied my repertoire to be sure my voice would not be pulled downward. Yes, I *could* have sung Norma again, though admittedly it would have been an enormous challenge, just as it had been the first time around. But why do it? As we used to say in vaudeville, never try to top your own act *with* your own act.

During the give-and-take with Eddie Johnson I eventually agreed to sing *Gioconda, L'Amore dei tre re, Cavalleria rusticana, Carmen, L'Africaine,* Donna Anna in *Don Giovanni,* and *Traviata.* I added but one caveat: I asked the Met to revive Francesco Cilèa's *Adriana Lecouvreur* for me. This was the first and only revival I ever requested, and it seemed entirely reasonable to Libbie and me, especially since Eddie had been talking about revivals, what with *Otello* and *Norma.* For me, however, *Adriana Lecouvreur* would have been a forward step, a step in the same direction as *Traviata* and *Carmen* had been. Like them—and unlike the musically-beautiful but dramatically-stilted *Norma* —*Adriana* was a flesh-and-blood character.

Those who know this masterpiece of Cilèa will know why it has consistently attracted actress-singers of every generation since its premiere in 1902. Its libretto (based, as with so many great operas, on a play by Eugène Scribe, this one coauthored by his colleague Gabriel Legouvé in 1849) centers on the famous eighteenth-century Parisian actress Adriana Lecouvreur, whose rival for the love of Maurice de Saxe (or Maurizio in the opera) is a member of the royalty, Princess Bouillon. Cilèa's score—basically akin to those of Puccini in its fluid but electric melodic lines, affording rich opportunities for lyrical as well as dramatic singing—was as much a treat for me as the acting possibilities inherent in the title role.

Ziegler made known to Eddie Johnson that he would vehemently oppose *Adriana Lecouvreur* on box office grounds. He claimed history as his defense: the opera had last been heard at the Met when Lina Cavalieri had sung it opposite Caruso in the 1907–8 season. If Cavalieri and Caruso hadn't been able to keep it in the repertoire in 1908, he argued, neither could I three decades later.

Libbie and I countered on the grounds that the times were not comparable. For one, Oscar Hammerstein's Manhattan Opera Company had been a factor in *Adriana*'s fate in 1908. For another, Lina Cavalieri, great artist that she was, had been a poor vocal choice for the title role; she had too lyrical a voice for the score's dramatic demands.

Ziegler counterargued by reminding Eddie Johnson that in 1908 the country hadn't emerged from a nearly catastrophic depression. The uncertainty of New Deal prosperity in 1937–38, plus the cost of such revivals as *Otello* and an augmented budget for Wagnerian operas, led Eddie to go along with Ziegler and say no to me.

I couldn't find it in my heart to forgive Eddie for this. I began to feel that he, like Ziegler, somehow had it in for me, that he had chosen to forget how hard I'd worked for the Met in *Forza del destino, Ernani, Gioconda, La Vestale, Norma, Don Giovanni, Traviata,* and the other major productions in which I'd starred—not to mention the disastrous *Legend* and misfired *Notte di Zoraima,* my two "world premieres."*

Eventually, I tried another strategy. Since the Metropolitan's "no" had been based on economic considerations vis-à-vis the uncertainty of *Adriana*'s drawing power with the public, I offered to sing the first twelve performances without any salary. This, too, Eddie and Ziegler vetoed: they claimed it would save them only thirty thousand dollars, a drop in the bucket compared to the cost of the total production. While I could see their point, in terms of dollars and cents, I began to suspect that nothing I could offer would make them change their minds.

Thanks to a well-meant but badly timed gesture on the part of a wealthy Metropolitan patron, relations between Eddie and me grew strained in mid-March 1937. The patron, Robert De Biccari, hand-delivered a two-page letter to Johnson's secretary. The letter carried the signatures of eighty-one other Met patrons, among them radio magnate Atwater Kent. The letter stated that De Biccari and his fellow "regular and enthusiastic patrons of the opera, would respectfully request that among other revivals you may be planning for next season, that also Cilea's *Adriana Lecouvreur* be included and [we] suggest that the leading role be entrusted to that famous, gifted and talented artist, Miss Rosa Ponselle."

The letter went on to say that although *Adriana* "has not been given since the days of Lina Cavalieri and Caruso, we feel confident that such a revival with Miss Ponselle should be a practical novelty and of tremendous interest to the present opera-goers of the Metropolitan Opera House." De Biccari concluded the body of the letter by assuring Eddie that the group's thoughts were being sent in "the interest and continued success and future of the Metropolitan Opera Association."

* *Ponselle's growing distrust of Johnson and the Met adminstration was evident when she fell prey to rumors Edith reported that another soprano had bribed Ziegler to oppose a Ponselle* Adriana *so that the role could be saved for her. That the rumor was nonsense (the rumored soprano did not have the star stature to assume the role, and the amount of the alleged bribe was a paltry thousand dollars) did not dissuade Ponselle from believing it for a time.* J.A.D.

Eddie was on the phone with Libbie the day the letter arrived. He blamed me for instigating it. I didn't dignify his charge by answering it; I told Libbie truthfully that I knew nothing about it and had in no way prompted it. Johnson claimed otherwise because the letter addressed the Cavalieri-Caruso matter —private information that only the principals in the negotiations would have knowledge of, said Johnson. Libbie reminded him that the opera company was a small world, and that patrons like De Biccari could, with little trouble, find out what the management was thinking.

The matter ended with Eddie Johnson drafting a polite but firmly worded response to De Biccari and his co-signers, noting that while he appreciated their interest and respected their views, the management had much to take into account before embarking on a new production of *Adriana Lecouvreur*.

By the time he drafted and sent his response, I had already sung my last performances of the 1936–37 season. *Carmen* was the very last, a touring performance sung in Cleveland on Saturday, April 17, 1937; ironically, tenor Giordano Paltrinieri, bass-baritone Louis d'Angelo, and conductor Gennaro Papi, who had all been a part of my debut nineteen years earlier, performed with me that last time. Earlier that week I had sung a *Cavalleria* in Cleveland, a double-bill outing that brought a record nine thousand people to the city's Public Hall to hear my Santuzza followed by Lily Pons's Queen in *Le Coq d'or*. My last in-house performance at the Met had been a mid-February *Carmen*, followed by a Sunday Night Concert appearance the next month. During the concert, interestingly, my last group of songs concluded with "When I Have Sung My Songs to You (I'll Sing No More!)."

All that was left me, unless Johnson would reconsider *Adriana,* was a series of summer concerts. If he refused to reconsider, I knew I would be in for a long wait. I was prepared for it mentally, as I really didn't want to leave the Metropolitan on those terms. Still, deep inside me I couldn't shake the feeling that Johnson was somehow punishing me by refusing to trust my artistry and box office power in a revival. If he could trust Martinelli's in *Otello,* why not mine in *Adriana Lecouvreur?* I concede that the two works may not be comparable musically, but I would have appreciated the vote of confidence anyway.

Feeling estranged from the Met, I sang my final concerts of the year, extending through the fall of 1937. The reviews I received assured me that if nothing else I still had a voice. "Surely this voice is one of the rarest beauties of the generation!" exclaimed the Worcester, Massachusetts, *Evening Post*'s critic after I sang there in October. "The familiar rich hue, the warm vibrancy and rounded tone all remain as we have heard them many times; moreover, with the years exemplary vocalism had been added to the natural opulence of tone."

On October 15, Atlanta received me with open arms, taking me back to the days when I had sung there with Caruso in *Forza del destino*. The Atlanta *Constitution* said I had "returned to recapture the city which worshipped at [my] feet." The critic who wrote those words, Moselle Horton Young, called my program one "of utmost artistry and unexcelled interpretative genius

. . . She leaves not one detail of one phrase untouched by the highly-sensitive artistry that will always keep her a great singer."

Will always keep her a great singer . . . those words gave me terrific confidence at a time when I needed to hear them. Here I was, forty years old, in the nineteenth season of my career, having suffered at the hands of critics over *Carmen,* and now in the middle of a battle to keep my place at the Metropolitan. In this frame of mind, warm words from a critic boosted my spirits immeasurably.

The day after a concert I sang in Washington—Monday, October 18, 1937— Libbie wired me through Carle at Eddie Johnson's urgent request. The Met had been pressuring her for a decision whether I would sing at all the next season, and she didn't want to speak for me. I positively hated making decisions under pressure and waited till the very last minute to make up my mind. "I hoped to have [her] Metropolitan decision by now," Libbie told Carle in her wire. "Their prospectus must go to press at three o'clock this afternoon. They cannot possibly hold it up any longer."

I phoned Libbie from Hollywood, where I was staying, and asked her advice. "Leave your name on the rosters," she told me. "Johnson and Ziegler will go along with that, and we'll negotiate what you'll sing afterward. But count *Adriana* out. Johnson hasn't backed down yet, and he's not going to."

An hour before the three o'clock deadline, Libbie informed Eddie Johnson that I wanted my name kept on the rosters for the next season. She said he accepted the decision indifferently.

Just when I least needed another complication in my life, Edith had a falling-out with Carle and I found myself in the middle. In retrospect, she and Carle were bound to have trouble because, until he entered my life, she had been the organizer of my life, and I the focal point of hers. Suddenly, she felt her status eroded by a man—and, at that, a man I hadn't really known very long, and who wasn't about to become a "Mr. Ponselle" type of husband.

Once we were married, Carle could see no reason for my keeping Edith. Libbie could take care of my business, he argued, and one or the other of his secretaries could handle my personal mail. He found an ally in Libbie, who tended to be wary of Edith, feeling that as a secretary she had far too much control over me. I had feelings for all of them and wanted no one hurt.

A new man entered Edith's life about the time I married Carle. Albert Sania was single, handsome, and a successful life-insurance executive when Edith was introduced to him. Officially, their engagement became her reason for resigning as my secretary; privately, our close friends knew that the real reason was her inability to get along with Carle.

Edith left me in June 1937. She was bitter, and from July till late September we neither saw each other nor exchanged any kind of communication. It was not my doing; she made clear that she never wanted to see or hear from me again, that she felt I should have stood up to Carle and kept our relationship intact.

A mutual friend, Mina Horne, tried to patch up things by writing Edith and telling her how despondent I was over our breakup. She showed me the letter before she mailed it. "I phoned Rosa," she wrote, "and sure enough she was alone and begged me to come over. I went about four o'clock and found Edith Mason and her daughter there. We all went out walking, and then took Edith Mason home. Then we walked back through the park. We had a long talk about you, naturally. She's really heartbroken over it; she had tears in her eyes, and continually insisted how much she loved you. I assure you, the house seems empty and forlorn now; I hate to say this, but it seems as though there was some death in the house, and an air of mourning hung all over the place."

I asked Mina to add a sentence, underscoring what the source of the trouble was. "Rosa sure misses you, honey," she wrote at the bottom of the page, "but as long as Carle will be around, he will be the boss, and no one will be too near her."

Mina's letter arrived near the end of September 1937. When Edith didn't respond, I tried another way to let her know I cared for her. From Baltimore, where I was staying with Carle, I sent her a letter and a check. I kept the message simple, hoping she'd call. I said the check was a token of my appreciation, and that I intended to call her soon rather than to continue writing letters.

The check was for three thousand dollars—no small fortune, to be sure, nor was it meant to be. I was desperate to try anything to patch up relations with her, and money seemed one way to do it. The amount itself wouldn't be important, I thought, because Albert Sania was quite wealthy and the two of them were about to be married.

Edith's return letter utterly devastated me.

The letter began pointedly. "This token—as you call it—was a bit staggering," she wrote. "I really had anticipated you in a more generous mood when one considers all the facts and circumstances." She went on to charge that I had used her over the years and was nothing less than a completely thoughtless person. To deepen the hurt, she attached two canceled checks I'd written to Pippo several years before; they totalled thirteen thousand dollars, which led her to infer that he had been more important in my life than she had.*

---

* *The contents of the letter reveal much about Edith's and Rosa's relationship, as the former viewed it in retrospect:*

"I must clear myself first and for all time," Edith wrote, "but before I do, I want you to feel as I do, without rancor. And if the truth hurts a bit, remember, it's the truth.

"I'm going to start about nineteen years ago with the real Rosa. The one I would have given my life for, if necessary. At 307 West 97th Street, when you made your debut. Think hard and you will recall the promises you had made me. For one entire year you did not pay me salary because you earned such a nominal sum, and I was satisfied. Your future was most promising. You were to rise to great heights, and I was to be with you and share in all your joys and sorrows. You as the Prima Donna and I as the friend, companion, secretary, Mother, sister, nurse, maid, and chief cook and bottle washer.

"Knowing that you would become the greatest living woman singer of the century (and my judgment was justified) I put all my eggs in one basket, as it were. I gave you everything it was humanly possible to give—loyalty, devotion, friendship, consideration, and sisterly love. I was at your beck and call—day and night—everything and everyone

She ended the letter with a thinly veiled threat. "By the way, it is strange how quickly news travels," she said coyly. "I am sure you will be interested to know that a newspaper syndicate has heard that we have severed our connections and has made me a very flattering offer for a series on 'My Life with a Prima Donna.' It is needless for me to tell you that I shall anxiously await your reply."

I never answered the letter. Her words cut far too deeply; they paralyzed me and for a moment made me wish we'd never met.

When the hurt passed I reread her letter and felt she had written it only to cause me pain. There was so little truth to what she said that I couldn't come to any other conclusion. She claimed that she'd taken almost no salary, especially in our early years, and had "put all her eggs in one basket"; she had so much faith in me, she claimed, that she was sure I would one day provide a comfortable living for her. True, she did take very little salary at first; and, yes, she probably did put all her eggs in one basket. But in my own defense I had to say that my "basket," as opposed to any other Edith might have chosen, was by far the more plentiful. How else could she have led a life of lavish parties, exquisite food and clothes, abroad at posh resorts, international celebrities for company, and all of the other pluses that my career afforded?

I couldn't figure out what it would take to renew our relationship. Did she want more money—say thirty thousand dollars instead of three thousand dollars? Was that the only salve for a nineteen-year association? Or did she want some sort of public apology, some admission of guilt for all the world to see?

We remained estranged till her wedding day, May 19, 1938. Carle and I wired our congratulations from Baltimore, and later in the day he and Albert arranged a phone call between us. We had a tearful reunion in New York the next day. From then on we remained warm friends as couples, though Edith and I never completely regained our closeness.

My strained relations with her made me want to throw in the towel and quit—quit worrying, quit negotiating with Johnson and Ziegler, quit every-

---

was pushed aside. You and your career were of the greatest importance. Nothing else mattered.

"And further: That after nineteen years of unswerving loyalty and honesty—honesty when I know other people without the love and interest I had in you, might have been dishonest—I find myself practically destitute. That for fifteen years while your income was increasing in leaps and bounds under my care, I did not receive an increase in salary. Even under normal business circumstances where the contact is not so personal, honest effort is rewarded in raises in salary and bonuses.

"But all these years I never deviated from the one cardinal feeling I had, that someday you would make an arrangement whereby my future would be made comfortable. This hope was almost a religion with me, because I was so sure that you would stand by me, and the thought that you would not fulfill this hope never occurred to me. That was the degree of faith I had in you.

"Rosa, in considering the above, do you honestly feel in your heart of hearts that you could on the Day of Judgment say that you had kept faith with me? Could you then too say honestly that you love me as much as you claimed when you spoke to Albert, Mina Horne, Tony and Lydia and a few others? Think over carefully all that I have written and you will agree with me." J.A.D.

thing. The thought of life in the rolling hills of the Greenspring Valley, being Mrs. Carle A. Jackson, appealed to me more and more as 1938 wore on. The more Libbie pressured me for a decision about next season's concert dates, and what I wanted to sing at the Metropolitan, the more appeal country life held for me.

My name had no more than reappeared on the Metropolitan's rosters when a reporter from the Associated Press caught me in a black mood and got me to say in print that I might retire. I was feeling particularly low that day, and even said that I wasn't sure whether I'd be able to make a concert date in Boston the very next week. A few days later I paid dearly for my remarks when the columns of *The Breeze,* a Boston-area society magazine, reminded Bostonians that I had once canceled a *Cavalleria* there:

> Frankly, we can't help wondering about the Rosa Ponselle concert on November 4th at Symphony Hall . . . The point being that Mrs. Ponselle-Jackson has pulled one of those tricks she's been using far too much the past few years. The trick this time was giving out, as she hopped on an Eastbound train, a statement that she 'hoped' to be able to give her concert in Boston. Nice of her to hope: and not too reassuring to [those] who will remember all too clearly an incident of the Metropolitan Opera's Boston season last spring, when Liz [*sic*] Rethberg just about had time to catch the train from New York so as to arrive in time for the Saturday matinee of *Cavalleria Rusticana,* which Rosa had had to relinquish.

This was merely a prologue to the brutal comment that followed. "We understand that among the critics of the town," this editor wrote, "there are bets as to the identity of the artist who will actually sing Miss Ponselle's recital. In case you want to take the risk—and don't be the least affrighted by taking such a risk, for the unknown will probably be better than the scheduled singer—they're still selling tickets up at Symphony Hall."

What have I done to deserve all this? I said to myself in disbelief. So I had had to cancel a *Cavalleria* that Rethberg eventually sang thrillingly! Wasn't I entitled to get sick like the rest of the world? Yes, I had canceled a handful of concert dates because I was under too much strain; again, I wasn't made of stone and things didn't roll off my back like they did others'.

Now Libbie turned against me. That horrible editorial in *The Breeze* did it. She fired off a letter to Carle, rather than me, tacking onto it a copy of the column. "The enclosed is most distressing and most damaging," she said. "This in addition to all the verbal talk that is going the rounds is what has made the situation so difficult and what forces me to ask you not to allow Rosa to make any statements about her not wishing to sing at the Metropolitan."

In the letter she said she was convinced that my not going back to the Met would irreparably damage my concert and recording careers. "If Rosa does not wish to sing any more," she concluded, "that is her affair—but because of my deep devotion to her career it has been and is my wish that she step down from her throne gracefully, instead of letting it topple as it has been doing."

Libbie's letter made me realize that for the first time in my adult life I was totally alone. I had no one to turn to for comfort but Carle—and he wasn't enough. How could he be, having just come into my life? Mamma was dead; Carmela was no longer a part of my daily life; Edith left me bitterly. Even Gatti was gone—away in Italy in his retirement. And now, Libbie.

Having no one to rely on but Carle, I let him answer Libbie's letter. I was both angry and hurt by her remarks, and impulsively told Carle to let her know who was boss in our dealings. He took me literally and sent her a letter that should've been typed on asbestos. "I am certainly getting bored and upset with receiving nothing but adverse criticism from you," he wrote. "I am not telling you how to run Rosa's career but I believe it has gotten to a point that if you would spend more time to build her up than that which you spend sending me letters and clippings from various cities, you would all make far more money if that is what you are interested in."

Carle underscored his growing intolerance of her ways in his final paragraph. "I personally am not interested in whether you ever book Rosa for a concert or an opera," he said bluntly. "As far as I am concerned, as long as you are her manager just tell me the results of what you have done and not what you had to overcome to do it."

Though Carle had signed the letter, Libbie assumed that the sentiments, if not the words, were mine. From then on she refused to communicate with me unless by telegram or certified letter. It was now the winter of 1938, and I hadn't sung one performance at the Met all season, either in-house or on tour; the Cleveland *Carmen* of the previous April was the last opera I'd sung. Other offers came my way, but none intrigued me enough to want to give up the freedom of my life with Carle.*

In the fall of 1938 I needed an escape from the pressures I was feeling in New York. Carle and I went to Hollywood, where I reopened film negotiations with M-G-M. Paramount's Adolph Zukor was also interested in filming my *Carmen,* which gave me another reason to stay in Brentwood for a while. Carle and I rented Barbara Stanwyck's and Frank Fay's spacious home on Bristol Avenue, and we were soon immersed in the Hollywood social scene. My days were one long series of parties, tennis games, and swimming sessions; I interrupted them only to vocalize an hour or so each day. I had plenty of

---

* As word spread in management circles that Ponselle might officially leave the Metropolitan, lucrative offers came from the Chicago and San Francisco opera companies, both of which she rejected without comment. RCA Victor tried to lure her back into the recording studios in 1938, but she put them "on hold" till she could arrive at a final decision about staying with the Metropolitan. Meantime, both NBC and CBS had reportedly offered her a season-long contract as a radio soloist (the Paley interests were said to offer five thousand dollars per broadcast for her services), which she also turned down. Amid such offers, Libbie was forced to conclude that Ponselle simply didn't want to perform anymore, but couldn't consciously admit it to herself. J.A.D.

company when I practiced; Irene Dunne, Irene Rich, Gloria Swanson, and Joan Crawford were all studying voice at the time and came over to listen to me go through my paces.

I had never had this kind of an active, intense, day-and-night social life before. In retrospect I think I felt lost without career obligations to contend with; I felt a sudden need to be seen, probably as a substitute for the demands upon my time I'd gotten used to when I was performing. Carle was more accustomed to this kind of life and adjusted easily to it. The film colony received us generously, and we met as many of the studio heads, producers, and backers as we did stars.

I had a restful stay in Hollywood until the first week of October 1938, when a telegram arrived from Eddie Johnson. The time had come to compile a roster for the next season, and he wanted a final decision about my status with the company. "Libbie tells me," he wired, "that Carle told her definitely that you had no interest in singing at the Metropolitan during the coming season . . . In view of this, do you want your name retained in our prospectus? Please telegraph collect at once your decision, as we are about to go to press with the prospectus."

I slept on it overnight, weighed the advantages of my private life with Carle and my public life as a singer, and wired Johnson the next day. "Dear Eddie," my telegram read, "I deeply regret that in view of the fact that we could not get together on a repertoire last season, and inasmuch as the situation remains the same, I think it best that you eliminate my name from your artists list this year. Affectionate greetings to Mr. Ziegler, Earle and you, with best wishes for a most successful season. Rosa."

That was it.

No great fanfare.

No memorable retirement performance.

No tearful farewells from colleagues.

No final tribute from the critics.

My career had begun as a sunburst twenty years earlier. Now it flickered out in the plastic phrases of a sixty-two-word telegram.

THE MUSIC STOPPED

MY LEAVING THE Met put an end to my relationship with Libbie. Not that I wanted it that way; in the end, she forced the issue. All along she argued that without the imprimatur of the Metropolitan I would no longer be marketable. I disagreed, but to her it was a moot point: the fact was, I was her most important client, and without me her income dropped sharply; she wasn't collecting sizable enough commissions anymore. She asked not to renew our contract when it expired in June 1939. The date came, and it all ended rather bitterly. Her parting shot was to inform me by letter that she would sue me if I tried to sing in New York under someone else's management.

Feeling estranged, I stayed away from Manhattan entirely for several months. When I did go back it was at Giuseppe de Luca's request. Still in rich voice at sixty-four, he came back to the Met to sing a handful of the roles that had made him one of the most respected performers in the company's history. He invited me to the farewell *Barber* he was to sing on March 23, 1940, with Lily Pons, Nino Martini, and Pinza in the cast. I accepted gladly.

Carle was unable to go, so Edith went with me. It was eerie going to the Metropolitan Opera House and no longer being a part of its goings-on. Technically I was just a guest at the performance, but to my happy surprise, the audience applauded me as I entered the box I had been assigned. At intermission several dozen well-wishers came for autographs; they helped relieve some of the awkwardness I was feeling.

I would have enjoyed the performance if I hadn't caught sight of Eddie Johnson during the last intermission. The very sight of him made me angry—and Edith knew why. A few months earlier, in a newspaper interview, he had been asked which of the Met's principal singers had been its most valuable assets in the recent past. He gave a fairly predictable list that included Flagstad, Melchior, Tibbett, Martinelli, Pons, and the rest. My name never crossed his lips; instead, he cited Florence Easton as one of the company's greatest dramatic sopranos.

Privately, it had gotten back to me that when one of the interviewers pressed Eddie for an off-the-record assessment of Easton and me, he had said, "Well, let's just say that Miss Easton met her obligations to the public and never caused the management any grief."

Edith, knowing me as she did, sensed that my seeing Eddie Johnson, what with the mixed emotions I felt sitting through a performance as an outsider, had put me in a black mood.

"Look, Rosa, why don't we cut our backstage visit short?" she suggested. "Let's go back and congratulate de Luca and the rest of the cast and then leave."

I agreed, and the plan worked—until just before going backstage I found myself face to face with Eddie Johnson. I completely lost my temper.

"So Florence Easton didn't cause anybody any grief, did she?"

I caught him completely off-balance. He just stared at me quizzically.

"And Easton met her obligations, did she?" I went on, delivering my words at a machine-gun clip. "Well, did Florence Easton sing *Norma* for the Met? Did she do *Vestale,* too?"

He tried to interrupt me. "Rosa, I don't know what you're talking about, but I don't think this is the time or the place to—"

I cut him off with a pointed remark. "Why don't you just go ahead and admit that you and Ziegler wanted me out?"

"Look, Rosa, I'm not sure what's gotten into you," he said pointedly, his stare turning steel-hard. "Whatever it is, you'll do yourself a favor by taking it up with me privately, in the confines of my office."

With that, he turned away from me. I honestly don't recall the sequence of what happened next. All I know is that I completely lost my temper, and felt desperately sorry afterwards. I do have my limits—and when those limits are reached, which hasn't been many times in my life, I react. That evening, Eddie Johnson saw me at my worst.

Mind you, I had nothing against Florence Easton. In fact, if I myself had been asked which colleagues who shared my repertoire I most admired, Florence Easton would have been near the very top of my list. Except from the critics, I never felt she got quite the acclaim she deserved. She was one of the most versatile singers in the Met's history, and a most considerate colleague.

No, it wasn't the mention of Florence Easton that set me off; I was never prone to that sort of thing and did my best to diffuse any press attempts to fuel rivalries. What did it, I guess, was Eddie's unwillingness to acknowledge to a reporter what my nineteen seasons had meant to the Metropolitan. I felt he could have talked about my record as an artist without getting into any management differences that he and I might have had. Add to all of it my oversensitive nature, and the atmosphere was ripe for an explosion. It came and went, and I was left standing in the midst of a deadly silent group.

I knew I had done and said things I shouldn't have. By the time I got control of myself, Eddie had gone to his office, wanting to be alone. It was his way of calming down. I knew I had to apologize to him, yet I could do nothing but stare at the floor. Finally, I got up the courage to go to his office. I knocked lightly at the outer chamber's door.

"It's open," I heard him say. I found him seated at his desk, staring aimlessly at one of the walls.

"I—I need to talk to you, Eddie. I just don't know what to say."

"That's odd," he said in a monotone. "A few minutes ago you certainly had no trouble finding words."

His indifference, understandable as it was, numbed me. The whole scene began to haunt me. Ten years before, I had come to this same office to make up with Gatti over a *Norma* incident that I felt Ziegler had prompted. Gatti understood me and received me with open arms. Ten years later, there sat Eddie Johnson in Gatti's chair. He seemed impenetrable, unreachable.

"Eddie, I'm asking you to forgive and forget," I said, trying to maintain my composure. "I know it's asking a lot, considering what I just did and said. But I'm asking you anyway."

"I doubt this will make any sense to you, Rosa, but why should I?"

"Because . . . because to tell you the truth, Eddie, I've had a tough time in the last couple of years. Sometimes I have trouble keeping myself in one piece. That's why I'm asking you to forgive me."

I watched his steeliness disappear as he let me talk.

"I can see now that there were times when I should've handled myself a lot differently," I admitted. "But to be fair, there were a few times where I felt sure I was getting a bad deal from the Met. I guess it's all past history now, but my feelings won't give me any peace."

"Rosa, the only thing I can say is that none of this is doing anybody any good. Not you, not me, and not the Metropolitan. There's nothing to gain and everything to lose by being at each other's throats."

A smile came as he added an afterthought. "If the critics counted for anything, you and I had two pretty good throats between us."

Eddie never knew what that afterthought, that momentary play on words, meant to me. Suddenly, he reminded me—and perhaps himself—who we were. First and foremost, we were artists. The years had passed and our lives and careers had gone different ways, but our differences weren't enough to put an end to our friendship.

"I guess what I'm suggesting, Rosa, is that forgiving and forgetting is a two-way street. I'll do anything you're willing to do."

"You have my word, and I mean it," I said as I made my way to the door.

Eddie took my hands in his, kissed my cheek and said goodbye to me. "Promise me you'll think about coming back, won't you?"

"The way I've been feeling, I can't make those kinds of promises," I told him wistfully. "Maybe I'm a 'no come back' girl. I just don't know anymore."

I never did go back. But that day I left with something rich and wonderful: the renewed friendship of Eddie Johnson, a fine artist and a great man, a general manager whose long reign was one of the Metropolitan's greatest assets. I stayed in contact with him until, in 1959, he died in Ontario.

Carle's father, Mayor Jackson, is owed the basic credit for making me a Baltimorean. Carle was with me in Hollywood in the fall of 1939 during my negotiating sessions with Paramount. The negotiations went nowhere, ultimately, but we had a good time in the process. Mayor Jackson, with one of his city's largest insurance firms to look after, grew impatient with Carle as the months went on; he was needed in the company, his father said, hinting that Carle would lose his place to his brother Riall if he stayed in California much longer. The mayor wrote again, this time issuing an ultimatum: Carle could either play tennis in Hollywood and have no income, or else he could come home and sell insurance. He had one month to decide.

By November 1 we were on our way back to Baltimore. All the way there, Carle kept trying to sell me on the merits of the city. For several months I couldn't find any; I was sure all that Baltimoreans did was eat: the women had garden parties and lunches in the middle of the day, and at night their husbands had dinner parties. As I look back, particularly after living happily here for forty years, I'm amused at my first reactions to such a culturally vital city. At the time I was distressed at the thought of losing the excitement of Hollywood—and, of course, most anything would have paled in comparison to the lavish treatment Carle and I were receiving in Hollywood.

Like every great city, Baltimore had a vitality distinctly its own. It was rich, both industrially and artistically, and its many-faceted charms had lured (and often kept) an array of celebrities. The acerbic H. L. Mencken made his home in Baltimore, and for a time F. Scott Fitzgerald lived in the picturesque Rennert Hotel, at Saratoga and Liberty streets. Lillian Hellman, Ogden Nash, and Dashiell Hammett also lived in Baltimore at different times. John Charles Thomas—like Mencken, a native—had property along the Eastern shore. Soprano Mabel Garrison and her husband, conductor George Siemann, were also Baltimoreans. Lionel Atwill, the film star, had a lovely estate, Rainbow Hill, on the Greenspring Valley Road, not far from the home I eventually built.

Theater, music, and art all prospered in Baltimore during the New Deal, just as they had since the last century. Two of the most colorful art collectors of their day, the Cone sisters, enriched the city with a collection whose scope rivaled those of their equally colorful friends, Gertrude Stein and Alice B. Toklas. (Miss Stein, it happened, met one of the Cone sisters when the two were studying medicine at Johns Hopkins.) Thanks to the repertory companies then active in the city, a covey of newcomers to the stage—Pat O'Brien, Spencer Tracy, Katharine Hepburn, Henry Fonda, Margaret Sullavan, Frank McHugh, and Baltimore's own Mildred Dunnock and Mildred Natwick— had launched their careers here in the late 1920s and early 1930s.

The theaters where they performed—Ford's, which had opened in 1871, the Maryland Theater, the Lyric, and others—offered a full array of dramatic and musical presentations. Ford's Theater, in fact, had been the site of the rehearsals for the American premiere (in Washington in 1906) of Puccini's *Madama Butterfly*. I had sung at the Lyric, in concerts and on tour with the Metropolitan, and after I moved to Baltimore I remember hearing my friend Margarete Matzenaeur at the Maryland Theater in the production of *Il Trova-*

tore. Thanks to a wealth of touring companies like the Columbia Opera, the Philadelphia La Scala, the Charles Wagner Company, the San Carlo Opera, the Boston Opera, the German Opera Company (which Johanna Gadski had founded) and, of course, the Metropolitan and Chicago Opera tours, it was possible to hear as many as fifteen different opera productions a year in Baltimore.

Although the smaller companies varied in their repertoires and in the length and frequency of their tours, they brought an array of first-rate artists to Baltimore over the years. Most of them followed a similar format: they would mount a production around a well-known artist, whom they would surround with younger talent—or, as often happened, European artists who hadn't become established with American audiences as yet. Alexander Sved, Ferruccio Tagliavini and his wife, Pia Tassinari, and tenor Alessandro Granda were but a few of the European stars who were heard in Baltimore in touring-company productions. Others were built around such well-known artists as Giovanni Martinelli, Licia Albanese, Richard Bonelli,* Carlo Morelli (with whom I'd sung *Cavalleria* at the Met, a brother of the Chilean tenor Renato Zanelli), Bruna Castagna, Ebe Stignani, Tito Schipa, and many others. Through Gadski, whose German Opera Company usually began its touring season in Baltimore, Jacques Urlus, Friedrich Schorr, Karl Jörn, and other luminaries of her era were also brought here.

Baltimore had been an important stop for the Metropolitan—so much so that before World War I, Met performances were heard every other Thursday night in the city. (Baltimore, in fact, had been one of the company's earliest stops when it launched its tours in 1883.) While I was with the Met I sang, in Baltimore, *Trovatore, Cavalleria rusticana, Forza del destino, Norma, Aida, La Juive* (opposite Martinelli's Eléazar, when the Met revived it for him in 1929), *Traviata, L'Africaine,* and, of course, *Carmen.*

Symphonic music could be heard almost as frequently as one wanted, as played by the resident orchestra, the Baltimore Symphony, or the Philadelphia Orchestra under Leopold Stokowski, or else Washington's National Symphony, then under the direction of Dr. Hans Kindler. As with the Philadelphia, the National had a subscription season in Baltimore. The New York Philharmonic-Symphony and eventually the NBC Symphony (under Toscanini, who conducted in Baltimore during his one-and-only tour with the NBC) also came here several times a year. The Peabody, the city's great conservatory (and the oldest in this country), supplied new generations of performers not only to Baltimore but to the Americas and Europe. The Peabody's well-acclaimed "Candlelight" recital series was a fixture in Baltimore for nearly fifty years.

Bonelli was one of several singers whose first acclaim could be traced directly to Baltimore—in his case to the efforts of promoter John J. Carlin, founder and owner of Carlin's Park, once located in Baltimore's Park Circle area. Carlin, who had come to Baltimore as a law student near the turn of the century, sponsored the George de Feo Opera Company's local apperances, in one of which Bonelli received early acclaim. Carlin's "Opera Under the Stars" series prospered in Baltimore for many years. J.A.D.

On radio, Baltimore's station WFBR brought the city into the mainstream of commercial broadcasting. One of its most popular musical programs was a daily broadcast of light classical and popular music, conducted by Joseph Imbrogulio, who was then WFBR's musical director. Robert Weede and Rosemary Kullman were among the local soloists whose reputations grew because of their exposure on Joe's programs. Joe and his wife, Betty, were friends of mine, and I always enjoyed his broadcasts. Eventually WFBR was a starting place for Arthur Godfrey and, a bit later, Garry Moore.

New Year's Day 1940 marked a turning point in my feelings about Baltimore. That day Carle and I made an offer on a tract of land in the rolling hills of the Greenspring Valley. Originally the land was part of an estate called "Nacirema"—nothing foreign, just "American" spelled backwards. It had been built before the Civil War and was owned by Felix Agnus, a prominent industrialist. An influential man whose pastime was raising horses, Agnus was important enough in Washington to entertain, at Nacirema, a list of presidents that included William McKinley, Theodore Roosevelt, and William Howard Taft.

In the fall of 1937, a local land developer named Carter, who had bought the estate after Felix Agnus' death, tried to subdivide it. Some irregularities in the bidding put an end to his plans and the entire parcel, one hundred fifty acres, was put up for sale. With two of our friends as co-investors, Raymond and Louise Clark, Carle and I bought the estate. We recorded the deed on January 22, 1940, my forty-third birthday.

The immense home that had been the focal point of Nacirema was long gone by 1940. The developer had razed it, and all that was left on the front acreage were two frame houses. One was a yellow clapboard house, smallish and run down; the other was a more spacious frame house that could be lived in. We moved in while we drew plans for our own custom-designed home.

The home became a project all its own. I already had a name for it: Villa Pace, after the "Pace, pace mio Dio" in *Forza del destino*. I wanted it to look like the lovely villas I had seen in Tuscany—smooth stucco on the outside, a red tiled roof, ornate wrought ironwork, with massive windows and high ceilings inside. I hit upon an interesting shape for the house. It would be built in the form of a cross. I had religious as well as practical considerations in mind; I wanted excellent ventilation, which the cross-shape design guaranteed.

The architects delivered a preliminary set of drawings in mid-March 1940. The interior would encompass, on the first floor, a music room, library, dining room, enclosed porch, guest quarters complete with bathroom and a mirrored dressing room, an immense kitchen and adjoining breakfast room, plus an apartment for a butler and cook. The focal point of these first-floor rooms, the center of the cross, would be a fifteen-by-eighteen-foot foyer whose vaulted ceiling would rise twenty-two feet from the floor.

The second story would feature a master bedroom twenty-eight feet long, with an adjoining bathroom and separate dressing room for me. There would be a second guest suite with bath and dressing area. Carle would have a dressing room, bath and wardrobe storage area as well.

Plans for the surrounding grounds called for three garages, a swimming pool twenty-five by sixty feet (spring-fed, at my urging, because I liked to swim in cold water), tennis courts, a horse barn, a chicken house, meat house, and dairy building. In the basement a cedar-lined storage room would be built for my Metropolitan costumes.

We rejected two sets of plans before we agreed on a final design. We approved the third set and soon Villa Pace was under way. Next came the pleasant task of furnishing it—I wanted to do it entirely on my own, item by item, preferably from New York City sources.

One of the more memorable buying trips I made took me to the Anderson Gallery to price select antiques. Myron Ehrlich, who had been a fan of mine since he was nine, and who was now living in Manhattan, volunteered to chauffeur me in Carle's absence. While we were making our way through the gallery, I heard a man behind me humming a melody from *La Juive*. The music was too out of the ordinary and the sound too perfect to escape my notice. Impulsively I turned around, and there stood Giovanni Martinelli—a bit older, a bit grayer, a trifle overweight, but the rage of the Metropolitan as Otello. We embraced as long-lost friends.

"Look two aisles over," he said. "There's Frances Alda."

Giovanni knew I was wary of Alda, so I said goodbye to him and told Myron to get me out of there before Alda saw me. It was too late. Suddenly the air was filled with exclamations of "Rosa dear" and "Frances darling."

"They say you're building a place in Baltimore," Alda said, introducing me to her new husband. "If you want to see a *real* house, I insist you and your guest come with us to my new place at Madison Avenue and Sixty-third. It's positively gorgeous and you *must* see it!"

Before I could think up an excuse I was sitting next to Alda in her limousine, listening to her pontificate about anything that crossed her mind. Myron got her going when he tried to pay her a tribute.

"Madame Alda," he said confidently, "when you, Rosa, Chaliapin, Ruffo, and Caruso were singing at the Metropolitan, it was truly a Golden Age. I hesitate to say this, but I think that we're now living in a Tin Age."

Alda picked up the cue immediately.

"This man's youth belies his wisdom," she said to me with a nod. "Not long ago I went to see a performance of *Tosca*—and if ever there was clear proof that this is an Age of Tin, that performance was it. Grace Moore, that *goat,* was in it—and if the son of a bitch who sang Scarpia had barked one more note, I'd have left!"

I had barely regained my composure when the limousine pulled up in front of her home. It *was* beautiful. Once we got inside, Alda reached for a bellcord and summoned her five servants. They stood in front of her like an army at attention. In an unbroken string of words she said to them, "This is Rosa Ponselle, the greatest soprano who ever lived, so have a look and get back to work!" Like obedient soldiers, they gawked, smiled, did an about-face, and then left. That was Alda for you—outrageously unpredictable all her life.

The opening of the tennis courts at Villa Pace was a momentous occasion. One of my friends was Alice Marble, who was then among the top-ranked women players in tennis. I invited her for a weekend and scheduled a large party for the opening of the new courts. She had designed them for me and was eager to try them out. We marked the event with a Falstaffian lunch, from which we all recovered about three in the afternoon. We were sitting by the swimming pool when Alice announced she was ready to play tennis—with me as her opponent.

"Are you out of your mind?" I laughed.

"Maybe so," she said with a wicked smile, "but either you play opposite me or I won't play at all."

In a few minutes we were dressed and on the courts. I never scored a point. Alice had me running all over the place, and I hardly hit the ball.

Later that day, at dinner, the conversation turned to music, and several of the guests asked Alice how she was doing in her "second career." She aspired to a nightclub career as a pop singer, and was then trying her luck in the Rainbow Room at Rockefeller Center. In her act she played a guitar and sang popular ballads.

After dinner, as always happened, I was asked to sing. It was the moment I'd waited for and I used it to the fullest.

"I won't sing unless Alice sings first," I announced.

A bit later, after Alice sang "You Stepped Out of a Dream," I raised the roof with an all-out performance of Teresa del Riego's song, "Homing." From then on, Alice did the tennis-playing and I did the singing at Villa Pace.

I had just begun to enjoy Villa Pace when my whole world seemed to turn upside down. Pearl Harbor and the outbreak of war made everything topsy-turvy—including my politics. For a while I flirted with Lindbergh's brand of isolationism, mainly because I didn't want the United States to go to war against Italy. I had no appreciation for the intricacies of world politics; I hated killing and violence, even if it was done in the name of national defense. But once the Japanese devastated Pearl Harbor, I had no recourse but to change my mind. If the Nazi-Japanese alliance could produce that kind of ruthlessness, it seemed to me that we had a moral obligation to stop what Churchill was calling their "long night of barbarism."

What hurt me during the war was Mussolini's siding with Hitler. I had met Benito Mussolini, and intially I felt sure that he had been duped by pro-Nazi staff members. I couldn't conceive that he and his *fascisti* might be as cold-blooded as his allies in the Third Reich. The politics of war aside, Italy was my parents' homeland. Now, their country and everyone in it—my relatives, colleagues, and friends included—was at war with my own.

Carle, a fighter from the word go, couldn't wait to get into a uniform. He enlisted in the Navy the day after Pearl Harbor; the same afternoon, his younger brother Riall enlisted in the Army Air Corps. I was terrified of Carle's enlisting and begged him not to go; he was all I had and I couldn't face the thought of losing him. He went anyway; like his Galloway ancestors, he wanted adventure. As it was, the Navy kept him Stateside for a few months. Then he was sent to St. Augustine, Florida, for sea duty. He spent the greater part of the war years as a lieutenant commander in the European theater's troop movement detail.

While Carle was overseas, troubles emerged within my family—troubles I hardly needed under the circumstances. Carmela, to use today's language, was "born again" religiously. In her middle age she grew mystical and ethereal and began "seeing" Christ's work everywhere. She got involved with a group of Fundamentalists around 1940 and sang throughout the war years on a religious radio program in and around New York City. By 1942 she had amassed a great number of composition books, like the ones children use in schools; on the lined pages she had written out prayers, biblical quotations, and what she called "fleeting glimpses into the Divine."

Her periodic "glimpses" led to frequent phone calls for money to "spread the message of Jesus Christ." She used a code when she called; she would phone me and say, "Toodles, send me my flowers," which I was supposed to understand as a request for more money. (Once, someone in my household answered her call and actually sent her flowers!) After that, her code became, "I miss those birds flying up from the South." I thought it harmless at first, though eventually it cost me thousands of dollars. If it made her happy, or helped others, it was worth every cent. She supplemented it with income from concerts for the blind and deaf, in and around New York City.

Carmela's problems were moderate compared to Tony's and Lydia's during the war. Tony had had one failure after another in business and was on the verge of bankruptcy. Carmela, I found out later, had lent him whatever extra money she had. Now he was forced to ask me for money—which he hated to do because of his pride. This time, he was about to lose not only his own house but also our family home on Springdale Avenue, where Papa was still living. To help out, I bought both homes and took over most of Tony's debts.

Sadly, Lydia eventually broke under the strain of their financial problems. Early one morning, Meriden police found her wandering aimlessly through the downtown area. She had had a complete nervous breakdown and had to be hospitalized. She never recovered, and died not long afterward.

Nino Romani and his young wife, Ruth, whom he married in 1938, were my consolation during this long, stressful period. Carle and I had persuaded them to stay with me at Villa Pace while he was in the Navy. Carle and I were living in Hollywood then, and I learned that M-G-M was looking for a voice teacher and coach for Ilona Massey. Naturally, I told Louis B. Mayer about Nino—and though Nino wasn't eager to give up his teaching in Manhattan, he reluctantly agreed to move to Hollywood. Eventually he either taught or coached Joan Crawford, Douglas McPhail (whose warm baritone voice had impressed Larry Tibbett, who recommended him to Nino for study), Eleanor Powell, Deanna Durbin, and Ann Sothern. He stayed in Hollywood after Carle and I left, but gradually Nino grew to miss New York. Because it was the musical capital of the world in those days, Manhattan was far more interesting to him than Hollywood was.

Nino and Ruth moved into our guesthouse in the summer of 1941, after Carle and I had begun living in Villa Pace. They stayed only for the summer, at first, but when they went back to Manhattan, Ruth was expecting. When the baby—a boy, christened Romano Romani, Jr.—was born the next March, I was proud to be his godmother.

The baby's livelihood was one of the reasons Carle had used to convince Nino and Ruth to live with me while he was away. Rationing, particularly of meat and milk, was a wartime fact of life. The thought of not being able to buy milk for the baby made Nino anxious. We kept cows and goats at Villa Pace, so our milk supply was guaranteed, rationing or no rationing. It was a great comfort to Nino and Ruth, and it made us happy to be able to provide this kind of security for the new baby.

When Carle came home from the Navy in 1946, we began to rebuild our relationship as husband and wife. It was almost like starting over, but this time without the romance of our courtship; the war had made everything different, and it took some time to readjust to each other. It was a common problem among wartime couples, but it was a small price to pay for having a husband return home without the scars of the battlefield.

Near Thanksgiving Day of 1946 my life changed irretrievably It's a time in my life that even today I find hard to talk about. Friday, the day after Thanksgiving, several of Carle's cronies and their wives showed up for a card party; it went on till the early morning hours. As with so many other evenings like it, I felt like a stranger in my own home. I was never as comfortable as Carle in giving parties—and card-playing held little interest for me. Occasionally, I'd go to the piano and sing for myself, for want of an audience. This was hardly the life I'd been used to.

That Saturday in November, after Carle left for an early-morning fox hunt in the valley, I was upset and couldn't get to sleep. I was taking tranquilizers under a doctor's orders, but this time I forgot how many I'd taken. Accidentally, I took too many. Carle found me, and immediately called the doctor. He and Nino helped him get me out of bed and walk me till I was given an injection to counteract the pills' effects. I was rushed to an emergency room and was put in a hospital for almost four months.

As of the winter of 1947, when I finally went home to Villa Pace, I hadn't sung a note for months. After I recuperated I decided to go to New York for a change of scenery. While there, I found myself the center of attention at several rounds of parties given me by Jim and Bess Farley, Fannie Hurst, and other Manhattan figures. One of Fannie's parties was particularly wonderful because I found myself with two old friends, Giovanni Martinelli and Giuseppe de Luca. Inevitably, they were asked to sing, and performed the "Solenne in quest' ora" from *Forza* and the last-act duet from *La Bohème*. Afterward, Guiseppe de Luca turned to me and said, in so many words, "It's your turn."

I couldn't say no, even though I was afraid what I would sound like.

We picked music we had sung before—the Nile Scene from *Aida,* beginning with Amonasro's and Aida's duet, "Rivedrai le foreste imbalsamante!," which de Luca and I began. From there through the stirring "Pur ti riveggo," "Tu! Amonasro!," and Martinelli's climactic "Sacerdote! Io rest' a te!" we sang as if we were onstage. Afterward, I was ecstatic. There I was, not having sung anything that demanding for nearly a year, but still able to get through some of the most challenging music Verdi ever wrote. It pleased me no end that both Martinelli and de Luca found my voice essentially unimpaired after ten years' retirement.

Word of our impromptu *Aida* spread quickly through New York. When Constance Hope gave a party for me, she made sure that the guest list contained enough musicians to induce me to sing again. Leonard Bernstein, a promising young protégé of Serge Koussevitsky at the time, was one of Constance's guests. He told me that I'd been one of his earliest musical inspirations, and he offered to accompany me in anything I wanted to sing. I said a tactful "no thank you" at first, until he played the entrance to "Ritorna vincitor!" from *Aida*. Robert Merrill and Blanche Thebom were standing in the bend of the piano, and I was sitting next to Lenny Bernstein at the keyboard. I sang "Ritorna vincitor!" and a number of duets. Bob Merrill brings it all back to me whenever we talk.

Singing, even for a handful of friends, was a breath of spring in an otherwise unsettled life. Carle and I grew more and more estranged in 1947, and though we were legally still married we lived separate lives. We were still very much in love, as we had always been. But love is only one ingredient in a marriage—even if it's one of the most important. Beyond love, there is the chemistry between the two people involved, and the need for mutual interests of various kinds. In the end, Carle and I were too dissimilar to sustain a marriage.

Our parting was as intense and dramatic as the beginning of our relationship fourteen years earlier. No one incident caused our breakup, though our friends could see it coming. In retrospect, I guess we could too. We were both clinging to something that was slowly ruining our lives. It all came apart one night in 1949, while we were sitting in the library of Villa Pace. It was just like any other evening. There were only the four of us—Carle and I, and Nino and Ruth. I hadn't even expected to see them, until Carle told me that he'd called and invited them for dinner. We were having a glass of wine while the meal was being prepared.

Suddenly, Carle announced that he was leaving me.

At first I didn't know what to say. Then I got angry, but I couldn't cry. Before I could speak, he said his bags were already in the car. With that, he started to get up from his chair. He was still holding his wineglass.

I completely lost my temper and slapped the glass out of his hand. The rim of the glass cut his lip; he wiped away the blood but said nothing. A few moments later he walked out of Villa Pace forever.* I filed for divorce in August 1950; on February 27 of the next year, the Second Circuit Court of Baltimore dissolved the marriage.

As my marriage collapsed I turned more and more to music for solace, and I began to enjoy singing again. I had sung at a few social events since leaving the Metropolitan (once Marion Telva and I were at a party and sang the *Norma* duets, to Alec Templeton's accompaniment), but my stamina wasn't what it once was, owing to retirement. In 1949 a visit from Ida and Louise Cook made me think about getting my voice in shape again. Ida and Louise had renewed our acquaintance just after I was released from the hospital in the winter of 1947. When they visited me again two years later they brought with them a young physician, Dr. Dick Alexander, and his wife, who were fans of mine. At Ida's and Louise's urging, Dr. Alexander brought with him an early-model wire recorder.

Ida Cook, though a writer by profession, was, like her sister Louise, a great devotee of the opera. At Villa Pace she got me to sing one of my favorite songs, "Fa la nana bambine," into Dick Alexander's machine. It's a song that requires controlled *mezza-voce* singing, and since the *mezza voce* is the immediate indicator of whether or not I'm in voice, I chose it instead of something more musically complex.

I'll never forget my thoughts as I heard it played back. My singing had been recorded before; an admirer, Gideon Stieff, had made wire recordings of Telva's and my *Norma* duets, as well as parts of my *Traviata,* but I'd never listened to them very intently. Circumstances forced me to listen this time. I asked if I really sounded that bad.

"Well, it's pretty accurate in the main," the doctor said before Ida or Louise could think up a more tactful response.

I was heartsick.

"You mean I'm that rusty and my *pianissimi* aren't at all what they should be?"

There was a long silence and then Louise Cook spoke up.

"There's nothing that a few weeks of practice wouldn't put right," she said confidently.

I credit the Cook sisters with having given me a further reason to rebuild

---

* *Carle's leaving had a curious postscript to it. As soon as he walked out, Rosa went to pieces emotionally. An hour passed before her doctor arrived with a sedative. Her friend Sonia Parr, who arrived about that time, recalled a remark that had undercut the seeming formality of Carle's departure. Nino Romani, who had known Rosa's and Carle's moods intimately, had made the remark to Sonia as Rosa was being sedated.*

"Miss Parr," he said quizzically in his broken English, "why Carle no leave after dinner? Now his guests go hungry!" J.A.D.

my stamina. I had no goal in mind other than personal accomplishment; I had no plans to perform again. I just wanted to see for myself how much voice I had as I approached my fifty-third birthday.

Though I had begun to sing again, I had no involvement *with* singing. Leigh Martinet took care of that. Leigh was the son of the founders of the Baltimore Civic Opera Company, Eugene and Mary Martinet. The elder Martinet studied voice with John Charles Thomas' teacher and had tried a career on his own. He tasted just enough of Broadway to want to go back to Baltimore. He founded the local opera company after he'd managed a small company in Montreal. With his wife as his accompanist, he taught voice in and around Baltimore, but devoted most of his time to running what amounted to a showcase for local talent.

Leigh's father's death in 1947 brought him into the organization just as the opera company was on the verge of dissolving. Leigh had a music degree from Columbia University and had done a tour of duty with the Army Air Corps Band. He was teaching music in the Baltimore school system when he took his father's place in an attempt to keep the company alive. With the help of Anthony Stivanello, a New York costume-and-sets supplier, and with a small but effective board of directors, Leigh got the company going again.

He was producing *La Traviata* when he invited me, timidly, to attend one of the rehearsals. I went—and I *loved* it. Though none of the surroundings were at all the same—the Maryland Casualty Company building, with its seven-hundred-seat auditorium, was hardly the Metropolitan Opera House—the atmosphere of an opera company, or at least the beginnings of one, was inescapably there. Though I was still a "star" to the young singers in the production, I seemed to be able to put them at ease and make a few suggestions about the staging and singing. I felt so good I sang through several parts of the score for about an hour.

Struggling as it was, I was intrigued with the little company. I asked Leigh Martinet what his next production would be. *Aida,* he said. I thought he was joking. If he'd have said *Hansel and Gretel,* I'd have nodded my head; certainly a small company could manage that. *La Bohème?* A little risky but, yes, with the right singers it might have worked. But *Aida*—that Spectacle of Spectacles in Italian opera? I just stood there shaking my head.

The story got more outlandish as Leigh went on. On paper, he and Tony Stivanello had already put the production together. They intended to use a ten-piece orchestra and a theater organ. The stage of the auditorium they were going to use had a maximum depth of only fifteen feet. There was that much space between the curtain and the outer backdrop in any of the major opera houses.

Tony Stivanello's attitude toward an *Aida* on a fifteen-foot stage was admirably philosophical.

"What the hell," he told Leigh. "We'll pack thirty people on that stage and it'll seem like a crowd!"

A *Traviata* in the spring of 1951 was the first of the company's productions that I could take any real credit for. I coached the singers and discovered I could teach and see steady progress in those I worked with. Better scenery and costumes, as with other sophisticated touches, would come when we began to make money. Meantime, in *Traviata*, which featured Phyllis Frankel in the title role, I helped her costuming as Violetta by lending her some of my own jewelry and accouterments. Phyllis became my first real voice student. She was a lyric soprano with only local experience when we began, but eventually she sang the leading roles in nine of our productions and went on to the opera and concert circuit in New York, under Columbia Artists' management. Today she heads the opera workshop at Towson State University near Baltimore.

Fortunately, the *Traviata* production was a financial as well as critical success. It was the proverbial shot-in-the-arm the little company needed. I was having so much fun that, when the Board of Directors invited me to become a member of their group, I said yes without any hesitation. From then on Villa Pace became a rehearsal hall, coaching studio, cafeteria, party house, hotel, and entertainment center.

Especially during the early days, when we were striving to shape local and regional talent into nationally recognized singers, I couldn't find enough hours in the day for my opera work. From 1951 to 1953 we did two productions each season; by 1952 we had moved to the Lyric Theater, the company's current location, giving us the first genuine theatrical facilities we had ever had. We usually found enough local talent to double-cast the lead roles, so that we could get through the run of performances in case of illnesses. We were non-union in those days, which helped cut costs but kept us from hiring the best orchestra players and technicians. One of my earliest recommendations was that we become a union company. When we did, we made the transition from an amateur to professional organization.

We needed money to get on our feet, and it took a special kind of leadership among the Board of Directors to raise it. During my early tenure, the presidency of the board passed from Charles Duff to Hugo Hoffman, then to Charles Newland and Gerald Wise. All were highly successful business executives, and the Baltimore friends we tapped for funding—the Walter Porters, the Guy Campbells, the Morris Mechanics, the Chase Ridgelys, the Bryson Tuckers, the Sam Schleisners, the Charles Dunnings, the Wendall Allens, the Joseph Carters, Dr. Frank Marino, Katherine (Mrs. C. Redman) Stewart, Mrs. Harold Duane Jacobs, Mrs. Henry Rosenberg, Mrs. Sidney Lansburgh, Mrs. Gideon Stieff, Howard De Muth, and Sonia Parr—came through handsomely. In no small way, they and others like them built the Baltimore Opera.

Though I was able to tap one or two prominent New York singers to help our ticket sales (Herva Nelli sang an *Aida* for us just before she joined the Met, and the veteran Robert Weede, a Baltimorean who had known Leigh's father, repeated his well-acclaimed Rigoletto for us), most of our casts featured local talent. As with Phyllis Frankel, many of them—Bette Hankin, Joshua

Hecht, Richard Cassilly, Eva Bober, Charles May, Richard Cross, Spiro Malas, and Norma Heyde—went on to have prominent careers as performers or teachers. Others like Eddie Ruhl, Shakeh Vartenissian, and Victor Laderout made commercial recordings (often under the batons of widely respected conductors), though their prominence as performers (outside Baltimore, at least) might have been less than that of, say, Spiro Malas, Richard Cassilly, or Richard Cross. A number of others—Beverly Sills, Albert d'Acosta, Enrico di Giuseppe, Martha King, Gabriella Ruggiero, and Lili Chookasian, among them—were "adopted out-of-towners" who came to me at the beginning of their careers, and whom I prepared in various roles.

I coached these young artists in a predictable repertoire—*Bohème, Manon, Madama Butterfly, Rigoletto, Traviata, Trovatore, Cavalleria rusticana,* and *Pagliacci,* the operas that draw best at the box office. As our budget permitted, we mounted revivals of such works as *Thaïs* and the Puccini *Trittico,* and even gave the American premiere of Rossellini's *La Guerra* and, in April 1976, the world premiere of Thomas Pasatieri's *Ines de Castro.* As time went on I inherited new titles—Director of Auditions, Artistic Advisor, then Artistic Director—as my work with the company increased. I had a great deal of musical help. Leigh, who had studied for a time with Giuseppe Bamboschek, did the conducting and most of the rehearsing in those early days. Lili Chookasian rightly described Leigh as "a singer's conductor"—a high compliment from an artist who has sung under many of the great contemporary conductors.

Igor Chichagov, the exquisite Russian pianist and teacher, joined us in the spring of 1950, first as an accompanist for coaching sessions and rehearsals (Mary Martinet, Leigh's mother, still did some of the rehearsal accompanying as of 1950–51), and subsequently as a conductor, sharing the baton with Leigh for a number of performances. He also became the pianist for my private sessions. He is profoundly musical: he understands both opera and voice, he is a master of languages (Italian, French, German, and, especially, Russian), and he knows operatic traditions (and I use "traditions" in the purest sense of the word) quite thoroughly. Though he is not a singer, he has always amazed me with his complete grasp of the technique of singing: he can watch and listen and detect flaws or signs of danger in a singer's production. Just as important, he knows both how to place and build a voice. He and Nino Romani are almost the only two non-singers who, in my experience, understood and were able to demonstrate and explain vocal technique without being performers themselves.

Igor has since lent his considerable expertise to opera companies and their workshops throughout the country. He teaches singing in New York City, using methods and techniques he learned from me during the many years of our professional association. He is the only artist I groomed as a coaching assistant and teacher—and, for the record, is therefore the only teacher who can speak authoritatively of my own "method."

Igor had married Kira Baklanova, a magnetic *spinto* soprano who had escaped, like him, from Russia to Germany. There she appeared with the Hamburg orchestra, achieving a respectable following with the critics, although in those days her singing overemphasized the chest register. This she got from her years as a ballad singer, specializing in Russian and gypsy songs. I worked extensively with her and grew very fond of her—"my little Chaliapin," I used to call her. Her voice was electric, heavy-toned, and fully resonant, both in its upper reaches (her high Cs were nicely covered and were of dramatic-soprano size) and in her lower tones (her chest voice was always one of her glories). She had a well-defined trill and amazing agility, which served her particularly well in the Rossini arias she prepared with me. Her repertoire included Carmen, Cio-Cio-San, Elisabeth, Giorgetta, Lisa, Liù, Maddalena in *Chénier*, Manon Lescaut, Marina, Mimi, Santuzza, Tatiana, and Tosca, among others. Most of these she sang in Baltimore. Her accomplishments aside, what I admired most about her onstage was her complete identification with the characters she portrayed, and her ability to project a great variety of moods. These were among the many qualities that had led Tullio Serafin to sponsor her in Italy, where he presented her on equal footing with Renata Tebaldi.

The opera company was in full swing by the summer of 1958, when Nino Romani came to visit. He was living in Italy at the time but would teach singing in this country, mainly in New York, during the summer months. He and I had seen too little of each other in the early and mid 1950s, so his visit gave us a chance to catch up on each other's lives.

Near the Fourth of July he and his athletic-looking teenage son, his namesake, arrived at Villa Pace. They were treated to several rounds of parties by Sonia Parr and other Valley society people. That year, the Fourth fell on a Friday, and he and I spent most of the day lolling about the pool, reminiscing and talking about music.

Later in the day I had several of my younger singers come by to perform for him; he put them through their paces and had me sing several exercises as demonstrations. One of the singers, Celina Sanchez, asked for more time with him. Celina was a highly intelligent artist whose voice showed a great deal of promise. She had an almost instinctive grasp of technique, and never let an opportunity to learn pass her by. She was very well organized and was always thorough, both as an aspiring artist and as a person. For extra money, she was helping my secretary with typing and filing. Because of her promise, Nino agreed to meet her at Villa Pace the next afternoon for an extended work session.

I was having lunch on the patio outside the music room when she arrived. I listened intently as Nino accompanied her in familiar vocalises. As I was listening I couldn't help thinking back to the Riverside Theater; that was forty years ago, when Carmela and I were still with the Keith Circuit in vaudeville. I remember how handsome he looked when he called on us in our dressing rooms, assuring us that we'd someday sing at the Metropolitan.

The sight of young Nino swimming laps in my pool made me realize how much time had passed since then. Inside, I heard Celina singing the last phrases of a vocalise that Nino had taught me in those early days. It was a simple little exercise, with one syllable of each word sung high, followed by others in a descending pattern—*amore, deh vieni, andiamo . . . addio.*

Then the music stopped.

There was a thud, as if the fall board on the piano had been slammed shut. In the instant it took me to turn toward the music room, the young girl inside called out to me. Quickly my eyes took in the scene. Nino's arms were dangling lifelessly near the floor. His head rested on the music rack of the piano, his mouth agape. His eyes, half closed by now, were locked in a stare.

Twenty minutes later, in the very bed in which he'd slept the night before, he was pronounced dead. A part of me died with him.

MY PET PROJECT

THE BALTIMORE OPERA remained my pet project through the 1950s and 1960s. During those years, because of the energy and leadership of our Board of Directors, we grew into a nationally acclaimed organization. Russell Wonderlic became president of our board in 1961 and took the company to the next level in its development. Our accomplishments during those years were immense. We launched a fund-raising drive to enable us to build our own productions. We created a Vocal Awards Contest to help us locate promising young talent. We engaged the excellent Baltimore Symphony, and as time went on our chorus (and, for that matter, the rest of the company) became more a staff of professionals and less a group of mutually interested volunteers. We even changed our name: "Civic," some board members thought, sounded a bit amateurish, so we became simply the "Baltimore Opera Company."

The singers we engaged, especially as we grew, were regionally or nationally recognized. A number of them, I'm happy to say, are international stars today. I can claim a small amount of credit for nurturing at least four of them. One is James Morris, the elegant bass-baritone whose Don Giovanni has earned such favorable reviews from the critics. Jim was a teenager when he was brought to me for an audition. (He was almost close enough to be considered family. His mother, who had since remarried, was once Carle's sister-in-law.) I could hear the promise in Jim's voice and worked with him as time permitted, though at the time I had confined my teaching and coaching largely to established singers. He was a beginner, but because of my other commitments I didn't feel I could take the responsibility for shaping his talents.

Nicola Mascona, whose rich bass voice had been an asset to the Metropolitan since the 1937–38 season, gave Jim the excellent direction and training his youthful talent deserved. In Baltimore he began as a *comprimario* in *Contes d'Hoffmann, Forza del destino, Gianni Schicchi, Boris Godunov, Traviata,* and other staples, and was soon singing Ramfis in *Aida,* the villains in *Hoffmann,* and *Don Giovanni.* He was engaged by the Metropolitan almost at once, but his debut was marred by a sad event similar to one I had gone through: just as my mother never lived to hear me sing in Italy, Jim's father died before his son's Metropolitan debut.

Jim's devotion to me has meant more than I can adequately express. I don't think he'll mind my relating an example of his and his darling wife Joanne's generosity and caring. After his performance in the Metropolitan telecast of *Don Giovanni* had created a sensation, I told him that I enjoyed it so much I wished I could see it again. Soon he arrived at Villa Pace with a wonderful gift: a videotape machine, complete with tapes of *Don Giovanni* and other Metropolitan telecasts, which I can see and hear whenever I want. Thoughtfulness of this kind is second nature to Jim and Joanne Morris.

Sherrill Milnes had sung only in concerts when Lili Chookasian brought him to Villa Pace. A Midwesterner, he had the rugged build of a farm lad but had just the rights looks for the stage. His voice was large though capable of refined lyricism. I groomed him for his operatic debut as Gérard in *Andrea Chénier,* opposite Kira Baklanova as Maddalena. He was an instant success and was soon engaged by the Met, but came back to Baltimore to sing Valentin in *Faust* and Rigoletto. To his own generation of American baritones, Sherrill is what Leonard Warren and Robert Merrill—or, in an earlier day, Lawrence Tibbett and John Charles Thomas—were to theirs.

Raina Kabaivanska came to me through Ida Cook, who had known her in London. As part of a tribute to Giovanni Martinelli, the Metropolitan's management had asked her to sing the "Suicidio" from *Gioconda,* and she came to me for guidance. In Italy she had been told that her voice would be suited best to the German repertoire, so she felt completely uneasy about singing Gioconda. I listened to her voice and, sure enough, its timbre was non-Italian; it had a distinct Slavic edge to it, just as she had been told all along. I was sure that the proper vocalises, combined with extensive humming exercises (humming brings the vocal registers together and places the voice "in the mask"), would give her voice a more Latin timbre and would lead to the overall improvement of her technique.

Initially, we had only a weekend to work together, owing to her busy schedule. From Friday through Sunday we worked into the wee hours of the morning, and I'm pleased that she has since credited much of her vocal transformation to that weekend. Our immediate goal was, as I say, to enable her to sing a laudable "Suicidio" for the Martinelli tribute. I had to admit that I was surprised that she had been given the aria to sing. Zinka Milanov was the reigning Gioconda of the day, but had been asked to sing one of the last-act arias from *Otello,* probably to allow her to display her famous *mezza voce.* So Raina was given the "Suicidio"—admittedly a poor choice for her voice, because she didn't have the power and weight for Ponchielli's music. But, being new to the Metropolitan, and thus being a bit insecure about her position, she agreed to do it.

My first task was to analyze her voice and decide what would be technically safe, artistically successful, and dramatically exciting, given the parameters of her basic voice and technique. To my surprise I found that she had never sung a genuine *pianissimo*—and she knew it. She didn't know how to produce one. By Monday morning, when she left, she could execute a seamless *diminuendo* at will, and could sustain a *pianissimo* line wherever the music called for it.

Working on the "Suicidio," which was a great advantage because I had sung the aria so often, I explained that there were at least three tendencies she would have to overcome: one would be to force the voice because of the demands of volume and range. Being carried away by the emotion of the drama was another potential problem. So was the possibility of being enveloped by the sweep of the music itself. Raina has great musical intelligence, which made all this so much the easier to work around. We outlined a pattern for her to call upon when singing "Suicidio," a pattern featuring contrasts in colors as well as dynamics. We worked especially hard on precise attacks, sweeping phrasing, diction, and mood changes in the aria. After that weekend, she worked with me on several other roles, whenever she could.

Later I learned that the difference in her singing was immediately noticed in New York. When she was asked what accounted for her improvement, she attributed it to our weekend's work. Later, the Met management phoned to congratulate and thank me for what I had done. Recognition of this kind is a great lift for any teacher.

Beverly Sills was all of twenty-three when in 1952 my friend Giuseppe Bamboschek, the conductor, encourage her to audition for me in Jules Massenet's *Manon.* I took to her the moment I saw her. Like Raina, Beverly is very musical, and had already acquired a formidable technique by the time we met. Opera was new to her but the stage was not. I worked closely with her and rarely enjoyed any coaching sessions quite so much.

"You treat me differently than the others," she told me over lunch one afternoon.

I asked her what she meant.

"Well, the others I've worked with like Désiré Defrère for instance, just tell me what to do and expect me to do it without questioning them. You, though, you let me argue with you. I like that."

Beverly sang not only a splendid Manon for us, but came back as Donna Anna and again in *Tales of Hoffmann.** She was already a star by then. She had gotten her first national attention when *Time* labeled her "A Singer to Watch" in 1956. She was in touch with me almost weekly in those days, writing a string of letters every chance she got.

She was single then, and her flame-red hair and sparkling personality made her the object of a great deal of male attention. For a while I tried to play matchmaker but failed rather badly. One of my fiascos involved two handsome, wealthy brothers who were dying to meet her. Sure enough, they looked her up in Manhattan. "Those devoted brothers *and their wives* have notified me that they'll be at my next performance," she wrote, tongue-in-cheek. "Boy,

---

* *Sills shared Manon with Phyllis Frankel, since the production was double-cast. For maximum exposure in the press, Ponselle saw to it that Giovanni Martinelli was in the audience for both performances. Local reviews of Sills were uniformly laudatory. "Beverly Sills has a lovely voice, freely produced, of varied dramatic color, and capable of the cleanest coloratura I have heard for fifteen years," wrote Baltimore critic Katherine E. Conger.* J.A.D.

as a marriage broker, you're awful. Gawd! Wives and children yet!" If I failed her, she did very well without me. On November 17, 1956, she became Mrs. Peter Greenough, marrying the associate editor of the Cleveland *Plain Dealer*.

For all the affection, charm, and wit that Beverly Sills displayed in the beginnings of our friendship, she paid me a marvelous tribute in a letter she wrote after she'd made her first trip to Villa Pace. I knew her words came from the heart:

> I'm so very grateful for this opportunity to "talk" with you that I would like to tell you something. I've been singing since I was seven years old. I suppose I was a little precocious and by the time I was twelve I guess I imagined myself quite the artist. Then my father bought me one of your recordings. "When you can sing," he said, "with the perfection and beauty of this woman, then you'll be an artist." I have never called myself an artist since.

Today, with Luciano Pavarotti, she is probably the most recognized opera singer in America. Though she has closed the curtain on her singing career, she is beginning a new one as General Manager of the New York City Opera Company. She'll succeed because she knows her craft well.

As the Baltimore Opera's Artistic Director, I've enjoyed a fine association with a number of present-day singers who hold a special charm with the critics and public. I first met Birgit Nilsson when I co-sponsored a Baltimore performance of *Tristan und Isolde;* later, I had the pleasure of bringing her back to Baltimore in *Turandot.* Vocally, her tones are somewhat narrower than Kirsten Flagstad's or Frida Leider's, but they have enormous carrying quality. Her top tones are easier than Flagstad's, and have the same Nordic timbre as those in her middle voice. I grew immensely fond of Birgit as a person. She is gracious, undemanding, and has a terrific sense of humor—something often missing among opera singers. My only regret is that we weren't able to bring her back to Baltimore as Salome, one of her very best roles.

Joan Sutherland deserves every accolade she has received—and they are so numerous by now that I'm sure she's lost count! She is a true dramatic coloratura whose voice has grown more expansive in color and depth, without any real loss to her upper range. Her *Norma,* among her many great roles, is not only beautifully sung, but is also a penetrating characterization on her part.

I hadn't the pleasure of hearing Joan during her formative years. I first heard her in a Metropolitan broadcast, but when she arrived at the Met she was already a star. Had she done nothing more than display her brilliant technique in a limited number of predictable roles, her place in history would have been secure. But refinement is a byword with Joan, and her voice, technique, and artistry have grown year after year. I know of few other singers who can make that claim.

To think of Joan is to think of Richard Bonynge, her husband, and the many young careers the two of them have nurtured. Jim Morris and Spiro Malas, both of whom began with me in Baltimore, are but two of many who have benefited from Richard's and Joan's interest in their artistic development. Richard is a "singer's conductor"—a rarer commodity today than in my era—who has a thorough understanding of the singing voice. In this regard he's in a league with Tullio Serafin, Nino Romani, Wilfred Pelletier, and Igor Chichagov. Richard is a complete student of the *bel canto* repertoire, and has few peers in his grasp of the French tradition.

Leontyne Price and Montserrat Caballé currently share honors in the repertoire that Muzio, Raisa, Rethberg, and I once shared. Leontyne Price's voice is a large lyric soprano that has grown in size over the years without any loss in basic quality; her 1979 White House concert underscored this handily. I met her at the beginning of her career when Dr. Peter Adler, the conductor, brought her to Villa Pace. She made a splendid impression on me, even at that early stage in the development of her artistry. I never had the opportunity to work with her, much to my regret, but over the last twenty-five years or so we have never been out of touch. Once I recall discussing her assets with Rosa Raisa; this was after Leontyne had sung to great acclaim in Chicago. As I hope she knows, both Rosas gave her a full vote of confidence. Beyond her artistic accomplishments—which are pheonomenal and have earned her a permanent niche in opera history—I have a special liking for her, on two counts. The first is that she is a warm, thoughtful, unassuming person. The second has to do with the parts we played—not the ones we shared on the opera stage, but the ones we played in American opera itself, a generation apart. Just as I was destined to pave the way for American-born singers with no European experience, fate chose Leontyne Price to open the doors of our own opera houses to black artists.*

Montserrat Caballé's voice, if what one hears of it on radio and recordings is accurate, is both lyrical and agile, making it finely suited to the *fioritura* demands of the great *bel canto* roles. I have not heard her in person, but her secure production reassures me that for all its lyricism her voice carries very easily in the heavier lyric roles. Early in her career I noticed a tendency not to want to sing *fortissimo* where the music seemed to call for it. Whether this was because she wanted to make the effect with her remarkable *mezza voce*, I can't say; but I did notice that she often reversed the dynamics other sopranos followed in certain musical moments. Later, as she assumed heavier roles, she began to use her full voice more and more. Though her artistry is best displayed in the timeless *bel canto* roles (her Norma, like Joan Sutherland's, is exquisitely sung), she also sings commendably in the *verismo* repertoire. Her husband, tenor Bernabé Martì, with whom I worked in *Tosca*, gave us a splen-

---

* *Ponselle, as with a number of her operatic colleagues, lent her support to the career of Roland Hayes, the black tenor whose concert and oratorio appearances were much heralded in the 1920s, both here and in England. In the 1950s, when he attempted to launch a career for his daughter, Hayes again wrote to Ponselle, who followed young Africa Hayes's career with interest.* J.A.D.

did and manly Mario, and was an endlessly cooperative artist. The quality of his Baltimore performances leads me to wonder why he had not sung more in American opera houses.

What Caballé, Price, and Sutherland are among sopranos, Luciano Pavarotti and Placido Domingo are among tenors. I know and love both of them. I met Placido when he was just beginning his American career; we engaged him for *Les Contes d'Hoffmann* in our 1966–67 season. There was a boyishness to his personality that I found warmly compelling, and his voice had a youthful lyricism to it. He was an excellent musician (these days he's a part-time conductor) and had a ringing middle and upper voice that often reminded one of Jussi Björling's. With maturity Placido's voice has grown larger and more baritonal, enabling him to take on weightier roles. Like Beverly Sills and Raina Kabaivanska, Placido can work mentally from a score. Although I can't speak of his method of preparing new roles (Hoffmann was already in his repertoire when he sang with us), I can say that he was an absolute dream to work with—even in the patience-draining environment that our primitive stage equipment represented. Though there is sometimes a certain reserve to Placido's acting, he has portrayed Otello most convincingly. It will be interesting to see what his future holds. His promise, even at the height of his career, is immense, and he undertakes new roles with the frequency and rigor of Caruso.

Luciano Pavarotti was inspired both by Jussi Björling and Giuseppe di Stefano. He wanted to strive for Björling's flawless vocalism and style, and di Stefano's ability to communicate with an audience. Luciano's father, a "singing baker" in Modena, surrounded his athletic son with recordings of Caruso, Gigli, Lauri-Volpi, Schipa, and the other great artists; that sort of environment made it natural for him to want to be a famous tenor.

Luciano's voice is distinctive—he simply sounds like no other tenor. A dozen years ago, when he was just beginning to be known in America, his voice was reminiscent of Björling's in its sparkling silvery timbre, yet like di Stefano's (though smaller and softer tonally) in its lyrical exuberance. His top is reminiscent of Lauri-Volpi's; he has no trouble with the high C in "Che gelida manina," nor even the D in "A te, o cara, amor talora" from *I Puritani*. Today he still has his high notes, and his voice retains its sparkling, silvery color. With the years its timbre has darkened, letting him venture such weighty roles as Manrico in *Trovatore*.

Great as his voice is, it is his artistry and his ability to cradle an audience in his hands that commands comparison even with Caruso. Although he and Caruso have little in common in their voices (Caruso's was a large dramatic voice, rich and baritonal in color), their ability to communicate musically is perhaps equivalent in comparable roles.

Luciano has that certain indefinable something that crosses the footlights and makes its way into a listener's very being. Only a handful of singers have ever had that quality. Offstage, like Placido Domingo's, his feet are firmly planted on the ground; there is no pretense, no narcissism in his ways. He's a boy at heart, capable of unrestrained fun when at play; otherwise, he is an intensely serious, very articulate, highly intelligent man whose characterizations reflect his many qualities. His gifts as a singer are as sizable as his capacity for work and study. Because of his popularity, today's listeners will probably carry his name to their grandchildren, much as my generation did Caruso's.

Phonograph records preserve for future generations the flawless vocalism of Jussi Björling, who remains a major influence on today's tenors. Björling was still in his twenties when he made his Metropolitan debut as Rodolfo in *La Bohème*. I first heard of him through my longtime friend Milton Cross, who had introduced him to the American radio public in 1937. In Baltimore after the war, I saw his Rodolfo, with Licia Albanese an ideal Mimi. Among all the tenors of his day, at least for the sheer perfection of his singing, he had first claim to the company of the great tenors of my time. He combined the best of their assets in his singing and boasted one of the most perfectly produced voices ever heard. It was shimmering and silvery, but when used *fortissimo* it rang out like a finely cast bell. Had he been a more inspiring performer onstage, he might've been compared with Caruso. Yet his good taste was so apparent that one overlooked his rather workman-like characterizations. Though his life, like Caruso's, was much too brief, he kept his magnificent voice and technique till the very end.

He hardly lacked for competitors. Giuseppe di Stefano, whom I saw and heard several times, was more popular with some of the public than Björling because he was a better actor and communicated more warmth to an audience. Through the mid-1950s his singing had such freedom, such verve, that he became Gigli's rightful heir to the great lyrical roles. I admired di Stefano, as I did another of his comtemporaries, Ferruccio Tagliavini. (I was also an admirer of Pia Tassinari, Mrs. Tagliavini offstage, because of her great dramatic projection.) Although they sang a wide range of lyric and *lirico-spinto* roles, I liked di Stefano and Tagliavini best in the lyric repertoire.

I admired Franco Corelli, a protégé of Lauri-Volpi, for the singular quality of his voice, his command of *mezza voce,* and the sun-like brightness and warmth of his tone. I also admired Mario del Monaco, who like Corelli was quite handsome, and whose large but compact tone enabled him to convey high degrees of tension and strife in dramatic situations.

The war years produced two American tenors who in their different ways ranked among the very best. One was Richard Tucker, the successor to Josef Rosenblatt as a cantor, and the possessor of a ringing *lirico-spinto* voice. Paul Althouse refined his singing for opera, and on his own Richard developed surely and steadily as a dramatist. With his lovely wife Sara at his side, he went on to conquer the world's great opera houses. At the time of his death, Baltimore was eagerly awaiting his Eléazar in *La Juive;* his sudden passing in 1976 robbed us of the privilege. I would love to have heard his Eléazar, which, by all rights, should have been definitive. Richard was often called "America's Caruso," and deservedly so.

Jan Peerce's fluid lyrical voice showed itself brilliantly, especially under Toscanini's baton. The Maestro picked him for some fifteen productions, most of them broadcast "live" over NBC. Peerce's unerring musicianship and technique never failed him during those high-pressure moments. Toscanini requested him season after season—the highest compliment to his musicianship, artistry, and reliability.

Among tenors, Carlo Bergonzi warrants special mention, both because of the quality of his voice and his refined grasp of diverse styles. Especially at home in the Verdi-Puccini repertoire (as Radames he even negotiated the *"ppp morendo"* Verdi wrote at the end of "Celeste Aida"), he had a well-placed voice that put him in a league with Björling, Corelli, di Stefano, and the others. Like Alfredo Kraus, Nicolai Gedda, and Canadian-born Jon Vickers, who is at ease both in Verdi and Wagner, Bergonzi's career is still spoken of in present tense.

Sopranos—what a covey to choose among in the generation after mine! Several were called the "new Ponselle," and I crossed my fingers for their success. Gina Cigna, in the sense that she took over most of my roles, was my immediate successor at the Metropolitan. I first heard her in Florence, at the *Maggio Musicale,* and was very impressed with her God-given looks and superb, natural dramatic-soprano voice. The American critics seemed less impressed than Italy's, objecting that her voice was marred by a tremolo, and that she carried the chest voice too high. In so doing, they overlooked many of her best points. The Italian critics unfailingly warmed to her singing.

Zinka Milanov was often compared to me—perhaps unfairly to both of us. I felt we were too different to be compared; mine was an Italian voice of dramatic proportions, while hers, at least to my ears, was distinctively Slavic and of a higher *tessitura* and lighter tone than mine. If she warranted a comparison with anyone, it would have been with Rosa Raisa for the quality of her voice, and Elisabeth Rethberg, with whom she shared a complete mastery of the high *pianissimo.*

Milanov's was an amazingly beautiful voice, probably rivaled in later days only by Renata Tebaldi's for ease of production. When she first came to this country, the Metropolitan sent her to Nino Romani, from whom I heard much about her. Her acting was rather routine, but, as Nino testified, her endurance in studio sessions was something else. In *Gioconda,* for instance, she could sing through the entire score two or three times, in full voice, and still be fresh afterward. (I admit I couldn't do that, even in a studio, because I would've spent myself emotionally the first time around.) In the end, she earned a place in opera history and it was an Olympian one. I will say emphatically that her Leonora in *Trovatore,* among other roles she sang splendidly, was the peer of any soprano's in my experience. (Yes, my own included.)

In an era that lay claim to the superb vocalism of Milanov, Tebaldi, Cigna, and the rest, Maria Callas reigned supreme as the most talked-about dramatic figure on the operatic stage. She came to my attention through Tullio Serafin, our mutual mentor, who sent me some private recordings of her when she was young. At that stage of its development her voice was a pure but sizable dramatic coloratura—that is to say, a sizable coloratura voice with dramatic capabilities, not the other way around. Its flexibility and scope enabled her to sing several of the great classical roles I had sung, plus many others that few sopranos had touched since the nineteenth century.

What did I think of her?

First, I'll comment on her voice and technique. To do so I have to make a few more or less technical comments of my own. Although there is some disagreement about the number and kinds of registers in the singing voice, I have always found it accurate, as I've said elsewhere here, to dissect the voice into "chest" and "head" components. In various segments of a voice's overall range, either the head or chest sound can be emphasized, for any number of reasons. But use of the chest voice should be somewhat cautious, especially as regards how high it is carried into the middle and upper parts of the range. Although it is often used to effect color contrasts and can be employed as a way of resting the voice in low passages that demand power, the chest voice should not be carried too high into the range, as it will eventually cause a break in the vocal "column" that cannot be disguised.

What I heard when I listened to the recordings Serafin sent me of the young Maria Callas was a voice that, when allowed to flow freely, projected an intensely personal quality that suggested a pervasive sadness. Her tone could be limpid and quite full, and her great musicality, marvelous dramatic instincts, and way with words and colors were already much in evidence. Unfortunately, so were some obvious faults in her production. For instance, she consistently misused her chest voice, not for purposes of coloring or resting the voice in low passages, but rather to try to enlarge the sound of her lower-middle range. As a result, she carried her chest voice upward to notes that surely would lead to future problems. Her way with high notes also worried me; I was afraid that her approach would eventually cost her steadiness of tone and reliability of pitch. Her repertoire in those days concerned me even more. Coloraturas who sing, as she was then doing, such heavy roles as Turandot, Kundry, Isolde, and Brünnhilde tend not to keep their voices very long.

Whether my observations were right or wrong I must leave to those who heard her in the opera house as her career progressed. As it was, I heard her only on records, radio, and, at least once, on television. If memory serves me right, it was on Ed Sullivan's *Toast of the Town,* where she sang excerpts from the second act of *Tosca,* in costume. I could see her grace, her physical beauty, and her intense ability to communicate—there was no mistaking it, even on television, including her dramatic reactions to Scarpia's every word. Yet as I watched I became aware of what seemed a studied rather than spontaneous delivery. For instance, I kept being distracted by the way she took care of the train of her dress; she fussed with it, moved it around, as if to improve its line for some questionable visual reason. I realize, of course, that any number of extraneous factors—the cramped studio space, the unfamiliar set, the wires, cables, and other television paraphernalia—could have accounted for it. But it made me wonder what she was thinking, vis-à-vis the libretto. Surely a woman of Floria Tosca's period would be used to the minor problems of maneuvering the train of a gown—and wouldn't be bothering with it, especially in the heat of the drama with Scarpia. But, again, this was television and not the opera house.

I would have loved to work with Maria when she prepared *Norma*. Serafin urged her to study it with me, but her independent nature made her want to go it alone. I respected her stance and admired her dramatic (if not vocal) creation of Norma as it is heard on records. There is no question that Serafin greatly improved her singing; and arguments about her technique aside, her vocalizing had a vitality and drive that left its stamp on the harshest of critics. As it was, she and I never had the chance to meet face to face. We were introduced once by telephone, and I was very grateful for the tributes she paid me. Her death in 1977 stunned me. It's almost impossible to believe that someone as young and vital as she is gone.

The life and career of Elisabeth Schwarzkopf, fortunately, have been long and wonderfully productive. As a girl she studied with another legend, Maria Ivogün, making her debut as one of the flower maidens in *Parsifal* at the Städtische Oper in Berlin. In 1942 she went from Berlin to Vienna, where she sang both coloratura and lyric-soprano roles. America claimed her in the mid-1950s (San Francisco first, then Chicago), after she had sung brilliantly for a number of seasons at Covent Garden. I became a fan of hers by radio, thanks to a late-night New York City radio station that played her early 78 records from time to time. Eventually, I came to know her when she sang as guest soloist with the Baltimore Symphony. She was married to the late Walter Legge, the critic and recording executive, of whom colleagues on two continents have nothing but wonderful memories.

I can't leave sopranos without paying tribute to those two exquisite artists of the postwar years, Licia Albanese and Bidú Sayão. Inevitably, one speaks of them together because they were the two leading lyric sopranos of their day. I can't recall another time when two artists in the same company reached the very pinnacle of critical achievement and, with much the same repertoire, had such equivalent success with the public. Each was a master of diverse styles and traditions, and both projected a vulnerable feminine quality—an overtone to their incredible acting abilities. But despite these similarities, they were entirely different performers, at least in my estimation. To compare them as, for example, Mimi or Violetta was fascinating, not only to critics and specialists but to the general public as well. Business prospered as a result of their popularity; fans of one felt compelled to hear the other in the same roles, for comparison.

Bidú, Brazilian by birth, was one of Jean de Reszke's last pupils. She began her career as a coloratura (Rosina was her debut role in Italy), but despite her success as Lucia, Elvira, Amina, and Lakmé, she longed for more than soubrettes and madwomen. Both the French and Italian traditions eventually satisfied this longing: she was superb as a singer of Mozart, Pergolesi, Donizetti, Rossini, Gounod, and Debussy, and her Manon was virtually definitive. She chose her repertoire with great wisdom, utilizing to the fullest a basically lyric-soprano voice with highly developed coloratura capabilities. Her production was flawless because of her technique kept her free of all forcing, and enabled her to be heard easily over very heavy orchestrations. Her *pianissimo*—unequaled in my experience—could be heard anywhere, lyrical though her voice was.

Licia made her debut in Parma, as Cio-Cio-San, having studied with Giuseppina Baldassare-Tedeschi. Shortly after she made her Covent Garden debut, she got an early break by recording a complete *Bohème* with Gigli. Her youthful beauty, stage presence, and, to a certain extent, her limpid lyrical voice, called to mind Bori's singing—an association fostered by the roles they shared in common. Licia became one of our century's greatest Puccini interpreters, and was Toscanini's first choice for the much-heralded postwar "live" recordings of the famed NBC broadcasts commissioned for the Maestro. Just as Bidú sang the definitive Manon, Licia sang the definitive Manon Lescaut, in my judgment. Today she and Bidú, who have always been close friends and, I'm happy to say, are both dear friends of mine, pass on the wisdom of their careers (often with Stella Roman and Giuseppe di Stefano) to tomorrow's performers. They are artists whose greatness transcends the era in which they sang: others may sing their roles, but Licia Albanese and Bidú Sayão can never be replaced.

The lower voices, both male and female, were much in abundance during the postwar years. Ettore Bastianini's marvelous voice called to mind the days of Danise and de Luca, although his acting and interpreting were not always on a par with theirs. Leonard Warren, who like Bastianini died much too young, had a singular if not ravishingly beautiful voice. Some called him the successor to Titta Ruffo, which, to be fair to both, is not accurate. Ruffo's voice was larger, more dramatic; he had not only a voice but instinctive artistry and dramatic talent. In Leonard Warren's case, these were less a matter of nature, and more one of hard work. Eventually, his ceaseless efforts to improve himself yielded a voice that was more equalized than Titta Ruffo's. Through a fortunate association with Wilfred Pelletier, who groomed him till the very night of his death in 1960 (Pellie was in the audience when he was stricken in *Forza del destino*), Warren became one of the greatest singers of his time.

Robert Merrill might have pursued a baseball career had his promise as a singer been less than it was. With the general public he was the most popular baritone of the postwar years, both in opera and in Broadway music. He had virtually everything on his side—good looks, a ringing voice, instinctive musicanship, a warm and entertaining wit, everything required to "make it big." He did—especially as Germont in *Traviata,* in which he rivaled Richard Bonelli. In the mid-1970s, his television and concert-hall appearances with

Richard Tucker showed how two great voices could remain great, even in the twilight years of a career.

Cesare Siepi and Jerome Hines earned my lasting respect in the bass and bass-baritone roles, as did Fedora Barbieri, Rosalind Elias (especially in Samuel Barber's *Vanessa*), and Marilyn Horne, among mezzo-sopranos. I first heard Fedora Barbieri in the telecast of *Don Carlos* or the opening night performance of Rudolf Bing's first season at the Met. Nino and Ruth Romani were watching with me, and we were all quite impressed with her artistry—an impression borne out when she sang Azucena in Baltimore, on tour with the Metropolitan.

Marilyn Horne—"Jackie" to her family and friends—has one of the most beautiful voices heard today, and has successfully revived a number of *bel canto* roles (Rossini works, in particular) that have eluded other mezzos. I think it's no secret to Jackie that she's one of my very special pets. I'm particularly proud of her for resisting certain appealing roles she might have sung to great acclaim with the public, choosing instead to maintain her supremacy in a repertoire no one else can approach.

Barber's *Vanessa* served not only Rosalind Elias but also Eleanor Steber, who joined the Metropolitan after winning the 1940 *Auditions of the Air*. A pupil of Paul Althouse, Eleanor made her debut as Sophie in *Der Rosenkavalier* and eventually went on to sing the Marschallin. She had an innate feeling for Mozart and Strauss, and had a loveliness of tone that recalled the voice of a great predecessor, Edith Mason. Baltimoreans will remember Eleanor's Countess in *Figaro*, where her performance of the Countess's well-known aria earned her one of the largest ovations I have ever heard.

One of the more difficult challenges I faced as the Baltimore Opera's Artistic Director came in the 1967–68 season, when we produced *Boris Godunov*—a work I had heard sung definitively by Chaliapin during my own career. Our Baltimore production invariably leads me to remember Norman Treigle, who sang the title role. The untimely death of this marvelous singing actor robbed us of one of the truly great bass-baritone voices of modern times. His was a large and distinctive voice, and I had come to admire it early on in the NBC televised operas; I wanted him for Baltimore, but ten years were to pass before we were to engage him. We signed him for *Mefistofele*, where his sinister and fascinating characterization earned plaudits from the critics. In addition to *Boris*, he also sang a superlative *Don Giovanni* for us. I would have loved to bring him back to Baltimore for *L'Amore dei tre re*, though, as the history of modern singing sadly records, he died at the crest of his powers. Even today, though we are blessed with an abundance of basses and bass-baritones, no one yet seems destined to take his particular place.

I had the pleasure of coaching William Warfield in *Boris*, though he was already a seasoned artist by the time I worked with him. He had made a considerable name for himself in American concert circles (he was one of very few who could draw full houses for recitals), yet his popularity spread as far as

Europe, Australia, and even Russia. In America, concertgoers flocked to hear his spirituals and sacred songs; he sang them as a baritone, though his voice was already darkening through the normal process of maturing. He had already mastered an enormous repertoire of masses and oratorios, and classical as well as popular songs. His voice, as I quickly discovered when working with him, was not only highly expressive but had the power and body required for Boris.

So much has been written about the power of Chaliapin's voice and acting as Boris that I hardly need to say more. Sheer volume, however, has never been a feature I particularly value in a singer. With Chaliapin, in fact, what I loved most was the way he used his *mezza voce* and *pianissimi* to make some of his most telling effects; they were poignantly colored and were so soft they could barely be heard, though they carried to the back walls of the old Met or Covent Garden. William Warfield understood this approach, and together we worked out some intensely dramatic points this way. Throughout our coaching sessions we worked easily together, sharing and refining our ideas and approaches to the music.

The same season Norman Treigle appeared in *Boris,* Adriana Maliponte sang Violetta in *Traviata* for us. The season before, 1966–67, she sang *Bohème* for us, impressing everyone with the quality of her artistry. She was already an established singer and was then trying to get a Metropolitan contract. After working with her I put in a call to the Met and suggested they hear her. An audition was arranged and eventually she got her contract. In all, she coached Mimi, Manon, and Violetta with me; she was anxious to learn, always receptive to my ideas, and a pleasure to work with. Especially with *Traviata,* a profound interest in the history of the role was apparent in her many questions to me. Not only did she want to know everything about my own Violetta; she was just as curious about Gemma Bellincioni's characterization as well.

Adriana's fluid lyric-soprano voice reminded me a little of that of Victoria de los Angeles. Complemented by her fine acting and commanding musicianship, her singing has been an asset to the Metropolitan ever since they awarded her a contract. My fondness for her, I readily admit, goes beyond her singing because, like me, she loves all animals and is devastated by their suffering. When she first came to Villa Pace there were about six dogs, eight cats, and three squirrels in residence; she fell in love with all of them, and her obvious feelings led them to respond similarly to her. In Italy, Adriana has both a large country villa and a roomy city apartment, in each of which she keeps a half-dozen dogs and cats. If she sees an abandoned or suffering animal, she rescues it from the street. One such pet, a little dog, she found in New York City. She took it home to her villa in Italy, where it regained its health and became a constant companion to her.

Gilda Cruz-Romo, like Adriana, is one of today's highly acclaimed artists. Fans of Metropolitan telecasts in recent seasons will recall her Desdemona, sung to the awesome Otello of Jon Vickers. There, as in other roles, she displayed her admirable mastery of the *pianissimi* and *mezza voce*. Her voice is essentially lyrical rather than dramatic, but because it is well focused she can negotiate rather heavy music. Unlike Adriana, with whom I worked extensively, I hadn't the opportunity to become similarly involved with Gilda. Though I was present at a number of *Tosca* rehearsals (she sang the title role in our 1975 production), and though I came to know her as a person and an artist, both my position and my usefulness were steadily—and stealthily—being limited by the Opera Company.

I resigned as Artistic Director in June of 1979. As reported in the press, it may have seemed sudden. But my close friends know my decision capped nearly seven years of a stressful, degenerating relationship between Bob Collinge, the General Manager, and me. Unpleasant as some parts of it are, my side of the story—if only because of the conflicting rumors that began to circulate after I resigned—remains for me to tell.

A LASTING MARK

THE BALTIMORE OPERA celebrated its silver anniversary with a world premiere in 1975–76. Though the Opera's roots extended to the early 1930s, when Eugene and Mary Martinet first began producing full operas, the Board of Trustees dated the silver anniversary from the 1950 charter that Leigh Martinet had overseen, creating the Baltimore Civic Opera. The world premiere twenty-five seasons later—of *Ines de Castro,* an opera set in fourteenth-century Portugal, written by Thomas Pasatieri with libretto by Bernard Stambler— proved to be my last real involvement with the Opera.

From 1969 through 1971, Bob Collinge, out of personal interest, had researched the story of Dona Ines de Castro, originally of Castile, and Dom Pedro of Portugal, whose tragic love story was the foundation of Pasatieri's and Stambler's work. When Bob presented a detailed outline of the story to me early in 1971, I was impressed and thought it would be good theater. A few months later, the story went from a mere idea to a funded project when my longtime friend Clemmie (Mrs. Duane L.) Peterson commissioned the writing of *Ines de Castro.* Clemmie, who paid me a great honor in 1967 by creating the Rosa Ponselle Club, a fund-raising wing of the Opera Company, is one of Baltimore's most dedicated patrons of the arts, and one of its greatest philanthropists. Her grant for *Ines de Castro* enabled us to secure young Tom Pasatieri to compose the opera, and Tito Capobianco to produce and direct it.

Tom Pasatieri was only twenty-eight when he began working on *Ines de Castro.* A Juilliard graduate, he had written a handful of operas (*Black Widow, The Trial of Mary Lincoln, Calvary, The Penitentes,* and *The Seagull,* among them), which had earned him national recognition. He was clearly gifted, but was unassuming, very devoted, and an exceptionally hard worker. It was he who brought Bernard Stambler, one of his professors at Juilliard, into the project as librettist. A medieval scholar and an authority on Dante, Professor Stambler had shared in the Pulitzer Prize for the opera *The Crucible,* based on Arthur Miller's play.

Tito Capobianco, whose productions have been seen in nearly every major opera house in Europe and the Americas, had given us *Turandot, Les Contes d'Hoffmann,* and *Boris Godunov* in Baltimore in the mid-1960s. Tito is without question one of the most imaginative and most efficient producers and directors

I have ever known. His efficiency, especially with rehearsal time, is legendary and saves a company a great deal of money. He is undaunted by a theater's limitations (not even the shallow stage of our Lyric Theater could undermine his plans), and he can choreograph extremely quick scenic and costume changes, even with a chorus as large as the one in *Turandot*.

We chose Christopher Keene to conduct the premiere cast, whose principals included Richard Stilwell, Lili Chookasian, James Morris, Sheila Nadler, and Evelyn Mandac in the title role. Keene, who was then conducting at the New York City Opera, had been assistant conductor to the San Diego and San Francisco Opera companies. He had been invited to conduct abroad at the Festival of Two Worlds in Spoleto, and had ascended to the post of Music Director of the Festival. Jim Morris and Lili Chookasian were internationally known by the time they appeared in *Ines de Castro;* they sang the parts of King Alfonso and Queen Beatrix, parents of Dom Pedro. Sheila Nadler, who portrayed Dona Blanca, had worked with me since the late 1960s, and has one of the finest (and largest) mezzo-soprano voices heard today. Richard Stilwell and Evelyn Mandac, who created Dom Pedro and Dona Ines de Castro, were both known to me by reputation. I had remembered Richard Stilwell from our annual auditions, where I'd made a mental note to find a vehicle for him. Dr. Peter Adler had presented Miss Mandac with the Baltimore Symphony, and she had been seen in a national telecast of *Pique Dame*.

Ines de Castro was in every sense a success, and enhanced the reputations of everyone connected with it. Whether it will find a niche in the standard repertoire is obviously too early to tell. Whatever its future, it was a high point in the recent history of the Baltimore Opera. In fact, considering the twists and turns the company has taken ever since—uneven productions, less-than-admiring reviews by the critics, questionable direction, and the tiresome "palace intrigue" that seemed to infect Bob Collinge and some of his staff—the case could be made that *Ines de Castro* was the high point in the opera company's immediate past.

Bob Collinge himself, I'm sorry to have to say, was directly responsible for the dark clouds that began to obscure the Opera's previous accomplishments. Bob, once a department-store window dresser, had been named General Manager when the Board of Trustees created the position. Though he had no musical or dramatic credentials, he had worked his way into the trustees' confidence through a long series of events, beginning with his assisting as a wig fitter and costumer. He was hired as production director a bit later, paving the way for his becoming General Manager.

With the board's acquiescence, Bob slowly and irretrievably changed the production philosophy I had fashioned since joining the company as Artistic Director. Perhaps because of my experience during the Depression, I had never been completely optimistic, even in the best of times, about funding for the performing arts. It's a sad fact of life (as we're now seeing again) that in times of economic stress the arts are among the quickest to be labeled "frills." As a result, previously healthy companies often falter and close, despite their clear importance to their communities. My plan had always been to concentrate local fund-raising efforts into the nurturing of local talent. Of necessity we started small, but as one generation of our singers made their marks in major opera companies throughout the country, our base of support increased dramatically and we were able to expand our budgets.

Never, though, did we lose our original focus—the nurturing of local talent. But this was exactly what Bob Collinge threw aside. There was no question that by the mid-1960s we had the formula and the raw material to have built a distinctive professional company. We had earned a reputation for mounting productions with up-and-coming nationally known artists, whom we surrounded with local singers we were carefully developing. (I'm confident that the singers I discussed in the last chapter will make my point that our formula had worked.) Bob Collinge changed our philosophy: in place of local talent, except in some minor roles, he substituted high-priced "name" singers, whom he surrounded with lavish, expensive scenery.

By 1980, then, the bulk of the Opera Company's money was being spent for visual and publicity gains, primarily—spent, in other words, on costly scenery and imported singers, neither of which could do anything for the long-term future of the company. Our philosophy had different aims, and took into account that funds might someday begin to dry up. If so, the musical quality of the company—not the scenery, but a level of musical quality reinforced continuously by the development of new talent—could enable it to survive. This approach, which was certainly not novel among regional companies, had proven itself long ago. But under Bob Collinge's administration this philosophy, this tradition, all but disappeared. In the process, he gradually undermined my position and my usefulness.

I am no longer in a position to say what this change in philosophy may have cost the Baltimore Opera. But I can say what Bob Collinge and his machinations have cost me. Until I finally took hold of the situation and, through Elayne Duke, looked at it for what it was and made a decision to resign my post, my relationship with Bob Collinge cost me plenty.

Though I've known Elayne Duke for some twenty-five years, she began to play a direct role in my daily life in 1972. Her parents, Milton and Henriette Duke, were well-known Baltimoreans and were near-neighbors of mine in the Greenspring Valley. Milton was my friend and financial advisor until his death in 1973. His wife, Henriette, was invaluable in coordinating a base of support for the Opera. Her decades of leadership in nearly every artistic organization in our city—the Baltimore Symphony Guild, the Baltimore Music Club, the Maryland Federation of Music Clubs, and the Women's Board of the Peabody Institute, all of which she served as president at various times—gave her a deep familiarity with Baltimore's cultural affairs and the inner workings of the city's performing arts groups.

In 1972 I was hospitalized with a severe bacterial infection—an infection so serious that the doctors, unknown to me, gave me very small odds for a complete recovery. In the midst of my long hospitalization and recuperation, I had to delegate authority for my many involvements—the Baltimore Opera, my activities with other arts groups, my coaching, and, of course, the particulars of my finances, my home, my correspondence, and the like—to someone in whom I could have complete confidence. Trusting Elayne implicitly, both because of my long acquaintance with her and her family and because of her professional stature (she was then an assistant professor of art history and was also head of the Department of Fine Arts at a nearby college), I gave her power of attorney and appointed her my personal representative. Though my full recovery astounded the doctors, and enabled me to rescind power of attorney had I wished, Elayne's great efficiency, energy, and drive led me to reaffirm my decision year after year.

Elayne and some of my close friends were witnesses to the series of incidents that finally led me to resign my artistic directorship. The first of these happened near my seventy-fifth birthday, at a time when I was still very much involved with the day-to-day operations of the company. Each spring we held audition sessions that extended over a two-week period, each session lasting about three hours. I always looked forward to them, both because of the thrill of hearing promising young voices and because my philosophy of developing new talent depended on these sessions. I made it a point to be the first to arrive and the last to leave, since I was a judge who had been prominent herself and the young singers we auditioned were interested in how I responded to their performing. During each session I dictated copious notes on all the singers to Elayne, and afterward I would talk with each one and share the comments I had made.

The format and procedure of the annual auditions had long been established by the time this first regrettable incident happened. Early in the proceedings, Bob announced from the stage of the Notre Dame College auditorium (where the event was then held) that the judges should be aware that balloting would be as usual, with one exception: I would not be a member of the final judging panel.

I was astounded—Bob had said nothing to me in advance, so, like the rest of the judges he was addressing, I was hearing this for the first time. I said nothing to him, as it was neither the time nor place to resolve what I was sure was a procedural mistake on his part.

Hugh Johns, a fellow judge, rode with me to Villa Pace that night. Two other friends—Dr. Dragi Jovanovski, and Bette Hankin, one of our best mezzos and one of my "pets"—were to meet us at my home for a traditional nightcap. We were nearing Villa Pace when Hugh gingerly brought up Bob's remark. I didn't really want to talk about it because I had no explanation for such an arbitrary decision. "Don't get into it," I told Hugh; I said I would take care of it on my own. Later that night Hugh repeated this to Bette and Dragi, who wanted to join him in lodging a protest on my behalf.

I phoned Bob the next afternoon and asked for an explanation. He told me that he had decided that local judges should not serve on the final judging panel. "This sort of thing just isn't done," he said firmly. I don't like arguments, and I could see that he'd done this intentionally—it wasn't an "oversight" or any such thing, and nothing was going to change his mind. I couldn't see his reasoning, though; it seemed to me very arbitrary that he was now considering me a "local" judge, and since I had always served as a final judge, a precedent—a tradition, if you like—had already been established in our company.

Bob carried out his decision on the night of the final judging. While the performers and their audience—some members of the Opera board, the Opera's administrative staff, or friends of the singers, and others—walked across the foyer from the auditorium to the gymnasium, where refreshments were being served, the judges went to a nearby room to deliberate. I was handed a camp-stool to sit on—outside the room, in the foyer, in plain sight of the performers and the others.

I was bewildered. I just sat there, saying nothing.

Inside, I later found out, George London asked where I was. George, who was then director of the Kennedy Center for the Performing Arts, had driven in from Washington to serve as a final judge; he had been with us before and had looked forward to serving with me again. He asked Bob Collinge where I was; he got no satisfactory answers but didn't want to begin the deliberations without me. Finally, Bob had to tell him I wasn't going to be included. George, I'm told, had the last word. "The most qualified judge among us is sitting outside this room," he said forcefully. "I came here to serve with her, and if she's being excluded I'm going to my car and drive back to Washington." Soon I was invited into the judges' room.

This incident was plainly humiliating. But years later another, much more hurtful incident happened during the auditions. I was older and, much as I don't like to think about it, my health had begun to deteriorate.* I was having problems with my legs, and my walking became awkward and uncertain. Bob took note of my unsteadiness—not out of sympathy or concern, but rather to imply that I was becoming more of a burden than an asset.

The auditions had been moved from Notre Dame to the Peabody Institute, in Baltimore's Mount Vernon Place. Because of its center-of-town location, parking was a problem. Elayne would drive me to the sessions, would stay with me and take down my comments, and would drive me home. But for me to go to and from the car, which might be parked several blocks away from

---

* *Her health especially declined from March 1977 onward, during which she was hospitalized ten times—twice as an outpatient, eight times for stays ranging from two to twenty-eight days. Since 1972 she was hospitalized thirteen times, beginning with the long stay occasioned by the bacterial infection (endocarditis, according to the diagnosis) she spoke of earlier. She continued to suffer from a malignant blood disorder, which made her extremely susceptible to viral infections. She was never told of the seriousness or complexity of her illnesses.* J.A.D.

the auditorium, I needed an escort. During this particular session, I asked Bob to have one of his staff members help me. He promised one, but the next evening—a Wednesday, midway through the sessions—no one was there to help me. My walking, which to my embarrassment had been reduced to an almost childlike gait, caused me to have to spend as much as a half hour to go from the auditorium to the car when the sessions were over. With no escort to help me—even though Bob had promised one—I was absolutely exhausted by the time I got to the car. On top of everything else, I had a virus that kept getting worse; throughout the judging sessions my temperature rarely went below 101°.

That night as I lay in bed, sick and unable to sleep, I couldn't get my mind off Bob Collinge and his thoughtless treatment of me. This wasn't the first time I'd been hurt by his slights and rude treatment, but I was upset and I couldn't find any acceptable reason for his behavior. Though it was past midnight, I phoned Hugh Johns; I was both hurt and angry and it showed throughout our long conversation. I told him that I was going to confront Bob the next evening and get all of this out in the open.*

When I did confront him, he was soothing and cooperative for the moment, even promising me an escort for the rest of the sessions. Things went fairly well until the final session, when a deep sense of duty kept me there, despite a temperature of 103°—enough to make me almost delirious at certain moments. At the close of the session, when balloting was to begin, Bob announced another change of plans: instead of deliberating in the auditorium, as we always had, he was going to move us to a room beneath the Peabody's stage—an area accessible only by a rather steep, winding stairway. He did this even though he knew I couldn't negotiate staircases anymore—I'd even had a convalescent "elevator chair" installed at Villa Pace. It was hard for me not to see this as a calculated move to keep me out of the deliberations.

I was too sick to protest, so Elayne acted for me.

First, she got two of Bob's assistants to try to help me from my seat, hoping that once I was on my feet I might be able to at least talk to Bob and see if he might let the judges deliberate in the auditorium. When that failed—I was so ill I fell to the floor when the two men lifted me—Elayne implored Bob to leave things as they were.

"We don't need her," he told her rudely. "Just send her ballots downstairs."

Elayne would have none of this. She threatened to go directly to the judges if he didn't inform them that I wasn't in any condition to negotiate the stairs.

---

* *Johns recalled that the call came at 1:30 A.M. and lasted till 4:30 A.M., when he reluctantly told her that he had to get ready for a workday. "Rosa was very upset when she called, and I felt bad that my own schedule—I had to be at work at 7 A.M.—had prevented me from staying after most of the sessions, so I could help escort her. She was very upset about Collinge because she felt he was being disrespectful to her. She didn't mean 'disrespectful' because she was Rosa Ponselle. She said to me, 'He doesn't respect me in any way—not as a woman, nor as an elderly woman, nor as a woman who is sick enough to be in a hospital.' Nor could she understand why any of his staff let these indignities happen. Over and over she said, 'It's just not the same company it used to be!' "* J.A.D.

Bob knew from past dealings that Elayne was decisive, and that when she said she would do something she meant it. Wisely, he asked the other judges to return to the auditorium. Once they saw how sick I was, they were only too happy to stay with me. At the end of our deliberations we declared Maria de Castro Alberti, a fine young artist with a promising *lirico-spinto* voice, the winner of the auditions.

After the auditorium had emptied, I sat awaiting the escort Bob had promised. Though I was feverish and weak, I managed to spend a small amount of time talking with Miss Alberti, who told me that she had been a longtime admirer of my recordings. Elayne and her mother and one of my maids, Betty Thompson, were waiting with me, gathering up my belongings. Just as I was in the midst of my brief talk with Miss Alberti, Bob ordered the lights turned off in the auditorium—another example of sheer thoughtlessness on his part, as he could see very plainly that I was sitting there.

In the darkness of the auditorium, I waited and waited for the promised escort. No one came.

When it became clear that I would have to get to the car with no male help, Elayne brought the car to the Charles Street side of the auditorium. When she came back inside, she, her mother, and my maid tried to lift me from my seat but couldn't. I was too weak to try to stand. One of the Peabody's security guards, an elderly fellow, also helped but to no avail. Though they were able to get me to the edge of my seat, I collapsed on the floor and couldn't get up.

I had no alternative but to crawl on my hands and knees from my seat to the closest exit.

I crawled to the door facing Charles Street. I hoped and prayed that I'd be spared the embarrassment of having to crawl down the sidewalk to the car. I couldn't believe that Bob Collinge, even in his worst moments, could have allowed this to happen to me—especially when he'd promised over and over that there would be someone there to help me.

At the door the elderly guard again tried to help me to my feet, but I collapsed on the sidewalk.

Elayne, Henriette, and my maid were helpless to do anything, much as they tried. At this point I was so delirious I hardly knew where I was.

During those humiliating moments, as I lay on the sidewalk, several passersby thought they recognized me. Several of them helped get me into the car, ending that part of the ordeal.

Elayne had phoned ahead to Villa Pace, where Bette Hankin and her son were waiting for us. All of them tried to help me from the car to the house, but I fell at the entranceway and couldn't get up. Elayne quickly called an ambulance and soon I was on my way to the emergency room of the St. Joseph's Hospital.

I was finally released one month and three days later.

While I was in the hospital I thought things over and felt the time had

As Carmen, in the Card Scene in Act III.
The costume, designed by Valentina, had a burgundy appliqué.
I sang this scene more slowly than most other Carmens,
at Albert Carré's suggestion. "This is the only place
where a truly beautiful voice can unfold in *Carmen*," he said.
"You have the reserve of breath to shape these phrases broadly."

Our *gran signor,* Giulio Gatti-Casazza, at the farewell party
I gave in honor aboard the S.S. *Rex,* 1935.
Seated at Gatti's left is his wife, Rosina Galli.
Carmela is standing behind him,
and at far left is Edith Mason.

At the London premiere of Romano Romani's *Fedra,*
Covent Garden, 1931. My costume was gold, and the toga
purple and gold. Most of the jewelry was of blue sapphires
set in bronze. Later, I donated the costume to the
museum at Covent Garden.

Backstage at the
my first *La Vestale*
Metropolitan performan
hair, in keepin
in Florence I play
a slight break with tra

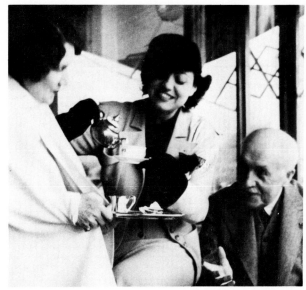

With Marguerite and Albert Carré while I was
preparing *Carmen*, taken at
the Grand Hotel, St. Moritz, June 1935.

unale, Florence, after
ɔ *Musicale* in 1933. In my
I played her with short dark
al tradition. But
ɪng, light brown hair—
a more pleasing effect.

Santuzza, as I portrayed her
near the close of my career. Valentina
designed this costume in 1935.

With Carle and his parents, Mayor and Mrs. Jackson,
backstage at the Lyric Theater in Baltimore after *Carmen*, April 4, 1936.

With Carle as newlyweds, New York City, December 1936.

With *(left to right)* Edward Arnold, Boris Morros, and George Jessel in Hollywood, 1939.
I was negotiating both with M-G-M and Paramount for a film version of *Carmen*.

At a Hollywood gathering in 1936, with *(left to right)*
Gladys Swarthout, Irene Dunne, Grace Moore, and Rhea (Mrs. Clark) Gable.

Backstage at the Hollywood Bowl, after a concert I sang in 1938.

On the M-G-M lot, with Clark Gable and Joan Crawford
still in costume from an afternoon's shooting. At Joan's left is Louis B. Mayer.

The music room in use. An informal recording session in the early 1950s, supervised by Addison Foster *(left)*, with Nino Romani at the piano. RCA Victor's engineers used almost the same placements for the microphones and piano when they recorded me in October 1954.

The music room of Villa F
Gold is the predominant c
to the sculpted-gold carpe
of hand-pa

The master bedroom, as it appeared in 1955. A silver and crystal crucifix is set into the tufted white silk headboard. The mauve-colored draperies at one end of the room open to a panoramic view of the rolling hills of the Greenspring Valley.

Seated at the piano
The piano, a gift of the k
to compleme

n from the foyer.
he Scalamandré draperies
ulted ceiling is made
t panels.

The dining room at Villa Pace.
High-backed chairs finished in blue leather accent the
hand-carved walnut table. Gold draperies match the gold silk
Fortuny wall coverings. The ceiling, like the music room's,
is of hand-painted walnut panels.

oom at Villa Pace, 1941.
ny, was custom-designed
oom's décor.

A summertime luxury—my spring-fed swimming pool,
which I have enjoyed since 1941. A large ceramic clamshell
was the source of the aerating fountain when this was taken
in 1956. The intricate wrought-iron gatework came
from my Manhattan penthouse.

Informal portrait taken on my seventieth birthday, January 22, 1967, in the foyer of Villa Pace. The staircase, which is dominated by deep blue Cuban tiles set into the steps, leads to a balcony that surrounds most of the foyer. One of my pleasures has always been to vocalize from the balcony or from the stairs, because of the foyer's marvelous acoustics.

come for me to resign. My health was far less a factor than the insensitive treatment I was receiving at Bob Collinge's hands.

I phoned him and invited him to dinner at my home, where we could talk things over calmly. We were to dine at seven. The hour came and went. Eight, then nine o'clock passed, with no phone call or any other word from Bob. He never came.

When he failed to call the next day to apologize, I phoned him and spoke very directly. "In view of the way things have been going lately, Bob, I think it's time I resigned as Artistic Director. I want to resign in a quiet, orderly way, so that I don't hurt any of the company's dealings."

I knew that the Opera was still using my name for fund-raising purposes, so I didn't want to undermine any of their campaigns.

Bob spoke up. "We want you to stay," he told me. "Now, just as much as ever, the Opera Company needs you."

I admit I was rather taken aback by this, though I found it reassuring. I agreed to stay on, but I stressed to Bob that my uncertain health would prevent my accepting any responsibilities that would require me to deal with the public. He said he understood and would respect my wishes.

He did—for a while. But in 1979—when, as he knew, I had been very ill and had been in and out of the hospital—he committed me without my knowledge to the honorary chairmanship of a major arts festival in Baltimore. I learned about it when Bob's staff finally got around to forwarding a congratulatory letter from the festival's director, thanking me for accepting and asking me to contact him so that we could coordinate our schedules. I sent word to him that I was too ill to accept such an important responsibility, though I would lend my name to it, if that would help. Fortunately, my dear friend Licia Albanese came to my aid and represented me to the festival's committee.

For some time Bob and his staff had been handling the mail I received at the Opera Company's offices. They had often been lax in forwarding it to Villa Pace—which often caused me problems. When a whole year's efforts at remedying the situation got me nowhere, I turned the matter over to Michael Abromaitis, my attorney, who asked Bob in writing to forward my personal mail unopened, within a reasonable time of its arrival at the Opera's offices.

Michael's letter yielded this blunt response from Bob, dated May 29, 1979:

> Your letter *re* Rosa's mail has arrived and to comply with the request poses for us some problems . . . Although she no longer takes an active role in the company's operations, we have continued her listing as a tribute to her and as a means of keeping her name before the public. Personal mail is always referred to Villa Pace as are requests for personal auditions, autographs, records, photos, personal appearances, etc.
>
> To comply with the request in your letter would create an extra

expense for the Opera Company in the cost of double handling of such business mail and the added postage involved as well as the loss of time in handling routine business matters.

The only way I can see to prevent such an inefficient handling of the company's business would be to remove Rosa as Artistic Director. Her inactivity in the past several years because of her illness creates the false impressions that she is still active in the Opera Company's artistic management. (As I said before, her name is there as an honor to her.)

Under such circumstances all Ponselle mail would be personal and could be then forwarded to Villa Pace unopened. If this avenue is acceptable to Rosa, please let us know and we shall be happy to comply. Please know however that it will take several months to delete Rosa's name from all national listings. I await your further reply.

If ever I had needed written evidence of Bob Collinge's callousness, this letter was it. Sick as I was, I couldn't believe that his way of dealing with a simple administrative problem was to declare that my resignation would be the most effective way to solve it. Some part of me could have accepted his convoluted logic if he hadn't added the insulting aside, "we have continued her listing as a tribute to her *and as a means of keeping her name before the public.*" God forbid if all that kept me from being forgotten by the public was Bob Collinge's efforts to keep my name before them! This hurt me more than I can say—it hurt my pride and insulted my intelligence. It forced me to make a decision, and I made it. I resigned.

Though I had no way of knowing it at the time, neither Harry B. ("Gus") Cummings, Chairman of the Board of Trustees, nor any of his colleagues on the board had seen the Collinge letter until its contents appeared in a newspaper story written by columnist Stephen Cera. Gus, whose sensitivity and guidance I had always admired, begged me to reconsider. As a first step to resolving problems he asked me to put in writing any and all concerns I might have. On June 22, 1979, I signed a long draft that Elayne prepared for me, at my direction. "As to my reasons for my decision to resign," I wrote, "the Collinge letter speaks for itself. Since there is repeated reference to the usage of 'us' in the contents of the letter, I assumed it to be conveying the sentiments of the Board as well. I did not for a moment think that Mr. Collinge would have acted unilaterally without the acknowledgment and approval of the Board." By this time, of course, Michael Abromaitis had, on my instructions, already delivered my resignation in writing. Gus's invitation for me to air my concerns at least afforded a way for me to communicate directly with the board, without the filtering and misrepresentation of Bob Collinge and some of the staff with which he surrounded himself.

Unfortunately for all of us, the details of my resignation spilled into the columns of the Baltimore *Sun* and *News American*. Because Collinge was so clearly at fault in the incident that triggered my decision, I felt that the board should make some sort of apology to me in the press. Unwisely, Bob had made some disparaging remarks to reporters. At a special meeting during the last week of June 1979, the trustees agreed to clarify my position as Artistic Director in relation to Collinge's as General Manager. But the group hesitated to oppose his actions, at least in any public statements. Instead, in a conciliatory letter addressed to me by Board President Donald L. DeVries and by Gus Cummings as Board Chairman, the trustees made a nominal attempt to calm things down. They made clear that they wanted me to stay on as Artistic Director, or to assume the title "Artistic Director Emeritus" or any similar title I might be happy with. They added a proviso that they would send a small delegation to interview me about my intentions. Unfortunately, my health continually prohibited it.*

Apart from my personal differences with Bob Collinge, I was still deeply concerned about the future direction of the company. As before, I did not want to do anything that would jeopardize the board's planning. Though I let my resignation stand, I was willing to accept the emeritus title, as my name might still be useful for fund-raising campaigns. But because I felt so strongly about the developmental philosophy I had stood for, I asked the board if, as part the details of my vacating my current title, I could propose a successor. Naturally, I had in mind someone whose artistic stature would parallel my own, someone who would share my basic philosophy. When after an unwarranted lapse of time this too fell through, I concluded my dealings with the Baltimore Opera Company.

If there is an unsettling postscript to all of this, it is that Elayne became the brunt of criticism over my resignation—not just from Collinge and his staff but even from a few of my friends. They should know better, because they are aware how much her care and dedication have meant to my comfort. For nine years she has administered every aspect of my daily life—from overseeing my business affairs with my attorneys and trust officers, to selecting and supervising my nursing and household staffs, to seeing to it that during my many hospital stays I have had every conceivable comfort, and the best possible care. She has done all this with a thoroughness and professionalism that are beyond criticism.

I accept a certain amount of the blame for any stress or concern my resignation might have caused my friends, my associates, or the loyal supporters of the company who have been at my side over the past thirty years. I accept some of the blame because I tolerated slights and abuse from Bob Collinge for too

---

* *Ponselle had no more than received DeVries' and Cummings' letter when she suffered a series of strokes on July 3–4, 1979, leaving her with impaired speech for several months afterward. Somewhat earlier, major abdominal surgery had been required to relieve an intestinal problem. During her long hospitalization and recovery, on written orders from her physician, Aidan E. Walsh, M.D., visits of any stressful nature were prohibited. This precluded her meeting with the Opera Board to resolve any conflicts with Collinge.* J.A.D.

many years before I went through with my resignation. I stayed on because since my retirement from the Metropolitan nothing has meant more to me than the discovery and nurturing of young talent. When I did resign it was because I saw in black-and-white prose, over Bob Collinge's signature, that I was being kept on not because I had anything artistic to contribute any longer, but only because my title was "an honor" to me. When the Board of Trustees acquiesced, even to the point of not appearing willing to have me recommend a successor, there was nothing further for me to say or do.

Yet I learned an important lesson from all of it, a lesson about decisiveness. As I look back upon my eighty-four years, on three occasions I have been in stressful situations that required me to be decisive. On two of those occasions— my dealings with Eddie Johnson and the Met in 1937, and my marital problems with Carle ten years later—I couldn't bring myself to face reality and make a final decision. As a result, I let events dictate to me, not vice versa.

This time, I made a decision and let it stand.

My troubles with Bob Collinge aside, my life has been very rewarding over the past several years. It has been especially rewarding to become aware, through articles, books, and other sources of critical analysis which friends have sent me, that I seem to have made a lasting mark on performing in our time. Harold C. Schonberg particularly flattered me with this assessment of my singing, written when I turned seventy:

> She had the low notes of a contralto, and a knock-out high-C. And there were no artificial registers in the voice—it went from bottom to top in the smoothest, most seamless of scales, with no shifting from chest to head. And that trill: that articulated br-r-r-r- which no singer today is able to come near matching! And the emotionalism of her singing, combined with good taste! And the power when she let loose! And the delicacy of her pianissimos! And the flexibility in coloratura work! And the accuracy of intonation! And the handsome figure onstage!

How many of Mr. Schonberg's exclamations are merited? I can't honestly say. Certainly, some must be true; I can't dismiss them as sheer flattery heaped on an aging soprano by a benevolent critic. (Mr. Schonberg, being a distinguished critic, is not especially known for benevolence anyway!) Nor can I dismiss Tullio Serafin's statement, at the end of his long and productive life, that he had known but three miracles in singing: Caruso, Ruffo, and Ponselle. I can be far more objective about Caruso and Ruffo than I can about myself; but I'm proud that Serafin included me in their illustrious company.

Thinking about whatever assets I might have had, I am aware that the unusual quality of my voice is what gave me an immediate edge over some of my colleagues, especially with the critics. I can't, of course, claim any credit for my voice. What made it unusual (and Mr. Schonberg's comments allude to this) was its color and range. Its color was distinctive because my timbre was dark and could take on the hues of a mezzo or contralto, yet I had the flexibility and ease of a lyric soprano. My range was unusual because of my low tones; in my prime I could sing from the equivalent of the male bass-baritone range, through the soprano's high D flat, in an unbroken sequence of scales.*

Physiologically, I have no idea what accounts for my voice. There was no history of it in our family, although someone who checked Papa's roots in Italy claimed there was a priest among the Ponzillos, supposedly a monsignor, who had a fine baritone voice. During my career my singing was the object of much analysis, but the results never told me anything special. One researcher took an impression of my oral cavity and found it was larger than any other soprano's he had measured. (Elisabeth Rethberg, incidentally, had the smallest.) Other than verifying that I had a big mouth (so to speak) I don't know what that proved.

Another time, a newspaper photographer took a sequence of shots of me singing a scale. What the photos showed was hardly a surprise: I opened my mouth wider for the high C than I did for a middle C. Any singer would do that.

In my case, since I haven't sung in public for more than forty years, phonograph records—and sometimes rather primitive ones, at that—are the only evidence of what I sang like. Some comments about my recordings are therefore in order. I've often been asked by interviewers whether I listen to my records now that I am retired and have the time to study them leisurely. The truth is, I don't; in fact, I don't even own that many of them.

It's not that I dislike them—although there are several that I *do* dislike. It's just that they mean less to me than they would to someone else. I think most singers feel that way about their recordings. Phonograph records, like photographs, are artifacts that enable us to recapture moments in the past. They're valuable if only for that reason. But they strike you differently if you were there, if you were the one in the snapshots—or, in my case, the one on the recordings. Because I was the one doing the performing, and because I'm blessed with a good memory, my records aren't as significant to me as they seem to be to others.

My recording career began in the spring of 1918, under Nino Romani's direction at the Columbia Graphophone Company's studios in the Woolworth Building in Manhattan. The very first title I recorded (though it wasn't meant for release commercially) was the "Pace, pace mio Dio" from *Forza del destino*. Not long ago that unpublished "take," as it was called, was located; since then, it has been rerecorded and released privately to collectors.

---

* See the Discography, *p. 263, for Ponselle's 1954 RCA recording of Farley's "The Night Wind," on which she sings a rapid descending scale from high A natural to a bass-baritone's low D.* J.A.D.

God forbid that anyone should have to make recordings the way we did then!

The strongest memory I have of my early recording sessions is of the gigantic clock that every studio sported. The clock was the god we were taught to worship and everything we recorded had to be tailored to fit it. At the time a standard 78 rpm record played anywhere from three to five minutes, depending on the diameter of the disc. That meant that virtually everything we wanted to record, from simple songs to operatic ensembles, had to be sung in less than five minutes. Because of time limitations we were forced to speed up tempos or sometimes leave out entire pages of the score.

And we were limited in other ways. In lieu of a microphone (this, remember, was well before the days of amplifiers, microphones, and the other paraphernalia that eventually became commonplace in recording studios), we had to sing into a funnel-shaped metal horn. The horn fed the sound to a thin, pliable diaphragm that had a cutting stylus attached to it. When sound waves from the voice or from the instruments of the studio orchestra struck the diaphragm, it would vibrate, then the cutting stylus would engrave impressions of the sound onto a thick wax disc. Primitive as it was, that's how we made recordings before 1925—and, frankly, few were truly representative of our voices and artistry.

Among the records I made under the old process ("acoustical recording," it was called) were the ones I did for the Columbia Company between 1918 and 1923. Those available to listeners on today's long-playing discs are, among others, the "Selva opaca" from *William Tell*, "Mi chiamano Mimi" from *Bohème*, "Voi lo sapete" from *Cavalleria rusticana*, "Il va venir" from *La Juive*, "Elsas Traum" from *Lohengrin*, "Un bel di vedremo" from *Madama Butterfly*, "In quelle trine morbide" from *Manon Lescaut*, "Scenes That Are the Brightest" from *Maritana*, the "Ballatella" from *Pagliacci*, "A Song of India" from *Sadko*, "Vissi d'arte" from *Tosca*, and the "Bolero" from *I Vespri siciliani*—none of which I rerecorded, and many of which I never sang in the opera house.

Of them I like the *Tell* recording best. Also special to me is the *Trovatore* duet I recorded at Columbia with my friend and colleague Riccardo Stracciari. Although the record doesn't do justice to either of us, it gives a hint of the diamond-like brilliance of his voice and of the fire we struck as Count di Luna and Leonora. Unfortunately, the limitations of the old process prevented our being as communicative as we might have been.

Columbia had Carmela and me record some of the high points of our vaudeville act. "O sole mio," which we recorded in September 1921, is one of our finest duet recordings and is sung just as we performed it on the Keith Circuit. The "Barcarolle" from *Les Contes d'Hoffmann* was also part of our act; so is "Comin' Thro' the Rye," which we made in 1919 using the arrangement I wrote for our vaudeville debut. In all of these Columbia duets (and later a Schubert "Serenade" we made at Victor in 1926) the "family resemblance" in our timbres is evident. I regret that we didn't record other operatic duets.

The first real operatic recording I made by the new process turned out to be a best-seller: the Tomb Scene from *Aida,* which I recorded with Giovanni Martinelli, the most popular Radames of the day. Actually, we had first recorded together in *Aida* in the winter of 1924; we did both the Tomb Scene and parts of the Nile Scene. Neither of us liked them, so they were never approved for public release. Two years later Victor brought us together again to record an electrical version of the Tomb Scene. This one, though it was better than the 1924 one, was still unsatisfactory to me. My main concern was that our voices sounded out of balance. Finally, the Victor executives set up a conference-type phone call so that we could all talk about the discs.

"Look, Rosa," Martinelli said to me, "it's great singing, and the public will accept the balance problem."

I okayed their release, and, needless to say, he was right.

Among my Victor electric discs I like the "Pace, pace mio Dio," "Ernani, involami" from *Ernani,* "Ritorna vincitor" from *Aida,* the Finale from *Forza del destino* with Martinelli and Pinza, and my two recordings from *La Vestale,* "Tu che invoco" and "O nume tutelar."

As to ones I don't particularly like, I'm not very fond of Martinelli's and my "Miserere" from *Trovatore* (there too the balance could have been a lot better), nor do I like my Victor electrical recording of the "Casta Diva" from *Norma.* (My best *Norma* recording is the "Mira, o Norma!" duet with Marion Telva.) I positively dislike the "Vergine degli angeli" with Pinza. An anonymous engineer, not content with letting my voice record *piano* (the way a prayer should be sung), boosted the volume so that it would match Pinza's. That destroyed the effect I wanted to achieve and I've never liked the record because of it.

Among those of my other Red Seals I like are the two arias I recorded from *Otello*—the lovely "Ave Maria" and the "Salce, salce" made in 1924; though they were made by the old process, they are good performances by my standards. Several songs also number among my favorites. I like my Red Seal issues of such Italian gems as "Maria, Mari'," "Luna d'estate," and " 'A vucchella"; among sacred songs I particularly favor the Bach-Gounod "Ave Maria" I recorded under Rosario Bourdon's baton in 1926. Though I made a number of "Ave Maria" recordings over the years (including, in my Columbia days, the one adapted from the "Intermezzo" to *Cavalleria rusticana*), I like best my record of the Bach-Gounod prayer.

Those who prefer the simplicity of the Franz Schubert "Ave Maria" must go to my radio broadcasts and private recordings for the best version I made. Though I recorded it commercially for RCA Victor in 1939, while Carle and I were living in Hollywood, I wasn't pleased with the disc and am now sorry that Nino Romani (who accompanied me in my last Red Seal 78s) and I didn't rerecord it. I completely missed the mood of the piece.

Many of my radio appearances were recorded, all or in part, and most have since been released on special collectors' labels. In the early 1930s, when I was doing most of my radio work, the networks and sponsors commissioned what were called "airchecks"; these were off-the-air recordings that were done mainly to check the balance of the sound and the smoothness of a program. Artists sometimes commissioned airchecks too, but I rarely did. Fortunately, Larry Tibbett was farsighted enough to have our January 1935 *Traviata* recorded (it was a Saturday matinee broadcast, sponsored by Listerine in those days), which enabled my Violetta to be heard after we'd all assumed it had been lost.

From 1931 to 1937 I sang Metropolitan broadcasts of *Norma, Il Trovatore, Don Giovanni, L'Africaine, La Traviata,* and *Carmen,* all of which might exist somewhere, someplace; so far only the *Carmens* (four in all, one splendidly rerecorded for the Metropolitan "Historic Broadcast" series by Dario Soria and RCA in 1980), fragments of a *Don Giovanni* (missing, sadly, the "Non mi dir" aria), and the *Traviata* have been located.

Listeners to these and other Metropolitan broadcasts from the mid-1930s may be tempted to think they were among the first done of full operas. Actually, one of the first was a January 1910 *Tosca* with Olive Fremstad in the title role. In that same period, under Dr. Lee DeForest's supervision, a Caruso *Pagliacci* was broadcast, also from the Met stage. Both of these could only be heard within a radius of forty to fifty miles. By the time Carmela, Anna Roselle, Dimitri Dobkin, and León Rothier broadcast *Aida* from the Bronx in 1923, the radius had been extended to a thousand miles. Regular broadcasts of the now familiar "Saturday matinee" format began with a Christmas Day performance of *Hansel and Gretel* in 1931. At first, either (and sometimes both) Deems Taylor or Milton Cross served as commentators, crowding in their running descriptions of the action whenever the orchestra played several measures on its own. By 1933, Milton was on his way to the longest-running program in the history of radio, with his plot summaries and insightful comments being limited to the beginning of each act.

Although I can't place my very first radio appearance as a solo artist, I can remember listening to Frances Alda, Geraldine Farrar, Margarete Matzenauer, Maria Jeritza, and Mary Garden on the radio. The earliest of my appearances that I can document was on New Year's Eve 1928. Between then and May 1938, I can confirm twenty-nine radio appearances. Many were on *The General Motors Hour,* where a typical program might include the "Habanera" from *Carmen,* "Pace, pace mio Dio" from *Forza,* and the "Casta Diva" from *Norma,* which I might follow with piano-accompanied versions of "The Nightingale and the Rose," the "Swiss Echo Song," and Sadero's "Tuscan Lullaby." Often I would appear with the Metropolitan Opera Orchestra and Chorus, under Giulio Setti's direction.

All of these broadcasts originated from theaters in the Times Square area of Manhattan, and there were no real rehearsals for any of them. A full audience attended each broadcast, with tickets provided merely for the asking by the sponsor. Because all programs originated live in those days, two broadcasts were necessary—one for the Eastern and Midwestern audiences, and an identical one transmitted from three to five hours later for the West Coast. In my case, I had to turn over the delayed broadcast to other artists who sang their own selections (usually Lawrence Tibbett, but sometimes the golden-voiced Grete Stueckgold) as I found it impossible to summon the same mood twice in so short a span of time. Had my second program been different, I could have done it easily. But the networks required the same content for both coasts. As a result, until I did a coast-to-coast radio tour with Milton Cross—culminating in Hollywood, where we were fêted by Mary Pickford, Edward G. Robinson, and other friends and acquaintances from the film world—my voice was never heard live on radio on the West Coast.

My fondest memories of radio involve André Kostelanetz, whom I remember from the Metropolitan when he was courting Lily Pons. He was a thorough student, and his arms were always filled with opera and symphonic scores, which he would pore over while Lily rehearsed. By the mid-1930s, along with Frank Black, Gus Haenschen, Don Voorhees, Eugene Ormandy (who began as a young associate of Black's and Haenschen's in the recording industry), and Nathaniel Shilkret, André was one of the most important personalities in classical, light classical, and popular music as it was heard on radio. He did much to spread an understanding and acceptance of serious music among average listeners.

André was a complete musician who had both the technical facility and the inspiration to produce outstanding orchestrations on short notice. I thought his arrangement both beautiful and complementary to the singing voice, always enhancing but never detracting from the vocal line. As a "singer's conductor" he was in a class second only to Serafin; he was sensitive to any problems that arose, and he encouraged a spontaneous give-and-take that added immeasurably to the quality of his programs. His absolute reliability and perfect command of the orchestra gave a singer complete confidence—a necessary ingredient for the singer, considering the lack of rehearsal time and the pressures of live performing.

A few years ago, in *Opera News,* as I recall, André talked about our broadcasts together and mentioned that he had discovered a sort of "stereo" effect in his attempt to place microphones to pick up my voice. Whereas most sopranos were "miked" close-up, so that they sang almost directly into the microphone, the resonance of my voice, owing to the acoustics of the Manhattan Theatre, from which our shows originated, made my full tone very hard to capture. To try to remedy the problem, André experimented with several microphone placements, ultimately deciding that my voice sounded best when it was picked up by a microphone in the second or third row of the audience. He and his engineers would then mix this microphone with the ones used for the orchestra onstage. The effect gave my voice the full resonance that studio audiences were used to, because of the room resonance of the hall; as a result, my appearances with André on *The Chesterfield Hour* (which, I should say, was a sustained program with me as the only guest for a number of seasons) were often superior in sound to my other radio appearances—including my Met broadcasts, which contain some irregular dynamics because of the placement of the microphones in relation to my changing positions onstage.

All in all I'm pleased with those of my radio appearances which have survived, and I'm always delighted when another one is located by a fan.

I confess that the only time I thoroughly enjoyed making recordings was in the autumn of 1954, when RCA Victor offered me a contract to make two long-playing albums of songs. This time, there was no traveling to Camden, New Jersey, RCA's home studios, and no rearranging my schedule to record in Liederkranz Hall in Manhattan, which Victor used as a studio in the late 1920s. Instead, RCA brought the studio to me: the master recordings were all made at Villa Pace.

The contract came about in an interesting way. In September 1952, "Ike" Eisenhower was running for the presidency; he and Mamie were friends of mine, so he asked me to join them at a Baltimore rally. John Charles Thomas had been engaged to sing to the crowd until Ike and Mamie made their appearance. John got the crowd in hand with "Home on the Range," "Danny Boy," and other gems until he practically ran out of songs. He knew I was in the audience so he took a chance.

"There's a little girl here tonight, a little girl I sang with at my Metropolitan Opera debut in *La Traviata* many years ago," he said to the audience. "I wonder if you might help me persuade her to come to the microphone."

Several minutes of deafening applause followed me to the stage; hastily I asked John what he wanted me to sing. We agreed to do a harmonized "Old Folks at Home," and it went reasonably well. Then I sang Schubert's "Ave Maria," a favorite of Ike's. Unknown to me, my voice was being carried over loudspeakers outside. Ike and Mamie were just arriving in their limousine.

"That's Rosa," he said to Mamie. "I'd know her voice anywhere."

Once he was safely inside the auditorium, I thought fast and brought him to the stage in a rather creative way. I launched into the popular "Some Enchanted Evening" from *South Pacific*. Overhead was a massive portrait of Ike. When I came to the end of the song I changed the lyrics and pointed upward: "Now *we* have found him . . . Never let him go!" It brought the crowd to its feet, and Ike to the stage, all in the same moment.

An admirer of mine, Lloyd Garrison, recorded my appearance at the rally and had a private album made of it, at my request. It was titled *Rosa's Christmas Gift,* and I had one hundred copies of it printed in long-playing form, which I gave that year as Christmas presents. The album made its way to RCA through friends and admirers. The next year, 1953, Lloyd and an associate, Cass Falkanar, recorded an impromptu Christmas concert at Villa Pace; I sang, as did many of the Opera's young singers, and even Carmela sang. I had long-playing discs made from these master tapes and allowed them to be sold to raise money for the Baltimore Symphony. These also made their way to New York City and soon I received inquiries from Capitol Records and RCA Victor. Since Victor had been my artistic "home" on phonograph records since 1923, I went with past loyalties and agreed to talk with their representatives. Soon we signed a contract.

The recording engineers arrived on October 17, 1954 and began setting up their equipment in the dining room at Villa Pace. When the first set of equipment failed (they said my voice was simply too large for what they'd brought), the engineers sent for the Philadelphia Orchestra's recording equipment and it proved ideal. The resulting LPs were very well received by the critics.*

My phonograph records, whether good or bad, convey something of my voice and a little of my artistry. I was said to have had a great voice; my recordings, especially the ones taken from radio broadcasts, captured what I had rather faithfully. But voice and artistry are separate matters. Having a great voice in no way guarantees being an artist; it guarantees only that the voice will probably appeal to an audience. Artistry is something beyond that. Caruso had the formula for it. He gave it to anyone who asked him what it took to become an artist.

"Work, work, and again, work," he used to say.

Part of what artistry involves is probably inborn. The rest is an alchemy of self-confidence, willpower, proper guidance, and, as Caruso said, hard work. For nineteen seasons at the Metropolitan, from *Forza del destino* through *Carmen,* I tried to achieve that alchemy. Whether I succeeded, only history, not I, can judge.

---

* *This is an understatement, to be sure. "That Ponselle should have agreed to emerge from her self-imposed retirement and to record again for RCA Victor is a surprise and a very heartwarming one," wrote record critic Aida Favia-Artsay when* Rosa Ponselle Sings Today *was released in the spring of 1955. "But that she should make her comeback with the freshness of voice she had at the zenith of her career—that is staggering!" One of Ponselle's favorite tributes to her new LP came from a different source. "I have just played your recording and, next to Eleanor Roosevelt perhaps, I think you are the most wonderful woman in America," the writer said. Typewritten on* The Carolina Israelite *stationery, the letter was signed by its tough-minded editor, Harry Golden.* J.A.D.

POSTSCRIPT

THE PUBLIC LAST glimpsed Rosa Ponselle in January 1979, when she turned eighty-two. Her birthday was marked by a week-long series of tributes. On January 20, during its telecast of Verdi's *Luisa Miller,* the Metropolitan Opera paid tribute to her on national television. The late Francis Robinson narrated and co-produced the segment, interweaving photographs, recordings, her M-G-M screen test as Carmen, and footage from a CBS filmed interview on her eightieth birthday. Two nights later, on January 22, Joan Sutherland, Richard Bonynge, and Luciano Pavarotti, through announcer Martin Bookspan, conveyed birthday wishes during their joint concert on public television. At the end of the week ("Rosa Ponselle Week" in Baltimore, as the city's mayor officially pronounced it), the Peabody Institute paid tribute to her in a standing-room-only event that featured some of the singers to whom she had been a mentor.

Maryland's Democratic senator, Paul R. Sarbanes, was on the dais at the Peabody event and conveyed a tribute from the White House. The day before, Sarbanes' Republican colleague, Senator Charles Mathias, awarded her a special congressional citation for her prominent role in American music.

As a gesture of thanks and a way of raising funds for the Peabody, Ponselle allowed Villa Pace to be opened to the public for three hours a day during that special week. The last time Villa Pace had been opened to the public was in 1962. In the intervening years a new generation had grown up and was curious about the Mediterranean estate and its infrequently seen owner. They toured all but the kitchen wing and servants' quarters in the cross-shaped villa, admiring the art works and antiques, buying LP reissues of her recordings, taking in the expansive view from the glass doors of her bedroom's balcony, and, no doubt, hoping to see the Great Lady in person.

Though she entertained different groups of critics, reporters, and colleagues when, at two o'clock each afternoon, the doors were closed to the public, she hadn't the stamina to greet everyone in person. Rather than favor any one group of visitors, she chose to spend the mornings and early afternoons in private. Tributes and honors were, after all, hardly new to her, even in later life. In May 1965, the Peabody voted her an honorary doctor's degree—an honor that Our Lady of Notre Dame of Baltimore and, in 1980, the University of Maryland would confer in absentia. In 1968, for having "enhanced the progress and well-being of country and mankind," she was elected to the United States Hall of Fame Society. The next year, on January 27, 1969, Italy awarded her the coveted Order of the Commendatore, making her the third woman (and the first American-born) to have been so honored.

Her seventy-fifth birthday, in 1972, had been a major news event for the wire services. "It is most fitting," wrote President Nixon, in a letter widely quoted afterward, "that on your seventy-fifth birthday so many grateful citizens acknowledge the brilliant contributions you have made and the joy that your singing has brought to millions, both here and abroad." Nixon had never forgotten the moral support she had given the 1952 Eisenhower campaign.

Three years after the Nixon citation, the American Committee on Italian Migration presented her its Achievement in the Arts Award. The late Ella Grasso, governor of her home state, Connecticut, was present for the occasion. At the formal ball following the event, the lady being honored astounded everyone by giving a flawless impromptu performance of several American ballads.

Much as she treasured all these honors, she never lost sight of the fact that they were tributes not so much to the aging lady who gratefully accepted them, but to the Rosa Ponselle who had achieved stardom a half century earlier, under the long-ago tutelage of Gatti-Casazza and Caruso. In that sense, the honors merely underscored the passing of the years. Life for her had reached its twilight, and she knew it. Much as she hated to confront the thought that one day it would come to an end, circumstances made her face it. One by one her colleagues slipped away—Stracciari, Ruffo, Pinza, de Luca, and Gigli in the 1950s, Farrar, Bori, Galli-Curci, Telva, Matzenauer, Danise, Tibbett, and Martinelli in the 1960s, and nearly all the rest by the end of the 1970s. As she marked her eighty-fourth birthday in January 1981, only a handful were still living.

She grieved genuinely and deeply for them—so much so that whenever she saw portraits of former colleagues in the newspapers she would initially turn away from the page, fearing that she would be reading their obituaries. Six deaths in particular—those of Lily Pons, Lotte Lehmann, Milton Cross, André Kostelanetz, Walter Legge, and Francis Robinson—profoundly upset her. She accepted their passing as a sad fact of life. Except for the ritual of prayer, religion held no ultimate comforts for her in such circumstances. Though her basic Catholic faith made her hope for a Redeemer, and an afterlife, her experience led her toward skepticism. "To me, Jesus Christ is the one person we would all want to use as our model," she would say. "Whether or not he was God, I guess I have to leave to the theologians." She approached the issue of personal immortality much the same way: "I wish I could be sure of it, but I'm not."

Whether later or in the prime of her career, the twists and turns of Rosa Ponselle's life are relatively predictable to anyone inquiring into the people and events that shaped her basic personality. The events are reasonably few but sometimes misleading. Her childhood in Meriden is an example. A number of writers, perhaps bolstered by the imaginative accounts of her youth that her secretary or her managers provided, have suggested that music and singing were natural outgrowths of an Italian-American childhood in an essentially Italian community. The picture emerges of a Neapolitan child surrounded by native-born, transplanted Italians whose evenings were spent singing folk songs to mandolin accompaniment, and whose meager earnings might have gone to the purchase of Caruso and Tetrazzini recordings. As any ethnic historian will attest, this image of Italian-American life at the turn of the century, at least as regards life in ethnically mixed communities such as Meriden, is highly stereotypical. In Ponselle's case it is simply erroneous: except for Anna Ryan's teaching (an Irish teacher, at that) and five concerts to which her mother took Carmela and her, Ponselle's formative years were essentially non-musical. Not even the phonograph record played any part in her development. Only one family on Springdale Avenue, a family of German immigrants, owned a phonograph. Tony Ponzillo recalled that the only records its owners played were cylinders of Sousa marches.

Much of Rosa's childhood and adolescence, except for the basic values and self-image she derived from them, must be downplayed in explaining her career and adult life because Carmela, not Rosa, made most of her decisions. "My sister had all the ambition I lacked," Rosa said in numerous interviews. "She pulled me by the hand, and I went along with whatever she said. She was my sister, she knew the ropes in New York, so to me she always knew best." All of that changed when, on November 15, 1918, Rosa made her first entrance onto the Metropolitan Opera House stage.

Her debut was certainly the first key event one can point to in shaping her adult life, but it too can be misleading, since it must be understood in the context of her vaudeville career. The significance of the Ponzillo Sisters' vaudeville success is often misunderstood—as is vaudeville itself to generations weaned on radio and television, where, in particular, the world of vaudeville is portrayed in terms of straw hats, striped coats, and soft-shoe routines. Factually, Rosa and Carmela Ponzillo accomplished by the singularity of their vocal endowments a near-impossible feat in the harsh, competitive world of big-time vaudeville: in just a year and a half they went from being virtual unknowns in the Bronx to headliners at the famed Palace Theater.

Though only twenty-one when she stepped onto the Metropolitan stage opposite Caruso, Ponselle was therefore a well-seasoned stage figure to whom the sound of applause was second nature, and whose endurance as a singer had been conditioned by two-a-day vaudeville performing. Both at the Palace and on tour through the North and South, she and Carmela sang a string of opera arias, duets, and Italian songs—often twice a day, four days in a row. Then they boarded a train and went on to their next engagement. Though in a different medium, it was excellent training and discipline for a future opera singer.

The significance of her debut in *La Forza del destino* is that it propelled her into the musical medium that her singular endowments naturally fitted. (The word "propelled" is carefully chosen, in that Ponselle always felt that her voice, wherever she revealed it, led others to advance her career for her. Whether it was Anna Ryan, Jimmy Ceriani, Carmela, or, eventually, Giulio Gatti-Casazza, the fact remained that she saw herself as merely going along with others' plans for her voice. Like a perfectly endowed natural athlete, a simile she always favored, she let the trainers dictate how these natural endowments would be developed and used.) Of equal significance to the musical triumph it came to represent is the confidence-shattering effect of her Metropolitan debut. Though she pulled herself together as the performance progressed (here again her stage experience at the Palace cannot be overemphasized), it left her with a permanent case of stage fright. Fortunately, her worst fears were left behind once she got onstage, although her pre-performance nervousness never abated no matter how successfully she sang.

The severity of her nervousness, particularly in the last years of her career, has long been a matter of record. Helen Noble, in her autobiographical *Life with the Met,* provides this account of Ponselle's condition before a performance:

> She was petrified with fear each time she stood in the wings waiting for her cue. She was so nervous she made all about her nervous. She was sure she would never make her high notes—yet they always came over without fail, pure and wonderful and magnificent. It was no good for anyone to stand next to her as she waited, encouraging her, assuring her; no, she had this terrible phobia about high notes. How many times Mr. Ziegler and I would discuss it, and so many times he would say: "She sings her high notes with such ease, just like water running off a duck's back. Whatever is the matter with that woman I will never know."

The moment she got onstage, Miss Noble records, "she certainly never gave any impression of nervousness [and] always seemed in perfect command." To be sure, this offstage-onstage dichotomy is hardly unique to Rosa Ponselle; it plagued Caruso and most other great artists from whom the paying public expected absolute perfection, performance after performance.

High notes were not the source of her anxiety. Miss Noble somewhat overstates matters by labeling this rather commonplace anxiety a "terrible phobia" on Ponselle's part, although Ponselle herself did much to contribute to such a notion, especially in interviews during her retirement. On her eightieth birthday, for example, when she gave her last filmed interview, she was asked which of her roles were the hardest to sing. She replied, truthfully, that usually she had no trouble negotiating anything in an operatic score. But, her interviewer asked, what of scores with high notes? "Well, I just crossed my fingers and hoped for the best," Rosa replied. She hardly meant it seriously, but after making enough such comments over the years, some of them stuck. To be sure, in the "O patria mia" from *Aida,* she became preoccupied with the approach Verdi had written to the high C; but otherwise, either she sang what was written or, as was common then and now, she sang in a transposed key. Many of her greatest roles had abundant high notes—the high Cs in *Norma,* the D flat in *Trovatore*—and, as is evidenced by at least one aircheck from her commercial radio appearances in 1937, she was still able to sing the E flat above high C. Her fears aside, her technique made her high notes secure. Plus which, as with any artist of her caliber, while she was singing her attention was focused on the meaning of the text. In such moments, the placement of notes on a musical staff was psychologically unimportant.

The root of her fears lay not in anything as fundamental as high notes, but rather in the awesome responsibility she felt when she was engaged by the Metropolitan. To view this responsibility in the same proportions that she came to view it is first to distinguish fact from fiction in the "legend" that quickly surrounded her phenomenal stardom. Her career was in its fourth year when her hometown newspaper, the Meriden *Daily Journal,* published this first-person account of her rise to fame:

> When I was sixteen, the course of my life was greatly influenced by the family mortgage. Oh yes, we had one and the banker, true to form, was threatening to foreclose. So when a motion picture exhibitor offered me money to sing for his patrons, I lost no time in accepting, though I did wonder if I could possibly be worth so much money.
>
> Then came a proposition from a leading hotel in New Haven— fifty dollars a week—think of it! That was too good to believe! We soon disposed of the mortgage.
>
> By this time I was nineteen. Carmela and I went into vaudeville, doing what they call 'big time.' Then we made a big sacrifice. We were both making plenty of money, but we decided to quit and devote all our time to study . . .
>
> One day a wonderful thing happened. Caruso heard me sing. Then later in the spring he arranged for me to sing before Gatti-Casazza and the Metropolitan. The next high spot in my life came when I made my Metropolitan debut . . . with Caruso in the cast.
>
> In the months following my engagement there I worked harder than I ever worked in my life, and I've slaved ever since.
>
> My story of "how I did it," you see, is just the record of a poor

girl who was forced by circumstances to reach her goal by a different path than the accepted one.

Though this account appeared under Rosa's name, it was written by Edith Prilik and was only slightly less imaginative than some of the other ones that she or Libbie Miller concocted. The story at least followed the general thread of actual events—the pathway from the nickelodeons to the Cafe Mellone in New Haven (wrongly identified as a "hotel"), to vaudeville, and finally to the Metropolitan—though most of the motives given in the story were exercises in creative thinking. Ben Ponzillo had not been hounded by creditors at the time, nor had his daughters left vaudeville to "devote all our time to study."

One paragraph in the otherwise embellished account is, however, inarguably accurate: "In the months following my engagement there I worked harder than I ever worked in my life, and I've slaved ever since." When one scrutinizes the contract she signed in June 1918, one can easily see why. The actual contract, which has only come to light recently, tends to dispel the rosy glow of wonderment that Ponselle herself (or, rather, Edith Prilik) could evoke by writing, "One day a wonderful thing happened: Caruso heard me sing." For the sum of $150 per week—less than a fourth of the Ponzillo Sisters' weekly earnings at the Palace—and for a minimum of three performances and maximum of four per week for the full Metropolitan season, Rosa agreed, in the contract's eleventh clause, "to sing and perform as the Company or its representative may require, in the following roles or parts: Aida, Leonora in 'Il Trovatore,' Santuzza in 'Cavalleria Rusticana,' Eleonora [*sic*] in 'Forza del destino,' Gioconda, Tosca, Amelia in 'Un Ballo in Maschera,' and Verdi's Requiem."

Were the list of roles not awesome enough in itself, the contract specified that five of them—*Aida, Cavalleria rusticana, Trovatore, Forza del destino,* and the Verdi *Requiem*—were "to be ready for production by the artist by November 11, 1918." It could hardly be doubted, then, that during the summer of 1918 Ponselle "worked harder than I ever worked in my life." With the hard work came the source of the eventual nervousness that marked her performing. For, unlike any other Metropolitan star of her time, Rosa Ponselle arrived without a repertoire. She had to learn new roles while performing ones she had mastered only a few months earlier. Except for *Norma,* which she took two summers to prepare, this was the pattern she followed virtually throughout her career. Over the years it took its toll.

Viewed in the light of her 1918–19 contract, her engagement can hardly be seen as a casual investment by America's foremost opera company in "a poor girl who was forced by circumstances" to pay off her family's mortgage by singing in cafes and vaudeville houses. Rather, it was a shrewd (if last-minute) investment in a stage-wise young woman whom Gatti-Casazza, in his autobiography, described as being "extremely musical and very sure of herself." But

229

in thrusting upon her the kind of responsibility she seemed to want, he and his co-administrators tapped her ungovernable sense of responsibility. Gatti personally recognized this, and helped shepherd her through the proverbial tortures of the damned she suffered every time she performed. "She is a woman who is very conscientious, carrying this quality to a point where she frequently lets it upset her," he wrote. "But onstage she is absolutely sure."

Sure of herself or not, the years of outright hard work ultimately made her long for a more balanced life—hence her abrupt departure from the Met nineteen seasons later. Strictly speaking, Ponselle never actually "retired." That final-sounding word was tacked onto her Metropolitan biography after the fact, when it was clear that she would not return to the fold. She was only forty at the time. Age, however, is only an incidental factor in the length of a career. Melba sang past sixty, Schumann-Heink past seventy, and Martinelli and Lauri-Volpi past eighty. Others were finished at fifty because their voices and techniques had endured too much punishment. Ponselle was not one of them. At her last operatic performance in April 1937 she was still in excellent form.

Why, then, did she stop performing?

"I quit because I had disagreements with the Metropolitan, and then with my manager," she has said in various interviews. "When these events and situations became hurtful, I had to stop singing. I have never been able to tolerate bad feelings. I think if it weren't for my makeup, my career would have gone on." History records otherwise—not merely that she left the Metropolitan Opera Company, but that by 1939–40 she was no longer singing in public at all.

To understand why is first to take into account that to Rosa singing and performing had become different entities. Put simply, she never lost her love for singing, but grew increasingly weary of the rigors of performing—the years-in-advance scheduling, the endless nervousness before going onstage, the incessant preoccupation with the condition of the voice, all of the worries and frustrations that conceivably plague any opera singer. Eventually, these assumed monumental proportions; yet she couldn't bring herself to say aloud—even to herself, much less to the Metropolitan—that enough was enough.

Add to this scenario her emergent role in her immediate family, a role best understood in the context of her Italian-American identity, and one has all the ingredients for a premature ending to a stellar career. Her relationships with her parents are a case in point. Her mother, to whom she was totally devoted, died in 1932, leaving her to rely for any emotional support on her father, brother, and sister. Her father evinced no interest in her career, except for the money it earned her; to no surprise, she had little respect for him. When she became a Metropolitan star, however, her success and prominence caused her to displace her father as the head of her immediate family: she, not her father, had the money, status, and power to guarantee her family's well-being. Yet with her father's shady ways, Tony's persistent money problems, and Carmela's increasing dottiness, Rosa inherited, with her power, all the worries of a surrogate parent. It was not enough to have to lead her own life; now, she had others to lead as well.

For emotional support and fatherly guidance she relied not on Ben Ponzillo, but upon Gatti, whom she tended to describe in paternalistic terms. When the sudden death of Herbert Witherspoon deprived her of another fatherly general manager after Gatti retired—and when the next in line, Edward Johnson, was little more than a tenor colleague for whom her feelings were, at best, cordial and friendly but never much else—she grew to depend on her own inner circle, including Edith Prilik, Libbie Miller, and, in the early days at least, Carmela. Then she chose for a husband a strong, independent American whose conception of marriage made no room for such live-in advisers. With Carle firmly in the picture, she soon severed ties with Libbie, Edith, Tony, and almost everyone who had been close to her during her singing career. With Carle she assumed a new identity: far away from the Italian world of Italian opera, she became a Baltimorean immersed in country-club society, the celebrity-wife of the mayor's son.

Life with Carle in the Greenspring Valley had its rewards, especially after Villa Pace was completed, but singing wasn't one of them, at least not in any formal sense. Not that she lacked for opportunities, however. Her letters to Edith from 1938 to 1941 reveal the strategy she devised to turn down any offers that came her way. Early on, the Peabody Conservatory offered her a large sum to teach. She said no, but asked them to consider Nino Romani instead. "They certainly need someone like him here," she wrote to Edith. Why not teach at the Peabody herself? "I wish I had the patience to teach, but my confounded nerves won't permit such an undertaking."

Her "confounded nerves" continued to serve her in 1939–40. That season she was offered a new recording contract by RCA Victor, a series of high-paying radio appearances by NBC—and, with Paramount still pursuing her for *Carmen,* even Hollywood still held promise. To avoid accepting any one of these options, she played one against the other: she would accept no radio offers till negotiations with RCA were completed, and she would make no commitments to RCA until any film offers were settled. It was her way of refusing without actually having to say no, without making a real decision herself.

RCA's artists-and-repertoire men persisted until she agreed to make a handful of Red Seals at the company's Hollywood studios. "I have signed with RCA Victor," she wrote to Edith not long after Romani had accompanied her in a series of takes in late-October 1939. "They want me to make an album of three *lieder,* three French, three Italian, and three English songs. *Carmen* they definitely want to record sometime this fall, either in Washington or in New York."

No such recordings ever materialized because RCA had inadvertently given her a way out. Libbie's idle threats of lawsuits afforded Rosa a reason to rule out Manhattan recording sessions. "They want me in New York," she told

Edith, "but on account of Libbie I can't go—for, as I told them, I couldn't sing while I am worrying about her lawsuit." The RCA directors then suggested Washington or, if that wasn't suitable, Philadelphia; there she could record with the Philadelphia Orchestra. Now she used economics to prevent the sessions from taking place. "If I go to Philadelphia and record with their symphony, then I must share my royalties with the orchestra. Otherwise, I can only record with piano there, which I'm not willing to do."

RCA then reminded her that she could record in Washington. "They're trying to sign up the National Symphony with Dr. Kindler," she wrote to Edith, "and in that event I can record everything in Washington." She had asked RCA for Kindler, knowing full well that the National Symphony, like the Philadelphia Orchestra, would also want a share of her royalties. When the matter came up for discussion, she rejected the National, and with it the possibility of recording in Washington. She wouldn't record with piano only, and would not, she said, "make records with just *any* orchestra."

"As for me I'm at a standstill," she wrote to Edith in 1940, after she had turned down NBC and had successfully put off RCA Victor. "If I wasn't built this way, why, I could have gone on singing," she said in a letter to Edith. "But God gave me this super-sensitive character, and I can't hope to change at this time of life. Yet when it's all over, when I regain my self-confidence, then I'll do a few concerts now and then." She was pipe-dreaming and she knew it: she did not want to perform, whether on an opera stage or a concert platform. By the time she might have wanted to, both her marriage and her emotional health were in jeopardy.

Even in retirement, Rosa's prismatic personality—her warmth, her humor, her generosity, her sincerity both as a woman and an artist—made as well as kept her a celebrity. Those close to her always remembered her easy laughter, and her invariable willingness to prick the balloon of pomposity that often surrounds the medium of opera. In March 1934, she was one of the orchestrators of a long-remembered night at the Metropolitan, a raucous burlesque called "A Half-Century of Progress." Among the attractions was Lily Pons's appearance as a two-year-old tot, wheeled around in an oversized baby carriage by Antonio Scotti; the program identified the veteran baritone as "the Metropolitan's Best Chinaman." Lauritz Melchior swathed his three-hundred-pound frame in Salome's silks and satins, and did the "Dance of the Seven Veils" with not one but five severed heads—each carefully done in the likeness of a Manhattan critic. But, said the reviewers, "comedy honors fell to Rosa Ponselle for singing an aria from *Martha* while riding a bicycle around a Gay Nineties setting of Central Park."

Bicycling, though hardly fitting the image of a prima diva, was her favorite pastime and gave her an image "more like a collegian than a famous singer," the Providence (R.I.) *Bulletin* observed in 1934. Despite the protests of Gatti-Casazza & Company, she rode everywhere, winding her way through the ribbons of traffic on Riverside Drive, Broadway, Sixth Avenue, and other busy thoroughfares. Once, in a moment of particular daring, she rode her English racer through the lobby of the Old Met, directly into Gatti's office. Dressed in shorts, with her hair tucked under a bandanna, she let the bike gently bump his desk, nudging his attention from the paperwork in front of him.

"It's only me," she said with an innocent smile.

"And who else would it be *but* you?" he answered, shaking his head at her unpredictability.

Though she was always physically fit and robust during her career, her health, because of her voice, was an occasional source of worry—and, in at least one instance, of unintended humor. While touring in California in the mid-1920s, the threat of a smallpox epidemic led her, quite reluctantly, to be vaccinated. She was on a train to Atlanta from San Francisco when she noticed a middle-aged woman dressed in mourning clothes, standing near her door. Seeing the distraught look on the woman's face, she asked what had happened, thinking she might be able to comfort her.

"This is a very sad journey for me, Madame Ponselle," the woman said as she wiped away a tear with her handkerchief. "My son is dead and it's all because of that epidemic!"

"There, there," Rosa whispered as she stroked the woman's hand, hoping to console her, but not wanting to get quite so close to someone who might be infected herself. "This smallpox thing is terrible and I'm sad for you."

"Oh, it wasn't smallpox," the woman uttered through her tears, relieving Rosa that the poor lady hadn't been in direct contact with the disease.

"It was something else?" she inquired.

The answer she got was the very last one she could possibly have wanted to hear. Sobbing uncontrollably by now, the woman blurted out, "It was the vaccination that killed him!"

Hardly twenty minutes later—for psychosomatic reasons, surely—Rosa's temperature began to climb. She was convinced she was going to die, and kept cursing that she wasn't in New York, where Dr. Verdi could take care of her. Through Texas, Louisiana, Mississippi, and Alabama, she lay in her bed clutching a pearl rosary, her eyes locked open in fear.

Her secretary, by now used to her sometimes dramatic reactions, gave less credence to her condition each time the porters brought in the meals Rosa ordered. "Her appetite was always enormous," Edith remembered. "As long as her taste for food held out, you could be sure there wasn't much wrong with her." Nothing took away from the drama, however, and when the train pulled into Atlanta, an ambulance was there to whisk her away to the nearest hospital. She promptly recovered.

Although she wasn't generally given to such melodrama, except onstage, Rosa was a creature of extremes. To her closest friends, she always seemed larger than life. "A beautiful, wild animal," Valentina, her designer, said of her. "A Bohemian," Perle Mesta wrote. Her private life, though regular so far as the needs of her career were concerned, was a colorfully woven fabric of acceptable extremes. In it, her public image was openly wrapped, never shrouded. Whether in her politics, her charity, her business affairs, or even her daily living, her reactions were often spontaneous and completely carefree.

During her first Covent Garden season, for instance, she found herself with some unanticipated free time after rehearsals, and decided to spend it at the movies. Edith, Libbie, and her childhood friend Lena went with her, stopping at the first theater they passed. The afternoon's feature was *The White Hell of Piz Palu,* a mountain-climbing documentary filmed near St. Moritz. By the end of the impressive film, Rosa had decided to take up mountain climbing. Like a schoolgirl with an unlimited budget, she had Edith research and order whatever equipment they might need—and for guides she had Libbie hire the two climbers who had starred in the film. The group spent three memorable days in the same Alpine setting they'd originally seen in a London movie house.

A decade earlier, airplanes momentarily gripped her imagination. This was well before commercial flying was a reality, when open-cockpit biplanes of World War I vintage droned across uncrowded skies. In 1919, the Navy had sent its "flying boats" around the world. One of them, the *Falcon,* was moored in Memphis when she happened to be singing a concert there. Impulsively, she offered the pilot, a young lieutenant named Whitted, one hundred dollars to take her up in the plane. She talked Edith and her slightly squeamish accompanist, William Tyroler, into coming along. Much to their chagrin, Rosa wasn't happy until Lieutenant Whitted finally got the craft to an altitude of six thousand feet. After she landed, she admitted to waiting reporters that the day and date—November 2, All Souls' Day—might not have been the best choice to go flying for the first time.

For all her spontaneity and apparent accessibility—whether during her career or in retirement at Villa Pace, her telephone number was always listed—the power of her personality created an unwitting feeling of distance that even her closest friends were unable to traverse. Sonia Parr, who was as close to her as anyone, had first met her in Hollywood in 1936, at a time when the Parrs were well established in film-colony society. "Though I had lost the awe of meeting celebrities long ago," Mrs. Parr recalled, "I got so nervous when I was introduced to Rosa that I knocked over a highball into her piano." Mrs. Parr also recalled that when Rosa moved to Baltimore and became the center of Valley society, "She became the hub of a wheel in which her friends were the spokes. No one group necessarily knew who any of the others were, because that was the way she liked to keep it."

This sense of distance her friends experienced—a distance that Ponselle neither created nor understood when it was pointed out to her—often extended to equally famous colleagues. Giacomo Lauri-Volpi, one of the most imposing personalities in all of opera, remained puzzled by the dichotomy between Ponselle's accessibility and distance. And Rosa Raisa, whom she idolized, treated

234

her deferentially, even in retirement. Once Raisa felt awkward about seating herself in the music room of Villa Pace, for fear that Ponselle would "mind" where she sat.

Yet Ponselle was gracious to colleagues, even to the point of extremes. Nina Morgana once recalled a Ponselle concert in Detroit, to which Rosa had invited Morgana and her husband, Bruno Zirato. When at the end of the printed program a woman in the audience innocently requested "Caro nome" as an encore, Rosa pointed to the Zirato box and asked Morgana to take a bow. "Now *there* is the artist to sing 'Caro nome' for you," Rosa said to the woman. Morgana was taken aback by the compliment, especially under the circumstances.

Her generosity toward emerging talent, even at the zenith of her career, was well known among her colleagues. Baritone Dennis Noble, who had ascended to the role of Germont when Ponselle sang *Traviata* at Covent Garden, never forgot her kindness during his first curtain calls in the part. Though the order and sequence of the curtain calls were dictated by the stage director, Ponselle felt that Noble's performance warranted a solo moment onstage. After the curtain parted for Noble, tenor Dino Borgioli, and her to walk onstage, she said to Borgioli, "Come on, Dino, let's leave it for the kid." The two bowed quickly, left the stage, and gave Noble to the audience.

Even those who hadn't worked with her often paid unsolicited tributes to her artistry. Victor de Sabata, when he was conducting the New York Philharmonic, came to visit her at Villa Pace. Though he had never had the opportunity to work with her, he told her that he had attended all her *Vestale* rehearsals at the *Maggio Musicale* in Florence, a quarter century earlier. "Those rehearsals," he told her emphatically, "were the greatest musical experiences I have ever had in the theater."

Conductor Giorgio Polacco, in retirement, expressed a similar regret at not having worked with her. After listening to several of her recordings in the mid-1950s, Polacco was moved to write to her, saying that he thought her "the greatest singer of my era."

Two completely unexpected gestures from artists she profoundly respected all but left her speechless. Both Toscanini and Artur Rubinstein, at different times, made touring appearances in Baltimore after Ponselle had moved there. When she went backstage to pay her respects to them, each man dropped to his knees when she approached. Bruno Zirato was a witness to the Toscanini incident, and was quick to point out that this was hardly usual behavior on the part of the temperamental Maestro. "It was his way of letting her know how much he valued her artistry," Zirato recalled.

As Perle Mesta relates in her autobiography, Rosa lost none of her vitality and charm, even in retirement. In 1945 Mesta gave one of her glittering Washington parties, inviting Rosa and a predictable array of government powerbrokers—House Speaker Sam Rayburn, Minority Leader Joe Martin, Justice William O. Douglas, Senator Claude Pepper, and others—to a gala affair honoring Vice-President and Mrs. Truman. Scarcely a month later, Truman would be sworn in as President. The highlight of the evening, Mesta recalled, "came from two of the guests—Rosa Ponselle, [who] sang a few arias, and [who] persuaded the Vice President to accompany her as she perched on top of the piano and did an impression of the torch singer Helen Morgan."

Though she came to know each of the presidents from Harding through Nixon, Rosa's politics were Democratic, till she became an "Eisenhower Republican." Never in her life would she tolerate anyone overtly disrespectful of the America into which she was born. In November 1922, when the country's first "Red Scare" was still at its zenith, Isadora Duncan had inflamed Bostonians by proclaiming her sympathy for the Communist cause. When Boston's mayor discreetly made known that he wanted another celebrity to "stand up for America" on the same stage, Rosa not only volunteered but even agreed to pay the expenses of four Army veterans from Meriden to assist her. In the same theater where, the Boston *American* noted, Isadora Duncan had "flaunted her 'Red' progaganda," the four veterans now presented Rose Ponselle with "a handsome silk stars-and-stripes flag in recognition of her Americanism and as a rebuke to Miss Duncan." To make the point more dramatically, the *American* reported, "Miss Ponselle wrapped herself in the folds of the emblem and sang 'The Star-Spangled Banner.' "

Except for the Boston incident, Rosa rarely lent her name to causes. Like any celebrity's, her name had earning power with advertisers, though she rarely endorsed commercial products. Except for endorsements for Ampico and Duo-Art, the two leading reproducing pianos of the day—an endorsement that began with a Symphony Hall (Boston, again) concert in 1922, in which she sang "Vissi d'arte" to an Ampico's accompaniment—she avoided Madison Avenue almost entirely. She even declined an endorsement of Chesterfield cigarettes, despite their sponsorship of her appearances on *The Chesterfield Hour*. On the few occasions where her name was used without permission—even one as harmless as an Evansville, Indiana, produce company's newspaper ads quoting Rosa as saying, "I eat greens everyday!"—Libbie Miller would demand a printed apology. "Miss Ponselle never gave you any such testimonial," Libbie wrote to the hapless produce vendor, "and unless you indicate in print, for at least four consecutive days, that she has no connection whatsoever with your products, we will be forced to file charges."

Lending her name to charity events was another matter—especially when children were involved. On Christmas Day, 1924, she spent the afternoon singing carols to the staff and children of the New York Nursery and Child's Hospital. "Attendants and tots," said the United Press, "heard her hum million-dollar lullabies." Two years earlier, she had rented Cleveland's Public Hall for a free concert for the city's orphans. With the help of Columbia Graphophone's George Krauflich and several prominent Clevelanders, children from Catholic, Protestant, and Jewish orphanages heard an afternoon of classical and popular songs. Between selections, for many of which she played her own accompaniment, Rosa spoke about the meanings of the words and the lives of the composers. "This is merely an illustration of my belief in the importance of musical education for young children," she told the newspapers afterward. "A large part of their outlook on life depends on their understanding of beauty."

On one or two hurtful occasions, her charity work was momentarily forgotten, at least by the newswriters. An incident in Grand Rapids, Michigan, was a case in point. Late in October 1932, two of the city's newspapers, the *Herald* and the *Press,* ran headline stories on Rosa's cancellation of a Grand Rapids Armory concert appearance. The source of the trouble was the amount of money she was to be paid—$3,000, according to the contract she and Libbie signed with the series' management, but only $2,500 when it came time to perform. Rosa refused to accept the $500 difference—and paid for it in the editorial columns. "Most of us are glad to sing for our supper these days," said the *Herald.* "Well, it's nice to know that there are still folks to whom $3,000 is just a mere bag-o'-shells. To most of us, it's a couple years' salary."

Rosa's and Libbie's reasons for demanding the original sum would have done little, in Depression times, to change the newspapers' accounts. A few months earlier, the Metropolitan had reduced its fee schedule from a maximum of $2,500 to $1,000 per performance. This meant that artists of Rosa's stature had to supplement their reduced incomes by concert and radio appearances—hence Libbie's and her insistence that contractual sums be paid in full. But beyond the economics of her reasoning, at least as regards the city of Grand Rapids, there was a deeper issue in Rosa's mind: exactly ten years earlier, she had sung free of charge to crippled children in the Orthopedic Clinic at the Grand Rapids Hospital. Amid the Coolidge prosperity of the prior decade, the newspapers had idolized her generosity. "Rosa Ponselle will sing in joint recital with Beniamino Gigli in the Armory," they wrote. "But that is not all. She will sing for the children just as she does for the world's best musical critics." Her singing, they said afterward, "lured the dollars [that] eased the lives of many little crippled children."

If Rosa felt comfortable with her celebrity, it was partly because she was never at a loss to explain it: her voice was the reason for her fame, and she had no control over *having* the voice in the first place. The handful of great singers whose voices, like hers, have been praised as once-in-a-lifetime rarities, have tended to discuss their voices in disembodied terms. "The voice"—or, to recall Caruso's appellation, "the instrument"—becomes an entity in itself, presumably separable from the person possessing it. The voice comes to be described as a divine gift, a sign that God has blessed the individual and has destined him or her for a special life. This dualism of voice and person often allows such singers to see themselves in comparatively simple, secure terms as people. Their mission is to enrich others' lives through the medium of music—and, again, the mission is not of their own choosing, ultimately.

Though Rosa avoided personifying her voice, as a rule, none of its mystery was lost upon her. Near the end of her career, a reporter for the New Orleans

Item asked her what having a beautiful voice meant to her. "Great voices are Nature's gift," she replied, "but so are flowers. A beautiful, well-kept garden is the result of toil and constant care. A singer is great only after she has developed her gift to the highest degree possible." This was her version of Caruso's "work, work, and again, work" dictum.

The unrivaled beauty and virtual uniqueness of her voice escaped no one, whether contemporaries like Lotte Lehmann or legends like Geraldine Farrar, whose star stature had been reached the generation before Ponselle's. When leaving the Metropolitan after a Ponselle *Traviata,* Lehmann said to Farrar, "How is it possible to have a voice like hers?"

"Only by a special arrangement with the Lord," Farrar replied, "and then you must work very, very hard."

In quoting this gem of an answer over the years, many writers have inadvertently left out the second part—the "hard work" reference—of Farrar's comment. It has since fallen to one of Ponselle's collagues, the Russian baritone George Cehanovsky, to refresh memories on the subject of her self-refinement.

In an interview with the New York *Times*'s Harold C. Schonberg, Cehanovsky stressed that "Rosa was such a *student* of singing. She was always working to improve herself." Echoing Geraldine Farrar's comment years before, he said, "Rosa wasn't merely content with having a voice sent by God."

Though she retained a healthy mysticism about her voice, Rosa was seldom at a loss for words about the roles in which she used it. She had a realistic grasp of her artistry and knew, therefore, that it had complemented certain roles better than others. Bill Park, whose precision as a researcher led her to choose him as her discographer, once asked her to compare and contrast her many roles. On one of his visits to Villa Pace, he brought a stack of original programs from her Metropolitan performances. Initially, he asked her to autograph them, but then gently expanded his request to include a few lines about the operas themselves.

Of *La Forza del destino* she wrote, "This opera shall always be closest to my heart . . . my Alvaro was none other than the greatest of *all* tenors." Of *Oberon* she wrote, "I would have enjoyed this more if it were sung in German. Still I consider it a favorite." A few she passed over with little comment— *Cavalleria rusticana* was "one of my greatest roles," *Il Trovatore* she "adored," *La Vestale* was "a classic," *Andrea Chénier* "a great opera," and *Aida* "the greatest opera ever written—God bless Verdi!"

Others were intriguing either because of what she said—or else chose not to say. As with *Forza,* she could not write about *La Juive* without paying tribute to Caruso. "I loved this role," she said of Rachel, "and I cherish the memory of this more than words can say. Dear, dear Caruso departed this earth in 1921. It was his last role. How tragic!" Of *Ernani* she wrote, "A great showpiece and great music. Very demanding, vocally, but found it easy for me." Interestingly, she said nothing of *Le Roi d'Ys* except that she "loved Gigli's aria best of all." Three were obvious favorites—*La Gioconda* because it was "one of the heaviest and most demanding," *Norma* because "it was [revived] for me [and was] my pet." And *Carmen* had a special place in her memory because, she wrote, "Of all the roles I've sung, [it] gave me the fewest sleepless nights, and the most fun."

Four others held lesser places in her recollections. *L'Africaine* was "a great box-office attraction, good theatre, great cast, etc.—but not one of my favorites." Nor was *Luisa Miller*: "Anything Verdi wrote demands respect—but this was not one of my favorites." Montemezzi's soon-forgotten *La Notte di Zoraima* was dismissed with one exclamation: "No!" And Breil's *The Legend* also merited a one-word comment: "Terrible!" A half century after this ill-fated premiere had been relegated to a footnote in Metropolitan history, its Carmelita still could not mask her contempt for its banalities. Interviewing her about it, as Bill Park and others learned, rarely took more than a minute and yielded responses like this:

"Do you remember much about the premiere of *The Legend?*"

"No, thank God!"

"Did you like the score at all?"

"No."

"What was the music like? Is there a particular word you would use to describe it?"

"Yes: *bad.*"

"And what about the character Carmelita?"

"Worse."

"What was she supposed to be like?"

"I don't know—a peasant, I guess. In an opera like that, you don't get queens!"

"Did you ever look at the score in later years, just to see whether your opinion might have changed?"

"I couldn't."

"You mean you couldn't bring yourself to look at the score again?"

"No, I mean I *burned* it!"

Late in life, had her health and disposition permitted, Rosa might have returned to New York City and to Meriden, Connecticut—the two cities she had once called home—and would have seen how the principals in her life story finished their lives. A few words about them, and about her relationship to them during and after her career, are perhaps in order.

Carmela Ponselle died in New York City on June 13, 1977, a week after her ninetieth birthday. Though she had been frail for several years, her illness advanced so quickly that Rosa had little time to adjust to it, emotionally, and prepare herself for what might happen. X-rays showed that Carmela had suffered a broken hip. Surgery was inescapable but her age only worsened the risks. The doctors operated, but she never regained consciousness. In a moment of lucidness hours before the operation, she told Elayne Duke, who came to oversee her hospitalization, that she feared she would die. If so, she wanted to be buried in Baltimore, near Rosa. She was laid to rest in a mausoleum near the Greenspring Valley. Many years before, Giovanni Martinelli had spoken her epitaph as an artist: "She had the misfortune to be a sapphire mounted next to a diamond."

Rosa's own phenomenal success, as was suggested earlier, had unalterably changed her relationships with her sister and brother. Relations between Tony and Rosa had always been complicated, at least on his part. As his financial problems worsened in the late 1920s, he grew increasingly dependent upon his sister's generosity. Carmela, to whom he had always been close, seemed to understand his situation. She knew that he had made a number of ill-fated business judgments. But she never lost sight of the real problem in his affairs: his pride.

Though American-born, Tony was fundamentally an Italian male—and, at that, a male whose meager accomplishments had been wholly eclipsed by those of his sisters. Unlike them, he had no real alternative but to remain in Meriden. There his expansive ego could be bolstered by his last name. In Meriden he, like his sisters, had to seem larger than life. His home on Bradley Boulevard—awkwardly designed and the source of endless financial problems to him—had to be a showplace. His wife Lydia's dressing room, accented by lighted mirrors, was nearly as large as Rosa's. In business, even the delivery wagons he used for hauling coal had to be showpieces. Painted a cherry red in hand-rubbed lacquer, they were horse-drawn (Clydesdales only, two to a wagon) long after gas-powered trucks had come into use.

Carmela, understanding his pride, helped support him in his most troubled years. She helped him even when her own resources were comparatively limited, and when she was being sustained largely by Rosa. Tony could never bring himself to ask Rosa's support; it was less a matter of pride than one of past history, in which neither fully understood the other's situation. Rosa, her finances governed by Libbie, Edith, and a battery of accountants at the Fifth Avenue Bank in Manhattan, could not donate money except where tax law allowed. So, when Tony needed money, the accountants required him to take a loan from his sister—but which she never expected him to pay back. No matter how many times Rosa or her accountants explained her tax situation to him, he never accepted it. He began to feel less like a brother and more like a tax credit.

None of this was intentional on her part. Rosa, unlike Tony, had never known what it was to worry about money. Even when she was a teenager her earnings had always exceeded her needs. By the late 1920s her income was so large that occasionally she lost track of her holdings. Just as important, so far as her relationship with Tony is concerned, she had never tasted monetary failure. Nor could she put herself in the place of an admittedly insecure brother whose younger sister was a wealthy celebrity, whose duty it was—in his view—to share her bounty with him.

After Lydia's death in 1947, Tony and Rosa grew estranged. They rarely spoke and what each knew of the other came largely through Carmela and, occasionally, such childhood friends as Lena Angle, Sperando Ciotti and Giulietta Dondero. Heart failure led to his hospitalization in the spring of 1978, and his condition grew worse through the summer months. By Thanksgiving, Rosa received word that he was weakening. By Christmas he was gone; he was eighty-eight years old. Rosa buried him near his parents, next to Lydia, in the Sacred Heart Cemetery in Meriden.

Though Tony had inherited some of his mother's tenderness, to Rosa he seemed too much like her father—strongheaded, unbending, and prone to poor judgment in financial matters. Rosa had nothing in common with her father and was barely able to mask her less-than-ideal memories of him. Ben never remarried after Maddalena's death, and passed most of his remaining years in the family home at 159 Springdale Avenue. A few weeks after Maddalena's funeral he sent for his mercurial brother, Alfonso, who came to live with him. Ben had been unable to adjust to his loneliness and had offered to support Alfonso if he would come to Meriden. To the wayward Alfonso, this was an unexpected plus. A few years earlier, he had been tried (and, through a tough-minded Italian lawyer, acquitted) of the murder of his son-in-law, a Sicilian who partnered him in his bootlegging operation.

Alfonso had hardly moved into 159 Springdale when he displayed his temper in the neighborhood. Late one afternoon Tony stopped in to see his father and to deliver a dessert Lydia had made. Looking down at the backyard from one of the kitchen windows upstairs, he noticed Alfonso puttering near the back of the lot. A few minutes later he heard him shouting obscenities in Italian, and went to the window to see what was happening. Soon he caught sight of a neighborhood teenager, a brash young Calabrese who was taunting the old man by tossing empty tin cans onto the Ponzillo property. Knowing what might happen, Tony ran down the steps and out into the yard. He pleaded with the boy to go back into his house and mind his own business.

"Why should I?" the youth said smugly, lobbing another tin can over the fence.

"Because the old man might *kill* you! That's why!" Tony said nervously.

"Hah!" the stocky Calabrese said defiantly.

By this time Alfonso was walking toward him, a garden shovel hidden behind his back.

"I'm telling you, he shot and killed his son-in-law, and if you keep it up he'll kill you too!" Tony shouted.

Eying the business end of the shovel, the youth soon retreated to his house.

Eventually Alfonso went back to Waterbury. Ben lived alone, remaining in generally good health until his early nineties. When he began to fail mentally and physically, Tony had him moved to a local rest home, where he died at the age of ninety-six. At age ninety-one, when he was still living in the Springdale Avenue house, he seized a final opportunity to display the toughness he had learned from Alfonso in the saloons of Waterbury in the 1890s: he got into a fistfight with an irate neighbor, and had to be restrained by the Meriden police.

The other principals in Rosa's story lived out their years in relative tranquillity. Libbie Miller kept her office and home at the Franconia Hotel in Manhattan, where she had moved a year or so before she and Rosa had parted company. She wrote but did not publish her memoirs; in the manuscript's pages she deliberately excluded her years with Rosa, not wanting to reopen any doors to that part of her past. She died in New York City in the winter of 1978, on the eve of the sixtieth anniversary of Rosa's Metropolitan debut.

Edith, like Libbie, stayed in Manhattan, even after the death of her husband, Albert Sania. Though she and Rosa exhibited an outward affection for each other, their views of one another were often jaded. Especially in later life, Edith was prone to moments of plainly self-serving recollection. She accorded herself a more important role in the development of Rosa's career than any documents could substantiate. To those who admired her (and they were many), she seemed the essence of intelligence and organization, a woman whose ambition would have carried her far in today's equal-rights professional world. To those who distrusted her (and they, too, were many), she seemed bent upon establishing her own celebrity, often at Rosa's expense. In her later years she gave a few interviews, and sometimes participated in New York City tributes to Rosa. She remained in Manhattan until 1980, when she moved to St. Petersburg, Florida.

Lena Tamburini (Lena Angle to her Meriden friends) lived most of her life in a spacious home on North Street in Meriden's West Side, only a block or so from the Springdale Avenue home in which she had grown up. After the death of her husband, Henry Angle, she never remarried but remained very active in civic affairs in and around Meriden.

Carle Jackson married a fourth time in 1960, and by his own admission it was a turning point in his life. In business he had always been successful, partly because of the reputation his father's firm had built in Baltimore, and also because of his own intelligence and initiative. In later years, these same qualities served him well as the head of his own insurance firm. In his early seventies he retained most of the athletic looks that had attracted Rosa to him forty years earlier; only his thinning gray hair gave a hint of his age. Otherwise, he remained one of the most respected horsemen and competitive polo players in the Greenspring Valley. He and Rosa last saw each other in the late 1950s.

With two exceptions—one a tragic fire and the other her resignation from the Baltimore Opera Company—the final years of Rosa's own life were tranquil and rewarding. "Ex-Opera Star Rescued" was the New York *Times*'s headline for the fire that swept one wing of Villa Pace on Christmas Eve, 1979. The blaze, which originated in a shorted circuit in the home's library, destroyed art objects, antiques, and—worst of all for the lady whom the *Times* described as "devoted to her toy poodles and other pets"—the fire claimed five of her dogs and cats. Once rescued from the blaze, the news stories noted, "Miss Ponselle was taken to nearby Villa Julie [Convent], where she ate Christmas dinner with the nuns." Veteran critic Paul Hume, who visited her in May 1980 and saw the damage to Villa Pace firsthand, underscored the irony that the Metropolitan's first Leonora in *Forza* was given real-life refuge, sixty-two years later, by a religious community.

Hume capped his description of Rosa's life by noting, in the Washington *Post* in May 1980, "Now, at 83, one of the finest of all singers is waiting amid the remains for the insurance company and her lawyers to come to some agreement about the amount of damage done to Villa Pace by the fire that raced through its rooms." Hume, who had been acquainted with her since the early 1950s and who knew some of the unhappier sides of her story, went on to say, "Though life is not easy, it does not stop for Rosa Ponselle. It has not since that day in 1918 when she and Caruso sang a Verdi opera the Metropolitan had never previously presented." There remained, he wrote, "an indomitable will in Ponselle that sustains her in a time of trouble."

Unfortunately, both for her and in the end everyone involved, the circumstances surrounding her resignation as Artistic Director of the Baltimore Opera —her stepchild, whose growth she had overseen like a doting mother for twenty-nine years—tested this "indomitable will" beyond any reasonable bounds. Robert Collinge, whom she personally held responsible for the events that triggered her resignation, added a tasteless apostrophe to an already-deteriorating situation when, in February 1980, he did a mocking impersonation of Rosa at a party in a Baltimore bar. The *News American*'s Sylvia Boone described the scene in her February 12 column. "The saran-wrapped man who was the centerpiece for the food table gave one partygoer quite a fright; while sampling the food, he touched the centerpiece and it moved. Later, tired of lounging, the centerpiece changed into a black-sequined dress, which allegedly belonged to Judy Garland." Noting that during the evening "Bob Collinge, general manager of the Baltimore Opera Company, gave his best performance as Rosa," Boone capped the event with the tongue-in-cheek assessment "A gay old time was had by all. . . ."

Some ten days after the column appeared, former U. S. Attorney George Beall, who had begun representing Ponselle in her dealings with Collinge, addressed a letter to the chairman of the Opera Company's board, expressing Rosa's distress over the incident that the Boone column described. "At its best," said Beall in a February 1980 letter, "[the incident] exposes Miss Ponselle to ridicule at the hands of Mr. Collinge and, at its worst, confirms her previous expressions to the Board of the Baltimore Opera that her name is being disparaged by senior officials of the Company, as had previously been suggested. . . ."

A few months later, on May 22, 1980, Collinge died of an apparent heart attack. His hard-fought reputation as General Manager was tarnished at its close by his break with the woman who, as Artistic Director, had helped him achieve whatever prominence he had.

At the time of Collinge's death, Beall was negotiating the return of several items of *Carmen* memorabilia—among them a variety of tape recordings of coaching and audition sessions that Rosa had directed and that had obvious archival value. Beall, representing her in the ensuing dispute over the owner- ship of the memorabilia, contended that she had lent rather than given the items to Collinge. Jay Holbrook, Collinge's successor as General Manager and executor of his estate, argued that Ponselle had made a gift of the items, allegedly in front of fifty witnesses, at a birthday party for Collinge.*

(In depositions taken later, only two witnesses were produced—one an em- ployee of the Opera Company, and the other a personal friend of Collinge who shared an apartment with him for eleven years. Neither fully corroborated Holbrook's claims, and both denied that the items had been presented at a birthday party for Collinge. Had the dispute gone to court, Beall would proba- bly have attacked their credibility as witnesses, owing to their close associations with Collinge and the Opera Company.)

At Collinge's death the disputed ownership of the memorabilia became the focus of press attention when, as part of his estate, they were to be put up for auction (along with some of his personal belongings) in October of 1980. In a section from the legal correspondence surrounding the dispute, Beall sum- marized what occurred next:

> A letter was immediately delivered to the auction gallery, with copies to the personal [i.e., Jay Holbrook] and legal representatives of Mr. Collinge's estate, advising that some of the property to be auctioned was the subject of Miss Ponselle's previous claim filed with the Orphan's Court of Baltimore City and asking that these items not be put up to auction. This letter brought no satisfactory response.
>
> Accordingly, and regrettably, there was no choice for Miss Ponselle's representatives, if they were to prevent the items in dispute from being sold to strangers at a public auction, but to preserve the questions of ownership by stopping the auction of only those items . . . A temporary injunction was obtained preventing [their] sale.

The dispute was eventually resolved in late July 1981, through a compromise drafted by Beall and representatives of the Ponselle estate. The compromise brought to a conclusion all litigation and made careful provision for the *Car- men* items to be displayed in a "Rosa Ponselle Room" planned for the Lyric Theater in Baltimore; there, the items are to be identified as a gift from the

---

* *Holbrook, a close personal friend of Collinge, had served in various capacities in the Baltimore Opera since 1973, and was appointed Assistant General Manager in the summer of 1978. The Opera board named him General Manager on August 6, 1980.* J.A.D.

Baltimore Opera, in her memory. In the claims and counterclaims lodged by each side during the litigation, Joseph G. Mitchell, a friend with whom Collinge once resided, provided an apt footnote to the dispute. "The irony of this whole thing," Mitchell said in a court deposition on January 29, 1981, "is [that] Mr. Collinge knew very little about opera, and cared very little about opera as an art-form. It's ironic that he would have these things when there are people in this town whose tongues would hang out for it."

As the dispute over the *Carmen* memorabilia made its way into the press, Elayne Duke again became a target of criticism and suspicion in her handling of Ponselle's affairs. In this case, in view of the fact that the dispute was a legal one and that Ponselle had retained Beall to represent her interests, such suspicions seemed moot. But they had lingered since the early 1970s, when Ponselle's increasing illness made it necessary to limit the access of friends and associates to Villa Pace.

Ponselle had always regarded illness as a totally private matter. As early as 1947, when the first of a series of psychological depressions caused her to be hospitalized, she wanted no visitors; it was a simple matter of pride, not wanting to be seen when she was less than at her best. The same sense of privacy characterized her hospitalization, in the early 1950s, for a cancer operation, and again in 1972 when a bacterial infection irreparably damaged her heart. As she was again suffering from a depression, her physicians deliberately kept from her the extent of the damage the infection had done. When she returned home to Villa Pace, it became necessary to ask her friends to restrict their visiting time so that she could recuperate fully. At her physicians' suggestions it was decided not to confide the nature and extent of her illness to her friends, to preclude any possibility of her learning about it.

These prudent restrictions, medically ordered as they were, became necessarily more stringent from 1977 onward when, as has been explained, her health steadily deteriorated. Friends who could accept these necessary restrictions were welcomed repeatedly to Villa Pace whenever Ponselle's health permitted visitors. Those who could not accept them no doubt felt "screened," and went so far as to allege that Elayne Duke had prevented them from seeing Ponselle. A few who felt excluded formalized such allegations into a petition, intended for the Maryland State Attorney, in the summer of 1978. Though the petition never reached fruition, its allegations—specifically that Rosa was "being kept a prisoner in her own home" and was not permitted to use the telephone or to see any visitors—were deeply upsetting to her.

Those whom she did receive as her health permitted—artists including Licia Albanese, Bidú Sayão, Lili Chookasian, James Morris, Jerome Hines, Gilda Cruz-Romo, and Luciano Pavarotti, or longtime friends like Sonia Parr, Clemmie Peterson, Ida and Louise Cook, Myron Ehrlich, Leigh Martinet, George McManus, and others—buoyed her spirits and momentarily made her forget her illness. Because these visits were arranged and coordinated by Elayne Duke, it hurt Rosa to hear her criticized for her efforts. "Elayne is *my* representative," she said whenever such criticisms were made. She felt strongly that her choice of a representative—no matter who the person might have been—should have been respected by those involved with her, whether personal friends or professional associates.*

Elayne was with her when she died. Her transition was both sudden and peaceful: one moment she was reclining in bed, having just finished a late breakfast, and the next moment she was gone. The date was May 25, 1981—Memorial Day, a holiday she had helped initiate when, in 1919, Warren G. Harding had asked her to sing at the burial of America's Unknown Soldier. A few days earlier, she had gently reprimanded her four nurses—Mabel McArthur, Bettie Victory, Vernice Hollis, and Joyce Luna—for, as she put it, "working so hard to keep me alive."

"Why don't you just let me go?" she had asked them resignedly.

The night before she died, opera and life blended in her thoughts. *"La Forza del destino . . .* The Force of Destiny," she said over and over to Elayne, who had seen her through sleepless nights like this one. "Isn't it ironic," she said. "It's as if my whole life has been the Force of Destiny." Hours later, her own destiny was completed.

She lay in state in the music room of Villa Pace until Friday, May 29, when she was buried next to Carmela, near the Greenspring Valley. Thousands came to Villa Pace to pay their last respects—"a stream of mourners from Baltimore and around the nation [who] paid tribute to her voice, her beauty, [and] her influence on opera," said the Baltimore *Sun*. "As a flutist played selections from Bach, the mourners lined up in the estate's music room to view the legendary soprano one final time."

At her funeral Mass at the St. Charles Borromeo Catholic Church, where she had often sung on Christmas Eve, four of her former students—William Warfield, Phyllis Frankel, Kira Baklanova, and Bette Hankin—honored her memory in song. A thousand miles away, Luciano Pavarotti addressed the standing-room-only audience that erupted into applause when he stepped onto the stage of a Tulsa auditorium for a benefit concert. "Tonight I dedicate my singing to the memory of Rosa Ponselle," he told them.

---

* *Such criticism resurfaced when, a few months after her death, Jay Holbrook authorized advertisements for a production of* Carmen *"dedicated to the late Artistic Director Rosa Ponselle." Elayne Duke, in a letter to board president Charles S. Garland, requested that such advertisements be retracted, since a wrong impression would be given that disagreements between Ponselle and the Opera Company management had been resolved. Further, no such dedication of a* Carmen *had been agreed to in a September 1981 meeting among Garland, attorney Michael Abromaitis, and Elayne Duke. The Opera proceeded, nonetheless, with a tribute to Ponselle that appeared in the* Carmen *program. Whatever the author's intentions, the printed result was fraught with inaccuracies—e.g., identifying the "Pace, pace" aria from* Forza *as being in the first rather than last act, referring to "notables in this day" being "cannonized" [sic] by the media, wrongly identifying Luciano Pavarotti as a "soon-to-be notable" whom Rosa "brought to her doorstep" as Artistic Director—though the tribute nevertheless acknowledged that the Opera Company "couldn't have done it without [her]."* J.A.D.

During the funeral Mass in Baltimore, Paul Hume delivered the eulogy. When, near its end, he evoked visions of her voice leading a celestial choir, the congregation burst into applause. After the Boys' Choir of the Immaculate Heart of Mary Church sang, the pastor of St. Charles Borromeo, Father Martin Schwallenberg, spoke of Rosa's philosophy of music and life. "She believed that the great gift of her voice was from God, and was meant to be shared. Because of her belief, we all have beautiful memories."

In death as in life Rosa Ponselle's hold on opera history is secure. Her name will always be linked among the handful of opera's greatest singers, and greatest stars. Of her voice—so utterly distinctive in color and texture, range and flexibility—it seems safe to venture that there will never be another quite like it. Her voice was her passageway to immortality and she knew it—even if for more than half her lifetime she kept its shimmering beauty largely to herself.

November 1981   JAMES A. DRAKE

DISCOGRAPHY BY BILL PARK

THE RECORDED legacy of Rosa Ponselle is quite remarkable, considering not only the scope of what she recorded but also the span of years—1918 through 1977—in which she did so. This discography is the first authorized attempt to present as accurately as possible complete information about those of her recordings clearly known to exist. This includes not only her commercial records made either for the Columbia Graphophone Company or the Victor Talking Machine Company (or, as it was known after 1929, RCA Victor), but also the wealth of radio-broadcast material ("off-the-air" selections, as they are designated in these pages) and private recordings she made. The full scope of these latter recordings may never be known, although most of those listed in these pages have been traced from Miss Ponselle's own archives at Villa Pace and from the Rosa Ponselle Collection of the Library of Congress.

As with most legendary performers in opera, a number of her commercial recordings have been rereleased in LP form. While no effort has been made to list here all of these long-playing reissues, the titles and catalogue numbers of the major ones will be found here, and within the pages of the discography enough information is provided to enable the reader to determine which version of a selection is contained in any future reissues or in any that may have been omitted here.

Part I of the discography chronicles the Ponselle Columbia recordings, all of them made by the acoustical method between 1918 and 1923. Here one finds the test record she made for Columbia prior to her Metropolitan debut (No. 15), on which she first displayed the lushness of voice that would bring her international fame in a matter of months. Romano Romani, whose long career as a composer, conductor, and coach intertwined with hers, was her accompanist in this maiden appearance before the recording horn. The other titles listed in this section are those she recorded under the terms of her contract with Columbia Graphophone, and she was not favorably disposed to them as a rule. Despite her own lack of enthusiasm for them—an attitude perhaps explainable by her eventual break with William Thorner, who had originally lured her to Columbia for rather selfish reasons—critical opinion has favored these discs, sometimes more than the acoustical discs she made for the Victor Company between 1923 and 1925.*

In this opening section each title the singer recorded is assigned a discography number, and the number appears at the immediate left of the selection. The first column of the entry contains the title, its composer (where songs are concerned, but not necessarily for the more familiar operatic entries), any assisting artists involved in the recording, and a note whether the accompaniment is orchestral (*Or.*) or piano (*Pf.*); following this designation the name of the conductor or accompanist is also listed. The next columns list the precise catalogue information pertaining to the recording, and to avoid confusion over the technical terms generally used by record companies of Ponselle's era, the following information will be helpful:

1. In recording studios throughout the 1918–39 period covered by the commercial Ponselle releases, a thick wax disc was used by studio technicians to record the performance of an artist. In the parlance of the time, this wax disc was known as the *wax master*.

2. In the laboratories of the various record companies, technicians then dusted this wax master with powdered graphite, making it conducive to electroplating. The plate-like disc that resulted from the electroplating process was actually a "negative" of the original wax disc that had been recorded in the studio, and was called by recording technicians the *negative master* or, often more familiarly, the "mother" record.

3. This negative master was also put through the electroplating process and yielded a "positive" that resembled a metallic version of the wax disc used in the recording studio; this one could be played like an ordinary record for audition purposes. Technicians called this the *plate master*.

4. Ultimately, this plate master was electroplated and yielded what was called the *stamper*—actually a "negative" plate, like the "mother" but strong enough to be put into high-pressure presses and used to form the actual shellac-based discs sold to the public.

5. For the use of the artist in evaluating his or her performance before the recording horn, technicians usually pressed three or four shellac copies from the stamper, and these were identified with typewritten labels and given both to the artist and to the company's music executives to determine whether the record was sufficiently good to release to the public. These shellac samples, looking exactly like a commercial disc record except for their plain typewritten labels, were called *test pressings*. Because an artist usually recorded the same aria or song several times to ensure a good performance—these successive performances being called *takes*—test pressings of each take were usually made by the laboratory technicians. The artist, with the record company's music executives, would then choose which take would be released to the public.

* *For an authoritative comparison of Ponselle's Victor and Columbia releases, see articles by Aida Favia-Artsay in* Hobbies *magazine (October 1952) and in the now defunct English periodical* Record News *(January 1951).*

To return to the discography, using this information as a mental guide, it will be seen that each entry lists both the number assigned by the company to the *master record* involved in each session, and also the number of each *take* the session entailed. With the Ponselle Columbia discs, many of the titles she recorded were released in single- and double-sided form, and where the single-sided ones are listed it will be seen that the Columbia Company, for matters of record-keeping convenience, used the same number in their commercial catalogues as the technicians had used on the master recordings. Columbia abandoned this practice in its double-sided releases.

Each take of a Ponselle selection was of course a separate recording, and in a few instances neither she nor the Columbia management would permit any of the takes to be released. If one of those takes was published, however, its number will appear in bold face, and the commercial catalogue number(s) under which it was released is listed in the last column. (The date on which the takes listed were recorded appears in the second column.)

Part II lists all known information pertaining to Rosa Ponselle's Victor recordings, from the first of her "Red Seal" sessions on December 5, 1923, through the famous "LP" sessions that took place at Villa Pace October 16–22, 1954. The artist recorded both acoustically and electrically for the Victor Company, and the discography entries carry this identifying information to enable the reader to distinguish among them:

1. All *acoustical* recordings made for Victor by Miss Ponselle carry the prefixes "B" or "C" before their master numbers, "B" for ten-inch and "C" for twelve-inch master records.

2. All *electrical* Ponselle Victor discs, excluding her October 1954 LP recordings, carry the prefix "BVE" or "PBS" (ten-inch masters), and "CVE" or "PCS" (twelve-inch masters). The reader is advised that, except for the prefixes involved, the same master numbers were used in acoustical and electrical versions of the same selections, and thus without knowing the prefixes the company used they cannot be told apart unless by playing the actual takes. This does *not* apply to the Victor recordings she made in the company's Hollywood studios, which are prefixed "PBS" or "PCS," depending on their diameters. For reasons known only to Victor, both Ponselle and John Charles Thomas, and other artists who were recorded in their California studios, made takes that were not numbered consecutively by the studio personnel; if this was convenient to the Hollywood studio at the time, it has since caused discographers considerable headaches.

"VA," "VB," "ABHB," "DA," and "DB" are the prefixes used by Victor's then British counterpart, HMV (His Master's Voice), in releasing the Ponselle selections abroad. Further, the prefixes "LM," "LCT," "CBL," and "VIC" refer to long-playing discs issued by RCA Victor; the remaining prefix, "WCT," denotes 45 rpm collections. Numbers carrying the prefixes "EJS" or "ASCO" are also long-playing discs but refer to non-Victor issues.

Part III lists all known recordings of Miss Ponselle's appearances on radio, the greater number of which were recorded by networks and sponsors in order to check the quality of the broadcasts' transmission. The first column of the entries in Part III lists the discography number and the title of the selection. Different broadcasts of the selection are denoted *a, b,* etc. and list appropriate data regarding them, including, if they have been issued in any form, the record number(s) involved.

Part IV is a compilation of all known private recordings of Rosa Ponselle, most of which were recorded in her home. These may have been begun by the British collector Dr. Dick Alexander; the majority, however, were recorded by Lloyd Garrison, the first of them recorded on magnetic wire. As magnetic tape displaced wire recording, Garrison recorded Miss Ponselle on professional-type Presto equipment. It was these recordings which rekindled, on the part of RCA Victor and Capitol Records, an interest in the Ponselle voice and artistry. Garrison's efforts were continued by Leigh Martinet, Addison Foster, Hugh Johns, and Elayne Duke, among others. Data listed in this section follows the same format as that found in Part III concerning off-the-air recordings. A few of these private recordings were issued by Miss Ponselle for the benefit of the Baltimore Civic Opera Company, although most were not intended for public release.

Part V lists all of the albums of Rosa Ponselle including first edition LP releases and major LP reissues with discography numbers to indicate all of the selections contained in the albums.

The discography also contains indexes, the first of which, Index A, contains alphabetically arranged selections that Miss Ponselle recorded; these are followed by a discography number for the reader's reference and convenience. Index B contains notes of interest on entries in the discography. Index C contains listings of Rosa Ponselle's radio broadcasts. And Index D represents a complete discography of Carmela Ponselle, also listing information about the two known recordings of Anthony (Ponzillo) Ponselle, the one apparently a trial record made under Romano Romani's direction at Columbia,* and the other a radio duet with Carmela Ponselle (number 41).

Since this discography is the first and only one that Rosa Ponselle herself both commissioned and authorized, I express to her my special appreciation for having encouraged and assisted me during the many years this labor of love required. I wish to express a debt of gratitude on behalf of all future Ponselle discographers and devotees to Edith Prilik (Mrs. Albert) Sania, Miss Ponselle's career-long secretary and lifelong friend, through whose diaries and private

---

* *We must note that a controversy arose over this alleged Anthony Ponselle Columbia "test" shortly after it was released by William Violi on OASI 635. Not long after it was released, I received a letter from the well-known collector and discographer Lawrence F. Holdridge, of Amityville, L.I., declaring that the voice on the disc is that of the Mexican tenor Carlos Mejía, taken from a Victor blue-label acoustical disc. The authenticity of the item is in dispute.* J.A.D.

papers the dates of most of the singer's Columbia sessions were reconstructed decades after this information had disappeared from the company's own files.

I owe inestimable thanks to Elayne Duke, Miss Ponselle's personal representative and longtime friend, for having made available to me the entire scope of the Rosa Ponselle Archives at Villa Pace, so that I could leisurely study the many private recordings housed in the archives. Special help was given by Leigh Martinet, who assisted greatly in checking and helping confirm details of "private" recordings whose titles are reflected in these pages; and by Lloyd Garrison, who graciously checked my data against his personal recording files. Special thanks also go to that most knowledgeable "Ponselle-ite" and friend Hugh Johns, who remains the foremost authority on the career and artistry of Rosa Ponselle.

I am also grateful to Martine McCarthy of Columbia Records, John Pfeiffer and Bernadette Moore of RCA Records, and Ida Cook, James Alfonte, William Moran, Jim Cartwright, Harold Wright, Ronald Seeliger, William Collins, Dr. James Drake, Barbara Nuttall, William Violi, William Seward, Aida Artsay, Joseph Mitchell, Charlotte Brewer, and my family—Glenda, Wade, Wyatt, and Carla.

In dedicating my work to the beloved artist and dear friend who made this possible, I cite the tribute paid Rosa Ponselle and her recordings by the critic and historian Aida Favia-Artsay:

> To listen to these recordings is to be enchanted by a voice never equalled for its bewitching beauty, first giving shape to the musical composition with the care of a master sculptor and then, like him, passing on to the details, vivid or subdued, as the object being created may require . . . We have samples of her art in its progressive developments, and as hers was a perfectly phonogenic voice, we can enjoy it to our heart's content in all its resplendent glory.

PART I

COLUMBIA RECORDS
(*Acoustic*)

DISCOG. NO.		DATE	MATRIX/ TAKE	78 RPM CAT. NO.
	1. Abide with Me (Monk) (with B. Maurel) (Or. Romani)	9 July '19	78557-1, -2	36000D X245 (UK)
*	2. *Africana, L'*: Figlio del sol (In grembo a me) (Or. Romani)	1 Feb. '23	98059-1, -2	68000D
*	3. *Aida:* Ritorna vincitor (Or. Romani)	19 Sept. '23	98092-1, -2	68084D 7066M
	4. *Aida:* O patria mia (Or. Romani)	29 Nov. '18	49557-1, -2, -3, -4, -5	68036D 8910M
	5. *Aida:* O terra, addio! (with C. Hackett) (Or. Romani)	14 Jan. '20	49734-1	71000D 9010M
	6. *Blue Danube Waltz* (Strauss) (Or. Romani)	17 Sept. '21	49988-1, -2, -3, -4	68087D 7062M
*	7. *Bohème, La:* Sì, mi chiamano Mimi (Or. Romani)	13 Feb. '23	98062-1, -2	68000D 7035M
	8. Carolina Sunshine (composer?) (with C. Ponselle) (Or. Romani)	15 Jan. '20	78927-1, -2	(Unpublished)
	9. *Cavalleria rusticana:* Ave Maria (adapted from Intermezzo) (Or. Romani)	29 Nov. '18	49556-1	(Unpublished)
	10. *Cavalleria rusticana:* Voi lo sapete (Or. Romani)	9 Jan. '19	49570-1, -2	68039D 8909M
	11. Comin' Thro' the Rye (Trad.) (with C. Ponselle) (Or. Romani)	9 Dec. '19	78847-1, -2, -3	36002D
	12. *Ernani:* Ernani! Ernani, involami (Or. Romani)	9 June '22	98028-1, -2	68037D 7034M
	13. Flower of the Snow (composer?)	Bet. 20 Feb. '20 and 27 Feb. '20	49756-1	(Unpublished)

See the Notes on Discography Selections pages 293–95.

DISCOG. NO.		DATE	MATRIX/ TAKE	78 RPM CAT. NO.
14.	*Forza del destino, La:* La Vergine degli angeli (with chorus) (Or. Romani)	*2 Dec. '18*	49558-1, -2, -3, -4, -5, **-6, -7, -8**	68038D 8910M 7340 (UK) 7227 (UK)
* 15.	*Forza del destino, La:* Pace, pace mio Dio (Pf. Romani)	*3 April '18*	Test record, matrix number unknown	
16.	*Forza del destino La:* Pace, pace mio Dio (Or. Romani)	*5 July '20*	49859-1, **-2**	68038D 7033M
* 17.	*Gioconda, La:* Suicidio! (Or. Romani)	*14 Jan. '20*	49735-1, **-2**, **-3**	68039D 7034M (2)
18.	Good-Bye (Tosti) (Or. Romani)	*2 Dec. '18*	49560-1, -2, **-3**	68064D 70387
19.	Home, Sweet Home (Bishop) (Or. Romani)	*16 Feb. '21*	49335-**1**	68065D 7064M
* 20.	*Juive, La:* Il va venir (Or. Romani)	*28 Sept. '23* *11 Jan. '24* *14 Jan. '24*	98096-1, -2 **-3** -4	AF1
21.	Keep the Home Fires Burning (Novello) (with quartet—Harrison, Miller, Croxton, Sarto) (Or. Romani)	*15 Feb. '19*	49585-1, -2, **-3**	7038M
* 22.	Little Alabama Coon (Starr) (with quartet—Harrison, Miller, Croxton, Sarto) (Or. Romani)	*10 Sept. '21* *13 April '22*	79980-1, -2, **-3** -4, **-5**	33003D 2024M
* 23.	*Lohengrin:* Einsam in trüben Tagen (Or. Romani)	*21 Sept. '23*	98093-**1**, -2	AF1
24.	*Madama Butterfly:* Un bel dì vedremo (Or. Romani)	*9 Jan. '19*	49571-1, **-2**	68059D 7065M 7340 (UK) 7234 (UK)
* 25.	*Mademoiselle Modiste:* Kiss Me Again (Or. Romani)	*26 July '20*	49869-1, **-2**	68077D 7061M
* 26.	*Manon Lescaut:* In quelle trine morbide (Or. Romani)	*9 Sept. '21* *19 Sept. '23†* *11 Oct. '23*	79971-1, **-2** **-3** -4	36001D 2014M
27.	Maria, Mari! (Di Capua) (Or. Romani)	*26 July '20*	49870-1, **-2**	68064D 7035M
28.	*Maritana:* Scenes That Are Brightest (Or. Romani)	*9 Sept. '21*	49982-1, **-2**	68078D 7062M
29.	*Norma:* Casta Diva (Or. Romani)	*11 Dec. '19*	49720-1, -2, -3, -4	68060D 7063M
30.	Oh! That We Two Were Maying (Nevin) (with C. Ponselle) (Or. Romani)	*9 June '22*	80391-1, -2, **-3**	(Unpublished)

DISCOG. NO.		DATE	MATRIX/ TAKE	78 RPM CAT. NO.
31.	Old Folks at Home (Foster) (Or. Romani)	*15 Feb. '21*	49934-**1**	68065D 7064M
32.	*Otello:* Ave Maria (Or. Romani)	*9 June '22*	98029-1, **-2,** -3	68060D 7063M
* 33.	*Pagliacci, I:* Qual fiamma . . . stridono lassu (balletella) (Or. Romani)	*13 Feb. '23* *22 Sept. '23* *11 Jan. '24*	98063-1, -2 -3, -4, -5 **-6,** -7	68084D 7066M
34.	Rachem (Mana-Zucca) (Or. Romani)	*8 Jan. '21*	49925-1, **-2,** **-3**	7025M
35.	Rose of My Heart (Löhr) (Or. Romani)	*17 Sept. '21*	49987-1	(Unpublished)
* 36.	Rose of My Heart (Löhr) (Or. Romani)	*13 April '22*	80307-**1**	33003D 2024M
37.	*Sadko:* Song of India (Or. Romani)	*30 Dec. '20*	49920-1, **-2**	68077D 7061M
38.	Sole Mio, O (Di Capua) (with C. Ponselle) (Or. Romani)	*9 Sept. '21*	49983-**1**	9007M
39.	*Tales of Hoffmann:* Barcarolle (with C. Ponselle) (Or. Romani)	*9 Dec. '19*	78846-1, **-2,** -3	36001D
40.	*Tosca:* Vissi d'arte (Or. Romani)	*7 Jan. '19*	49569-1, **-2,** -3, -4, **-5**	68059D 7065M
* 41.	*Trovatore, Il:* Tacea la notte (Or. Romani)	*16 Nov. '22*	98051-**1,** -2	68036D 7033M
42.	*Trovatore, Il:* D'amor sull' ali rosee (Or. Romani)	*10 Dec. '18*	49559-1, **-2,** -3, **-4**	68058D 8909M
43.	*Trovatore, Il:* Mira d'acerbe (with Stracciari) (Or. Romani)	*30 Dec. '20*	49922-1, **-2**	71000D 9010M
44.	Values (Vanderpool) (Or. Romani)	*10 Jan. '20*	78920-1, -2, **-3**	
45.	*Vespri siciliani, I:* Mercè, dilette amiche (bolero) (Or. Romani)	*4 Nov. '19*	49686-1, -2, **-3**	68037D
46.	Where My Caravan Has Rested (Löhr) (with C. Ponselle) (Or. Romani)	*2 June '22* *13 June '22*	80391-1 -2, **-3**	36002D 2019M
* 47.	Whispering Hope (Hawthorne) (with B. Maurel) (Or. Romani)	*1 March '19* *9 July '19*	78325-1, -2, -3 -4, -5, **-6**	36000D 2019M X242 (UK)
48.	*William Tell:* Selva opaca	*1 Feb. '23*	98058-**1,** -2	68058D 7026M

† (*with recit: È ver, è ver!*)

PART II

VICTOR RECORDS
(*Acoustic and Electric*)

DISCOG. NO.		DATE	MATRIX/ TAKE	78 RPM CAT. NO.	LP CAT. NO.
49.	*Africana, L'*: Figlio del sol (In grembo a me) (Or. Bourdon)	*14 Jan. '25*	C 31710-**1**, **-2**	6496B	
* 50.	Agnus Dei (Bizet) (Organ, Chichagov)	*20 Oct. '54*	No number assigned		ASCO A-125
* 51.	*Aida:* Ritorna vincitor (Or. Bourdon)				
	a.	*5 Dec. '23*	C 29063-1, **-2**	74860	
		11 Dec. '23	**-3**, **-4**		
	b.	*20 May '26*	CVE 29063-5, **-6**		VIC 1507
		8 Dec. '27	**-7**, **-8**		
		18 Jan. '28	**-9**	7438A 8993 DB 1606 (UK)	
* 52.	*Aida:* O patria mia (Or. Bourdon)				
	a.	*5 Dec. '23*	C 29061-1, **-2**	(74861)	
		11 Dec. '23	**-3**, **-4**	6437B DB 854 (UK)	
	b.	*20 May '26*	CVE 29061-5, **-6**		VIC 1507
* 53.	*Aida:* Pur ti riveggo, mia dolce Aida (with Martinelli) (Or. Bourdon)	*7 Feb. '24*	C 29446-1, **-2**, **-3**	IRCC 126 VB 73 (UK)	LCT 1035
* 54.	*Aida:* Là tra foreste vergini (with Martinelli) (Or. Bourdon)	*7 Feb. '24*	C 29447-1, **-2**	VB 73 (UK)	LCT 1035
* 55.	*Aida:* La fatal pietra (with Martinelli) (Or. Bourdon)	*8 Feb. '24*	C 29451-1, **-2**	ABHB 3 (UK)	

DISCOG. NO.		DATE	MATRIX/ TAKE	78 RPM CAT. NO.	LP CAT. NO.
* 56.	*Aida:* O terra, addio! (with Martinelli) (Or. Bourdon)	8 Feb. '24	C 29450-1, -2	ABHB 3 (UK)	
* 57.	*Aida:* La fatal pietra (with Martinelli) (Or. Bourdon)	17 May '26	BVE 35459-1, -2, -3	3040A 1744A DA 810 (UK)	
* 58.	*Aida:* Morir! si pura e bella! (with Martinelli) (Or. Bourdon)	17 May '26	BVE 35460-1, -2, -3	3040B 1744B DA 810 (UK)	
* 59.	*Aida:* O terra, addio! (Part 1) (with Martinelli and chorus) (Or. Bourdon)	17 May '26	BVE 35461-1, -2	3041A 1745A DA 809 (UK)	
* 60.	*Aida:* O terra, addio! (Part 2) (with Martinelli, Elsie Baker, and chorus) (Or. Bourdon)	17 May '26	BVE 35462-1, -2, -3	3041B 1745B DA 809 (UK)	
61.	A l'aimé (de Fontenailles) (Pf. Romani)	31 Oct. '39	PBS 042207-2, -3, -5	2053A	
* 62.	*Amadis:* Bois épais (Lully) (Pf. Chichagov)	16 Oct. '54	E 4-RC-0701-1, -2		LM 1889
63.	Amuri, amuri (Sadero) (Pf. Ponselle)	17 Oct. '54	E 4-RC-0707-1, -2		LM 1889
* 64.	An die musik (Schubert, Op. 88, No. 4) (Pf. Chichagov)	20 Oct. '54	E 4-RC-0723-1		EJS 243
65.	Aprile (Tosti) (Pf. Chichagov)	18 Oct. '54	E 4-RC-0710-1		LM 1889
* 66.	Asturiana (De Falla) (Pf. Chichagov)	18 Oct. '54	E 4-RC-0727-1, -2		ASCO A-125

DISCOG. NO.	DATE	MATRIX/ TAKE	78 RPM CAT. NO.	LP CAT. NO.
67. Ave Maria (Bach-Gounod) (Or. Bourdon)	*19 May '26*	CVE 35470-1, **-2**	6599A DB 1052 (UK)	
68. Ave Maria (Kahn) (Or. Bourdon)	*2 June '27* *13 June '27* *16 June '27*	BVE 38856-1, -2, -3 -4 -5, **-6**	1456A	
* 69. Ave Maria (Luzzi) (Organ, Chichagov)	*20 Oct. '54*	No number assigned		ASCO A-125
* 70. Ave Maria (Millard) (Organ, Chichagov)	*20 Oct. '54*	No number assigned	(Unpublished)	
* 71. Ave Maria (Sandoval) (Organ, Chichagov)	*20 Oct. '54*	No number assigned		ASCO A-125
* 72. Ave Maria (Schubert, Op. 52, No. 6) (Pf. Romani; Violin, M. Violin)	*1 Nov. '39* *7 Nov. '39*	PCS 042212-2, -3, **-5** -9, -10	VB 74 (UK)	LCT 10
* 73. Ave Maria (Tosti) (Pf. Chichagov)	*20 Oct. '54*	E 4-RC-0722-**1**		EJS 243
74. Battitori di grano, I (Sadero) (Pf. Chichagov)	*17 Oct. '54*	E 4-RC-0706-**1**, -2		LM 1889
75. Beau soir (Debussy) (Pf. Chichagov)	*17 Oct. '54*	No number assigned		LM 2047
* 76. Beloved (Silberta) (Or. Pasternack)	*1 June '25* *4 June '25* *5 June '25*	BVE 32852-1, -2, -3, -4 **-5**, -6	VA 67 (UK)	
77. Bonjour, Suzon (Delibes) (Pf. Chichagov)	*17 Oct. '54*	No number assigned		LM 2047
78. Carmè (arr. De Curtis) (Or. Bourdon)	*11 April '24*	B 29878-1, **-2**, -3	(66256) 1013B	

DISCOG. NO.	DATE	MATRIX/ TAKE	78 RPM CAT. NO.	LP CAT. NO.
79. Carmen-Carmela (arr. Ross) (Pf. Chichagov)	*21 Oct. '54*	No number assigned		LM 2047
80. Carry Me Back to Old Virginny (Bland) (Or. Pasternack)	*2 June '25*	CVE 32856-1, -2, -3	6509A DB 872 (UK)	
81. Chevelure, Le (Debussy) (Pf. Chichagov)	*17 Oct. '54*	No number assigned		LM 2047
82. Colombetta (Buzzi-Peccia) (Pf. Chichagov)	*20 Oct. '54*	E 4-RC-0725-1	(Unpublished)	
83. Could I (Tosti) (Pf. Ponselle)	*21 Oct. '54*	No number assigned		LM 2047
84. Cradle Song (Wiegenlied) (Brahms, Op. 49, No. 4) (Or. Bourdon)	*8 Feb. '24*	B 29453-**1**	(66240) 1002A	
85. Cradle Song (Wiegenlied) (Brahms, Op. 49, No. 4) (Pf. Bourdon)	*8 Feb. '24*	B 29454-1	(Unpublished)	
86. Dicitencello vuje (Falvo) (Pf. Ponselle)	*21 Oct. '54*	No number assigned		LM 2047
87. Drink to Me Only with Thine Eyes (Trad.) (Pf. Chichagov)	*19 Oct. '54*	E 4-RC-0719-**1**		LM 1889
* 88. Elégie (Massenet) (Or. Bourdon)	*19 May '26*	CVE 35469-**1**, -2, **-3**	6599B DB 1052 (UK)	
89. Erlkönig, Der (Schubert) (Pf. Chichagov)	*19 Oct. '54*	E 4-RC-0715-**1**, -2		LM 1889
* 90. *Ernani:* Sorta è la notte . . . Ernani! Ernani, involami (Or. Bourdon) a.	*5 Dec. '23*	C 29062-1		

259

DISCOG. NO.		DATE	MATRIX/ TAKE	78 RPM CAT. NO.	LP CAT. NO.
		11 Dec. '23	-2, -3		
		23 Jan. '24	**-4**	(74867)	
				6440B	
	b.	*16 June '27*	CVE 29062-5		
		17 Jan. '28	**-6**	6875B	
				DB 1275 (UK)	
91.	Extase (Duparc) (Pf. Chichagov)	*17 Oct. '54*	No number assigned	(Unpublished)	
92.	Fa la nana bambin (Sadero) (Pf. Ponselle)	*Oct. '54*	E 4-RC-0708-1, **-2**		LM 2047
93.	*Forza del destino, La:* La Vergine degli angeli (with Pinza and chorus) (Or. Setti)	*23 Jan. '28*	CVE 41636-**1**	8097B DB 1199 (UK)	
94.	*Forza del destino, La:* Pace, pace mio Dio (Or. Bourdon) a.	*5 Dec. '23* *11 Dec. '23* *23 Jan. '24*	C 29060-1, -2 -3, -4 **-5**	(74866) 6440A	
	b.	*13 June '27* *16 June '27* *17 Jan. '28*	CVE 29060-6 -7 **-8**, -9	6875A DB 1275 (UK)	
95.	*Forza del destino, La:* Io muoio! (with Martinelli and Pinza) (Or. Bourdon)	*18 Jan. '28*	CVE 41625-1, **-2**	8104A DB 1202 (UK)	
96.	*Forza del destino, La:* Non imprecare (with Martinelli and Pinza) (Or. Bourdon)	*18 Jan. '28*	CVE 41626-1, **-2**	8104B DB 1202 (UK)	
97.	*Gioconda, La:* Suicidio! (Or. Bourdon)	*14 Jan. '25*	C 31709-**1**, -2	6496A DB 854 (UK)	
98.	Good-Bye (Tosti) (Or. Bourdon) a.	*11 April '24*	C 29876-1, **-2**	(74886) 6453A	

DISCOG. NO.		DATE	MATRIX/ TAKE	78 RPM CAT. NO.	LP CAT. NO.
	b.	*2 June '27*	CVE 29876-3, -4		
		13 June '27	-5, **-6**	6711B	
99.	Guitares et mandolines (Saint-Saëns) (Pf. Chichagov)	*20 Oct. '54*	E 4-RC-0726-**1**		LM 1889
100.	Happy Days (Strelezki) (Or. Pasternack)	*1 June '25*	BVE 32839-1, -2, -3		
		4 June '25	-4, -5, -6		
		5 June '25	-7, -8		
* 101.	Home, Sweet Home (Bishop) (Or. Pasternack)	*3 June '25*	CVE 32866-1, **-2**	VB 74 (UK)	LCT 10
102.	Homing (Del Riego) (Pf. Chichagov)	*19 Oct. '54*	E 4-RC-0718-1, **-2**		LM 1889
103.	Ideale (Tosti) (Pf. Chichagov)	*18 Oct. '54*	E 4-RC-0709-**1**		LM 2047
104.	In questa tomba oscura (Beethoven) (Pf. Chichagov)	*17 Oct. '54*	E 4-RC-0702-**1**, -2		LM 1889
* 105.	In the Luxembourg Gardens (Lockhart-Manning) (Pf. Chichagov)	*19 Oct. '54*	No number assigned		EJS 247
* 106.	Invitation au voyage, L' (Duparc) (Pf. Chichagov)	*17 Oct. '54*	No number assigned		EJS 243
107.	Jeune fillette (Weckerlin) (Pf. Chichagov)	*17 Oct. '54*	E 4-RC-0703-**1**		LM 2047
* 108.	Little Old Garden, The (Hewitt) (Or. Pasternack)	*1 June '25*	BVE 32850-1, **-2**, -3	VA 67 (UK)	
109.	Love's Sorrow (Shelley) (Or. Bourdon)	*11 April '24*	B 29875-1, **-2**	1057A	
110.	Lullaby (Scott) (Pf. Bourdon)	*23 Jan. '24*	B 29412-1		
111.	Lullaby (Scott) (Or. Bourdon)	*8 Feb. '24*	B 29452-**1**, -2	(66241) 1002B	

DISCOG. NO.		DATE	MATRIX/ TAKE	78 RPM CAT. NO.	LP CAT. NO.
112.	Luna d'estate (Tosti) (Or. Bourdon)	*18 May '26*	BVE 35467-1 -2, -3	1164B DA 1035 (UK) VA 68 (UK)	
113.	Marechiare (Tosti) (Pf. Chichagov)	*18 Oct. '54*	No number assigned		LM 2047
114.	Maria, Mari! (Di Capua) (Or. Bourdon)	*23 Jan. '24* *11 April '24*	B 29411-1, -2 -3, -4	(66255) 1013A	
115.	Mirar de la Maja, El (Granados) (Pf. Chichagov)	*18 Oct. '54*	No number assigned		LM 2047
116.	Mir träumte von einem Königskind (Trunk, Op. 4, No. 5) (Pf. Chichagov)	*18 Oct. '54*	E 4-RC-0712-1		LM 1889
117.	*Molinara, La:* Nel cor più non me sento (Paisiello) (Pf. Chichagov)	*18 Oct. '54*	E 4-RC-0721-1		LM 2047
* 118.	Morgen (Strauss, Op. 27, No. 4) (Pf. Chichagov)	*19 Oct. '54*	E 4-RC-0717-1		ASCO A-125
119.	My Dearest Heart (Sullivan) (Or. Pasternack)	*1 June '25* *2 June '25* *4 June '25* *5 June '25*	BVE 32853-1, -2 -3, -4 -5, -6, -7 -8, -9, -10		
120.	My Lovely Celia (Higgins) (Or. Bourdon)	*11 April '24*	B 29877-1, -2	1057B	
* 121.	My Lovely Celia (Monro) (Pf. Chichagov)	*19 Oct. '54*	No number assigned		ASCO A-125
122.	My Old Kentucky Home (Foster) (Or. Pasternack)	*2 June '25*	CVE 32857-1, -2, -3	6509B	
* 123.	Nana (De Falla) (Pf. Chichagov)	*18 Oct. '54*	E 4-RC-0728-1		ASCO A-125

DISCOG. NO.	DATE	MATRIX/ TAKE	78 RPM CAT. NO.	LP CAT. NO.
124. Nightingale and the Rose, The (Rimsky-Korsakov) (Or. Bourdon; Flute, Barone)	2 June '27	BVE 38857-1, -2	1456B	
* 125. Nightingale and the Rose, The (Rimsky-Korsakov) (Pf. Romani)	31 Oct. '39	PBS 042208-2, -3	16451A	
* 126. Night Wind, The (Farley) (Pf. Chichagov)	19 Oct. '54	E 4-RC-0720-1, -2		LM 1889
* 127. None but the Lonely Heart (Tchaikovsky, Op. 6, No. 6) (Pf. Chichagov)	16 Oct. '54	No number assigned (2 takes)		ASCO A-125
128. Norma: Sediziose voci . . . Casta Diva (Part 1) (with chorus) (Or. Setti)	31 Dec. '28 30 Jan. '29	CVE 49031-1, -2, -3, -4	8125A DB 1280 (UK)	
129. Norma: Ah! bello a me ritorna (Casta Diva, Part 2) (with chorus) (Or. Setti)	31 Dec. '28	CVE 49032-1, -2	8125B DB 1280 (UK)	
130. Norma: Mira o Norma (Part 1) (with Telva) (Or. Setti)	30 Jan. '29	CVE 49703-1, -2	8110A DB 1276 (UK)	
131. Norma: Cedi . . . deh cedi! (Mira, o Norma, Part 2) (with Telva) (Or. Setti)	30 Jan. '29	CVE 49704-1, -2	8110B DB 1276 (UK)	
* 132. Nozze di Figaro, Le: Voi che sapete (Pf. Chichagov)	21 Oct. '54	No number assigned		ASCO A-125

DISCOG. NO.		DATE	MATRIX/ TAKE	78 RPM CAT. NO.	LP CAT. NO.
133.	O del mio amato ben (Donaudy) (Pf. Chichagov)	19 Oct. '54	E 4-RC-0714-1, -2		LM 1889
* 134.	Old Folks at Home (Foster) (Or. Pasternack)	3 June '25 4 June '25	CVE 32865-1, -2, -3, -4	IRCC 126 (3) DB 872 (4) (UK)	
135.	On Wings of Dream (Arensky) (Pf. Romani; Violin, M. Violin)	1 Nov. '39	PCS 042213-1, -3, -5	16451B	
136.	Otello: Salce! Salce! (Or. Bourdon)	23 Jan. '24	C 29410-1, -2	6474A DB 807 (UK)	
137.	Otello: Ave Maria (double string quartet, Bourdon)	23 Jan. '24	C 29409-1, -2, -3	6474B DB 807 (UK)	
138.	Panis Angelicus (Franck) (Organ, Chichagov)	21 Oct. '54	No number assigned	(Unpublished)	
139.	Partida, La (Alvarez) (Pf. Chichagov)	18 Oct. '54	E 4-RC-0713-1		LM 2047
140.	Perfect Day, A (Bond) (Or. Pasternack)	3 June '25	BVE 32867-1, -2, -3	1098B	
141.	Plaisir d'amour (Martini) (Pf. Chichagov)	17 Oct. '54	No number assigned		LM 2047
* 142.	Psyche (Paladilhe) (Pf. Chichagov)	21 Oct. '54	No number assigned		ASCO A-125
143.	Rispetto (Wolf-Ferrari) (Pf. Chichagov)	20 Oct. '54	E 4-RC-0724-1, -2		LM 1889
144.	Rosary, The (Nevin) (Or. Pasternack)	3 June '25 4 June '25 5 June '25	BVE 32864-1, -2, -3 -4, -5, -6 -7, -8	1098A	

DISCOG. NO.	DATE	MATRIX/ TAKE	78 RPM CAT. NO.	LP CAT. NO.
145. Rosemonde (Persico) (Pf. Chichagov)	17 Oct. '54	E 4-RC-0704-1		LM 1889
* 146. Rosita, La (Dupont) (Or. Pasternack)	1 June '25	BVE 32851-1, -2, -3		
	4 June '25	-4, -5	VA 69 (UK)	
* 147. Se (Denza) (Pf. Chichagov)	18 Oct. '54	No number assigned		ASCO A-125
148. Serenade (Tosti) (Harp Lapitino) a.	12 April '24	C 29879-1, -2, -3	(74887) 6453B	
b.	2 June '27	CVE 29879-4, -5	6711B	
149. Since First I Met Thee (Rubinstein) (Or. Bourdon)	17 Jan. '28	BVE 41624-1, -2, -3	1319B DA 1023 (UK)	
150. Si tu le voulais (Tosti) (Pf. Romani)	31 Oct. '39	PBS 042206-2, -3, -5	2053B	
151. Songs My Mother Taught Me (Dvořák, Op. 55, No. 4) (Or. Bourdon)	17 Jan. '28	BVE 41623-1	1319A DA 1023 (UK)	
* 152. Spagnola, La (Di Chiara) (Or. Pasternack)	5 June '25	BVE 32873-1, -2, -3	VA 69 (UK)	
* 153. Ständchen (Schubert) (with C. Ponselle) (Or. Bourdon)	19 May '26	CVE 35471-1, -2		VIC 1507
154. Star vicino (Rosa) (Pf. Chichagov)	19 Oct. '54	E 4-RC-0715-1		LM 2047
155. Temps des lilas, Le (Chausson) (Pf. Chichagov)	17 Oct. '54	E 4-RC-0705-1		LM 1889
* 156. Tod und das Mädchen, Der (Schubert, Op. 7, No. 3) (Pf. Chichagov)	18 Oct. '54	No number assigned		ASCO A-125

DISCOG. NO.	DATE	MATRIX/ TAKE	78 RPM CAT. NO.	LP CAT. NO.
* 157. Träume (Wagner) (Pf. Chichagov)	19 Oct. '54	No number assigned		ASCO A-125
* 158. Tre giorni son che Nina (Ciampi) (Pf. Chichagov)	19 Oct. '54	No number assigned (2 takes)		ASCO A-125
* 159. Tristesse eternelle (Chopin, Etudes, Op. 10, No. 3) (Pf. Chichagov)	21 Oct. '54	No number assigned		ASCO A-125
* 160. Trovatore, Il: Miserere (with Martinelli and chorus) (Or. Setti)	23 Jan. '28	CVE 41637-1, -2	8097A DB 1199 (UK)	
161. Vestale, La: Tu che invoco (Or. Bourdon)	18 May '26	CVE 35464-1, -2	6605A DB 1274 (UK) VB 3 (UK)	
162. Vestale, La: O nume tutelar (Or. Bourdon)	18 May '26	CVE 35465-1, -2	6605B DB 1274 (UK) VB 3 (UK)	
163. Von ewiger Liebe (Brahms, Op. 43, No. 1) (Pf. Chichagov)	18 Oct. '54	E 4-RC-0711-1		LM 1889
164. Vucchella, 'A (Tosti) (Or. Bourdon)	18 May '26	BVE 35466-1, -2, -3	1164A DA 1035 (UK)	
165. Vucchella, 'A (Tosti) (Pf. Chichagov)	18 Oct. '54	No number assigned		LM 2047
* 166. When I Have Sung My Songs (Charles) (Pf. Romani)	31 Oct. '39	PBS 042209-1, -2, -3	VA 68 (UK)	CBL 100

PART III

OFF-THE-AIR RECORDINGS

DISCOG. NO.		DATE	LP RECORDINGS
167.	*Aida:* Ritorna vincitor (Or. Rapee)	*27 Sept. '36*	EJS 169, EJS 190, ANNA 1036, MDP-012
168.	*Alceste:* Divinités du Styx (Or. Kostelanetz)	*3 Dec. '34*	EJS 104, EJS 190, ANNA 1036, MDP-012
169.	Annie Laurie (Scott) (Or. Rapee)	*31 May '36*	OASI 635
170.	Auld Lang Syne (Trad.)	*31 Dec. '36*	
171.	Ave Maria (Kahn) (Or. Goossens)	*25 April '37*	OASI 635
172.	Ave Maria (Sandoval) a. (Or. Kostelanetz) b. (Or. Kostelanetz)	*19 Nov. '34* *25 March '36*	EJS 104, EJS 191, UORC 118, ASCO A-125, MDP-029
173.	Ave Maria (Schubert, Op. 52, No. 6) (Or. Rapee)	*31 May '36*	OASI 635
174.	Big Brown Bear (Mana-Zucca) (Pf. Henderson)	*3 Dec. '34*	ASCO A-125, MDP-029
175.	Blue Danube Waltz (Strauss) (Or. Kostelanetz)	*15 Oct. '34*	ASCO A-125, MDP-029
* 176.	*Carmen* (excerpts) (with Kullman, Pinza, etc.) (Or. Hasslemans) MET (NYC)	*1 Feb. '36*	EJS 219, ANNA 1037
177.	*Carmen* (complete) (with Maison, Pinza, Burke, etc.) (Or. Hasslemans) MET (Boston)	*28 March '36*	EJS 117, GFOPC P-1610, HRE 253-3
178.	*Carmen* (complete) (with Rayner, Huehn, Bodanya, etc.) (Or. Papi) MET (NYC)	*9 Jan. '37*	UORC 209

DISCOG. NO.		DATE	LP RECORDINGS

* 179.	*Carmen* (complete) (with Maison,
	    Huehn, Burke, etc.)
	    (Or. Papi)
	    MET (Cleveland)
		17 April '37	EJS 103/4 (excerpts),
			    OPA 10016/18, MET-7

180.	*Carmen:* Habanera
	    a. (fragment) (Or. Pasternack)
	    b. (with chorus) (Or.
	        Kostelanetz)
	    c. (with chorus) (Or.
	        Kostelanetz)
		7 Dec. '30
		
		26 Nov. '34
		
		25 March '36
			EJS 452
			
			EJS 190, MDP-012

181.	*Carmen:* Seguidilla
	    (Or. Kostelanetz)
		26 Feb. '36	EJS 190, ASCO A-125,
			    MDP -012

182.	*Carmen:* Chanson bohème
	    a. (with chorus) (Or.
	        Kostelanetz)
	    b. (with chorus) (Or.
	        Kostelanetz)
		8 Oct. '34
		
		4 March '36
			
			EJS 190, MDP-012

183.	*Carmen:* Air des cartes (Or. Kostelanetz)	*26 Feb. '36*	EJS 190, MDP-012

184.	Carry Me Back to Old Virginny
	    (Bland)
	    a. (Or. Rapee)
	    b. (with chorus) (Or. Black)
		24 May '36
		2 May '37
			
			EJS 192, ASCO A-125,
			    MDP-029

185.	*Cavalleria rusticana:* Ave Maria
	    (adapted from Intermezzo)
	    (with chorus)
	    (Or. Kostelanetz)
		8 Oct. '34	EJS 532, MDP-029

* 186.	*Cavalleria rusticana:* Voi lo sapete
	    a. (Or. Kostelanetz)
	
	    b. (Or. Rapee)
		11 March '36
		
		24 May '36
			EJS 190, ASCO A-125,
			    UORC 118, ANNA 1036
			MDP-012

187.	*Chocolate Soldier, The:* My hero
	    a. (Or. Kostelanetz)
	    b. (with Frank Forest) (Or.
	        (Goossens)
		8 Oct. '34
		
		25 April '37
			EJS 532
			
			OASI 635, MDP-029

188.	Clavelitos (Valverde)
	    (Or. Kostelanetz)
		4 March '36	EJS 191, ASCO A-125,
			    UORC 118, MDP-029

189.	Comin' Thro' the Rye (Trad.) (Or. Kostelanetz)	*11 March '36*	EJS 192, MDP-029

190.	Cradle Song (Wiegenlied)
	    (Brahms, Op. 49, No. 4)
	    (Or. Kostelanetz)
		15 Oct. '34	

191.	Cuckoo, The (Lehmann) (Or. Kostelanetz)	*1 April '36*	EJS 192, MDP-029

192.	Cuckoo Clock, The
	    (Griselle-Young)
	    (Or. Kostelanetz)
		1 Oct. '34	EJS 192, MDP-029

DISCOG. NO.		DATE	LP RECORDINGS
193.	Danny Boy (Trad.) (Or. Kostelanetz)	*4 March '36*	EJS 192, MDP-012
194.	Dicitencello vuje (Falvo) (Or. Kostelanetz)	*27 Sept. '36*	EJS 191, UORC 118, MDP-012
* 195.	*Don Giovanni* (excerpts) (with Pinza, Schipa, Müller, etc.) (Or. Serafin) MET (NYC)	*20 Jan. '34*	UORC 216, ANNA 1036
* 196.	*Don Giovanni:* Batti, batti (Or. Kostelanetz)	*1 Oct. '34*	EJS 104, EJS 190, ASCO A-125, ANNA 1036, MDP-012
197.	Dream, A (Bartlett) (Or. Kostelanetz)	*26 Nov. '34*	EJS 243, MDP-012
198.	Drink to Me Only with Thine Eyes (Trad.) (Pf. Ross)	*2 May '37*	
199.	Erlkönig, Der (Schubert) (Or. Kostelanetz)	*4 March '36*	EJS 191, UORC 118, MDP-012
200.	Estrellita (Ponce) (Or. Kostelanetz)	*19 Nov. '34*	
201.	*Fedra:* O divina Afrodite (Romani)		
	a. (Or. Kostelanetz)	*18 March '36*	EJS 104
	b. (Or. Black)	*2 May '37*	EJS 141, EJS 190, ASCO A-125, ANNA 1036, MDP-012
202.	*Forza del destino, La:* La Vergine degli angeli (with chorus)	*10 Dec. '36*	OASI 635
203.	Golondrina, La (Trad.) (Or. Kostelanetz)	*15 Oct. '34*	EJS 532, MDP-029
204.	Good-Bye (Tosti)		
	a. (Or. Kostelanetz)	*3 Dec. '34*	
	b. (Or. Kostelanetz)	*1 April '36*	EJS 191
205.	Here's to Romance: I Carry You in My Pocket (Grosvener) (with chorus) (Or. Kostelanetz)	*26 Feb. '36*	EJS 192, MDP-012
* 206.	Home, Sweet Home (Bishop) (Pf. Ponselle)	*2 May '37*	EJS 192, MDP-012
207.	Homing (Del Riego)		
	a. (Or. Kostelanetz)	*1 Oct. '34*	
	b. (Or. Rapee)	*27 Sept. '36*	EJS 192, UORC 118, MDP-029
208.	Humoresque (Dvořák) (with chorus) (Or. Kostelanetz)	*18 March '36*	EJS 192
209.	Ich liebe dich (Grieg, Op. 5, No. 3) (Or. Kostelanetz)	*25 March '36*	MDP-029

DISCOG. NO.		DATE	LP RECORDINGS
210.	I Love You Truly (Bond) (Or. Kostelanetz)	*1 Oct. '34*	EJS 192, MDP-029
211.	In the Luxembourg Gardens (Lockhart-Manning) (Or. Kostelanetz)	*8 Oct. '34*	
212.	Last Rose of Summer, The (Moore) (with chorus) (Or. Kostelanetz)	*29 Oct. '34*	
213.	*Mademoiselle Modiste:* Kiss Me Again (Or. Black)	*2 May '37*	EJS 192
214.	Marechiare (Tosti) (Or. Rapee)	*24 May '36*	EJS 191, ASCO A-125, MDP-029
215.	Mariä Wiegenlied (Reger, Op. 76, No. 52) (Or. Kostelanetz)	*3 Dec. '34*	MDP-029
216.	*Merry Widow, The:* Waltz (Or. Kostelanetz)	*19 Nov. '34*	
217.	Moonlight Bay (Wenrich)	*10 Dec. '36*	OASI 621
218.	Morenita, El (Buzzi-Peccia) (Or. Kostelanetz)	*1 April '36*	EJS 191, ASCO A-125, MDP-012
219.	My Old Kentucky Home (Foster) (Or. Black)	*2 May '37*	
220.	Night Wind, The (Farley) a. (Or. Kostelanetz) b. (Or. Goossens)	*25 March '36* *25 April '37*	EJS 192, UORC 118 OASI 635
221.	None but the Lonely Heart (Tchaikovsky, Op. 6, No. 6) a. (Or. Kostelanetz) b. (Or. Goossens)	*26 Feb. '36* *25 April '37*	EJS 191 OASI 635
222.	Old Refrain, The (Kreisler) a. (Or. Kostelanetz) b. (Or. Goossens)	*11 March '36* *25 April '37*	EJS 192, ASCO A-125 OASI 635
* 223.	*Otello:* Ave Maria (Or. Rapee)	*27 Sept. '36*	EJS 184, EJS 190, ASCO A-125, UORC 118, MDP-012, ANNA 1036
224.	Ouvre ton coeur (Bizet) a. (Or. Kostelanetz) b. (Or. Rapee)	*18 March '36* *27 Sept. '36*	EJS 191, ASCO A-125, UORC 118, MDP-012
225.	Rosary, The (Nevin) (with chorus) (Or. Kostelanetz)	*26 Nov. '34*	
* 226.	*Samson et Dalila:* Printemps qui commence (Or. Kostelanetz)	*29 Oct. '34*	EJS 243, ANNA 1037, MDP-012

DISCOG. NO.		DATE	LP RECORDINGS
227.	*Semiramide:* Bel raggio (Or. Rapee)	*24 May '36*	EJS 104, EJS 190, ASCO A-125, ANNA 1036, MDP-012
228.	Sleigh, The (Tchervanow-Kountz) (Or. Kostelanetz)	*19 Nov. '34*	
229.	Ständchen (Schubert) (fragment) (Or. Pasternack)	*7 Dec. '30*	EJS 452
* 230.	*Traviata, La* (complete) (with Tibbett, Jagel, etc.) (Or. Panizza) MET (NYC)	*5 Jan. '35*	EJS 107
231.	*Traviata, La:* Addio del passato (Or. Rapee)	*24 May '36*	EJS 190, EJS 104, MDP-012
232.	*Trovatore, Il:* Miserere (with De Filippi and chorus) (Or. Kolar)	*17 March '35*	UORC 105, MDP-012
233.	Ultima canzone, L' (Tosti) (Or. Kostelanetz)	*11 March '36*	EJS 191, UORC 118, MDP-029
234.	*Vestale, La:* Tu che invoco (Or. Kostelanetz)	*1 April '36*	EJS 190, ASCO A-125, ANNA 1037, MDP-012
235.	Violetera, La (Padilla) (Or. Kostelanetz)	*29 Oct. '34*	
236.	What's in the Air Today (Eden) (Or. Kostelanetz)	*26 Nov. '34*	EJS 243, MDP-029
237.	When I Have Sung My Songs (Charles) (Or. Kostelanetz)	*18 March '36*	EJS 192
238.	Will-o'-the-Wisp (Spross) (Or. Kostelanetz)	*15 Oct. '34*	

PART IV

PRIVATE RECORDINGS

DISCOG. NO.		DATE	LP RECORDINGS
239.	Adeste Fideles (Trad.) (O Come, All Ye Faithful)	25 Dec. '51	
	(with C. Ponselle)	25 Dec. '52	
	(with chorus) (Organ, Chichagov)	25 Dec. '53	E 4-KP-1517
		25 Dec. '55	
		25 Dec. '58	
240.	*Adriana Lecouvreur:* Io son l'umile ancella		
	a. (Pf. Romani)	16 April '50	
	b. (Pf.)	5 Sept. '53	EJS 243, ANNA 1036, MDP-036
241.	*Adriana Lecouvreur:* Poveri fiori		
	a. (Pf. Romani)	16 April '50	
	b. (Pf.)	5 Sept. '53	EJS 243, ANNA 1036, MDP-036
242.	*Adriana Lecouvreur:* O vagabonda (Pf.) (incomplete)	5 Sept. '53	
* 243.	Agnus Dei (Bizet)		
	a. (Pf. Chichagov)	24 Aug. '53	GR 103
	b. (Organ, Chichagov)	25 Dec. '53	E 4-KP-1517
* 244.	*Aida:* Act II, Scene 1, Aida/Amneris duet (complete)		
	a. (with Rock) (Pf. Chichagov)	6 July '53	
	b. (with Jones, Stewart, and Powers) (Pf.)	Fall '69	
	c. (with Nadler) (Pf.)	July '75	
245.	A l'aimé (de Fontenailles)		
	a. (Pf.)	19 June '52	
	b. (Pf.)	23 Oct. '52	
	c. (Pf.)	6 March '53	
246.	*Alceste:* Divinités du Styx (Pf. Romani)	'49	UORC 118B
247.	Altra sera la mia Nina, L' (Sadero)		
	a. (Pf.)	4 Oct. '52	
	b. (Pf.)	16 Oct. '52	
248.	*Amadis:* Bois épais (Lully)		
	a. (Pf. Chichagov) (3 takes)	4 Oct. '52	
	b. (Pf. Ponselle)	8 Nov. '52	
	c. (Pf.)	28 May '53	

DISCOG. NO.		DATE	LP RECORDINGS

249. *Amico Fritz, L':* Son pochi fiori
    a. (Pf.) — *26 May '51* — MDP-036
    b. (Pf.) — *19 June '52*
    c. (Pf. Romani) (incomplete) — *Jan. '52*
    d. (Pf.) — *24 Aug. '53*

* 250. *Amore dei tre re, L':* Dammi le labbra
    (Pf. Ponselle) — *26 May '51*

251. Amor è una pietanza, L' (Sadero)
    (Pf.) — *4 Oct. '52*

252. Amuri, amuri (Sadero)
    a. (Pf. Romani) — *'49* — UORC 118
    b. (Pf.) — *10 Jan. '51*
    c. (Pf.) — *27 June '51*
    d. (Pf. Romani) — *Jan. '52*
    e. (Pf.) — *31 Aug. '52*
    f. (Pf.) — *4 Oct. '52*
    g. (Pf.) — *23 Oct. '52*
    h. (Pf.) — *14 Dec. '52*
    i. (Pf.) — *6 March '53*
    j. (Pf.) — *22 Oct. '53*
    k. (Pf.) — *22 Nov. '53*
    l. (Pf.) — *22 April '54*
    m. (Pf. Templeton) — *28 June '54*
    n. (Pf.) — *23 May '58*

253. An die musik (Schubert, Op. 88, No. 4)
    a. (Pf. Chichagov) (2 takes) — *5 Sept. '53*
    b. (Pf.) — *6 Sept. '53*

254. *Andrea Chénier:* Vicino a te
    (with Khanzadian) (Pf. Yanuzzi) — *Spring of '72*

255. Annie Laurie (Scott)
    (Pf. Ponselle) (2 takes) — *25 Dec. '57*

256. Après un rêve (Fauré)
    a. (Pf.) — *15 May '50* — EJS 191
    b. (Pf.) — *18 Feb. '53*
    c. (Pf.) — *24 Aug. '53*

257. *Arlesiana, L':* Esser madre
    (Pf.) — *5 Sept. '53* — ASCO A-125

258. Auld Lang Syne (Trad.)
    a. (with Tibbett, Crooks, Melchior, Carminati, and Yurka) (Pf.) — *31 Dec. '35*
    b. (Nelson Eddy's house) (Pf.) — *31 Dec. '36*
    c. (3 takes) — *4 Jan. '52*
    d. (Pf.) — *25 Dec. '52*
    e. (with Keeler, Kelly) — *?*
    f. (with Bampton, Albanese, Roman, Guilford, Stokes, and Baklanova) (Pf. Chichagov) — *22 Jan. '77*

DISCOG. NO.		DATE	LP RECORDINGS
g.	(with Albanese, Roman, Guilford, etc.) (Pf. Chichagov)	23 Jan. '77	
*259.	Ave Maria (Luzzi)		
a.	(Pf. Chichagov)	24 Aug. '53	GR 103
b.	(Organ, Chichagov)	25 Dec. '53	E 4-KP-1517
c.	(Pf. Chichagov)	7 Dec. '53	EJS 191
d.	(Organ)	11 Jan. '54	
260.	Ave Maria (Millard)		
	(Organ, Chichagov)	22 Nov. '53	
261.	Ave Maria (Sandoval)		
a.	(Organ/Chimes, Chichagov)	7 Dec. '53	E 4-KP-1517
b.	(Organ, Chichagov)	3 Jan. '54	
262.	Ave Maria, (Schubert, Op. 52, No. 6)		
a.	(Organ, Barstow) (Sacred Heart Catholic Church)	24 Dec. '50	
b.	(Pf. Romani)	16 Jan. '51	
c.	(Pf. Ponselle)	25 Sept. '52	
d.	(Pf.)	25 Dec. '52	
e.	(Organ/Harp, Belvedere Hotel)	8 May '53	
f.	(Organ, Chichagov)	25 Dec. '54	
g.	(Organ, Chichagov)	25 Dec. '55	
h.	(Pf.)	23 May '58	
i.	(Organ)	25 Dec. '58	
j.	(Pf. Ponselle) (incomplete)	4 April '76	
k.	(Pf. Chichagov)	23 Jan. '77	
263.	Ave Maria (Tosti)		
a.		15 May '50	
b.		19 June '52	
264.	Away in a Manger (Luther)		
a.	(with chorus) (Pf. Chichagov)	Dec. '52	
b.	(with Frankel) (Organ, Chichagov)	25 Dec. '54	
265.	Beau soir (Debussy)		
a.	(Pf.)	?	
b.	(Pf.)	22 Nov. '53	
266.	Berceaux, Les, (Fauré, Op. 23, No. 1)		
a.	(Pf. Romani)	15 April '50	
b.	(Pf.)	19 June '52	
c.	(Pf.)	18 Feb. '53	
267.	Bohème, La: Addio (Bada, sotto il guanciale notte) (fragment coaching unknown soprano) (Pf.)	13 Sept. '52	
268.	Bohème, La: Quartet: Addio, sognante vita (with Doubleday) (Pf.)	31 Aug. '52	

DISCOG. NO.		DATE	LP RECORDINGS
269.	*Bohème, La:* O Rodolfo (Pf. Serafin)	*23 Oct. '52*	
270.	*Bohème, La:* Vecchia zimarra, senti (Pf. Serafin)	*23 Oct. '52*	
271.	*Bohème, La:* Sono andati? (Pf. Serafin) (2 different Oct. rehearsals exist)	*23 Oct. '52*	
272.	*Bohème, La:* La mia cuffietta (Pf. Serafin)	*23 Oct. '52*	
273.	*Call Me Madam:* I hear singing (with Stritch & Smith) (Pf.)	*13 Jan. '53*	
* 274.	*Carmen:* Habanera		
	a. (Pf.) (screen test)	*13 April '36*	
	b. (Pf. M. Martinet)	*27 June '51*	
	c. (Pf. Chichagov)	*27 Oct. '51*	
	d. (incomplete) (Pf.)	*28 May '53*	
275.	*Carmen:* Enfin c'est toi! (with Kelly) (Pf.)	*14 Dec. '52*	
* 276.	*Carmen:* Chanson bohème (Pf.) (screen test)	*13 April '36*	
277.	*Carmen:* Melons! Coupons! (Trio, Act III, inc. Air des cartes) (with Kemp, Nuttall) (Pf.)	*7 Dec. '53*	
278.	*Carmen:* Air des cartes (Voyons, que j'essaie à mon tour)		
	a. (Pf. M. Martinet)	*27 June '51*	
	b. (Pf. Chichagov)	*27 Oct. '51*	
	c. (Pf.)	*14 Dec. '52*	RPX 102
	d. (with Kemp, Nuttall) (Pf.)	*7 Dec. '53*	
279.	*Carmen:* Si tu m'aimes, Carmen (with Kirkham) (4 takes) (Pf.)	*15 March '57*	
280.	*Carmen:* C'est toi? C'est moi!		
	a. (with Kelly) (Pf.) (2 takes)	*14 Dec. '52*	
	b. (with Khanzadian) (Pf. Yanuzzi)	*Spring '72*	
281.	Caro mio ben (Giordani) (with Pavarotti) (Pf. Ponselle)	*4 April '76*	
282.	Carry Me Back to Old Virginny (Bland)		
	a. (Pf.) (2 takes)	*3 April '53*	
	b. (Pf.) (3 takes)	*4 May '54*	
	c. (incomplete) (Pf. Ponselle)	*4 April '76*	
283.	*Cenerentola, La:* Nacqui all' affanno e al pianto (coaching Baklanov) (Pf. Chichagov)	*23 Nov. '52*	
284.	Chanson triste (Duparc) (incomplete) (Pf.)	*15 May '50*	
285.	Chevelure, Le (Debussy) (Pf.)	*24 Nov. '52*	

DISCOG. NO.		DATE	LP RECORDINGS
286.	Comin' Thro' the Rye (Trad.) (Pf. Romani) (2 takes)	*Jan. '52*	
287.	Contemplation (Widor) (Pf. Chichagov)	*19 Nov. '58*	
288.	Could I (Tosti)		
	a. (Pf.)	*1 Oct. '49*	EJS 532
	b. (Pf.) (Deutsches Haus)	*23 May '52*	
	c. (Pf.)	*14 Dec. '52*	
	d. (Pf.)	*6 March '53*	
	e. (Pf.)	*22 April '54*	
289.	Deck the Halls (Trad.) (with chorus) (Organ, Chichagov)	*25 Dec. '54*	
290.	Deh vieni (The Gem) (R. Ponselle) (Pf. Ponselle)	*18 March '53*	
* 291.	Dicitencello vuje (Falvo)		
	a. (Pf. Romani)	*'49*	UORC 118
	b. (Pf. Romani)	*Jan. '52*	
	c. (Pf.)	*15 April '50*	
	d. (Pf. Ponselle)	*23 Oct. '52*	
	e. (Pf.)	*6 March '53*	
	f. (Pf. Chichagov)	*28 May '53*	
292.	*Don Giovanni:* Là ci darem la mano		
	a. (with Hecht) (Pf.)	*3 May '53*	
	b. (with Hensen) (Pf.)	*3 May '53*	
	c. (with Pinza) (Pf.)	*8 May '53*	EJS 243, ANNA 1037, MDP-012
	d. (with Hecht) (Pf.)	*22 April '54*	
	e. (with J. Morris) (incomplete) (Pf. Yanuzzi)	*'71*	
293.	Dream, A (Bartlett) (sung as duet with Caruso record) (2 takes)	*31 Aug. '52*	
294.	Drink to Me Only with Thine Eyes (Trad.) (Pf.) (2 takes)	*4 Jan. '52*	
295.	Elégie (Massenet) (Pf. Romani)	*18 Feb. '53*	
296.	Erlkönig, Der (Schubert)		
	a. (Pf. Romani)	*15 April '50*	
	b. (Pf. Chichagov) (2 takes)	*5 Sept. '53*	
297.	Eros (Grieg) (Pf.)	*9 Dec. '51*	
298.	Extase (Duparc)		
	a. (Pf.)	*9 Dec. '51*	
	b. (Pf. Romani)	*Jan. '52*	
299.	Faith (Mana-Zucca) (incomplete) (Pf. Chichagov)	*23 May '58*	

DISCOG. NO.			DATE	LP RECORDINGS

300. Fa la nana bambin (Sadero)
  a. (Pf. Ponselle) — 27 June '51
  b. (Pf. Chichagov) — 27 Oct. '51
  c. (Pf.) — 11 Nov. '51
  d. (Pf. Romani) — Jan. '52
  e. (Pf.) (2 takes, sung in English) — 1 June '52
  f. (Pf.) — 18 Feb. '53
  g. (Pf.) — 6 March '53
  h. (Pf.) (incomplete) — 22 April '54
  i. (Pf. Templeton) — 28 June '54
  j. (Pf.) (incomplete) — 23 May '58
  k. (Pf. Ponselle) — 24 Dec. '68

301. *Fedra:* O divina Afrodite
  a. (Pf. Romani) — '49 — UORC 118
  b. (Pf. Romani) — 15 April '50

302. First Noël, The
  a. (with chorus) (Organ, Chichagov) — 25 Dec. '52
  b. — 25 Dec. '54
  c. — 25 Dec. '55
  d. (with Baklanova, Sanchez, Amparan, and Hankin) (Organ, Chichagov) — 25 Dec. '57
  e. — 25 Dec. '58

303. *Fortunio:* La maison grise
  a. (Pf. Chichagov) — 30 March '57 — RPX 102, EJS 243, ANNA 1037, MDP-036
  b. (incomplete) (Pf.) — 23 May '58

304. *Forza del destino, La:* La Vergine degli angeli
  a. (with Hecht) (Pf.) — 3 May '53
  b. (with Pinza and chorus) (Pf.) — 8 May '53 — EJS 243, ANNA 1037, MDP-012

305. Gesù Bambino (Yon) (with Nuttall and Vartenissian) (Organ, Chichagov) — 25 Dec. '53 — E 4-KP-1517

306. *Gianni Schicchi:* O mio babbino caro
  a. (Pf.) — 19 June '52
  b. (Pf. Ponselle) — 30 June '52 — RPX 102, MDP-036
  c. (Pf.) — 31 Aug. '52
  d. (incomplete) (Pf.) — 4 Oct. '52
  e. (Pf.) — 23 Oct. '52

307. Hark! the Herald Angels Sing (Mendelssohn)
  a. (with C. Ponselle) (Organ, Chichagov) — 25 Dec. '51
  b. (with chorus) (Organ, Chichagov) — 25 Dec. '52
  c. (with chorus) (Organ, Chichagov) — 25 Dec. '55

		DATE	LP RECORDINGS
	d. (with Baklanova, Hankin, Amparan, and chorus) (Organ, Chichagov)	25 Dec. '57	
308.	Heureux Vagabond, L' (Bruneau)		
	a. (Pf.) (3 takes)	8 Nov. '52	
	b. (Pf.) (2 takes)	3 April '53	
	c. (Pf.)	5 Sept. '53	
309.	Home, Sweet Home (Bishop) (Pf. Romani)	Jan. '52	
310.	I Love You Truly (Bond) (Pf. Ponselle)	24 Dec. '68 22 Jan. '77	
311.	In questa tomba oscura (Beethoven)		
	a. (Pf. Chichagov)	27 Oct. '51	
	b. (Pf. Romani)	Jan. '52	
	c. (incomplete) (Pf. Ponselle)	24 Dec. '68	
	d. (incomplete) (Pf. Ponselle)	4 April '76	
312.	In the Luxembourg Gardens (Lockhart-Manning) (incomplete) (Pf. Chichagov)	23 May '58	
313.	Invitation au voyage, L' (Duparc)		
	a. (Pf.)	15 May '50	
	b. (Pf.) (3 takes)	24 Aug. '53	
314.	It Came Upon the Midnight Clear (Trad.)		
	a. (with C. Ponselle and chorus) (Organ, Chichagov)	25 Dec. '51	
	b. (with chorus) (Organ, Chichagov)	25 Dec. '52	
	c. (with chorus) (Organ, Chichagov)	25 Dec. '54	
	d. (with Baklanova, Sanchez, Hankin, and Amparan) (Organ, Chichagov)	25 Dec. '57	
315.	J'ai pleuré en rêve (Hüe)		
	a. (Pf.)	15 May '50	
	b. (Pf. Chichagov)	5 Sept. '53	
316.	Jardin d'amour (Vuillermoz) (Pf.)	5 Sept. '53	RPX 102
317.	Jeanne d'Arc: Adieu, forêts		
	a. (Pf. Romani)	'49	UORC 118
	b. (Pf.)	31 Aug. '52	
318.	Jingle Bells (with children's chorus) (Organ, Chichagov)	25 Dec. '54	
319.	Joy to the World (Handel) (with Werle and chorus) (Organ, Chichagov)	25 Dec. '54	
320.	Kiss Me, Kate: So in love		
	a. (Pf. Romani)	1 Oct. '49	RPX 102
	b. (Pf.)	5 Jan. '50	
	c. (Pf.) (incomplete) (Deutsches Haus)	23 May '52	

DISCOG. NO.			DATE	LP RECORDINGS
	d.	(Or.) (Deutsches Haus)	*23 May '52*	
	e.	(Pf.)	*3 May '53*	
	f.	(Pf.)	*8 May '53*	
321.	\multicolumn{2}{l}{Let's Go—Where do you want to go? (improvisation, vocalise) (with Pavarotti) (Pf. Ponselle)}		*4 April '76*	
322.	\multicolumn{2}{l}{Lullaby (Scott) (Pf.)}		*7 Dec. '53*	
* 323.	\multicolumn{2}{l}{*Madama Butterfly:* Lo so che (with Khanzadian and Hankin) (Pf. Yanuzzi)}		*Spring of '72*	
324.	\multicolumn{2}{l}{Mainacht, Die (Brahms, Op. 43, No. 2) (Pf. Chichagov)}		*24 Aug. '53*	
* 325.	\multicolumn{2}{l}{*Manon:* Je suis encore tout étourdie (with Sills) (Pf.)}		*20 Nov. '52*	
* 326.	\multicolumn{2}{l}{*Manon:* Pardonnez-moi/On l'appelle Manon (with Sills) (Pf.)}		*24 Nov. '52*	
* 327.	\multicolumn{2}{l}{*Manon:* Non! Je ne veux pas croire (with Sills) (Pf.)}		*24 Nov. '52*	
* 328.	\multicolumn{2}{l}{*Manon:* Adieu notre petite table}			
	a.	(Pf. Ponselle)	*20 Nov. '52*	
	b.		*24 Nov. '52*	EJS 243, ANNA 1037, MDP-036
	c.	(Pf. Romani)	*18 Feb. '53*	
	d.	(Pf.)	*6 March '53*	
	e.		*28 May '53*	
* 329.	\multicolumn{2}{l}{*Manon:* Le Rêve (Pf.) (2 takes)}		*24 Nov. '52*	
* 330.	\multicolumn{2}{l}{*Manon:* Gavotte (Pf.)}		*23 Nov. '52*	
331.	\multicolumn{2}{l}{Mariä Wiegenlied (Reger)}			
	a.	(Pf. Romani)	*'49*	UORC 118B
	b.	(incomplete) (Pf.)	*23 July '51*	
	c.	(Pf.)	*27 Oct. '51*	
* 332.	\multicolumn{2}{l}{*Messa da Requiem:* Recordatus (Verdi) (with Joan Crawford) (Pf.) (M-G-M)}		*Circa 1938*	CC 100/23
333.	\multicolumn{2}{l}{Mir träumte von einem Königskind, (Trunk, Op. 4, No. 5) (Pf. Romani)}		*15 April '50*	
334.	\multicolumn{2}{l}{*Molinara, La:* Nel cor più non me sento (Paisiello)}			
	a.	(Pf. Romani)	*Jan. '52*	
	b.	(Pf.)	*6 March '53*	
335.	\multicolumn{2}{l}{Morgen (Strauss, Op. 27, No. 4)}			
	a.	(Pf.)	*11 Nov. '51*	
	b.	(Pf. Chichagov)	*5 Sept. '53*	

DISCOG. NO.		DATE	LP RECORDINGS
336.	My Old Kentucky Home (Foster) (Pf. Yanuzzi)	'71	
337.	Nacht und Traume (Schubert, Op. 43, No. 2)		
	a. (Pf. Chichagov) (5 takes)	4 Oct. '52	
	b. (Pf.) (2 takes)	24 Aug. '53	
338.	Night (Tchaikovsky) (Pf.)	23 July '51	
339.	Night Wind, The (Farley)		
	a.	23 July '51	
	b. (incomplete) (Pf.)	27 Oct. '51	
	c. (Pf. Romani) (2 takes)	Jan. '52	
	d. (Pf.)	22 April '54	
340.	None but the Lonely Heart (Tchaikovsky, Op. 6, No. 6)		
	a. (Pf. Romani)	'49	UORC 118
	b. (Pf. Romani)	15 April '50	
	c. (Pf. Romani)	Jan. '52	
	d. (Pf.)	19 June '52	
	e. (Pf.)	22 Oct. '53	
	f. (Pf. Templeton)	28 June '54	
* 341.	*Norma:* Io stessa arsi così . . . /Ah! si fa core (with Nuttall) (Pf. Chichagov)	6 July '53	
* 342.	*Norma:* Mira, o Norma/Cedi . . . deh cedi!		
	a. (with Nuttall) (Pf. Chichagov)	28 May '53	
	b. (with Farrell) (incomplete) (Pf.)	22 April '54	
343.	Nussbaum, Der (Schumann, Op. 25, No. 3) (Pf.)	22 Nov. '53	
344.	O del mio amato ben (Donaudy)		
	a. (Pf. Romani)	Jan. '52	
	b. (Pf.)	23 May '58	
345.	O Holy Night (Adam)		
	a. (Pf.)	25 Dec. '52	
	b. (with Frankel, Hankin, and chorus) (Pf.)	25 Dec. '54	
	c. (Organ, Chichagov)	25 Dec. '55	
346.	Old Folks at Home (Foster)		
	a. (with J. C. Thomas) (Pf.)	25 Sept. '52	GR 101, EJS 531, OASI 527
	b. (Pf.) (2 takes)	3 April '53	
	c. (with Farrell) (one verse) (Pf.)	22 April '54	
	d. (Pf. Yanuzzi)	'71	
	e. (Pf. Ponselle)	April '77	
347.	O Little Town of Bethlehem		
	a. (with chorus) (Organ, Chichagov)	25 Dec. '54	

DISCOG. NO.			DATE	LP RECORDINGS
	b.	(with chorus) (Organ, Chichagov)	25 Dec. '58	
348.		*Pagliacci, I:* Qual fiamma (recit. only) (Pf.)	Oct. '52	
349.		Panis Angelicus (Franck)		
	a.	(with C. Ponselle, Nuttall, and Kemp) (Organ, Chichagov)	25 Dec. '53	E 4-KP-1517
	b.	(with C. Ponselle, Kemp) (Organ, Chichagov)	25 Dec. '54	
	c.	(with Laderoute) (Organ, Chichagov) (2 takes)	25 Dec. '55	
	d.	(with unknown soprano and alto) (Organ, Chichagov)	25 Dec. '58	
350.		Partida, La (Alvarez) (Pf. Romani)	Jan. '52	
351.		Plaisir d'amour (Martini)		
	a.	(Pf.)	24 Sept. '50	
	b.	(Pf.)	19 June '52	
	c.	(Pf. Templeton)	28 June '54	
352.		Psyche (Paladilhe)		
	a.	(Pf.)	15 May '50	
	b.	(Pf.)	31 Aug. '52	
	c.	(Pf. Romani)	18 Feb. '53	
	d.	(Pf.)	6 March '53	
	e.	(Pf. Templeton)	28 June '54	
353.		Rispetto (Wolf-Ferrari)		
	a.	(Pf. Romani)	Jan. '52	
	b.	(Pf.)	6 March '53	
354.		Rosary, The (Nevin)		
	a.	(with organ)	22 Nov. '53	
	b.	(with organ and chimes)	11 Jan. '54	
355.		Rossignol des Lilas, Le (Hahn) (Pf.)	18 March '53	
356.		Russian Gypsy Song (Trad.)		
	a.	(Pf. Chichagov) (rehearsal)	16 Oct. '52	
	b.	(Pf. Ponselle) (2 takes)	16 Oct. '52	
	c.	(Pf. Chichagov)	23 Oct. '52	
	d.	(Pf. Chichagov)	23 Nov. '52	
	e.	(Pf. Chichagov)	30 March '57	RPX 102, MDP-036
357.		*Samson et Dalila:* Printemps qui commence		
	a.	(Pf. Chichagov) (2 takes)	19 Oct. '53	
	b.	(Pf. R. Lawrence)	7 Nov. '53	RPX 102, EJS 243, MDP-036
358.		*Samson et Dalila:* Amour! viens aider ma faiblesse!		
	a.	(Pf. Chichagov)	19 Oct. '53	
	b.	(Pf. R. Lawrence)	7 Nov. '53	RPX 102, EJS 243, ANNA 1037, MDP-036

DISCOG. NO.		DATE	LP RECORDINGS
359.	*Samson et Dalila:* Mon coeur s'ouvre à ta voix		
	a. (Pf. Chichagov)	*19 Oct. '53*	
	b. (Pf. R. Lawrence)	*7 Nov. '53*	RPX 102, EJS 243, MDP-036
360.	Se (Denza)		
	a. (Pf. Ponselle) (2 takes)	*18 Feb. '53*	
	b. (Pf.)	*6 March '53*	
	c. (Pf. Chichagov)	*28 May '53*	
361.	September Song (Weill/Anderson) (Pf.)	*4 Oct. '52*	
362.	Silent Night (Gruber)		
	a. (with C. Ponselle) (Organ)	*24 Dec. '50*	
	b. (with chorus) (Organ, Chichagov)	*25 Dec. '51*	
	c. (with C. Ponselle) (Organ, Chichagov)	*25 Dec. '51*	
	d. (with C. Ponselle and chorus)	*24 Dec. '52*	
	e. (with C. Ponselle) (Organ, Chichagov)	*25 Dec. '52*	
	f. (Organ, Barstow—Sacred Heart Catholic Church) (with C. Ponselle)	*25 Dec. '52*	
	g. (Organ, Chichagov) (with C. Ponselle and chorus)	*25 Dec. '53*	E 4-KP-1517
	h. (with C. Ponselle) (Organ, Chichagov)	*25 Dec. '53*	
	i. (with C. Ponselle) (Organ, Chichagov)	*25 Dec. '54*	
	j. (with C. Ponselle) (Organ, Chichagov)	*25 Dec. '55*	
	k. (with Baklanova, Sanchez, Amparan, and Hankin) (Organ, Chichagov)	*25 Dec. '57*	
363.	Si tu le voulais (Tosti)		
	a. (Pf. Romani)	*'49*	UORC 118B
	b.	*19 June '52*	
	c. (Pf. Romani)	*18 Feb. '53*	
	d. (Pf.)	*6 March '53*	
364.	*South Pacific:* Some enchanted evening		
	a. (Pf. Romani)	*1 Oct. '49*	
	b. (Pf. Romani)	*5 Jan. '50*	RPX 102
	c. (Pf.)	*25 Sept. '52*	GR 101
	d. (with ensemble) (Pf.)	*3 May '53*	
365.	*South Pacific:* Bali Ha'i (Pf. Romani) (2 takes)	*1 Oct. '49*	
366.	Ständchen (Schubert)		
	a. (Pf. Romani)	*15 April '50*	
	b. (Pf.)	*24 Sept. '50*	
	c. (Pf.)	*5 Sept. '53*	
	d. (2 takes and fragment)	*4 May '54*	

DISCOG. NO.		DATE	LP RECORDINGS
367.	Star-Spangled Banner, The (Key)		
	a. (Pf.)	25 Sept. '52	GR 101, MDP-036
	b. (3 takes)	16 Oct. '52	
368.	Star vicino (Rosa)		
	(Pf. Romani)	15 April '50	
369.	*Suor Angelica:* Senza Mamma		
	a. (Pf.) (2 versions)	13 Sept. '52	ASCO A-125, ANNA 1037
	b. (Pf.) (incomplete)	Oct. '52	
370.	*Tales of Hoffmann* (Barcarolle)		
	(with Farrell) (incomplete)		
	(Pf.)	22 April '54	
371.	Tod und das Mädchen, Der		
	(Schubert, Op. 7, No. 3)		
	a. (Pf. Chichagov) (3 takes)	4 Oct. '52	
	b. (Pf.)	22 Nov. '53	
	c. (incomplete) (Pf.)	4 May '54	
372.	*Tosca:* Vissi d'arte		
	(Pf.) (2 takes)	9 Dec. '51	
373.	*Tote Stadt, Die:* Marietta's lied		
	a. (Pf. Ponselle)	27 Oct. '51	RPX 102, EJS 243, ANNA 1037, MDP-036
	b. (Pf.)	19 June '52	
	c. (Pf. Ponselle)	31 Aug. '52	
	d. (Pf.)	23 Oct. '52	
374.	Träume (Wagner)		
	a. (Pf. Romani)	Jan. '52	
	b. (incomplete) (Pf.)	31 Aug. '52	
375.	*Traviata, La:* Dite alla giovine/Imponete		
	(with R. Erwards) (Pf. Yanuzzi)	Fall '71	
376.	Tre giorni son che Nina (att. Pergolesi)		
	a. (Pf. Romani)	Jan. '52	
	b. (Pf.)	19 June '52	
377.	Treibhaus, Im (Wagner)		
	a. (Pf.)	31 Aug. '52	
	b. (Pf.)	6 Sept. '53	
378.	*Tristan und Isolde:* Liebestod		
	(Pf.)	6 Sept. '53	EJS 243, MDP-036
379.	Tristesse éternelle (Chopin, Etudes, Op. 10, No. 3)		
	a. (Pf. Romani)	June '52	
	b. (Pf.)	7 Nov. '53	
* 380.	*Trovatore, Il:* D'amor sull' ali rosee		
	(incomplete) (Pf. Ponselle)	26 May '51	
381.	*Trovatore, Il:* Finale scene		
	(with Khanzadian, Hankin) (Pf. Yanuzzi)	'71	

DISCOG. NO.		DATE	LP RECORDINGS
382.	Vergine è il Fabbro, La (Sadero)		
	a. (Pf.)	*4 Oct. '52*	
	b. (Pf.)	*16 Oct. '52*	
383.	Von ewiger Liebe (Brahms)		
	(Pf.)	*22 Nov. '53*	
384.	Vucchella, 'A (Tosti)		
	a. (Pf. Romani)	*'49*	UORC 118
	b. (Pf. Templeton)	*28 June '54*	
	c. (incomplete) (Pf. Ponselle)	*4 April '76*	
385.	Who Is Sylvia (Schubert)		
	(Pf. Chichagov)	*23 May '58*	
386.	Wiegenlied, (Strauss, Op. 41, No. 1)		
	a. (Pf.)	*23 July '51*	
	b. (Pf. Chichagov)	*27 Oct. '51*	
387.	Zueignung (Strauss, Op. 10, No. 1)		
	a. (Pf. Romani)	*Jan. '52*	
	b. (Pf.)	*31 Aug. '52*	

OTHER "PRIVATE" RECORDINGS ARE KNOWN TO HAVE BEEN MADE THAT ARE MISSING FROM THE VILLA PACE "ARCHIVES." AMONG THEM ARE:

Norma: Mira, o Norma/Cedi . . . deh cedi!
'46 (with Telva) (Pf. Alec Templeton)

Traviata, La: Addio del passato
'46 (Pf. Alec Templeton)

Aida: Act II, Scene 1, Aida/Amneris duet,
22 *April '54* (with Farrell) (Pf. Chichagov)
(Ponselle sings Amneris' music; Farrell sings Aida's)

Trovatore, Il: Act IV, Scene 2
Nov. '54 (with Giovanni Martinelli, Barbara Nuttall) (Pf. Chichagov)

Christmas Carols
Dec. '60 (with Norma Heyde) (Pf. Chichagov)
(Ponselle sings alto; Heyde sings soprano)
It Came Upon a Midnight Clear (Trad.)
O Little Town of Bethlehem
Panis Angelicus (Franck)
Away in a Manger (Luther)
First Noël, The

MANY HOURS OF "COACHING SESSIONS" EXIST ON TAPE. AMONG THE MOST INTERESTING ARE:

Carmen: Act II
11 Nov. '51 (with Niki Carruba) (Pf. Chichagov)

Aida: Act IV, Scene 1
5 Sept. '53 (with Barbara Nuttall) (Pf. Chichagov)
(Ponselle sings music of Radames, Ramfis, and chorus)

Forza del destino, La: Convent Scene
Feb. '57 (with Joshua Hecht, Gemi Beni) (Pf. Chichagov)
(Ponselle sings all of Leonora's music)

Trovatore, Il: Act IV, Scene 2
Feb. '68 (coaching Raina Kabaivanska) (Pf. Yanuzzi, Drucker, and Rias)
(three sessions . . . Ponselle sings Azucena's music)

Feb., Mar. '70 (coaching Ruby Jones, alto) (Pf. Yanuzzi)
(Ponselle sings Leonora's music)

Trovatore, Il: Act III, Scene 1
'70 (Pf. Yanuzzi)
(Ponselle sings all of Azucena's "scene")

Faust: Death of Valentine
Nov. '70 (with Sharon Edgeman, mezzo) (Pf. Chichagov)
(Ponselle sings Marguerite's music)

Amore dei tre re, L': Act I
'71 (with Ryan Edwards) (Pf. Yanuzzi)
(Ponselle sings all of Fiora's music, then Archibaldo's)

Tapes of "conversations" with many "personalities" such as Luciano Pavarotti, Bidú Sayão, Elisabeth Schwarzkopf, Walter Legge, Gloria Swanson, Ida and Louise Cook, among others, as well as countless "interviews" exist in Villa Pace's "Archives." Villa Pace also has movies of Ponselle with many other celebrities including Elisabeth Rethberg, Grace Moore, Valentín Parera, Romano Romani, Walter Pidgeon, Fanny Brice, Giovanni Zenatello, Gatti-Casazza, Rosina Galli. Miss Ponselle's 1936 M-G-M screen test is also there. It is interesting to note that this was not the first screen test. A letter from Libbie Miller dated May 9, 1935, to M-G-M's New York office indicates that earlier screen tests—probably January or February 1935—were made in New York. The letter details that in Test 1 Miss Ponselle sang "Carry Me Back to Old Virginny," "I Carry You in My Pocket," "The Locket Song," and in Test 2 "Elégie." Unfortunately, these earlier tests seem not to have survived.

Artists assisting on private recordings:

Licia Albanese (sop.)
Belen Amparan (alto)
Kira Baklanov (sop.)
Rose Bampton (sop.)
Ward Barstow (organ)
Tullio Carminati (tenor)
Igor Chichagov (Pf., organ)
Richard Crooks (bar.)
Elizabeth Doubleday (sop.)
Nelson Eddy (bar.)
Ryan Edwards (bar.)
Eileen Farrell (sop.)
Phyllis Frankel (sop.)
Nanette Guilford (sop.)
Bette Hankin (mezzo)
Joshua Hecht (bass)
Fred Hensen (bar.)
Delores Jones (sop.)
Ruby Keeler
Norman Kelly (tenor)
Patsy Kelly
Mary Jane Kemp (sop.)
Vahan Khanzadian (tenor)
Robert Kirkham (bar.)
Joseph Laderoute (tenor)
Robert Lawrence (Pf.)

Mary Martinet (Pf.)
Lauritz Melchior (tenor)
James Morris (bass)
Sheila Nadler (mezzo)
Barbara Nuttall (mezzo)
Luciano Pavarotti (tenor)
Ezio Pinza (bass)
Carmela Ponselle (mezzo)
Marie Powers (contralto)
Maud Key Shelton Rock (sop.)
Stella Roman (sop.)
Romano Romani (Pf.)
Celina Sanchez (sop.)
Tullio Serafin (Pf.)
Beverly Sills (sop.)
Ken Smith (bass bar.)
Phyllis Harris Stewart (mezzo)
Helen Stokes (sop.)
Elaine Stritch
Alec Templeton (Pf.)
John Charles Thomas (bar.)
Lawrence Tibbett (bar.)
Shakeh Vartenissian (sop.)
Judith Werle (sop.)
William Yanuzzi (Pf.)
Blanche Yurka

PART V

ALBUM TITLES

A. FIRST EDITION LP RELEASES

LM 1881	Rosa Ponselle Sings Today
LM2047	Rosa Ponselle in Song
RPX 102	Rosa Ponselle—By Request (issued by Miss Ponselle)
E4-KP-1517	Open House with Rosa Ponselle (issued by Miss Ponselle)
GR 101	10″ Eisenhower Rally LP (Miss Ponselle's Christmas Greeting to friends)
ASCO A-125	Rosa Ponselle—Soprano Assoluto

B. MAJOR LP REISSUES WITH DISCOGRAPHY NUMBERS

Rosa Ponselle in Opera
and Song—LCT 10/WCT 55
161, 162, 136, 137, 72, 101

Ten Great Singers
LM 6705
161, 97, 52a, 128, 129, 130, 131

The Art of Rosa Ponselle
CBL 100
161, 162, 90b, 53, 54, 97, 49, 128, 129, 130,
131, 93, 94b, 95, 96, 61, 150, 124, 135, 68,
148b, 98b, 164, 112, 88 (3), 166

Rosa Ponselle Sings Norma
and other Famous Heroines
VIC 1507
153, 51b, 52b, 57, 58, 59, 60, 160, 128, 129,
130, 131, 90b, 136, 137, 94b

Golden Age, Il Trovatore
VIC 1684
41, 42, 43, 160

Rosa Ponselle
RCA TVM 1-7202
90b, 93, 94b, 51a, 52a, 136, 128, 129, 130,
131, 97, 161, 162

Rosa Ponselle
RCA PVM 1-9047
51b (6), 52b (6), 57, 58, 59, 60, 160, 128,
129, 130, 131, 90b, 136, 137

Rosa Ponselle—Vol. I
Scala 803
26 (2), 40, 48, 24, 29, 7, 42, 28, 16, 14, 5,
17 (3)

287

Rosa Ponselle—Vol. II
Scala 838
20, 10, 4, 45, 43, 23, 37, 6, 18, 27, 25, 44, 39, 11, 47

Rosa Ponselle—Vol. III
Scala 851
3, 12, 41, 26 (3), 2, 32, 33, 19, 31, 38, 21, 34, 22, 36, 46, 1

Rosa Ponselle Sings
Verdi—Y31150
41, 43, 42, 12, 45, 14, 16, 3, 4, 5, 32
Note: Recording dates are incorrect.

Rosa Ponselle Operatic and Song Recital, Vol. I
OASI 595
14 (6), 17 (2), 38, 11, 25, 28, 6, 20, 23, 52a, 94a, 90a, 55, 56, 223, 51b (9), 111, 98a, 114, 120, 148a, 109, 84, 78, 108, 146, 76, 80, 122, 101, 152, 134 (3), 144, 140, 88 (1), 151, 149, 125, 72

Rosa Ponselle Operatic and Song Recital, Vol. II
OASI 621
26 (2), 7, 24, 40, 26 (3), 33, 37, 45, 17 (3), 10, 48, 2, 39, 29, 160 (1), 27, 21, 34, 18, 31, 19, 134 (4), 22, 36, 47, 1, 46, 44, 217, 15

Rosa Ponselle, Volume III
OASI 635
202, 220b, 222b, 173, 169, 221b, 171, 187b

Rosa Ponselle at the Villa Pace, 1954
HRE 236-3
All content of LM 1889 and LM 2047 and 1954 Victors contained on ASCO A-125 plus 257, 369a.

Rosa Ponselle—Live . . . In Concert, Vol. I
MDP-012
196, 292c, 227, 201b, 234, 186b, 168, 180c, 181, 182b, 183, 226, 224b, 167, 223, 231, 232, 304b, 199, 193, 194, 218, 197, 205, 206

Rosa Ponselle—Live . . . In Concert, Vol. II
MDP-029
185, 187a, 203, 175, 210, 191, 236, 174, 192, 188, 172b, 209, 214, 207a, 189, 184, 215, 233, 213

Rosa Ponselle—The Informal Recordings, Vol. III
MDP-036
378, 240b, 241b, 249a, 328b, 356d, 367a, 373a, 357b, 358b, 359b, 306b, 303a

Rosa Ponselle
Pearl GEMM 207
149, 151, 160, 161, 162, 128, 129, 130, 131, 51b, 52a, 57, 58, 59, 60, 80, 134 (4)

C.   PRIVATE ISSUES

EJS	—	The Golden Age of Opera
UORC	—	Unique Opera Recordings
OPA	—	Operatic Archives
ANNA	—	ANN Record Company

ALPHABETICAL LISTING OF SELECTIONS

INDEX A

Numbers following the titles are the discography numbers.

NOTES ON DISCOGRAPHY SELECTIONS

INDEX B

was Bori/Schipa Bohème: Death Scene) Blue card for this record in Victor files shows "Re-recorded from 3040 A&B and 3041 A&B." Five takes were required in the rerecording process on *7 July '31* (1 and 2). *4 Aug. '31* (3 and 4) and *16 Mar. '32* (5).

62.   Version 1 key of F sharp; Version 2 in F.

64.   Never issued by Victor.

66.   Never issued by Victor.

69.   Never issued by Victor.

70.   Never issued by Victor.

71.   Never issued by Victor.

72.   Master for Take 10 exists. Takes 9 and 10 have Pf. accompaniment only. Take 5 was never issued by Victor except on LP—LCT 10 (Rosa Ponselle in Opera and Song) and as 17-0351B in WCT 55 (45 release of same album).

73.   Never issued by Victor.

76.   Never issued by Victor; on EJS 192B.

88.   Take 3 issued on 6599B on *26 Nov. '26.* Take 1 issued on 6599B on *10 Aug. '42.*

90.   Test pressing of Take 1 exists.

101.   Never issued by Victor on 78. First issue LCT 10 (Rosa Ponselle in Opera and Song) and as 17-0350B in WCT 55 (45 release of same album.)

105.   Never issued by Victor.

106.   Never issued by Victor.

108.   This song also listed as "Sanctuary." Never issued by Victor; on EJS 192B.

118.   Never issued by Victor.

121.   Never issued by Victor.

123.   Never issued by Victor.

125.   The 10″ master was rerecorded onto 12″ master PCS 048926-1R and issued in that form only.

126.   Version 1 key of G sharp; Version 2 in D.

127.   Never issued by Victor.

132.   Never issued by Victor.

134.   IRCC 126 was privately issued by the International Record Collector's Club. Never issued by Victor.

142.   Never issued by Victor.

146.   Never issued by Victor; on EJS 191B.

147.   Never issued by Victor.

152.   Never issued by Victor; on EJS 191B.

153.   Test pressings exist of Takes 1 and 2. A composite of both takes was used for VIC 1507 due to the condition of the test pressings.

156.   Never issued by Victor.

157.   Never issued by Victor.

158.   Never issued by Victor.

159.   Never issued by Victor.

160.   Take 2 used on 8097A on all prewar pressings and for DB 1199. Take 1 was used for postwar pressings of 8097A.

166.   Never issued by Victor on 78. First release on CBL 100.

176.   ANNA 1037 contains: Habanera, Seguidilla, Chanson bohème, Air des cartes, Si tu m'aime and C'est toi? C'est moi.

179.   MET-7 is a deluxe boxed set issued by the Metropolitan Opera.

186.   MDP-012 is a composite of 186a and 186b.

195. ANNA 1036 contains Act I duet with Schipa, as does MDP-024.

196. MDP-012 contains spoken introduction by Ponselle.

206. MDP-012 contains spoken introduction by Ponselle.

223. UORC notes show this to be an "Unpublished Victor" but is the same broadcast performance.

226. MDP-012 contains spoken introduction by Ponselle.

230. Ah! fors' è lui/Sempre libera also on EJS 190 and ANNA 1036A; Dite alla giovine on ANNA 1036A.

243. GR-103 was a 12" 78 rpm private issue for Miss Ponselle.

244a. Ponselle as Amneris.

244b. Jones and Stewart alternating as Aida and Ponselle and Powers alternating as Amneris.

250. Sung in the manner of Claudia Muzio.

259a. See note on 243.

274a/276 These two selections were recorded for Miss Ponselle's screen test. Previously in 1935 there had been another M-G-M screen test. Among selections that were recorded for these tests were:
    1. Carry Me Back to Old Virginny.
    2. I Carry You in My Pocket.
    3. Elégie.
    4. A title referred to as Locket Song.
The above was noted in a letter to Mr. I. I. Altman of Metro-Goldwyn-Mayer Pictures, Inc., dated May 9, 1935.

291b. Library of Congress shows *12 Dec. '52.*

323. Ponselle sings Sharpless' music.

325. Coaching sessions—Ponselle sings des Grieux's music.

326. Coaching sessions—Ponselle sings des Grieux's music.

327. Coaching sessions—Ponselle sings des Grieux's music.

328. Coaching sessions.

329. Coaching sessions—Ponselle sings des Grieux's music.

330. Coaching sessions.

332. Both Miss Ponselle and Miss Crawford remembered recording the Barcarolle from Tales of Hoffmann at the M-G-M studio and there are pictures of the recording session. These were apparently personal mementos (although Miss Crawford thought they were issued commercially). Miss Crawford was studying with Maestro Romani at the time. Selection 319 contained in an album otherwise devoted to Joan Crawford.

341. Coaching session (Ponselle sings Norma's music).

342a. Ponselle sings Norma's music.

342b. Farrell sings Norma's music.

380. Sung in the manner of Claudia Muzio.

RADIO BROADCASTS OF ROSA PONSELLE

INDEX C

Index C is a partial listing of broadcasts beginning in 1927. Although the listing is not complete (except for the years 1934–37), it gives an interesting sampling of Miss Ponselle's broadcast career. Certainly broadcasts prior to 1930 are not likely to have been preserved, but many interesting ones may exist although not known to the discographer. Known existing broadcasts are marked with an asterisk.

Newspaper accounts of selections to be performed often differ from those actually sung. These have been corrected where broadcasts were preserved to check against the printed account. Listings for Chesterfield broadcasts were most often found in error.

Only Miss Ponselle's selections are listed for the broadcasts shown.

1 January 1927
VICTOR TALKING MACHINE
HOUR
New York, WEAF, 9–11 P.M.
(Other artists: McCormack, Cortot, and Elman) (Orch. Shilkret)
Ave Maria (Bach-Gounod?)
La Forza del destino: Pace, pace mio Dio
Elégie (Massenet)
Lullaby (?)
The Rosary (Nevin)
This broadcast was billed as "The radio debut of Rosa Ponselle."
(Pf.?)

1 January 1928
VICTOR TALKING MACHINE
HOUR
New York, WEAF, 9–11 P.M.
(Other artists: Martinelli, Pinza, Metropolitan Opera Orch. & Chorus, Cond. Setti)
Aida: Ritorna vincitor
Il Trovatore: Miserere (with Martinelli)
La Forza del destino: Trio finale (with Martinelli and Pinza)

3 December 1928
GENERAL MOTORS HOUR
New York
(Cond. Goossens)
La Forza del destino: Pace, pace mio Dio
Norma: Casta Diva
Carmen: Habanera
Mighty lak' a Rose (Nevin)
Fa la nana bambin (Sadero)
Swiss Echo Song (Eckert)
(Pf. Romani)

13 October 1929
ATWATER KENT RADIO HOUR
New York, WEAF, 8:15–9:15 P.M.
(Cond. Pasternack)
La Forza del destino: Madre pietosa Vergine
La Vestale: O nume tutelar
I Vespri siciliani: Bolero (with Orch.)
Rosalinda: Meco sulla verrai (Pastorale)
Tristeese éternelle (Chopin)
Heine (Blech)
La Chanson de la Cigale (Lecocq)
Swiss Echo Song (Eckert)

296

The Night Wind (Farley)
My Old Kentucky Home (Foster)
(Pf. Romani)

10 April 1930
RCA VICTOR HOUR
New York, WEAF, 10–11 P.M.
(Cond.?)
Ave Maria (?)
By the Waters of Minnetonka
  (Lieurance)
Mademoiselle Modiste: Kiss Me Again
The Night Wind (Farley)
Il Trovatore: Tacea la notte
The Fairy Pipers (Brewer)
Lullaby (?)
Swiss Echo Song (Eckert)
The Rosary (Nevin)

23 October 1930
RCA VICTOR HOUR
New York, WEAF
(Cond.?)
La Forza del destino: Pace, pace mio
  Dio
Angel's Serenade (Braga)
In the Luxembourg Gardens
Come unto These Yellow Sands (La
  Forge)
Carmen: Chanson bohème

7 December 1930*
ATWATER KENT RADIO HOUR
New York, WEAF
(Cond. Pasternack)
Fedra: O divina Afrodite
Mariä Wiegenlied (Reger)
Elégie (Massenet)
La Traviata: Addio del passato
I Vespri siciliani: Bolero
Annie Laurie (Scott)
The Cuckoo (Lehmann)
Ständchen (Schubert)
Swiss Echo Song (Eckert)
Carmen: Habanera
"Mr. Romano Romani will conduct the
  Romanza from his opera *Fedra*
  and accompany Miss Ponselle at
  the piano."

1 June 1931
ROYAL OPERA HOUSE, Covent
  Garden
London, WABC, 3 P.M.
Transatlantic broadcast
La Forza del destino (Cond. Serafin)
  (with Pertile, Franci, Pasero)

9 June 1931
ROYAL OPERA HOUSE, Covent
  Garden
London, WABC, 3 P.M.
Transatlantic broadcast
La Traviata (Cond. Serafin)
  (with Borgioli, Noble)

18 October 1931
ATWATER KENT RADIO HOUR
New York, WEAF, 9:15–10:15 P.M.
(Cond. Pasternack)
Ständchen (Schubert)
I Vespri siciliani: Bolero
But Lately in Dance (Arensky)
The Fairy Pipers (Brewer)
Angel's Serenade (Braga)
The Night Wind (Farley)
Fedra: O divina Afrodite
Marechiare (Tosti)
O Sole Mio (Di Capua)
(Pf. Romani)

26 December 1931
METROPOLITAN OPERA
New York, WEAF, 3:45–5:15 P.M.
Norma (Acts II and III) (Cond.
  Serafin)
  (with Lauri-Volpi, Swarthout, Pinza)

16 January 1932
METROPOLITAN OPERA
New York, WEAF, 3:00–4:00 P.M.
Il Trovatore (Cond. Bellezza)
  (with Lauri-Volpi, Danise, Petrova)

27 March 1932
GENERAL ELECTRIC
  TWILIGHT HOUR
New York, WEAF
(Cond.?)
The Rosary (Nevin)
I Passed by Your Window (Brahe)
Elégie (Massenet)
The Cuckoo Clock (Griselle-Young)
Ave Maria (Schubert)
Comin' Thro' the Rye (Trad.)
Mariä Wiegenlied (Reger)
Marechiare (Tosti)
The Last Rose of Summer (Moore)

17 December 1932
METROPOLITAN OPERA
New York, WJZ, 1:45–5:15 P.M.
Don Giovanni (Cond. Serafin)
  (with Pinza, Müller, Fleischer,
  Schipa, Pasero, Malatesta,
  Rothier)

19 January 1933†
Waldorf-Astoria
New York, 2 P.M.
Harlem Philharmonic (Cond.?)
 (with Borgioli)
Chi vuol comprar (Jomelli)
Die Tote Stadt: Marietta's Lied
Rispetto (Wolf-Ferrari)
Alceste: Divinités du Styx
La Traviata: Parigi, o cara
Freschi luoghi prati aulenti (Donaudy)
On Wings of Dream (Arensky)
Dedication (Schumann)
The Doll's Cradle Song (Moussorgsky)
Come unto These Yellow Sands (La
 Forge)

22 January 1933
GENERAL ELECTRIC SUNDAY
CIRCLE
New York, 9:00–9:30 P.M.
WEAF Orch. (Cond.?)
Swiss Echo Song (Eckert)
Home, Sweet Home (Bishop)
Naughty Marietta: Ah, sweet mystery
 of life (Herbert)
The Nightingale and the Rose
 (Rimsky-Korsakov)
Carmen: Habanera
Rose Marie: Indian Love Call

19 February 1933
GENERAL ELECTRIC SUNDAY
CIRCLE
New York, WEAF
WEAF Symphony (Cond.?)
Carmen: Chanson bohème
Cavalleria rusticana: Ave Maria
The Chocolate Soldier: My hero
Drink to Me Only with Thine Eyes
 (Trad.)
Ich liebe dich (Grieg)
Lullaby (Brahms)
Good-Bye (Tosti)
Aida: Ritorna vincitor

3 March 1933
PRE-INAUGURAL CONCERT
Washington, D.C., WEAF,
 8:30–9:30 P.M.
National Symphony Orch. (Cond.
 Kindler)
Aida: Ciel, mio padre w. Lawrence
 Tibbett

Die Tote Stadt: Marietta's Lied
Swiss Echo Song (Eckert)
Der Erlkönig (Schubert)
The Night Wind (Farley)

19 March 1933
GENERAL ELECTRIC SUNDAY
CIRCLE
New York, WEAF, 9–10 P.M.
WEAF Symphony (Cond.?)
Liebesträume (Liszt)
La Vestale: Tu che invoco
Comin' Thro' the Rye (Trad.)
I Vespri siciliani: Bolero
Serenade (Moszkowski)
In the Luxembourg Gardens
 (Lockhart-Manning)

7 May 1933
FLORENCE MAY FESTIVAL
Florence, Italy, 9 P.M.
La Vestale (Cond. V. Gui)
 (with Dolci, Pasero, Stignani,
 Pierobiasini)

15 November 1933
NBC 7th ANNIVERSARY
New York, WEAF, 10:30–11:00 P.M.
Drink to Me Only with Thine Eyes
 (Trad.)
The Cuckoo Clock (Griselle-Young)

11 December 1933†
New York, WEAF ?
 (with Heifetz)
La Vestale: O nume tutelar
La Traviata: Addio del passato
Carmen: Chanson bohème
Freschi luoghi prati aulenti (Donaudy)
Die Tote Stadt: Marietta's Lied
Rispetto (Wolf-Ferrari)
Slumber Song of the Madonna (Head)
My Lover He Comes on a Ski
 (Clough-Leighton)

24 December 1933
CADILLAC HOUR
New York, WJZ, 6–7 P.M.
Orch. and Met. Opera Chorus (Cond.
 Bodanzky)
Norma: Casta Diva (Bellini)
Good-Bye (Tosti)
Der Erlkönig (Schubert)
Mariä Wiegenlied
The Cuckoo Clock (Griselle-Young)
Adeste Fideles (Trad.)

† *Miss Ponselle's records show that this performance was broadcast. I have been
unable to verify this with any newspaper.*

13 January 1934
METROPOLITAN OPERA
New York, WEAF
L'Africana (Cond. Serafin)
  (with Jagel, Borgioli, Morgana,
    Rothier)

20 January 1934*
METROPOLITAN OPERA
New York, WEAF
Don Giovanni (Cond. Serafin)
  (with Pinza, Müller, Fleischer,
    Lazzari, Schipa)

28 January 1934
HEINZ HALL OF FAME
  PROGRAM
New York, WEAF, 10:30–11:00 P.M.
(Cond. Shilkret)
Naughty Marietta: Ah, sweet mystery
  of life
Cavalleria rusticana: Voi lo sapete
Mademoiselle Modiste: Kiss Me Again
Angel's Serenade (Braga)
Carmen: Habanera

2 April 1934
CHESTERFIELD HOUR
New York
(Cond. Kostelanetz)
Swiss Echo Song (Eckert)
Fedra: O divina Afrodite
A Perfect Day (Bond)

9 April 1934
CHESTERFIELD HOUR
New York, WABC
(Cond. Kostelanetz)
Carmen: Chanson bohème
Comin' Thro' the Rye (Trad.)
La Traviata: Addio del passato
Home, Sweet Home (Foster)

16 April 1934
CHESTERFIELD HOUR
New York, WABC
(Cond. Kostelanetz)
Songs My Mother Taught Me
  (Dvořák)
I Vespri siciliani: Bolero
La Paloma (Yradier)
The Nightingale and the Rose
  (Rimsky-Korsakov)

23 April 1934
CHESTERFIELD HOUR
New York, WABC
(Cond. Kostelanetz)
Come unto These Yellow Sands (La
  Forge)

The Old Refrain (Kreisler)
La Vestale: Tu che invoco

30 April 1934
CHESTERFIELD HOUR
New York, WABC
(Cond. Kostelanetz)
Naughty Marietta: Ah, sweet mystery
  of life
Die Tote Stadt: Marietta's Lied
Carry Me Back to Old Virginny
  (Bond)
Fa la nana bambin (Sadero)

7 May 1934
CHESTERFIELD HOUR
New York, WABC
(Cond. Kostelanetz)
Here's to Romance: I Carry You in My
  Pocket (Grosvener)
Alceste: Divinités du Styx
Ständchen (Schubert)
Love's Old Sweet Song (Molloy)

14 May 1934
CHESTERFIELD HOUR
New York, WABC
(Cond. Kostelanetz)
Carmen: Habanera
The Chocolate Soldier: My hero
Fa la nana bambin (Sadero)
Blue Danube Waltz (Strauss)

21 May 1934
CHESTERFIELD HOUR
New York, WABC
(Cond. Kostelanetz)
Mademoiselle Modiste: Kiss Me Again
La Bohème: Mi chiamano Mimi
My Old Kentucky Home (Foster)

28 May 1934
CHESTERFIELD HOUR
New York, WABC
(Cond. Kostelanetz)
Sadko: Song of India
  (Rimsky-Korsakov)
Ave Maria (Kahn)
The Night Wind (Farley)

4 June 1934
CHESTERFIELD HOUR
New York, WABC
(Cond. Kostelanetz)
Cavalleria rusticana: Voi lo sapete
The Cuckoo Clock (Griselle-Young)
The Rosary (Nevin)

11 June 1934
CHESTERFIELD HOUR
New York, WABC
(Cond. Kostelanetz)
Der Erlkönig (Schubert)
I Passed by Your Window (Brahe)
Danny Boy (Trad.)

18 June 1934
CHESTERFIELD HOUR
New York, WABC
(Cond. Kostelanetz)
O Sole Mio (Di Capua)
La Forza del destino: Pace, pace
Good-Bye (Tosti)

25 June 1934
CHESTERFIELD HOUR
New York, WABC
(Cond. Kostelanetz)
La Forza del destino: Pace, pace
Here's to Romance: I Carry You in
   My Pocket (Grosvener)
The Fairy Pipers (Brewer)
Annie Laurie (Trad.)

2 July 1934
CHESTERFIELD HOUR
New York, WABC
(Cond. Kostelanetz)
Marechiare (Tosti)
I'm Falling in Love with Someone
   (Herbert)
True (Samuels)

9 July 1934
CHESTERFIELD HOUR
New York, WABC
(Cond. Kostelanetz)
Dicitencello vuje (Falvo)
In the Luxembourg Gardens
   (Lockhart-Manning)
The Fortune Teller: Gypsy Love Song
   (Herbert)
Home, Sweet Home (Bishop)

1 October 1934*
CHESTERFIELD HOUR
New York, WABC, 9:00–9:30 P.M.
(Cond. Kostelanetz)
Don Giovanni: Batti, batti
I Love You Truly (Bond)
The Cuckoo Clock (Griselle-Young)
Homing (Del Riego)

8 October 1934*
CHESTERFIELD HOUR
New York, WABC, 9:00–9:30 P.M.

(Cond. Kostelanetz)
The Chocolate Soldier: My hero
Cavalleria rusticana: Ave Maria
In the Luxembourg Gardens
   (Lockhart-Manning)
Carmen: Chanson bohème

15 October 1934*
CHESTERFIELD HOUR
New York, WABC, 9:00–9:30 P.M.
(Cond. Kostelanetz)
Blue Danube Waltz (Strauss)
La Golondrina (Serradell)
Wiegenlied (Brahms)
Will-o'-the-Wisp (Spross)

22 October 1934
CHESTERFIELD HOUR
New York, WABC, 9:00–9:30 P.M.
(Cond. Kostelanetz)
Otello: Ave Maria
Swiss Echo Song (Eckert)
Ouvre ton coeur (Bizet)

29 October 1934*
CHESTERFIELD HOUR
New York, WABC, 9:00–9:30 P.M.
(Cond. Kostelanetz)
La Violetera (Padilla)
Samson et Dalila: Printemps qui
   commence
The Last Rose of Summer (Moore)

5 November 1934
CHESTERFIELD HOUR
New York, WABC, 9:00–9:30 P.M.
(Cond. Kostelanetz)
Humoresque (Dvořák)
The Cuckoo Clock (Griselle-Young)
Der Erlkönig (Schubert)

12 November 1934
CHESTERFIELD HOUR
New York, WABC, 9:00–9:30 P.M.
(Cond. Kostelanetz)
Jeanne d'Arc: Adieu forêts
Clavelitos (Valverde)
In the Gloaming (Harris)
Santa Maria (Lara)

19 November 1934*
CHESTERFIELD HOUR
New York, WABC, 9:00–9:30 P.M.
(Cond. Kostelanetz)
Ave Maria (Sandoval)
The Merry Widow: Waltz
Estrellita (Ponce)
The Sleigh (Tchervanow-Kountz)

*26 November 1934**
CHESTERFIELD HOUR
New York, WABC, 9:00–9:30 P.M.
(Cond. Kostelanetz)
Carmen: Habanera
A Dream (Bartlett)
What Is in the Air Today (Eden)
The Rosary (Nevin)

*3 December 1934**
CHESTERFIELD HOUR
New York, WABC, 9:00–9:30 P.M.
(Cond. Kostelanetz)
Alceste: Divinités du Styx
Mariä Wiegenlied (Reger)
Big Brown Bear (Mana-Zucca)
Good-Bye (Tosti)

10 December 1934
CHESTERFIELD HOUR
New York, WABC, 9:00–9:30 P.M.
(Cond. Kostelanetz)
Angel's Serenade (Braga)
Comin' Thro' the Rye (Trad.)
Fedra: O divina Afrodite

17 December 1934
CHESTERFIELD HOUR
New York, WABC, 9:00–9:30 P.M.
(Cond. Kostelanetz)
The Fairy Pipers (Brewer)
The Old Refrain (Kreisler)
Elégie (Massenet)
Don Giovanni: Mi tradi

24 December 1934
CHESTERFIELD HOUR
New York, WABC, 9:00–9:30 P.M.
(Cond. Kostelanetz)
Adeste Fideles (Trad.)
La Forza del destino: La Vergine degli
     angeli
Der Erlkönig (Schubert)

5 January 1935
METROPOLITAN OPERA
New York, NBC
La Traviata: (Cond. Panizza)
     (with Jagel, Tibbett)

9 February 1935
METROPOLITAN OPERA
New York, NBC
Don Giovanni (Cond. Panizza)
     (with Pinza, Müller, Fleischer,
     Lazzari, Schipa)

17 March 1935
FORD SUNDAY EVENING HOUR
Detroit, CBS, 9:00–10:00 P.M.
Ford Symphony (Cond. Kolar)
Jeanne d'Arc: Adieu forêts
Il Trovatore: Miserere (with de
     Filippi)
Carmen: Habanera
Sagesse (Panizza)
Ouvre ton coeur (Bizet)
Believe Me If All Those Endearing
     Young Charms (Moore)

27 October 1935
GENERAL MOTORS SYMPHONY
Detroit, WEAF, 10–11 P.M.
(Cond. Rapee)
Carmen: Habanera
Chanson bohème
Dicitincello vuje (Falvo)
You Tell It to Her
Blue Danube Waltz (Strauss)

21 November 1935
"TO ARMS FOR PEACE"
New York, WABC
(Cond. ?)
Carmen: Seguidilla
Jeanne d'Arc: Adieu forêts

*1 February 1936**
METROPOLITAN OPERA
New York, WABC
Carmen (Cond. Hasslemans)
     (with Kullman, Pinza, Fisher)

*26 February 1936**
CHESTERFIELD HOUR
New York, WABC
(Cond. Kostelanetz)
Carmen: Seguidilla
Air des cartes (Bizet)
Here's to Romance: I Carry You in
     My Pocket (Grosvener)
None but the Lonely Heart
     (Tchaikovsky)

*4 March 1936**
CHESTERFIELD HOUR
New York, WABC
(Cond. Kostelanetz)
Carmen: Chanson bohème
Clavelitos (Valverde)
Danny Boy (Trad.)
Der Erlkönig (Schubert)

11 March 1936*
CHESTERFIELD HOUR
New York, WABC
(Cond. Kostelanetz)
The Old Refrain (Kreisler)
L'Ultima canzone (Tosti)
Comin' Thro' the Rye (Trad.)
Cavalleria rusticana: Voi lo sapete

18 March 1936*
CHESTERFIELD HOUR
New York, WABC
(Cond. Kostelanetz)
Humoresque (Dvořák)
Ouvre ton coeur (Bizet)
Fedra: O divina Afrodite
When I Have Sung My Songs
  (Charles)

25 March 1936*
CHESTERFIELD HOUR
New York, WABC
(Cond. Kostelanetz)
Ave Maria (Sandoval)
The Night Wind (Farley)
Carmen: Habanera
Ich liebe dich (Grieg)

28 March 1936*
METROPOLITAN OPERA
Boston, NBC
Carmen (Cond. Hasslemans)
  (with Maison, Pinza, Burke)

1 April 1936*
CHESTERFIELD HOUR
New York, WABC
(Cond. Kostelanetz)
Good-Bye (Tosti)
The Cuckoo (Lehmann)
Morenita (Buzzi-Peccia)
La Vestale: Tu che invoco

24 May 1936*
LOS ANGELES PHILHARMONIC
Hollywood Bowl, WEAF, 10–11 P.M.
(Cond. Rapee)
Semiramide: Bel raggio
La Traviata: Addio del passato
Cavalleria rusticana: Voi lo sapete
Morenita (Buzzi-Peccia)
Carry Me Back to Old Virginny
  (Bland)
Marechiare (Tosti)

31 May 1936*
GENERAL MOTORS HOUR
San Francisco, California, WEAF,
  10–11 P.M.
San Francisco Symphony
(Cond. Rapee)
Alceste: Divinités du Styx
Ave Maria (Schubert)
Carmen: Seguidilla
Marechiare (Tosti)
Annie Laurie (Trad.)
Morenita (Buzzi-Peccia)

27 September 1936*
GENERAL MOTORS HOUR
Carnegie Hall, New York, WEAF,
  10–11 P.M.
(Cond. Rapee)
Aida: Ritorna vincitor
Dicitencello vuje (Falvo)
Otello: Ave Maria
Homing (Del Riego)
Ouvre ton coeur (Bizet)

10 December 1936*
"THEN AND NOW"
New York, WABC, 10:00–10:30 P.M.
(Cond.?)
La Forza del destino: La Vergine degli
  angeli
Moonlight Bay (Wenrich)

9 January 1937*
METROPOLITAN OPERA
New York, NBC
Carmen (Cond. Papi)
  (with Rayner, Huehn, Bodanya)

17 April 1937*
METROPOLITAN OPERA
Cleveland, NBC
Carmen (Cond. Papi)
  (with Maison, Huehn, Burke)

25 April 1937*
CINCINNATI SYMPHONY
  PROMS CONCERT
Cincinnati
(Cond. Goossens)
Ave Maria (Kahn)
The Chocolate Soldier: My hero (with
  Frank Forest)
The Old Refrain (Kreisler)
The Night Wind (Farley)
None but the Lonely Heart
  (Tchaikovsky)

2 May 1937*
RCA MAGIC KEY
New York, WJZ 2:00–3:00 P.M.
(Cond. Black)
Drink to Me Only with Thine Eyes
(Trad.)

Fedra: O divina Afrodite
Carry Me Back to Old Virginny
(Bland)
Mademoiselle Modiste: Kiss Me Again
My Old Kentucky Home (Foster)
Home, Sweet Home (Bishop)

A CARMELA PONSELLE DISCOGRAPHY

INDEX D

PART I
COLUMBIA RECORDS
(*Acoustic*)

Duets with Rosa Ponselle are listed in that discography.

DISCOG. NO.		DATE	MATRIX/ TAKE	78 RPM CAT. NO.	LP
1.	Alice, Where Art Thou? (Ascher) (Or.)	28 Dec. '22	80751	A3818 56M	
2.	Ave Maria (Bach-Gounod) (Or.)	10 Oct. '21	49995	A6215	
3.	Calm as the Night (Böhm) (Or.)	11 Dec. '23	81410-1	20009D	
4.	Caro mio ben (Giordani) (Or.)	26 Dec. '23	81438	(Unpublished)	
5.	Dream Faces (Hutchinson) (Or.)	2 Dec. '20	79547-1, -2	A3369	
6.	Heure exquise, L' (Hahn) (Or.)	11 July '23	81124-1, -2, -3	A3999 23M	
7.	Hidden Tears (Or.)	13 July '23	81134	(Unpublished)	
8.	Homing (Del Riego) (Or.)	22 Sept. '22	80451	A3732 55M	
9.	June's the Time for Roses (D'Lorah) (Or.)	11 Dec. '23	81411-1, -2, -3	20003D	
10.	Kiss Me with Your Eyes (Spencer) (Or.)	20 Nov. '23	81365-1, -2, -3	20003D	

DISCOG. NO.	DATE	MATRIX/ TAKE	78 RPM CAT. NO.	LP
11. Love Song (Minnelied) (Brahms) (Or.)	1 March '20	79008	A3369	
12. Moonlight (Schumann, Op. 39, No. 5) (Or. Bowers)	17 Dec. '23	81420	20009D 23M	
13. Oh, Promise Me (Op. 50) (De Koven) (Or.)	26 Sept. '22	80452-9	A3732 55M	
14. Plaisir d'Amour (Martini) (Or.)	11 July '23	81122-1, -2	A3999	
15. Rose of Old Castile (Or.)	20 Nov. '23	81364	(Unpublished)	
16. Serse: Ombra mai fu (Largo) (Handel) (Or.)	18 Jan. '22	49994	A6215 7026M	OASI 635
17. Somewhere a Voice Is Calling (Tate) (Or.)	28 Dec. '22	80750	A3818 56M	
18. Songs My Mother Used to Sing, Those (Smith) (Or.)	30 June '21	79921-1, -2	A3466	
19. Thinking of You (Eastman-Heltman) (Or.)	30 June '21	79922-1, -2, -3	A3466	
20. Voices of the Woods (Or.)	1 March '20	79009	(Unpublished)	
21. Who Knows? (Or.)	10 Oct. '23	81133	(Unpublished)	

Carmela Ponselle's original test record for Columbia (Matrix 62488–Rejected) was made on December 5, 1918. Title of selection is unknown.

PART II
OFF-THE-AIR/PRIVATE RECORDINGS

DISCOG. NO.		DATE	LP
22.	Agnus Dei (Bizet) (Pf.)	*25 Dec. '52*	
23.	Ascension (recitation)	*12 Oct. '58*	
24.	*Carmen:* Habanera		
	a. (Pf. Betty Dilling)	*'50*	
	b. (Pf.)	*14 Jan. '51*	MDP001
	c. (Pf. Chichagov)	*25 Dec. '52*	
25.	Chi vuol la zingarella (composer?) (Pf. Betty Dilling)	*1950*	
26.	Christmas Greeting (recitation)	*12 Oct. '58*	
27.	Come Back to Erin (Claribel) (Or.)	*1936/37 (?)*	MDP001
28.	*Don Carlos:* O Don Fatale (Pf.)	*1951*	MDP001
29.	Home, Sweet Home (Bishop) (Or.)	*1936*	
30.	Homing (Del Riego) (Or.)	*1937*	
31.	Kiss in the Dark, A (*Orange Blossoms*) (Herbert) (Or.)	*1936/37 (?)*	MDP001
32.	Last Rose of Summer (Moore) (Or.)	*1936/37 (?)*	MDP001
33.	Little Grey Home in the West (Löhr) (Or.)	*1936/37 (?)*	MDP001
34.	Lover Come Back to Me (*New Moon*) (Romberg)	*26 Feb. '27*	MDP001
35.	Love Sends a Little Gift of Roses (Crooke-Openshaw) (Or.)	*12 Feb. '37*	
36.	Love's Old Sweet Song (Molloy) (Or.)	*1936/37 (?)*	MDP001
37.	Mattinata (Leoncavallo) (Or.)	*6 Nov. '36*	MDP001
38.	Memories (Van Alstyne) (Or.)	*16 April '37*	MDP001
39.	Mother Machree (Young-Ball)	*?*	
40.	One Night of Love (Kahn-Schertzinger) (Or.)	*1936*	MDP001
41.	O Sole Mio (Di Capua) (Or.) (with Anthony Ponselle)	*11 Dec. '36* *1938 (?)*	MDP001
42.	Perfect Day, A (Bond)	*?*	

DISCOG. NO.		DATE	LP
43.	*Samson et Dalila:* Amour! viens aider ma faiblesse!		
	(Pf. Chichagov)	*25 Dec. '51*	
	(Pf. Chichagov)	*25 Dec. '52*	
44.	Se tu m'ami (Pergolesi)	*14 Jan.*	
	(Pf. Betty Dilling)		
45.	Silent Night (Gruber)	*1951*	
	(with Chorus) (Organ)		
46.	Silver Threads Among the Gold (Danks)		
	(Or.)	*1936*	
		12 Feb. '37	
47.	Song of Songs (Moya)	*1936/37 (?)*	MDP001
	(Or.)		
48.	Song of the Soul (Bereil)	*1936*	
	(Acapello)		
49.	Songs My Mother Taught Me (Dvořák)	*7 May '37*	MDP001
	(Or.)		
50.	The Coming of Christ Spirit (recitation)	*12 Oct. '58*	
51.	When You're Away (*The Only Girl*) (Herbert)	*19 Feb. '37*	MDP001
	(Or.)		

NOTE: *MDP001—Carmela Ponselle "In Live Concerts"*

NOTE: *Silent Night, Song of the Soul, and the three recitations made up a limited edition record entitled "Carmela Ponselle's Christmas Message."*

NOTE: *Carmela Ponselle performed in one Metropolitan Opera Broadcast (apparently not preserved):*

16 March 1935
METROPOLITAN OPERA
New York, WEAF
Aida (Cond. Panizza)
   (with Rethberg, Martinelli, A. Borgioli, Lazzari)

ANTHONY PONSELLE

52.	*Elisir d'amore, L':* Una furtiva lagrima	*20 Sept. '20*	OASI 635
	Matrix Number Unknown		
	(Or.)		

NOTE: *This was a "trial" record, not intended for publication.*

INDEX

"Ave Maria" (*Cavalleria rusticana*),
64, 219
"Ave Maria" (*Otello*), 219
"Ave Maria" (Schubert), 219, 222
"'A vucchella," 71, 219
Azucena. *See Trovatore, Il*

B

Babuscio, Angelo, 88
Bach-Gounod "Ave Maria," 219
Badini, Ernesto, 132
Bagby Foundation, 71
Baklanova, Kira, 189–90, 193, 246
Balanchine, George, 144
Baldassare-Tedeschi, Giuseppina, 202
Ball, Ernest, 33
"Ballatella," 218
Ballester, Vicente, 136
Ballo in Maschera, Un, 229
Baltimore, Md., xvi–xxv, 72, 159–61,
163, 164, 170, 171, 177–216, 224–25,
242–47 (*See also* Villa Pace);
Carmela buried in, 240; Eisenhower
rally in, 222; "Rosa Ponselle Week,"
224; Rosa's death in, 246–47
Baltimore *News American*, 215, 243
Baltimore Opera Company, xix,
187–90, 192–95 (*See also* specific
artists, productions); Rosa's
difficulties with Collinge,
resignation, 205, 206–16, 243–45
Baltimore Symphony, 73, 179, 192,
201, 207, 215, 223, 246
Bamboschek, Giuseppe, 95, 189
Bampton, Rose, 76, 132, 137, 138; at
Rosa's birthday party, xviii
Barber, Samuel, 203
Barber of Seville, The, 175; Sayão's
Rosina, 201; Stracciari's Figaro,
xxiii, 68
Barbieri, Fedora, 203
"Barcarolle," 32, 34, 64, 218
Barrientos, Maria, 37, 66, 67
Basiola, Mario, xxiii, 80, 133
Bastianini, Ettore, 202
Bayes, Nora, 33, 35, 39
Beall, George, 243, 244
"Beautiful Dreamer," 70
"Because," 164
Bekker, Paul, 152
"Bel dì vedremo, Un," 40, 64, 70, 218
Bellezza, Vincenzo, 120, 121

Bellincioni, Gemma, 124, 204
Bellini, Vincenzo. *See* specific works
"Bel raggio," 72
Benelli, Sem, 125
Benny, Jack, 35
Bergonzi, Carlo, 199
Berle, Milton, 35
Berlin, Ellin Mackay, 104, 138
Berlin, Germany, 201
Berlin, Irving, 104, 138
Bernard, Al, 37
Bernstein, Leonard, xvii, 185
Besanzoni, Gabriella, 65, 111
Bicycling, 232–33
Billings, Mont., 36
Bing, Rudolf, 203
Bizet, Georges, 142, 152; Carré and,
143
Björling, Jussi, 197, 198
Black, Frank, 221
Black artists, 196
Black Widow, 206
Bland, James, 71
Blois, Eustace, 119, 121, 125, 126
Bober, Eva, 189
Bodanzky, Artur, 77
Bohème, La, 75, 87, 93, 159, 182, 202
(*See also* specific arias); in
Atlanta, 67; Baltimore Opera and,
189, 204; Björling in, 198; Caruso
and bass aria, 49; Grace Moore in,
138
Bohnen, Michael, 80, 92
"Bolero" (*Vespri siciliani*), 218
Bonci, Alessandro, 49–50
Bonelli, Richard, 179, 202
Boninsegna, Celestina, 37
Bonynge, Richard, xix, 195–96, 224
Bookspan, Martin, 224
Boone, Sylvia, 243
Borge, Victor, xvii
Borgioli, Dino, 132, 133, 235
Bori, Lucrezia, 73, 94, 156, 159;
Albanese compared to, 202; in
Amore dei tre re, 125; death of,
225; in *Falstaff*, 136; in *Traviata*,
123, 124, 130, 152
Boris Godunov, 82, 155; Althouse in,
58; Baltimore Opera and, 192,
203–4, 206; Tibbett in, 136
Boscachiesa Nova, 133
Boston, Mass., 71, 172, 236
Boston *Advertiser*, 77–78

INDEX

V

"Vainement, ma bien aimée!," 87
Valentina, 144–45, 148, 164, 233
Vanderbilt, Mrs. Cornelius, 104
Vanderbilt, Grace, 104
Vanderbilt, Mr. and Mrs. Reginald, 99
Vanderbilt, Mrs. William K., 104
Vanessa, 203
Vanvitelli, Luigi, 1
Variety, 164
Vartenissian, Shakeh, 189
Vatican City, 100
Vaudeville, 30–39, 43, 67, 218–19, 226–27; Tony in, 96
Venice, 106
Verbeck, Mr. and Mrs. Howard, 98–99
Verdi, Bill, 43, 57, 131
Verdi, Giuseppe, 58, 59n, 70 (*See also* specific works); Met gala, 64–65; and Victor Maurel, 38
"Vergine degli angeli, La," 55, 64, 219
Vespri siciliani, I, 73, 218
Vestale, La, 103, 106–8, 109, 111, 235, 238; in Florence, 132, 133–34; "Tu che invoco," 70, 107n
"Vesti la giubba," 96
Vettori, Elda, 121
Viareggio, 101–3, 117
Vickers, Jon, 199, 204
Victor Records (RCA Victor; formerly Victor Talking Machine Company), 60, 63–64, 173n, 231–32, 248ff. (*See also* specific artists, works); discography of, 256–66
Victory, Bettie, 246
Villa Julie Convent, 243
Villa Pace, viii–ix, xxiv, 180–81ff., 193, 195, 196, 204, 209, 212, 213, 231, 235, 238, 245; archives, 248, 285n; Christmas concert at, 222; fire, 242–43; needlework pieces in, 70; open to public, 224; Romani's death at, 190–91; at Rosa's death, 246; Rosa's 80th birthday party at, xvi–xxi; Victor recordings made at, 223
Violi, William, 251n
"Vissi d'arte," 64, 70, 218, 236; Jeritza and, 90; Rosa sings for Puccini, 102
"Vivrà! contende il giubilo," 68
"Voce di donna," 40, 105

"Voi lo sapete, o Mamma!," 26, 40, 64, 218
Von Tilzer, Albert and Harry, 33
Vonynich, E. L., 70
Voorhees, Don, 221
Votipka, Thelma, 110

W

Wagner, Richard (Wagnerian repertoire), 60, 90, 117, 121, 140–41, 167 (*See also* specific artists, works); Gatti and, 155; Jeritza and, 91
Wagner (Charles) Company, 179
Waldorf-Astoria, 71
Walker, Danton, 152
Walküre, Die (Sieglinde), 58, 140
Wallace, Idaho, 36
Walla Walla, Wash., 36
Wally, La, 41
Walsh, Aidan E., 215n
Warfield, William, 203–4, 246
Warner Brothers, 157
Warren, Leonard, 202
Warren, Mrs. Whitney, 104
Washington, D.C., 72, 169, 178, 179, 232, 235–36
Washington (D.C.) *Herald*, 89–90
Washington (D.C.) *Post*, 243
Waterbury, Conn., 3–6
Wax masters, 249
Wayne, Richard, 162
WEAF, 96
Weber, Carl Maria von, 41, 59n
Weede, Robert, 180, 188
We Followed Our Stars, 129
Werrenwrath, Reinald, 68, 71
Wettergren, Gertrud, 147
WFBR, 180
"What'll I Do?," 138
"When I Have Sung My Songs to You," 168
"Whispering Hope," 64
White Hell of Piz Palu, The, 234
Whiteman (Paul) Band, 99
Wicker, Henriette, 151
Williams, Bert, 35
William Tell (Guillaume Tell), 93, 218
Wills, Nat, 35
Wilson, Stella, 126

327